Wicked Arts Assignments

Emiel Heijnen & Melissa Bremmer (eds.)

Wicked Arts Assignments

Practising Creativity in Contemporary Arts Education

Valiz

Introduction

Every arts educator knows, uses, and produces them: the assignments that are seemingly simple but challenge students and participants to the max. In daily life, wicked arts assignments are informally passed on to other arts teachers or artists, or live on in the form of memories and creative artefacts of students and participants. Localized in the grey area between the explicit and the hidden curriculum, these valuable pieces of curriculum embody both the formal demands of curricula *and* the norms, values and belief systems of today's arts educators.

Although we hypothesized that there should be an abundance of wicked arts assignments—tried and tested in all kinds of contexts—we wondered why they were so hard to find. This, in turn, sparked our idea of collecting the intangible gems of arts education and to introduce them to many. Not long after, we sent out a worldwide online call for challenging arts assignments. Arts teachers and artists submitted over five hundred of them—confirming our suspicions that they are productive educational designers.

But then began the daunting task of selecting assignments for our book. In a selection committee, we chose nearly one hundred of the most bold, unusual, contrary, funny, poetical, and socially committed ones. Moreover, through the selection process, we could compile those assignments that could reflect what we believe to be a contemporary arts education. Most of the arts assignments we chose are not restricted to a single medium or discipline. Instead, they encourage cross-disciplinary working and thinking. Also, they represent themes and ways of working recognized in contemporary arts and popular culture, from remix to engagement, from artistic intervention to hacking. The assignments are playful too, but can go against the grain just as much, touch on risky endeavours or invite intense introspection. They offer ways to learn about the arts, ourselves, and the world. Lastly, the selection process made clear that wicked arts assignments can be carried out in various contexts: from primary schools to higher education, from home to the (online) community, and from Bogotá to Istanbul.

The final result of the selection process lies in your hands: *Wicked Arts Assignments* reveals the arts educators' hidden oeuvre of arts assignments from different regions around the world. It has developed into a book that can be divided into two parts. The first part provides a theoretical perspective on the phenomenon of arts assignments and consists of two chapters and five interviews. In the first chapter, 'Scores, Instructions, Prompts and Briefs: The Assignment as an Artwork', an artistic perspective is given on the arts assignment. It follows the historical developments of assignments and instructions in the arts and education, how they are framed as conceptual artworks and used to stimulate democratic 'do it yourself'-practices. In the second chapter, 'Bridging Contradictions: the Design of Wicked Arts Assignments', an educational perspective is taken. It explores how wicked arts assignments can be designed and guided by arts teachers and artists. The five interviews reflect the views of contemporary scholars in arts and education on the arts assignment: Jorge Lucero (USA), Nina Paim (Brazil), Erik Schrooten (Belgium), Stephanie Springgay (Canada), and Pavèl van Houten (the Netherlands). Teaching and working in different contexts, their voices provide insight into contemporary arts and educational practices.

The second part of the book consists of the actual wicked arts assignments. Every assignment is accompanied by a short explanation, and one or more images of participants' results, related work of the author, or inspirational resources. To offer the reader a form of navigation, we clustered the assignments into twelve themes, such as 'Narrate', 'Hack', 'Make Some Noise', and 'Go Public'.

The very last section in this book we have named 'Too Wicked to Handle'. This selection is of assignments that were too unrealistic or too 'outrageous' to be carried out, or the assignments had not been 'tried and tested', but were still worthwhile as a wicked source of inspiration.

Lastly, we thank all arts educators for their generosity—for offering us a peek behind the scenes of their contemporary arts education and for opening up their practice for all. Moreover, we truly hope this book is not seen as an endpoint but as a starting point for (re)designing arts assignments. We invite you to live the wicked.

Scores, Instructions, Prompts and Briefs: The Assignment as Artwork

Emiel Heijnen and Melissa Bremmer

Trying to grasp arts assignments can feel like chasing a ghost. They are continuously thought up and carried out by arts teachers and artists, only to evaporate before they can be preserved as momentous slices of curriculum. As such, arts assignments constitute a living curriculum that is personal, dynamic, and embodied.[1]

Generally, arts curricula provide much freedom for interpretation, leaving space for the design of *personal* assignments that can relatively easily be implemented in the classroom. The collateral effect, however, is that these assignments can disappear into thin air when the teacher changes jobs. Arts assignments are *dynamic* too, as they are responsive to emergent events, themes or learning needs. Many arts teachers will constantly change, update, alter or remix their own or published assignments. Moreover, especially in theatre, music, and dance education, assignments are part of an *embodied* teaching practice, in which teachers communicate in physical ways:[2] their directions, prompts, and coaching strategies are often non-verbal and difficult to grasp in written assignments.

In contrast to these personal, dynamic, and embodied arts assignments, there is a vast body of them in textbooks for school curricula. Yet, these are often so generalized or standardized for a large group of teachers that they have become detached from the personal beliefs and practices from which they originated.[3] For our book we were looking for assignments that do have a strong personal signature, signifying a connection between the artistic ideas, values, pedagogical view, and local practice of the arts teacher or artist. These are the assignments by which you might remember a former arts teacher because you immediately recognize their authorship.[4]

The notion of an arts assignment as a personal and unique work raises the question if arts assignments themselves could be seen as works of art. Art and education scholar Elliot Eisner has emphasized the artistry in curriculum design and teaching, but the question remains if this also applies to the arts assignment itself.[5] In other words: can a set of instructions or prompts be seen as a work of art?

Do-it-yourself Artworks

Looking into the history of the arts, the answer is definitely 'yes': assignments can be seen as artworks. The most obvious and oldest examples of instructions as artworks are the traditional scores, texts, choreographies, and scripts written by composers, theatre makers, choreographers, and filmmakers. In the visual arts, where artists are used to carrying out their ideas themselves, instructions or scores used to be quite uncommon. This changed radically in the 1960s, when artists belonging to the international Fluxus group began to produce written and painted instructions as works of art. These works resemble the instructions in the performance arts, as they need others to perform or 'finish' a work, but there is also a big difference. While traditional instructions generally require skilled performers to bring a work to life, the so-called *event* or *word score*s by Fluxus artists such as Yoko Ono, George Brecht, and George Maciunas were directly aimed at the public. By activating the layman as a (co)author, these artists wanted to establish a connection between art and daily life. Any member of society could engage in the process of art making, outside arts' traditional contexts and institutions.

This production of instructions to be performed by laymen sparked a new movement. Yoko Ono imagined 'a Bronxville housewife saying to her guests "do add a circle to my painting before you have a drink"'.[6] The quote is taken from Ono's book *Grapefruit*—credited as one of the first artworks as a 'do-it-yourself kit'.[7] From exhibiting interactive works based on audience participation, Ono had taken the radical step to display only written directions as works at a Tokyo exhibition in 1962.[8]

PAINTING TO HAMMER A NAIL

Hammer a nail in the center of a piece of glass. Send each fragment to an arbitrary address.

1962 spring

1. Yoko Ono, *Grapefruit*, 1964 (excerpt, n.p.)

Grapefruit is a collection of these instructions, which can be simple and feasible (fig. 1), but can also have an absurd or poetic character, like: 'Send a smell to the moon' or 'Draw a map to get lost'. Similarly, fellow Fluxus member George Brecht wrote over a hundred scores on small cards, which he published, exhibited, or mailed to friends. His 'assignments' are even more open (or cryptic) than Ono's, as they often consist of just a few loose words (fig. 2).

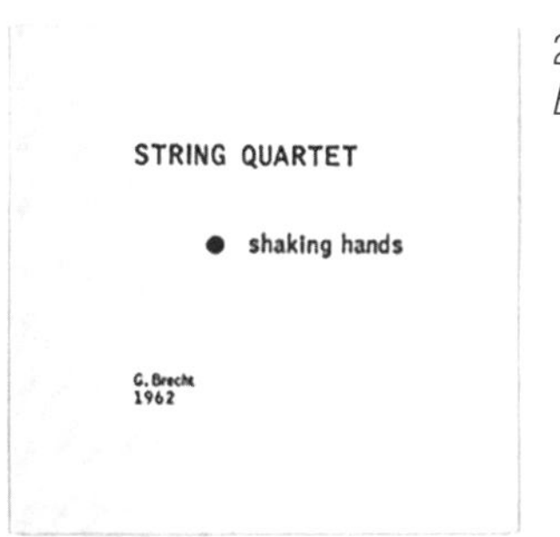

2. George Brecht, *Event Score*, 1962

The scores by Fluxus artists were heavily inspired by the Dada movement and experimental composer John Cage, whose classes at the New School for Social Research were attended by some Fluxus members. Cage had eliminated the divide between composer, performer, and listener by playing with chance in various works, including 4'33", a three-movement piece that consists solely of random noises in the concert hall, while the performer(s) do not play a single note.[9] The concept of chance was also explored by composer La Monte Young, as demonstrated in his self-published book *An Anthology of Chance Operations* (1963).[10] The book has a multidisciplinary approach featuring unorthodox instructions and graphic scores by different artists for improvised music, poetry, and dance (fig. 3).

INSTRUCTIONS FOR A DANCE:
One man is told that he must lie on the floor during the entire piece.
The other man is told that during the piece he must tie the first man to the wall.

3. Simone Forti, dance instruction in La Monte Young's *An Anthology of Chance Operations*, 1963

Fluxus artists took this playing with chance, the everyday, and participation further. To counter the 'elitist attitude' and abstract art of fellow artists, Fluxus wanted 'to promote living art, anti-art, promote non-art reality to be grasped by all peoples, not only critics, dilettantes, and professionals'.[11] Fluxus founder George Maciunas initiated Fluxus festivals or Fluxfests, where written scores were collectively carried out in real time. Just as with Ono and Brecht, Maciunas' scores consisted mostly of ordinary routines that required no special skills or artistic training (fig. 4). Maciunas also launched a mail order service that offered *Fluxkits*: boxes with scores, newspapers, games, and interactive objects from Fluxus members.

ICE TRICK
Pass one pound piece of ice among audience until it melts while playing a recording of fire sounds or actually a fire on stage.

4. George Maciunas, *Fluxfest Sale*, 1966 (excerpt)

The interdisciplinary Fluxus scores—as 'unrealized concepts'—cannot be detached from the advent of conceptual art, for which the development of concepts and ideas is more important than finished works.[12] This is underlined by the series of exhibitions initiated by curator and writer Lucy R. Lippard in the USA, Canada, and Argentina in the 1970s. Lippard saw the 'dematerialization' of art as a logical outcome of and based her art shows completely on written instructions on postcards that were mailed to her by various artists (fig. 5).[13]

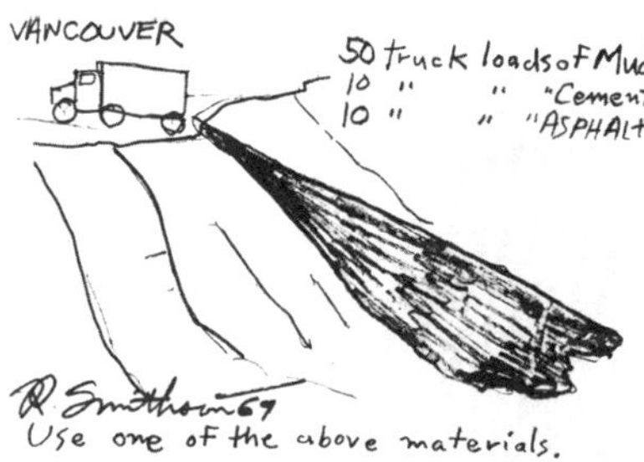

5. Robert Smithson, instruction postcard for Lucy R. Lippard's '557,087', 1969

The instruction postcards were printed as catalogues of these exhibitions, although some were carried out unrecognizably, or even not carried out at all.[14] Rather than the exhibited works, the conceptual backbone of the art shows was formed by instructions, as written 'promises' to be brought to life in the mind of the beholder.

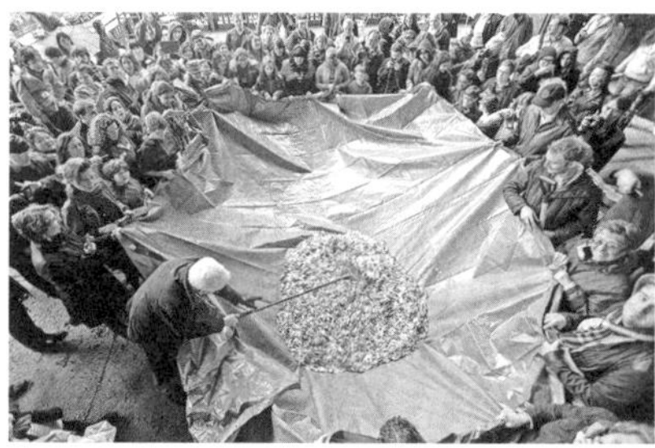

6. Alison Knowles, *Make a Salad*, performance in New York, 2012

The Fluxus movement and the rise of conceptual art inspired artists in the 1960s and 1970s to experiment with scores, instructions and directions, trying to create interdisciplinary artworks that were radically participatory and open-ended.[15] Notable examples are Alison Knowles' ongoing performance instruction *Make a Salad* (fig. 6) and Stanley Brouwn's *this way brouwn*; a collection of hand drawn city maps with directions, made by random passers-by.[16] And last but not least: Steve Kaltenbach's ads in *Artforum* magazine with assignments such as 'Start a rumor' and 'Perpetuate a hoax'.

The Social Turn

The emergence of participatory approaches in the arts often runs parallel with periods of radical political and societal change, as was the case in the 1960s and 1970s.[17] A second wave of 'do-it-yourself' practices appeared in the 1990s, in response to the rise of globalization, digitalization, and neoliberalism.[18] This demarcates the *social turn* in the contemporary arts, a (re)turn to socially engaged arts forms, involving people as 'material' to develop collaborative, often participatory work.[19]

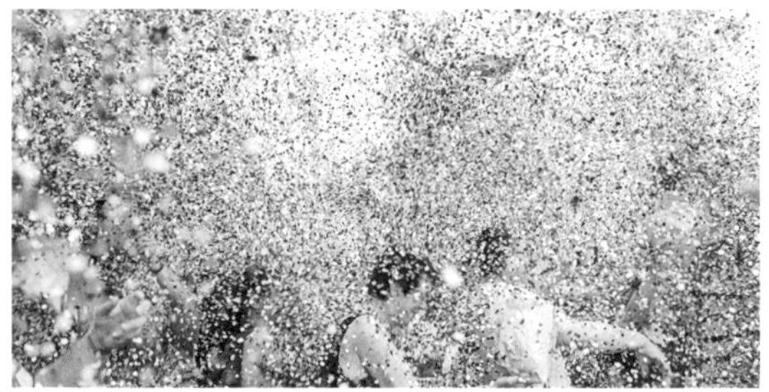

7. Opening party based on Amalia Pica's directions at *do it*, Kunsthal Rotterdam, 2012

To highlight the power of written instructions as a means of creating temporary participatory art events, Swiss curator Hans-Ulrich Obrist initiated *do it* in 1993. *Do it* is an ongoing international series of exhibitions, events, and publications that, up until now, has been hosted at over 45 museums and art centres in Europe, the Americas, Asia, and Australia. Its main branch is *do it (museum)*, exhibitions and events made with local people and materials, based on artist instructions. By no means should the artists or Obrist be involved in the realization of these exhibitions and all the works have to be destroyed afterwards. The instructions of *do it* are varied, including Fluxus-like prompts ('Sweep the desert' by Nasser al Salem), lighthearted invitations ('Throw a party' by Amalia Pica, fig. 7), socially engaged assignments (Suzanne Lacy's call to make a statement for abused women) and ethically questionable directions (Wilson Diaz' detailed cocaine recipe). *Do it* clearly celebrates instructions as artworks; what is actually produced is either destroyed or scarcely documented.

The project *Learning to Love You More* (2002–2009) by Miranda July and Harrell Fletcher took a different stance. *Learning to Love You More* consists of seventy assignments by July and Fletcher, published on an interactive website. Participants were invited to upload results of a completed assignment. July and Fletcher succeeded in collecting and documenting an astonishing five thousand texts, pictures, and videos from participants from all over the world.[20] Like many earlier instructions in the arts, the assignments of July and Fletcher are playful invitations to turn personal everyday experiences into interdisciplinary artworks. The difference is that *Learning to Love You More* has a therapeutic 'self-help' approach, as the assignments are meant as coping strategies for individuals in a globalizing and individualizing society.[21] Indeed, assignments such as 'Make the saddest song', 'Take a picture of your parents kissing' (fig. 8), or 'Act out someone else's argument' should literally help you to 'love you more'.

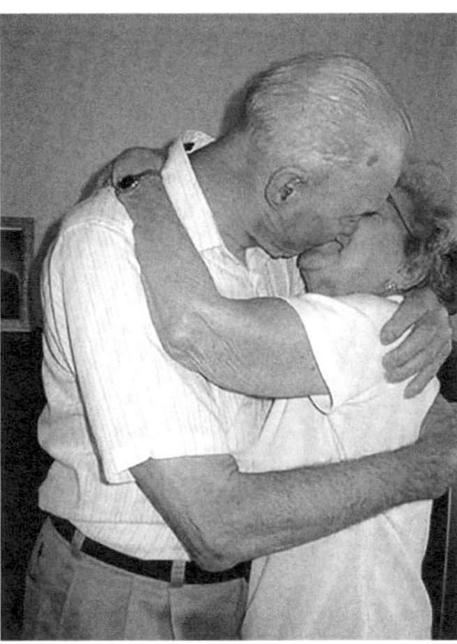

8. Judith Wigren-Slack, contribution in response to 'Make a picture of your parents kissing', n.d.

Doing or Learning Arts?

The cases discussed previously support our hypothesis that assignments or instructions can 'count' as artworks. However, when we take a closer look at these movements and initiatives from an educational perspective, we have to be critical. Many of the examples of instructions and assignments seem to be geared towards *doing* arts rather than *learning* arts. They include simple, repetitive or 'curatorial' operations that require little creativity or cognitive strain and offer little participant guidance. Yet, when we dive into the field of education, it cannot be denied that these types of assignments have permeated arts education. There, they have been used to spur on the artistic learning process of students.

8. Give police artist verbal description of Baldessari and have him do drawing. Perhaps everyone in class do verbal description.

48. Develop a visual code. Give it to another student to crack.

69. What art can come from the use of a set of walkie-talkie radios?

9. John Baldessari, *Assignment Sheet*, 1970 (excerpt)

A legendary example that keeps turning up in arts education's history is the list of 109 numbered assignments by conceptual artist John Baldessari.[22] Around 1970, Baldessari taught his so-called Post Studio Class at the California Institute of the Arts. His instructions (fig. 9) play with language and often challenge students to rethink the meaning, form and function of art. In assignment #45 the instruction even gets the form of a punishment, as students are asked to write lines like 'I will not make any more boring art' one thousand times on the wall. Baldessari's assignments are part of the book *Draw It with Your Eyes Closed*, which offers an overview of how conceptual assignments have entered the (American) art school.[23]

Another educational field where teachers experimented heavily with assignments, is graphic design. Being experts in communication, graphic designers understood how so-called *briefs* could form a meaningful intermediary 'work' for the exchange of ideas between teacher and student. Corinne Gisel interviewed several design teachers for *Taking a Line for a Walk*, a book that collected design assignments spanning over more than a hundred years.[24] Besides challenging assignments, the teachers recall interesting form experiments. For instance, Alex Balgiu's briefs in the form of small publications, and the assignment that students had to discover between the announcements in the Sunday's *News-Gazette* by Daniella Spinet, Neil Donnelly and Mary Voorhees Meehan (fig. 10). Another teacher, Chloé Briggs, experimented with remote teaching and sent her class weekly instructions without ever appearing in class.

ACT NOW

US: visiting dsgnrs, seeking "classified ad," 1 per pair of wkshop participants. YOU: talented Illini to offer/request svc; conduct transaction; solicit help/advice; find love OBO. Post ad in real or virtual world. Ads must have category. Conduct transactions at Fig One, Wed-Fri. Use 60 sq ft of wall at Fig One as you like. Kick off mtg: Wed 8am, Link Gallery, U of I. Closing party for ads + any results: Fri 6-9pm at Figure One, 116 N Walnut, 217-333-0786. XO, D + M + N.

10. Daniella Spinet, Neil Donnelly and Mary Voorhees Meehan, 'Act Now', assignment in Sunday's *News-Gazette*, 2011

Finally, we would like to highlight some assignment projects with a strong artistic signature, aiming to stimulate creative learning in the public domain. The influential *Oblique Strategies* (1975) developed by musician/producer Brian Eno and painter Peter Schmidt, is a boxed set of instruction cards. Each suggests an action or thought to assist in the (blocked) creative process. The card deck, also available as an app, contains directions such as 'Honor thy error as a hidden intention' and 'Use an old idea'.

More recently, we cannot ignore Keri Smith's signature publications such as *Finish This Book* and *The Guerilla Art Kit*, which inspire both children and parents to undertake assignments such as making your own secret headquarters, leaving books for strangers to find or making a 'moss graffiti'. Also noteworthy are the websites that feature assignments by contemporary designers and artists, like *designbriefs.ch* and *theartassignment.com*. Wypke Jannette

Walen and Oskar Maarleveld deserve a special mention too. Together with their class of pre-service art teachers, they managed to produce a box of 356 assignments, to be used as a 'daily art work-out'.

Contemporary Arts Education

What does *Wicked Arts Assignments* add to this discourse? It offers an artistic and educational perspective on assignments and reveals how instructions, prompts, and briefs are part of both the arts and education. It also provides an historical overview of assignments, thereby exemplifying the lingering traces in today's assignments of the experiments of artists and arts teachers of the past. But, most importantly, the *current* state of affairs of assignments in international arts education is showcased. These assignments can be seen as a collection of personal ideas, values, and pedagogical views that reflect the 'big ideas' of a contemporary arts curriculum.

NOTES

1 T. Grotzer, D. Vaughn, and B. Wilmot, *The Seven Principles of Living Curriculum* (2019), www.nais.org/magazine/independent-school/spring-2019/the-seven-principles-of-living-curriculum/.

2 M. Bremmer, *What the Body Knows about Teaching Music: The Specialist Preschool Music Teacher's Pedagogical Content Knowing Regarding Teaching and Learning Rhythm Skills Viewed from an Embodied Cognition Perspective* (Doctoral thesis, University of Exeter, 2015).

3 Ibid.

4 E. Wagner, 'Assignments', *Synnyt/Origins* 15, no. 2 (2019), pp. 637-652.

5 E.W. Eisner, *The Educational Imagination: On the Design and Evaluation of School Programs* (New York, NY: Macmillan, 1979).

6 Y. Ono, *Grapefruit: A Book of Instructions and Drawings* (New York, NY: Simon & Schuster, 1964), n.p.

7 C. Barliant, 'Yoko Ono's Instructions', *The New Yorker*, July 2013, www.newyorker.com/books/page-turner/yoko-onos-instructions.

8 B. Altshuler, 'Art by Instruction and the Prehistory of Do It', in *Do It: The Compendium*, ed. H.U. Obrist, pp. 29–40 (New York, NY: Independent Curators International, 2013).
9 C. Kravagna, 'Arbeit an der Gemeinschaft: Modelle partizipatorischer Praxis', in *Die Kunst des Öffentlichen*, ed. M. Babias and A. Könneke, pp. 28–46 (Dresden: Verlag der Kunst, 1998).
10 L.M. Young, *An Anthology of Chance Operations* (New York, NY: Jackson Mac Low and La Monte Young, 1963).
11 G. Maciunas, *Fluxus Manifesto* (New York, NY: Museum of Modern Art, 1963), n.p.
12 S. LeWitt, 'Paragraphs on Conceptual Art', *Artforum* 5, no. 10 (1967), pp. 79–83.
13 L.R. Lippard and J. Chandler, 'The Dematerialization of Art', *Art International* 12, no. 2 (1968), pp. 31–36.
14 L.R. Lippard, 'Curating by Numbers', *Tate Papers* 12 (2009), pp. 1–7.
15 A. Dezeuze, ed., *The 'Do-It-Yourself' Artwork: Participation from Fluxus to New Media* (Manchester: Manchester University Press, 2010).
16 W.A.L. Beeren et al., eds., *Actie, fictie en werkelijkheid in de kunst van de jaren '60 in Nederland*, exh. cat. Rotterdam: Museum Boymans-van Beuningen (The Hague: Staatsuitgeverij, 1979).
17 C. Bishop, *Artificial Hells: Participatory Art and the Politics of Spectatorship* (London: Verso, 2012).
18 Dezeuze, *The 'Do-It-Yourself' Artwork*.
19 C. Bishop, 'The Social Turn: Collaboration and Its Discontents', *Artforum* 44, no. 6 (2006), pp. 178–183.
20 A. Schorgl, *A Labor of Love: Art Production and Social Practice in Learning to Love You More Founded by Harrell Fletcher and Miranda July* (Master's thesis, University of Cincinnati, 2009).
21 A. Czudaj, *Miranda July's Intermedial Art: The Creative Class between Self-help and Individualism* (Bielefeld: Transcript Verlag, 2016).
22 J. Tumlir, 'Studio Crisis!', *Art Journal* 71, no. 1 (2014), pp. 58–75.
23 D. Petrovich and R. White, eds., *Draw It with Your Eyes Closed: The Art of the Art Assignment* (New York, NY: Paper Monument, 2012).
24 C. Gisel, 'Epilogue', in *Taking a Line for a Walk: Assignments in Design Education*, ed. N. Paim, C. Gisel, and E. Bergmark, pp. 3–37 (Leipzig: Spector Books, 2016).

Bridging Contradictions: The Design of Wicked Arts Assignments

Melissa Bremmer and Emiel Heijnen

For over ten years, we have given workshops around the globe in which we have played around with arts educators and invited them to design wicked arts assignments. You might wonder: why *wicked* arts assignments? Loosely based on the ideas of Rittel and Webber, we believe that arts education thrives on assignments that are wicked in nature: confusing, messy, complex, and challenging.[1] In our perception, wicked arts assignments are open *and* restricted, draw on personal fascinations *and* broaden one's horizon, leave room for exploration *and* provide guidance. What is more, these types of arts assignments are born out of authentic arts education—our main source of inspiration for this book.

Authentic Arts Education

In 2001, the educational researcher Haanstra coined the term 'authentic arts education', an approach that is firmly based on social-constructivist views on education. Broadly speaking, from an authentic arts education perspective, learning results in personal constructions of knowledge by students that are grounded in real life socio-cultural activities.[2] Thus, the word 'authentic' in the phrase 'authentic arts education' does not refer to *authentic forms of art* but to *realistic forms of learning*.[3]

More specifically, Haanstra described four principles underlying authentic arts education.[4] First of all, learning is aimed at the culture of the student, providing space for students' opinions, interests, and requirements. Secondly, communication and collaboration play an important role in the learning process: group tasks, student consultation, discussion, presentations and (peer) evaluations are regular features of this type of education. Thirdly, assignments are derived from and relate to activities performed by arts professionals in society. Lastly, learning takes place in productive learning environments, through complex and complete assignments that give scope for students' initiatives and explorations via global guidelines.

So, in theory, the assignment plays a central role in authentic arts education—it is the motor of the students' learning process. Yet, designing meaningful and challenging arts assignments is a wicked activity in itself, going beyond simply combining learning goals, content matter and media.[5] Therefore, this chapter takes a look at how arts educators might be aided with the design of wicked arts assignments, and how contradictions encountered during that design process might be bridged.

Open and Restricted

At times, some art educators might experience a stab of guilt because they feel they do not provide students with assignments that afford enough creative freedom. Especially secondary and college level students can voice that their creativity or personal expression is stifled by the constraints a specific assignment places on them.[6] Indeed, when the constraints of an assignment are formulated very tightly, focused on executing 'step-by-step' instructions rather than on experimenting, arts assignments can produce similar and uninspired outcomes.[7] Yet, given vast amounts of freedom, arts educators will also recognize that those same students seem paralyzed by that freedom and simply do not know how to begin working on an assignment, or they produce predictable results.[8]

In the view of Runco and Okuda Sakamoto, complete student autonomy does not necessarily promote students' creative activity, nor does it necessarily enhance their inquisitive behaviour.[9] They suggest that a 'controlled freedom', in which students are encouraged to explore problems within flexible limitations, holds the possibility to foster their creative potential.[10] Such limitations may actually prevent students from taking the most obvious path: one that is solely based on their existing knowledge, skills, and experience.[11]

Similarly, Davis and Sumara note that one of the most challenging tasks for educators is to produce *enabling constraints* that accompany an assignment: a set of limiting conditions that paradoxically open possibilities by narrowing down choices.[12] They, too, note that enabling constraints are not prescriptive but expansive, and operate by 'defining what cannot be done—thus opening the door to endless possibility by permitting everything else'.[13] Interestingly, designing assignments with enabling constraints as a means of challenging students' creativity is consistent with experimental studies on creative processes, which have found that *un*constrained assignments tend to result in less creative outcomes.[14] As such, finding a balance between limiting and enabling assignments becomes an art in itself.

How, then, could arts educators start thinking about constraints? They could design arts assignments providing a description of a problem with a list of one or more constraints that students must follow. Or, arts educators can formulate the core of an assignment in one or two sentences encompassing the constraints—such as is the case in this book. By robustly compressing an assignment into a short sentence, it turns into 'an anchor'. This makes it easier for arts educators and learners to relate additional explanations and demands to the assignment.

Depending on the focus of an arts assignment, the chosen constraints can prescribe themes (from a first-kiss film scene to post truth), or the use of tangible or intangible materials (anything from 3000 tons of sand to feelings of shame), or one or multiple art disciplines.[15] Constraints may also relate to the working process and can be found in the use of time limitations (a minute, an hour, a day, week or year), designated spaces (in a school, street or on the Internet), or in the number of collaborative partners. A combination of any of these constraints can challenge students to investigate political, personal, or poetic themes, use unorthodox materials and play around with time, space, and social relations.[16]

Personal Fascinations and Broader Horizons

From the perspectives of authentic arts education, to make arts assignments meaningful they should both challenge students or participants to work and think as conceptual, critical arts practitioners, *and* provide space for their fascinations, skills, and opinions.[17] Such meaningful assignments allow students to draw on their existing knowledge while at the same time having to expand their knowledge.

The idea of challenging students to work and think as conceptual, critical arts practitioners is not aimed at training them to become arts professionals. It is aimed at enabling students to experience how art works through the process of immersion, identification, and confrontation in and with art.[18] To allow for this, assignments should entice students to operate as artists and critics—roles derived from the professional arts world.[19] Many assignments in this book, for example, draw students into the way of working recognized in the conceptual and 'post medium' arts.[20] Although some assignments in this book seem at home in a certain arts discipline or take materials as a starting point, most depart from a concept that can be developed over time in different or interdisciplinary media. Such assignments immerse students in and confront them with the experience of being, seeing, and working as a conceptual artist.[21]

Furthermore, by allowing space in an assignment for students' fascinations, skills, and opinions, arts educators acknowledge that students develop expertise and artistic preferences beyond school, based on their personal areas of interest, which are often inspired by popular culture.[22] When arts educators connect to students' informal cultural production, it can motivate them to elaborate on their personal interests, and invite students to seek similarities with more unknown cultural works.[23] This process holds the possibility to lower the barrier to more complex or unknown forms of art, materials, or ways of artistic working and, thus, broaden students' horizons.[24] For instance, in this book, the assignment 'Create your own 3D Action Figure' joins students' interest in action figures found in popular culture with the world of Fablabs and 3D printing art. Or, the assignment 'Make a clair-obscure portrait with the light of your smartphone' connects students' intimate relationship with their smartphone to the lesser-known clair-obscure painting style stemming from the Renaissance.

Exploration and Guidance

One could say that an outcome of an arts assignment is a gain in students' competences: students start developing knowledge and skills they did not have before the assignment through treading unexplored artistic territory.[25] Yet, exploring unknown ground is not always easy for students as they can be confronted with complicated feelings, or become stuck during the (collaborative) creative working process.

Regarding feelings, some students may feel uncomfortable with the relative openness of an assignment and may become 'pissed' or 'frustrated' by it:[26] they do not know when or how to start, or fear they may fail. Others can feel overwhelmed by the contradiction contained within an assignment. For example, Hotze, Bremmer, Heijnen, Pijls, Beamer and Roos found that the tension between tenderness and technology in the arts assignment 'How can technology promote tenderness between people' caused heated discussions and confusion among students.[27]

Concerning the creative working process, students can experience design fixation when they get stuck on a first idea that is not necessarily interesting to explore further.[28] At the opposite end: students can keep on discussing ideas endlessly with each other, without actually realizing any of them.[29] Moreover, educators working from an authentic arts curriculum strive for long-term assignments overarching several lessons. However, students—not yet being able to oversee the amount of time needed for a creative working process[30]—may want to create something that is far too big for one work for the time provided ('we have plenty of time'), or rush to finish their work ('we hardly have enough time').

As visions of artworks, performances or installations do not always reveal themselves rapidly, nor materialize easily, it is important that students are purposefully guided, not simply left to their own devices.[31] When students embark on a wicked arts assignment, arts educators can guide them by not only providing students with feedback on the content of their work, but also by supervising their (collaborative) creative working process. For instance, arts educators can acknowledge the various emotions students may experience, which can range from interest, frustration, or confusion to excitement, and aid them to tolerate negative feelings by helping them frame those feelings as part of the creative working process.[32]

In the case of design fixation, a technique helping students to avoid fixating on one idea too early in the creative process, is by asking them to think up new ideas that are the opposite of their current idea, or by simply substituting one thing for another.[33] Furthermore, when students tend to infinitely talk about possible ideas for a work of art, or about their lack of ideas, arts educators can offer materials to work with. In general, ideas can emerge from working with the materials of an arts assignment, not only from thinking or talking about ideas in advance.[34] Lastly, arts educators can help students when, given the time allowed for an assignment, they choose an unmanageably broad approach. They should be guided so they realize that they have to narrow down the idea, concept, or narrative behind a work of art, sound sculpture, or artistic intervention.[35]

Wicked Arts Assignments in the Curriculum

We realize this book is not a ready-made arts curriculum: simply teaching these assignments one after the other does not make a coherent, meaningful curriculum. As such, a responsibility is placed on arts educators to think about how an arts assignment can be embedded in a series, how a preceding and following assignment connects to a current one.[36]

Another deliberation concerns the complexity and duration of assignments. In this book, we selected assignments that are not primarily designed as quick, simple exercises. However, arts educators may want to alternate between short or long, open or closed, more or less complex assignments, depending on what needs to be learned. They can also consider shortening, lengthening, or adapting an assignment to fit age, background, and context of students.

Finally, the operationalization of competencies that can be gained through wicked arts assignments, opens up possibilities for students' assessment. Assessment will pose various questions for arts educators: whether they want to assess students' competencies as an integrated whole, or would rather translate separate components into assessment criteria. Whether to assess the process, the product, or both. In any case, from an authentic arts education perspective, peer evaluations and group discussions are important vehicles for assessing works of art, performances, or artistic interventions.[37]

Think, Play, Learn

John Dewey, the 'godfather' of social constructivism wrote that '... thinking occurs when things are uncertain or doubtful or problematic'.[38] This book can indeed be seen as a collection of wicked problems that students or other participants have to solve *in*, *with* or *through* the arts. It is through the assignments that we envision a creative, cognitive, and conceptual approach to teaching and learning authentic arts education. Yes, wicked arts assignments are not neutral, and indeed, they may elicit feelings of discomfort and confusion. However, we are convinced that they challenge participants to mess around, to research, to experiment, to fail, to think, and to play. In other words: to learn.

NOTES

1 H.W.J. Rittel and M.M. Webber, 'Dilemmas in the General Theory of Planning', *Policy Science* 4, no. 2 (1973), pp. 155-169.
2 H. Franssen, E. Roelofs, and J. Terwel, 'Authentiek leren in de basisvorming', *Pedagogisch Tijdschrift* 20, no. 4-5 (1995), pp. 293-312.
3 E. Heijnen, *Remixing the Art Curriculum: How Contemporary Visual Practices Inspire Authentic Art Education* (Doctoral thesis, Radboud University Nijmegen, 2015).
4 F. Haanstra, 'Authentieke kunsteducatie: Een stand van zaken', *Cultuur + Educatie* 11, no. 31 (2011), pp. 8-31.
5 O. Gude, 'Principles of Possibility: Considerations for a 21st-Century Art & Culture Curriculum', *Art Education* 60, no. 1 (2007), pp. 6-17.
6 D.P. Sapp, 'Problem Parameters and Problem Finding in Art Education', *Journal of Creative Behavior* 31, no. 4 (1997), pp. 282-298.
7 A. Wilner, 'Fostering Critical Literacy: The Art of Assignment Design', *New Directions for Teaching and Learning* 103 (2005), pp. 23-38.
8 Heijnen, *Remixing the Art Curriculum*.
9 M.A. Runco and S. Okuda Sakamoto, 'Reaching Creatively Gifted Students through Their Learning Styles', in *Teaching and Counseling Gifted and Talented Adolescents: An International Learning Style Perspective*, ed. R.M. Milgram, R. Dunn, and G.G.E. Price, pp. 103-115 (New York, NY: Praeger, 1993).
10 Ibid., p. 114.
11 P. Rand, 'Design and the Play Instinct', in *Education of Vision*, ed. G. Kepes, pp. 156-174 (New York, NY: George Braziller Inc., 1965).
12 B. Davis and D. Sumara, '"If Things Were Simple ...": Complexity in Education', *Journal of Evaluation in Clinical Practice* 16, no. 4 (2010), pp. 856-860.
13 Ibid., p. 859.
14 R.K. Sawyer, 'Teaching and Learning How to Create in Schools of Art and Design', *Journal of the Learning Sciences* 27, no. 1 (2018), pp. 137-181.
15 E. Wagner, 'Assignments', *Synnyt*/Origins 15, no. 2 (2019), pp. 637-652.
16 Rand, 'Design and the Play Instinct'.
17 F. Haanstra, et al., 'A Review of Assessment Instruments in Arts Education', in *The Wisdom of the Many: Key Issues in Arts Education* (*International Yearbook for Research in Arts Education* 3), ed. S. Schonmann, pp. 413-418 (Münster: Waxmann, 2015); J. Wiggins, Teaching for Musical Understanding (Oxford: Oxford University Press, 2014).

18 Heijnen, *Remixing the Art Curriculum*.
19 Haanstra, 'Authentieke kunsteducatie'.
20 R. Krauss, *A Voyage on the North Sea: Art in the Age of the Post-Medium Condition* (New York, NY: Thames & Hudson, 1999).
21 M. Bremmer, E. Heijnen, and J. Lucero, 'School as Material: Modes of Operation for Teachers as Conceptual Artists, in *Researching the Arts*, ed. S. Blom et al., pp. 38-51 (Amsterdam: Amsterdam University of the Arts, 2018).
22 L. Green, *Music, Informal Learning and the School: A New Classroom Pedagogy* (Farnham: Ashgate Publishing Limited, 2008).
23 Heijnen, *Remixing the Art Curriculum*.
24 Green, *Music, Informal Learning and the School*.
25 Wagner, 'Assignments'.
26 Sawyer, 'Teaching and Learning How to Create in Schools of Art and Design', p. 163.
27 A. Hotze et al., 'ArtsSciences designathon: Pressure cooker voor aankomende leraren die vanuit verschillende disciplines samenwerken aan een vakoverstijgende ontwerptaak', *Velon* 40, no. 3 (2019), pp. 196–206.
28 B. Nicholl and R. McLellan, 'The Contribution of Product Analysis to Fixation in Students' Design and Technology Work', in *The Design and Technology Association International Research Conference 2007*, ed. E.W.L. Norma and D. Spendlove, pp. 71–76 (Wellesbourne: The Design and Technology Association, 2007).
29 Hotze et al., 'ArtsSciences designathon'.
30 Sawyer, 'Teaching and Learning How to Create in Schools of Art and Design'.
31 E.R. Halverson, 'Digital Art-Making as a Representational Process', *Journal of the Learning Sciences* 23, no. 1 (2013), pp. 121–162; P.A. Kirschner, J. Sweller, and R.E. Clark, 'Why Minimal Guidance during Instruction Does Not Work: An Analysis of the Failure of Constructivist, Discovery, Problem-Based, Experiential, and Inquiry-based Teaching', *Educational Psychologist* 41, no. 2 (2006), pp. 75–86.
32 G. Claxton, *Wise-Up: The Challenge of Lifelong Learning* (London, UK: Bloomsbury, 1999).
33 Sawyer, 'Teaching and Learning How to Create in Schools of Art and Design'.
34 Hotze et al., 'ArtsSciences designathon'.
35 Sawyer, 'Teaching and Learning How to Create in Schools of Art and Design'.
36 Wagner, 'Assignments'; Wiggins, *Teaching for Musical Understanding*.
37 Haanstra, et al., 'A Review of Assessment Instruments in Arts Education'.
38 J. Dewey, *Democracy and Education* (New York, NY: Macmillan, 2016), p. 173.

Interviews

‘No assignment is hopeless to me.’ Jorge Lucero

Interview by Sanne Kersten

What relation do arts assignments have to your practice?

There are many ways that art assignments are related to my practice. As a teacher—who thinks of his pedagogical practice as art—I test the materiality of what it means to give an assignment. I pay close attention to my students and try to formulate directives that are tight enough to be generative and loose enough to still manifest individual results. Even though I have given the same assignments more than once, I have never taught the same thing twice.

As an artist who thinks of his creative practice as a form of education, I work within limits—mostly conceptual, but sometimes material—to try to find the pliability of things that might appear to be concretized and immobile at first glance. I see this move as a pedagogical gesture. I'm drawn to the way that some things in the academy (e.g. banality and standardization, the rhythms of the school calendar, the textured relationality between differing stakeholders, and the constant bureaucratic oversight) map over a multitude of conceptual art discourses. In the academy we're faced with the readily available politics, pathos, angst, economic conundrums, utopian aspirations, and 'fields' for experimentation that many conceptual artists aspire to in their work. I see working in a school as a true art gift.

Which arts assignment have made an impression on you?

One of my first painting teachers told me to 'go talk to Paul Klee in the museum'—what he was really saying was go look at art and see what 'it' says to you. This is an assignment that I've yet to stop engaging with and it hasn't ceased to be a productive exercise. In many ways this has turned into a manner of studying anything: go 'listen' to it (whatever) and see what *it* says to you. The trick is to engage things slowly, repeatedly, over long stretches of time, and constantly think about how the thing you're looking at is constructed formally and leveraged conceptually. This constant and simultaneous formal and conceptual retreading opens up permissions within the observed works. It's almost as if the thing you're looking at finally says, 'This thing that you didn't know you could do; you actually can do it; if you want to.'

Who are your arts assignment 'heroes' or sources of inspiration?

The members of the performance group Goat Island were perhaps some of my greatest art teachers. Every *thing* generated something so there was never any wasted energy or useless encounter. Well, that's only half true. Everything 'gave' something because we, the observers, were encouraged to look with generative analysis, instead of stifled criticality. We were taught to *re-spect*—meaning to look again—over and over and over and over. If whatever we were analyzing lacked immediate intrigue or even was anti-aesthetic—regardless if it was student's work or some simple artefact/phenomenon in the world—the members of Goat Island taught us to find 'moments of wonder' and to work from there. This was a very fruitful, even hopeful process that avoided the stagnation that usually comes from critiques where the goal might be to identify and call out errors in the thing that is being critiqued. Goat Island would call it 'creative response' and I haven't stop using this method as a means to get students and myself to make from what is made, as opposed to just talk about what is or is not working.

What defines a good arts assignment?

I suppose a good art assignment is one that opens up a pathway for a student that ends up being a pathway of the student's own making. Believe it or not this does not exclude rote assignments with prescribed outcomes. Not unlike perfecting a specific dance posture or being taught how to pray by older relatives, sometimes a ritualistic or clearly delineated assignment can open up a personal pathway for an individual and therefore it can't be bad. The results may be predictable and perhaps quotidian, but with an eye towards generativity a good/slow/generative teacher (or observer) can catch the moments of difference, mistakes, and deviations in even the most uniform assignments to teach towards an expansion of the mind (and the world).

How has your perspective on arts assignments changed over time or throughout your career?

Since teaching in general has become a means by which I think about my creative work, assignments and their mechanisms have become that much more important and curious as a pliable material.

No assignment is hopeless to me. I understand an assignment not as a constriction, but as something that art can be launched from. A standard, for example, is not only a firm stipulation or a rallying point, but a means by which we can extend our thinking. Everyday I'm asked by different factions of the academy *and* the art world to complete tasks within certain parameters. The question that immediately ensues whenever an assignment emerges is: 'how do I do this thing in a way that is integral to what is important to me and how can I express who I am to the world through these mediations?' I pose a version of this question to my students with every assignment I give them and I pose it to myself with every task I take on, whether it's externally or internally given/mandated.

Jorge Lucero (1976) is an artist, teacher and Associate Professor of Art Education at the University of Illinois. He was born, raised, and educated in Chicago. One proposal Lucero makes in his work is that the teacher can be a conceptual artist through the permissions of conceptual art. Through the same thinking, the conceptualist is also a teacher.

‘An intriguing prompt can lead to a terrible learning experience.’ Nina Paim

Interview by Sanne Kersten

What relation do arts assignments have to your design practice?

I really strive to elicit critical thinking, and to bring social, political, and environmental discussions into the realm of design and the classroom. Therefore, my assignments usually revolve around problematizing the role of design and its entanglements with larger power structures, and systems of oppression. In my experience, design education in Europe, and especially in Switzerland, tends to happen as if design existed in a vacuum, dangerously disconnected from the world at large. In my teaching practice, I try to counter to this.

Which arts assignments have made an impression on you?

The example that immediately comes to my mind is an assignment back from primary school—third or fourth grade in Brazil. It was a language assignment. After learning the basic grammar rules, we were asked to go out in the streets and test our knowledge. We had to look for mistakes in signs all around the city, document those mistakes photographically, and then explain in each case what was wrong and why. I was maybe 11 or 12 years old, and it felt exhilarating to go out in the streets with a camera instead of being in the classroom staring at the blackboard. But afterwards, the teacher brought up a discussion that was even better than our initial photojournalist task. Departing from our own photographs, we problematized some of those 'mistakes'. Is a missing preposition from a hand painted sign equivalent to a mis-conjugated verb found in the city hall signage? We then talked about the adequacy of language, discussing different registers, types of speech, and styles. Eventually, our conversation entered the realms of literacy, and tackled issues of race, ethnicity, class, and power within speech. That was very important for me.

Who are your arts assignment 'heroes' or sources of inspiration?

In general, I'm sceptical of the notion of heroes altogether. But I definitely look up to a few ever-inspiring thinkers of education such as bell hooks and Paulo Freire, who have reflected on the emancipatory possibilities of education.

What defines a good arts assignment?

I don't really think there's such a thing as an intrinsically good or bad assignment. A seemingly 'banal' assignment can very well be a fantastic learning vehicle, depending on the teacher's ability to guide the class. In the same way, an intriguing prompt can lead to a terrible learning experience, in the absence of adequate teacher guidance.

I tend to see assignments as formulations or prompts that set classes in motion. They can function as frameworks for collective thinking, triggering conversations and joint investigations. Formulating a new assignment always starts with a reflection on what I, as a student, would be interested in thinking, examining, or making. It tends to be something that takes me out of my own comfort zone, something I'm not entirely familiar with, some sort of testing ground. And it also tends to react to specific events, news and to the specific local contexts of the institutions where I'm teaching.

A few years ago, Corinne Gisel, Emilia Bergmark, and I worked on the book *Taking a Line for a Walk: Assignments in Design Education*, bringing the assignment as a pedagogical element and verbal artefact of design education to the attention. We initiated this book not to select 'the best' assignments, but to showcase a wide variety of approaches to design education. We wanted to demonstrate how varied design education can be, and thereby 'open up' the field. At the same time, realizing how design education was becoming increasingly more exclusive, we wanted to democratize the access to such learning tools. We purposely ended our selection of 224 assignments with a prompt that called for picking any of the previous 223 exercises and redefining it so that it would make sense for one's own interests. I still very much hold on to this idea.

What is your current perspective on arts assignments?

Lately, I have been mentoring a few students in their BA and MA projects and theses, supporting them on a one-on-one level along the way. The work I try to do with these students is to really make them aware that they have agency to redefine an assignment, so that it makes sense to them. I think there is a huge pressure in design education for some form of validation. Students can ask me 'Is this good enough, is this what is expected?' How

I see my role as an educator is to actually help them answer those questions for themselves. Is this good enough for *them*, how would *they* like it to be? I think that's important to learn: not only how to evaluate, but how to frame your work.

Nina Paim is a designer, researcher, curator, and educator. She studied graphic design at Esdi (Brazil) and the Gerrit Rietveld Academie (the Netherlands). Paim works internationally and is a co-founder and project lead of the nonprofit design research practice *common-interest*, based in Switzerland.

‘A good assignment makes you smile, because it has something special.’ Erik Schrooten

Interview by Sanne Kersten

What does your teaching practice look like?

I have always had an adventurous teaching practice—doing experiments with students, working with incidental finds, giving confusing assignments. I used to divide my classes into two parts: one part craftsmanship, and one part creativity. Both parts had their own logic and didactic method. The didactics of craftsmanship is based on handing on a tradition, teaching skills in a systematic manner. That method has been increasingly developed and refined over time and therefore it has value. However, this strictly organized didactics is not suited to creativity. Creation does not follow a fixed plan and processes can be fuzzy. You may be working on something together for a while and nothing happens, while at other times things move very fast. Creativity, to me, covers a broad range—from adapting scores and giving out assignments to coaching students who contribute themes and ideas from their own fascinations. At the moment, I am not making this distinction all that strict, and craftsmanship, research, and creativity become more intermingled. I do still apply the golden rule that an original idea is always given priority.

Which arts assignments have made an impression on you, and why?

I'm a fan of the composer and producer Brian Eno. Eno was an important inspiration to David Bowie, U2, and many others. Since 1974, together with Peter Schmidt, he developed a set of cards called 'Oblique Strategies'. These cards contain bizarre assignments to help musicians get rid of ingrained patterns. The concept is quite simple. If you become stuck or need new impulses and ideas, you pick a card: *emphasize differences, change instrument roles, cluster analysis, use fewer notes*. Thereby Eno breaks your pattern to make room for new and interesting processes. For example, he taped Coldplay's Chris Martin's fingers together in order to force him to play the piano in a new way. Eno and Schmidt applied a whole set of tricks to *annoy* artists. They made me realize that these practices were not only interesting in an educational context, but could just as well be used to make really great art. Eno also used his card set when he helped develop Bowie's legendary Berlin albums.

Who are your arts assignment 'heroes' or sources of inspiration?

My heroes are those teachers who can make up their own assignments from their own context, goals, coincidence, or a theme they have chosen. One can only hope that all arts teachers will master the craft of designing assignments.

In music there is no real tradition in that area yet. The assignments that are now circulating are evergreens that keep coming back. In workshops I have teachers bring scores with them. The story of that composer, his style of writing and signature almost always provide material for making assignments. For example, my participants used the work of the Cuban composer Leo Brouwer. Brouwer frequently applies movable fingering for the left hand. Immediately, an assignment presents itself: choose a left-hand fingering and move it along the guitar neck. Listen, look for interesting combinations… and make a composition with just this one fingering.

What defines a good arts assignment?

A good assignment makes you smile, because it has something special, is unusual. A strong assignment is also sufficiently restricted to prevent students from drowning in a sea of possibilities. Personally, I like assignments that are made up of a number of consecutive instructions. Step one, step two, step three… You could call them guided assignments. Within the steps you allow total freedom, striking a balance between guidance and openness. As students become more skilful, your assignments can become more open. This means that a student's personal fascination can become the starting point for an original creation.

How has your perspective on arts assignments changed over time or throughout your career?

I have noticed a sort of wave-like motion with myself. Sometimes I work with very open assignments and then later I feel the need to work in a more focused and restricted manner… and then I tend to lean to the other side again. It has only been a few years since creativity is one of the end goals in the study programme of music in the arts faculties of Flanders. This means that we now have governmental permission to *play with the building blocks*, to allow for playfulness and adventure in the curriculum of a music academy. Many teachers of music still shy away from that: we haven't been properly trained for it, is what they say. This is because craftsmanship and virtuosity have been the supreme good in music education for so long. Changing that is a long-term process, but slowly but surely this is turning.

Erik Schrooten is an educator and guitar teacher in Belgium. He worked as a teacher trainer and policy-making assistant at the Flemish University colleges Leuven-Limburg. In 2016 he picked up his other great passion again: teaching guitar at the Art Academy Noord-Limburg. For the past ten years, he has been doing intensive research and has specialized in pedagogy of the arts.

‘I approach assignments as the “not yet known in advance”.’ Stephanie Springgay

Interview by Sanne Kersten

What is your view on the relationship between the arts and education?

I have been working as an academic for twenty years now at the intersections of artistic practices and pedagogy. I think there has always been the potential and the possibility to ask questions of a pedagogical nature through an artistic practice. Sometimes there’s friction, but that’s where the interesting possibilities between art and education emerge. I believe studying to become an artist and having an art practice is very different to thinking about pedagogical concepts and pedagogical practices. There are different kinds of literacies or languages, different value systems and tensions in both disciplines. However, rather than having one discipline turn into the other, I’m interested in the space between them where a new set of criteria and value systems are created in an emergent way.

'I approach assignments as the "not yet known in advance".'

Which arts assignments have made an impression on you?

I am not interested in narrowly defined assignments prescribed before the class begins, where students reproduce course material or assigned readings for the sake of obtaining grades. However, I approach assignments as the 'not yet known in advance'. These are assignments emerging from and in the context of the classroom, co-developed with students, involving reflection and feedback, and provoking discussion or action.

Furthermore, I am attentive to an 'aesthetic pedagogies' approach to assignments. For instance, students have 10-15 minutes to 'teach' the class something new, unusual, or creative that would not typically be part of a graduate seminar. This assignment asks students to consider 'class as art'. Aesthetic pedagogies have included: learning how to ferment cabbage, how to ride a unicycle, how to give a dog commands in Polish, how to make a beeswax candle, dry oregano, and many more.

In that similar vein, I will sometimes create conditions in my class for 'other ways of reading'. Students can bring something to read that resonates with the weekly assigned readings, and engage the rest of the class in an active and performative reading of this text. The texts can be academic, poetry, or anything really. For example, a student asked all of the class to meet in the University swimming pool. During the class we swam, performed synchronized swim movements, and read aloud a text about swimming.

More recently, I curated the 'Instant Class Kit', a mobile curriculum guide and pop-up exhibition which exemplifies this aesthetic pedagogy of the 'not yet known'. The 'Instant Class Kit' is a boxed edition of artistic curricular materials commissioned by fourteen contemporary artists, inspired by Fluxus. The contemporary artists strive to deliver a curriculum based on the values of critical democratic pedagogy, anti-racist and anti-colonial logics, and social justice. The lessons, syllabi, and classroom activities address topics and methodologies including queer subjectivities, Indigenous epistemologies, social movements, and collective protest.

Who are your arts assignment 'heroes' or sources of inspiration?

I have been working very closely with Vanessa Dion Fletcher, an Indigenous Canadian artist. A lot of her work is around Indigenous language revitalization, the ongoing legacies of settler colonialism and its violence against women's bodies, and indigenous textile practices. There's something very tactile about her art; for example, she works with porcupine quills that have a very strong odour. For someone like me who's really interested in the body and in the senses, I think her work is an inspiration.

An inspiring colleague of mine is Karyn Recollet, faculty member in 'Women and Gender' studies at the University of Toronto. She's an Indigenous Cree urban artist and scholar writing about Indigenous futurisms. There's a lot of resilience in her writing. I think her and Vanessa's work foregrounds the colonial legacies as well as the ongoing settler colonial violences, but then their work questions: 'What would a future look like?' and questions what that means. Recollet also uses concepts like radical relationality, writing about love, joy, and care—that I find significant in re-thinking what a future can become. Themes of these artists connect to 'The Instant Class Kit'. For example, the artist Syrus Ware added 'Activists' love letters' to the kit, that encourage you to think about reaching out to one person who moves you by what they do.

What defines a good arts assignment?

What interests me are assignments that are about experimentation and chance. Sometimes things fail, but failure to me is important. It means that there was some degree of risk and it opens up spaces for different kinds of conversations. I am compelled by assignments that create openings for different kinds of intimate encounters to take place, where learning is affective and curious. Assignments must be grounded in feminist, anti-racist and anti-colonial frameworks that are meaningful and attentive to fostering a better world.

How has your perspective on arts assignments changed over time or throughout your career?

During my entire academic career, I've been working in this same way, which is probably very much against the institutional norm. My pedagogical way of working with Masters and PhD students has been to rethink what a seminar looks like: how do we make class a work of art? That might mean that the kinds of things we do together look somewhere between a conventional seminar and an art class. I don't have a pre-planned idea of what's going to be happening from the first class to twelve weeks later. There are some propositions or enabling constraints that move the class along, like assigned readings. I don't believe that anything pedagogical can be repeatable, it would fail the next time because it only worked in the context of who was in that class and what we were trying to do together.

Stephanie Springgay is a Professor and the Director of the School of the Arts, McMaster University in Hamilton, ON, Canada. Their research is concerned with feminist, queer, anti-racist, anti-ableist, and anti-colonial contemporary art practices and their pedagogical and affective force. Springgay directs projects such as 'The Pedagogical Impulse' on socially-engaged art, and 'WalkingLab', an international collaborative that mobilizes critical walking methodologies.

‘Education can also be an artistic medium.’ Pavèl van Houten

Interview by Sanne Kersten

What relation do arts assignments have to your practice?

In my practice I concern myself with the question: how can you teach as *an artist*? In order to explore how didactics can be applied as an artistic medium, I conceived the ‘Didactic Experiment’. As a designer of a didactic experiment you are being challenged to play with the elements that make up a lesson or class. Think, for example, of time, location, instruction, division of roles, giving feedback, sound, test formats, or the subject of a lesson. But also think of certain rituals, such as: in each class there are students who need to go to the bathroom, how do you handle that?

I give students of Art in Education the assignment to work with one element of a lesson, to make it ‘extreme’, or tweak it. For example, I first give them a lecture about digestion and then the students may choose one aspect of that lecture and design an experiment based on that. The results can be very divergent. For instance, one group of students placed all the tables in a row in the shape of intestines, whereby the students represented the food and as everyone was crawling underneath the tables, the lesson was delivered. Another group of students tried to evoke the idea of a digestive tract by placing a bin with water over our heads. The stress induced by the fear of becoming wet can activate our bowels.

Which arts assignments have made an impression on you, and why?

I tasked students with designing their own feedback interview. One student asked me to lie down under the table while she was lying on top of it. Under usual circumstances a feedback interview can be tense and hierarchical, but this absurdist situation created room for a very open and creative discussion.

Another student pitched her work in five minutes, standing at the top of the stairs. I had to stand at the bottom of the stairs and run her work completely into the ground, but while ascending the stairs become increasingly positive about it. Having arrived at the top I was to praise her work euphorically as the best ever. The student knew: I'm being heavily criticized because it is necessary, but with this method she became the owner of the feedback process and got from it what she wanted.

Based on these forms of feedback we designed a card game. Sometimes, during the interview, students can hand me a card that may say: please be quiet for five minutes, or: give a tip, or: can you tell me a story? The game provides room to communicate about a student's needs, which allows them some measure of control over the feedback interview.

Who are your arts assignment 'heroes' or sources of inspiration?

I am interested in people such as Jorge Lucero and Maarten Bel, who operate on the intersection of art and education, because there are parallels with my own work. I find artists who dare to use restrictions inspiring. The Amsterdam artist Marieke Coppens, for example, created the work *Blue Creates the Open Space*, in which she organized seven 'healing' nights, informed by elements from a sect. In this setting, texts were read out and people sang together, but there was also almost half an hour of silence. Taking the liberty to do that and then see what happens, despite feelings of awkwardness, that takes guts.

What defines a good arts assignment?

Education is different in each situation. The dynamic of a Monday morning class is different from that on a Friday afternoon. I think that it is important to have a flexible way of teaching: be well prepared, but also open to what happens spontaneously. Don't be afraid to interrupt your class if you feel that it's not working. Run up and down the stairs together three times, go for a walk, or have students draw an animal that is inspired by the model you just discussed.

I also think that the degree of freedom in an assignment is important. Students often think that they want to work on assignments in all freedom, but paradoxically that can be very restricting. I once designed a plan in which all the elements of the lessons were empty. The plan only showed inspiring spaces on various locations, such as a roof terrace, a gym, and so on. The rest of the plan was completely free and the students found that very complicated. Still, I think it's important for them to experience this because as an artist you are confronted with much emptiness. If you work as an autonomous artist, the need to create something must be felt *from inside*. You begin to doubt everything and are confronted with very basic questions such as: why am I here? What am I doing here?

How has your perspective on arts assignments changed over time or throughout your career?

Teaching influences my art practice, and vice versa. I find that I am more and more working *with* students instead of *for* students. And I notice that art disciplines are becoming increasingly hybrid, both in the art world and in art education, but the study programmes are still lagging in this respect. It is now my mission to see how the teacher training programmes at art academies can come to be regarded as more of a positive force. Art teachers don’t just teach about art but can also be the creators of education as such. They possess the skills to make this happen. Education can really also be an artistic medium.

Pavèl van Houten (1984) studied at the Gerrit Rietveld Academie (BA) and the Sandberg Instituut (MA). He is a teacher at the Willem de Kooning Academy and other institutes. His projects take place in public and semi-public space. He documents and analyzes his research objects with both fanaticism and relativism, while stylizing and ritualizing his methods. He treats educational spaces (schools) in the same manner. His work has been exhibited in the Stedelijk Museum Amsterdam, Museum De Hallen Haarlem, TENT Rotterdam, and other art venues.

Assignments

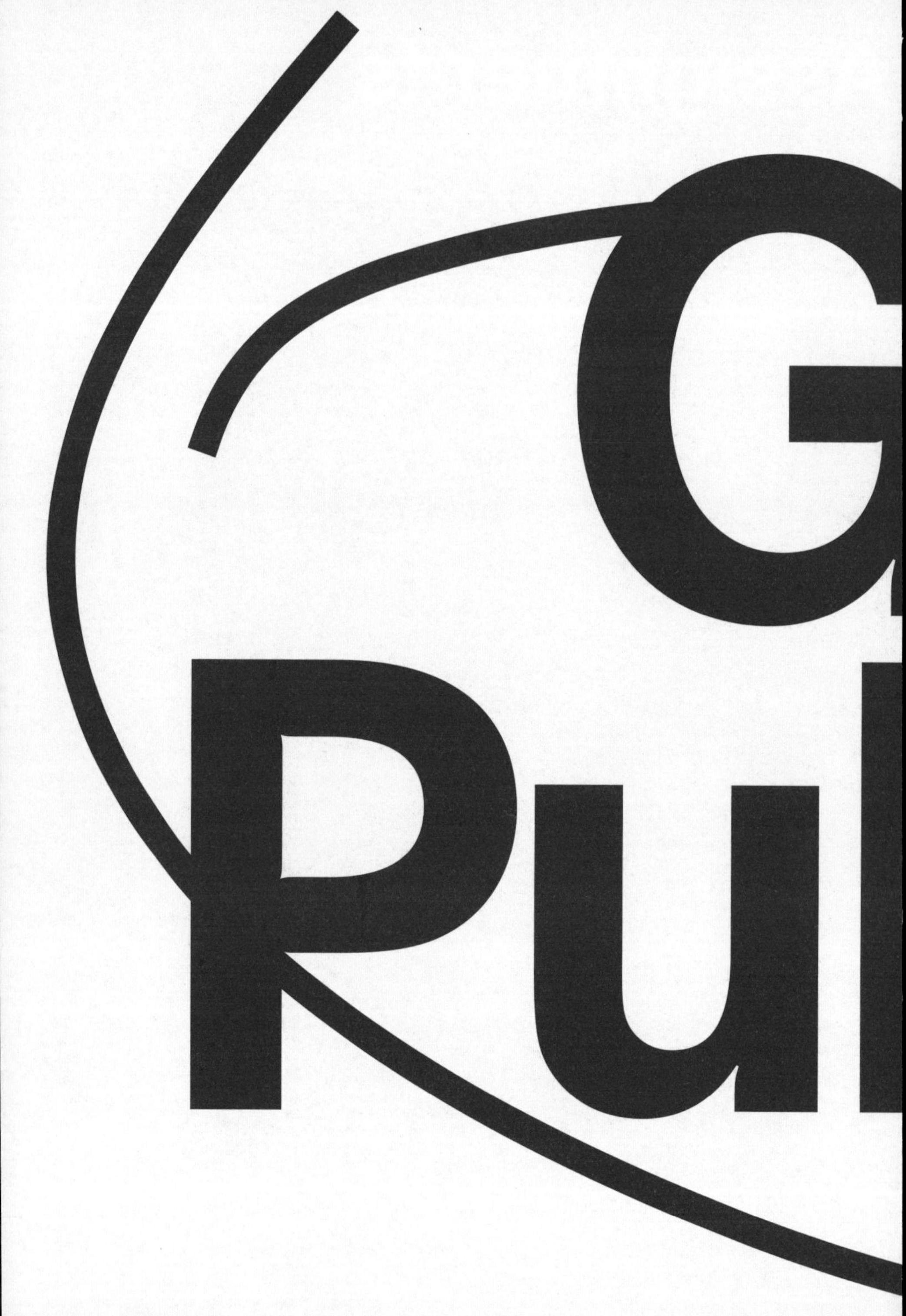

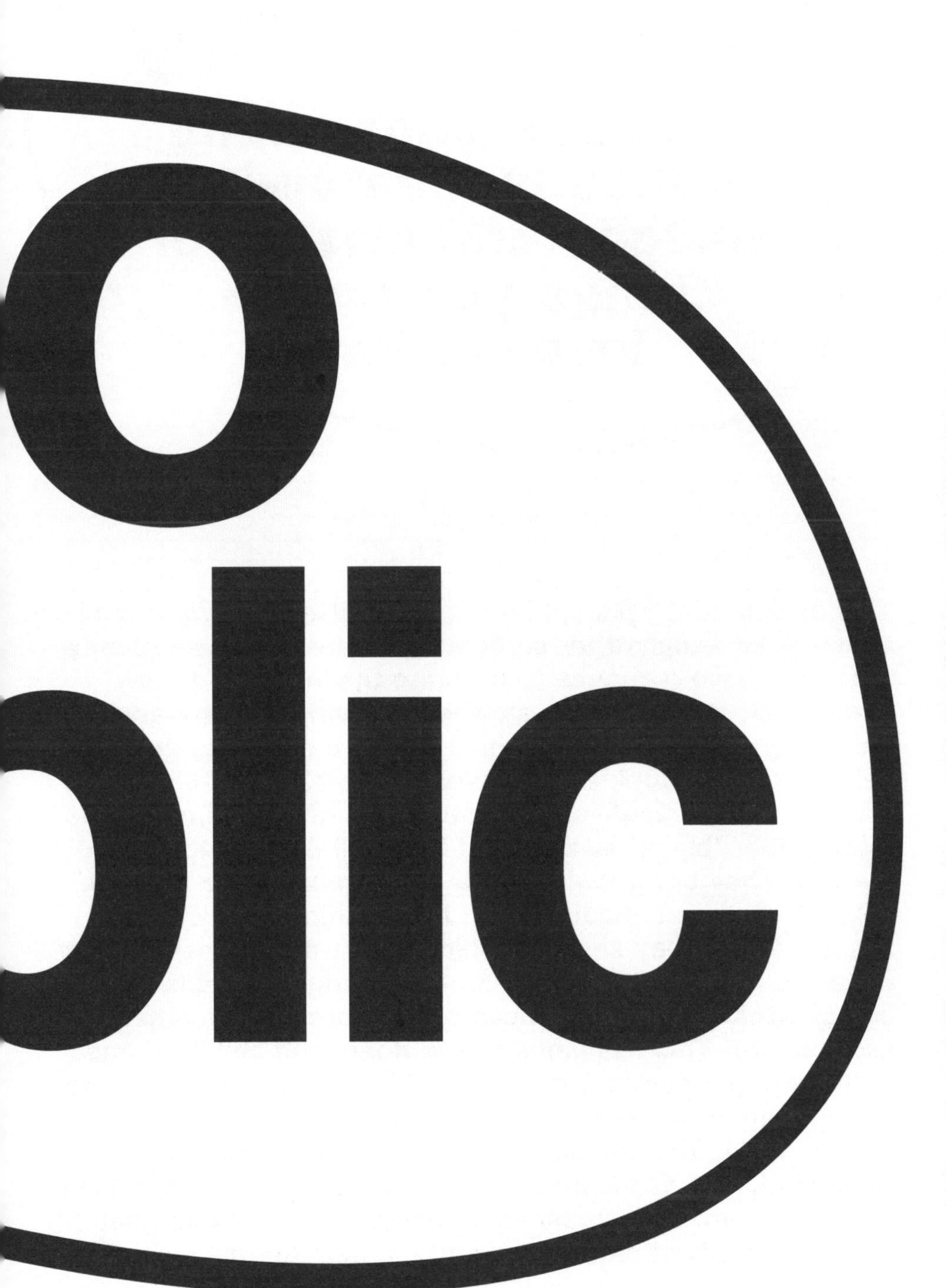
o
blic

Assess the City

Evaluate your public space by bestowing badges and prizes for things you notice, love, or hate.

Anne Thulson
Denver, CO, USA

This assignment asks students to appraise and award public space. It is designed for students who are tested frequently, but never have a chance to evaluate the world that tests them. First, students discuss when and why they are assessed and describe the forms in which they are compensated or penalized. They look at examples of trophies and blooper prizes and discuss divergent categories of assessment. They make paper 'blank' awards that they will present to parts of the city. They bring their awards on a walk, where they are asked to keep a critical eye out for anything they want to assess. When they see something they want to assess, they write the name of the award on their badge and affix it to the object or site. Then they move on to more opportunities for assessment. This assignment was done with children, aged 5–10, during a summer day camp. They enthusiastically and thoughtfully taped many badges around town. Some of the badges read: 'the stinkiest trash can', 'the longest cross walk light', 'the saddest statue', 'most columns', 'best rolling down hill', 'not bad', 'best lunch parks', 'number one goat statue', 'smellyist bathroom', and 'coolest bridge'.

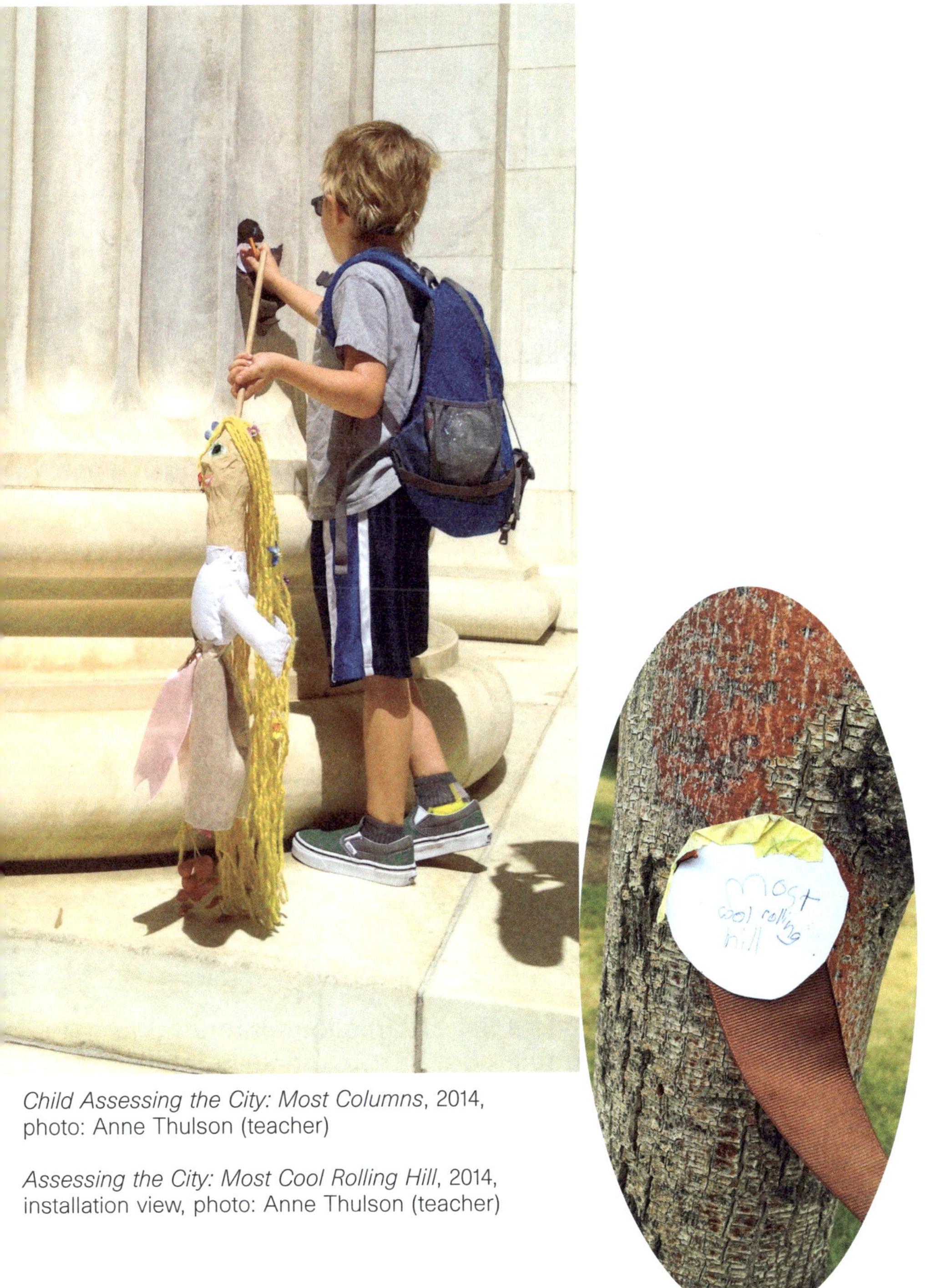

Child Assessing the City: Most Columns, 2014, photo: Anne Thulson (teacher)

Assessing the City: Most Cool Rolling Hill, 2014, installation view, photo: Anne Thulson (teacher)

Who Is Your Soulmate?

Find artworks that best respond to a list of unlikely, counterintuitive, and humanizing questions.

Maura Flood and Sam Ramos
Chicago, IL, USA

Who Is Your Soulmate? is a list of questions intended to help participants access and talk about art, especially in a gallery. The questions are bizarre, sentimental, funny, romantic, and political, and can be used, like a deck of cards, in any number of ways or combinations to help individuals and groups reflect upon, and discuss, their own unique experiences with art. Examples include helping teens gain confidence talking in galleries, prompting art students to pair questions with their own work, and asking pairs or groups to write their own questions in response to our supplied list.

Which artwork will cry with you?
Which artwork do you want to take on a walk?
Which artwork would you introduce to your parents?
Which artwork do you want to whisper, "Everything will be okay," to?
Which artwork do you want to enlarge to the size of a building?
Which artwork would you bury?
Which artwork dances balls-to-the-wall alone in its apartment?
Which artwork is impatient?
Which artwork should be your best friend?
Which artwork misses its grandmother?
Which artwork came to America with nothing but ten dollars and the shirt on its back?
Which artwork takes more than it gives?
Which artwork gives more than it takes?
Which artwork was bullied as a child?
Which artwork has insomnia?
Which artwork dreams of falling?
Which artwork will someday run a cupcake shop?
Which artwork is a cloud?
Which artwork adores its friends?
Which artwork is a pale blue light?
Which artwork should the aliens see first?
Which artwork would you take on your time machine with you?
Which artwork would you go into battle with?
Which artwork knows karate?
Which artwork would you deliver into the ocean from whence it came?
Which artwork do you want to save from the coming storm?
Which artwork will you walk on?
Which artwork is vomit?
Which artwork is rainbows?
Which artwork doesn't care if you look at it or not?
Which artwork sings beautifully?
Which artwork stays up late writing poetry?
Which artwork had its heart broken long ago and has been a little different ever since?
Which artwork will break your heart?
Which artwork is damn proud?
Which artwork do you want to touch with your hair with your eyes closed?
Which artwork once was lost but now is found?
Which artwork do you want to possess? Not own or keep. Possess.
Which artwork is yesterday?
Which artwork is today?
Which artwork is tomorrow?
Which artwork will fulfill your wildest dreams?
Which artwork will be with you when you die?
Which artwork brings moons on moonless nights?
Which artwork is haunted?
Which artwork bites its fingernails?
Which artwork does the cutest thing with its lip?
Which artwork slouches when it sits?
Which artwork is afraid to dress the way it really wants to?
Which artwork listens to achy music?
Which artwork is your guardian angel?
Which artwork will you kiss in public no matter who is around?
Which artwork will you kiss in hiding?
Which artwork talks back?
Which artwork falls? Rises? Floats? Which artwork destroys? Which artwork creates?
Which artwork wants more than it can have? Which artwork waits?
Which artwork watches you watching it?
Which artwork would you marry?
Which artwork stills your heart?
Which artwork represents your deepest anxiety?
Which artwork do you want to destroy?

100 Metre Malmö

Conduct a guerrilla marketing or arts intervention on a stretch of 100 metres.

Ewa Berg
Malmö, Sweden

The assignment concerns selecting a specific stretch of a hundred metres in Malmö, Sweden. Having selected it, decide to conduct either guerrilla marketing or an arts intervention. Then, choose something you want to market, or intervene with. Execute your project and document what happens with your intervention.

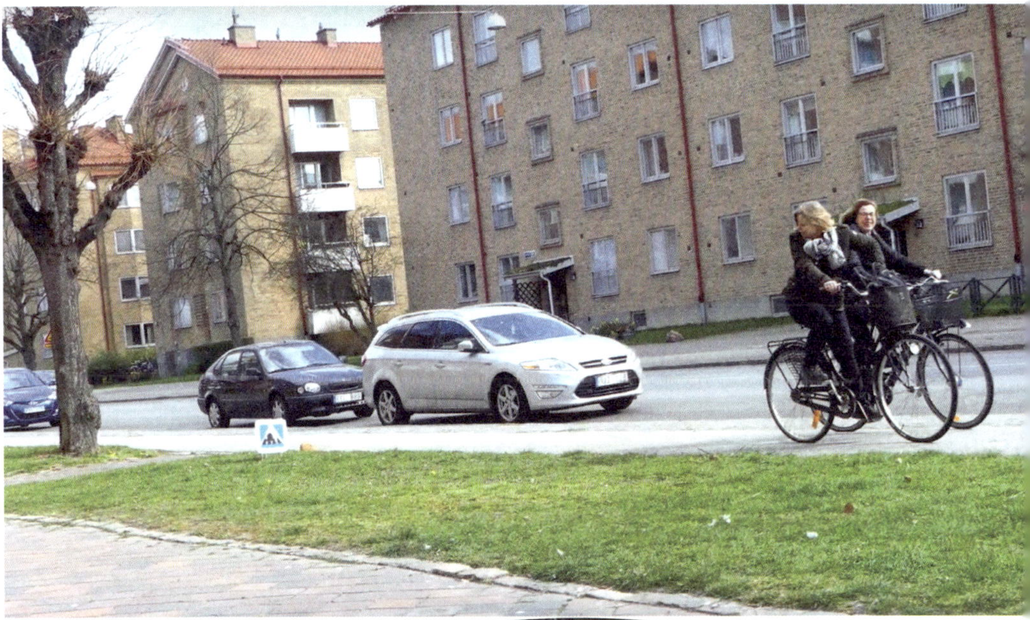

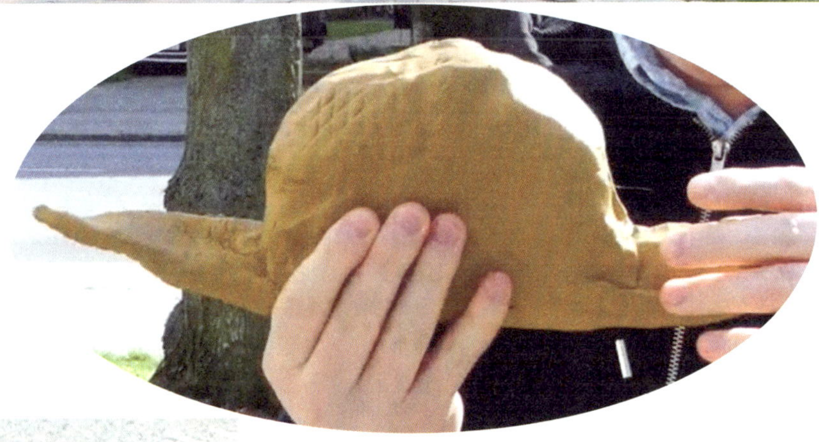

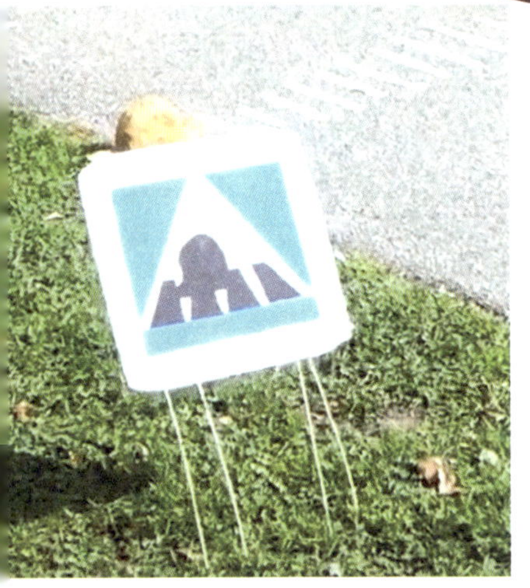

Hampus Hagnell Crossing for Snails,
2019, film still

Colour Intervention

Make a colour intervention in a public space without doing something illegal or unethical.

Olivia Gude
Chicago, IL, USA

Rather than affirming those things that we, artist-educators highly value—nuanced perception, artistic investigation, and confidence in one's own creative capacities—the Western colour teaching tradition is often structured to constrict, control, and regulate colour, mandating limited pseudo-scientific experiments in which students must replicate predictable results by solving predictable problems. Thus, much traditional colour curriculum functions as a primal repression of art education. 'Repression' in the sense of keeping down something that is powerful and energetic, something that without the exertion of force might burst forth, perhaps disrupting social order. Wild colour.

An earlier colour investigation asked each student to bring in between thirty and fifty objects that 1) they can carry, 2) are not precious, 3) are not bio-degradable. Roll out a long and wide strip of black paper on the floor. Students collaboratively sort and discover for themselves the problems and nuances of colour classification.

In the later investigation, each student makes a colour intervention in a public space, bringing the results to class through a tour of a nearby site or through contextualizing photo/video documentation. When asked about the parameters of the assignment, I say only, 'Make an impact. Be principled. Be safe.'

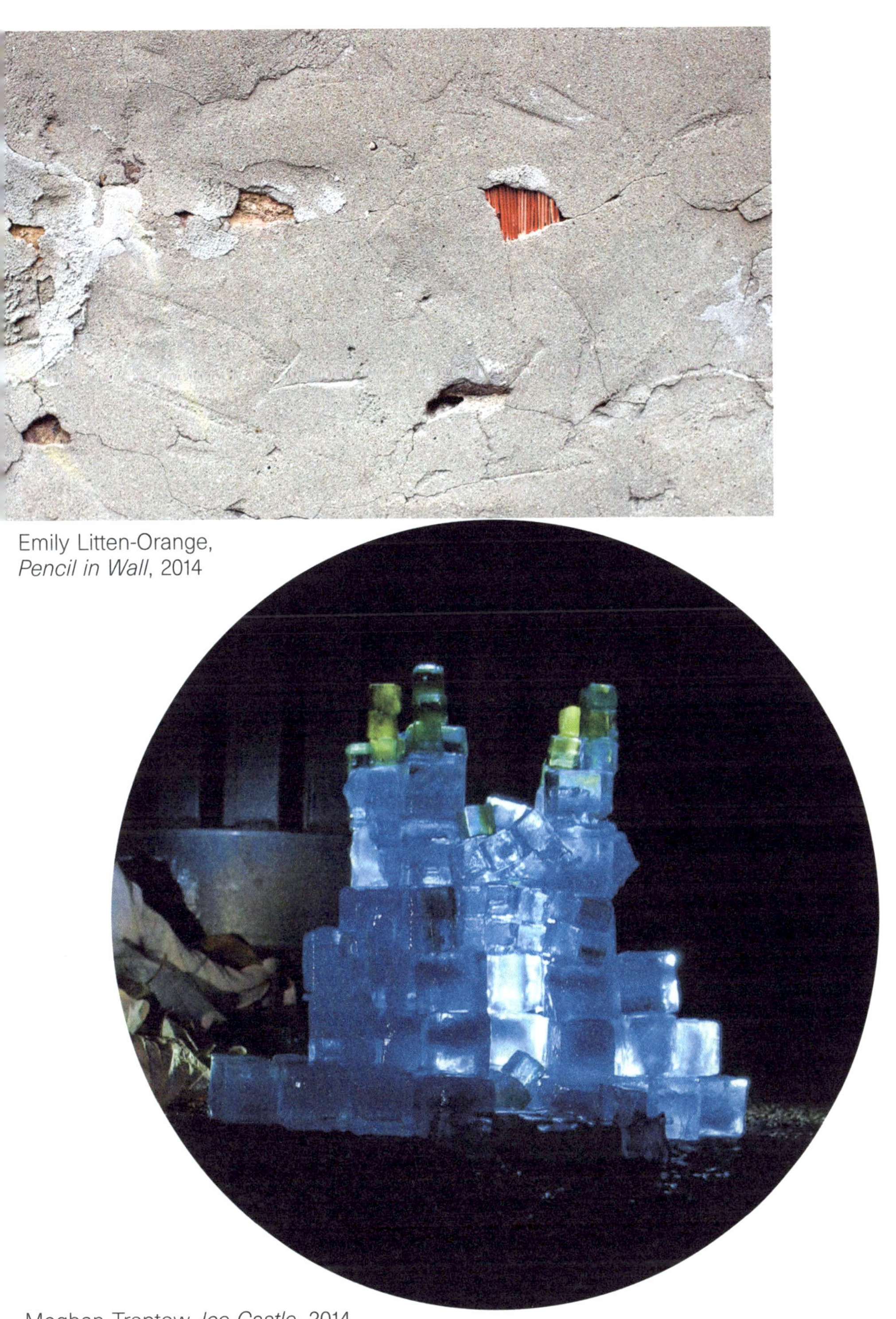

Emily Litten-Orange,
Pencil in Wall, 2014

Meghan Treptow, *Ice Castle*, 2014

Drive-by Art

If you notice a desolate place that you pass by each day, enliven it with an ephemeral installation.

Erin Tapley
Cullowhee, NC, USA

While aesthetic values may differ among individual people, most can agree that misplaced trash or neglected old buildings can be spruced up through simple means. 'Drive-by' suggests quick interactions with a site that will generate both visual interest and a sense of freshness and care with the site's transformation. Many artists have embraced these transformations as art (Mierle Laderman Ukeles, Gordon Matta-Clark, and Tyree Guyton). Most landowners seem not to mind if an ephemeral decoration/clean-up is done.

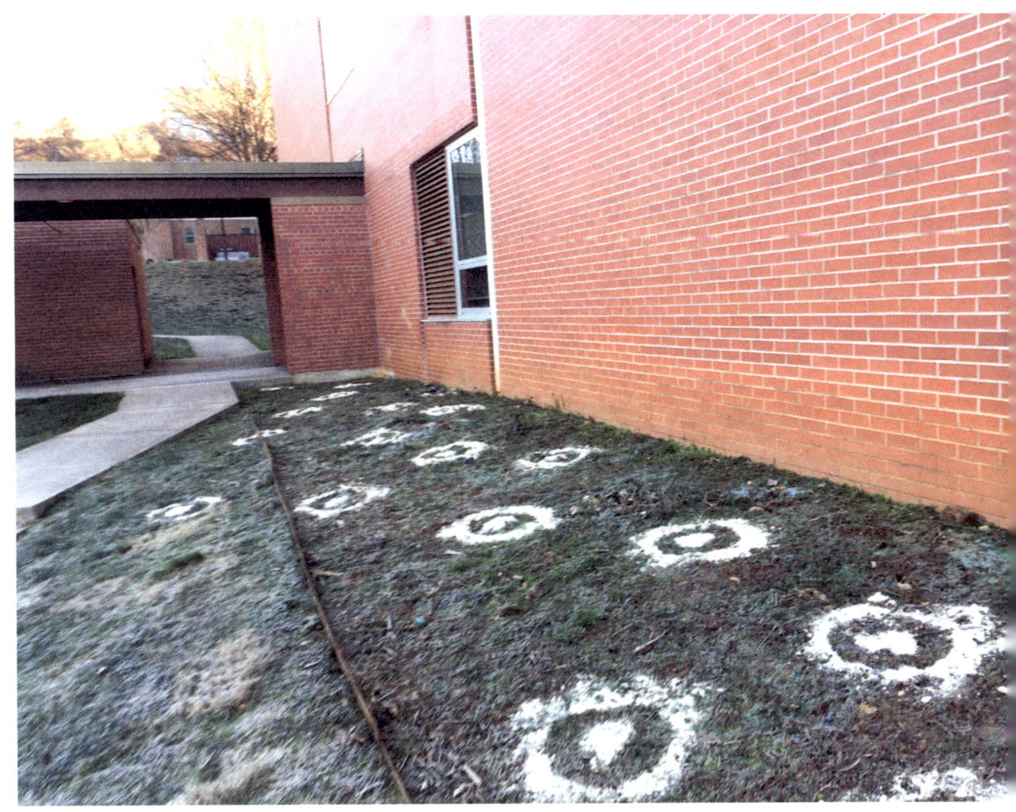

Erin Tapley, *Drive-by Art*, 2020, course example, Western Carolina University, photo: Erin Tapley

Fake News

Bring fake news into the world.

Wilke van der Molen and Chris de Man
Zwolle, the Netherlands

This assignment was developed by preservice teachers of the Hogeschool Viaaa and teachers of primary school De Sprankel in Zwolle. At the time, there was a news item about a Dutch cabinet member who had lied to Parliament about having attended a meeting with the Russian President Putin. We decided to make an assignment around the theme of fake news for 9-to-10-year-olds. The children were given an open group assignment to 'bring fake news into the world'. They went at it with enthusiasm and in their very own way. One group reported about a dolphin that had been spotted in the IJssel River; they even had a video by an eyewitness. Another group hung up posters in the neighbourhood, reporting an escaped snake. And a couple of girls produced diagrams for the Education Minister, visualizing how homework impacted stress levels and children's night rest. All this resulted in great conversations about credibility and about what is fake.

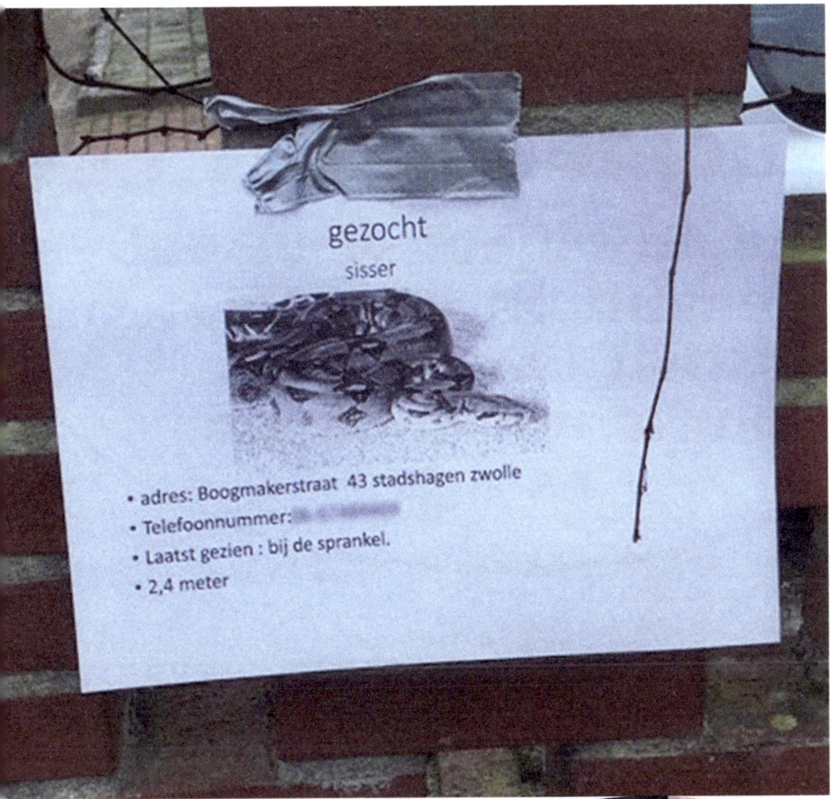

gezocht

sisser

- adres: Boogmakerstraat 43 stadshagen zwolle
- Telefoonnummer:
- Laatst gezien : bij de sprankel.
- 2,4 meter

Pupils of De Sprankel, Zwolle, *Missing Poster for Escaped Snake*, 2018

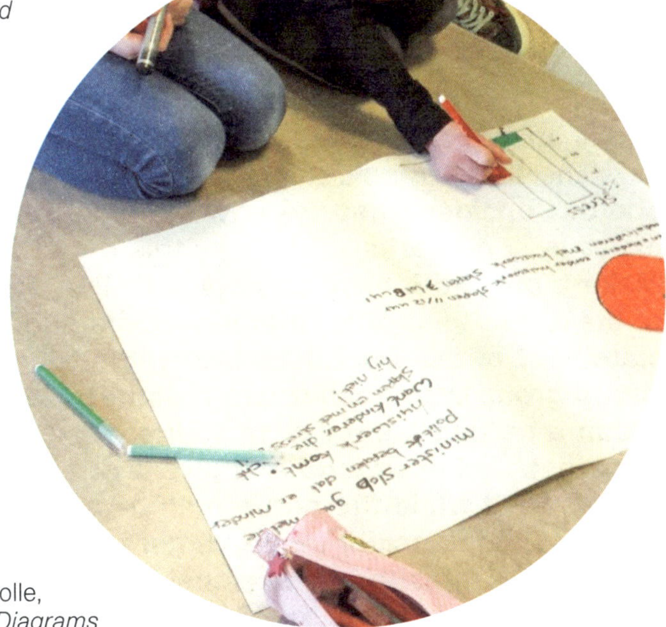

Pupils of De Sprankel, Zwolle, *Homework Stress Levels Diagrams*

Accidental Art I

Find an object or visual element on the street that can be art but is not intended as art.

Oskar Maarleveld
Amsterdam, the Netherlands

Look for an object or visual element on the street (or in public space) that could be art but is not meant to be art. Take the time to look closely at the object and take a nice photo. Consider what the artwork could be about if it were made by a real artist. Why was this material or place chosen? Make a placard for the artwork with the, self-invented, name of the artist, year, title, material and a short explanation/ statement of the work. It is preferable to do this assignment with a group with each group member seeking out a work within a certain area and, in a kind of art tour, alternately show each other around and give a brief explanation in the role of artist while the group members can ask questions. Variation: find accidental art within a given theme such as accidental protest art or accidental social art. Explain what issues the work wants to raise.

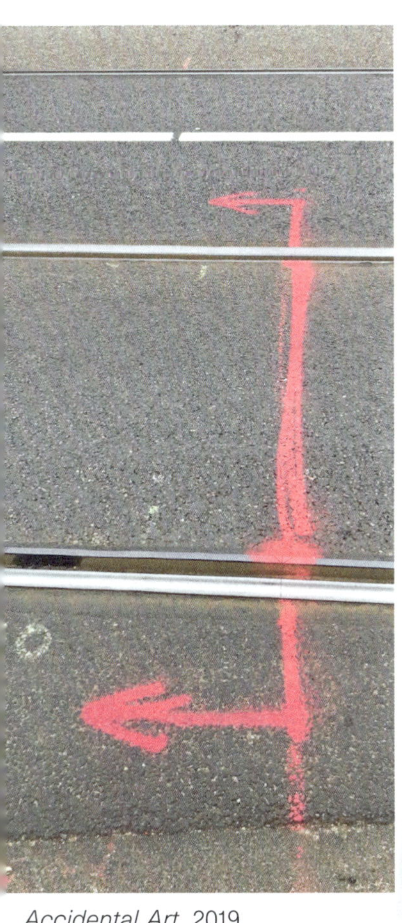

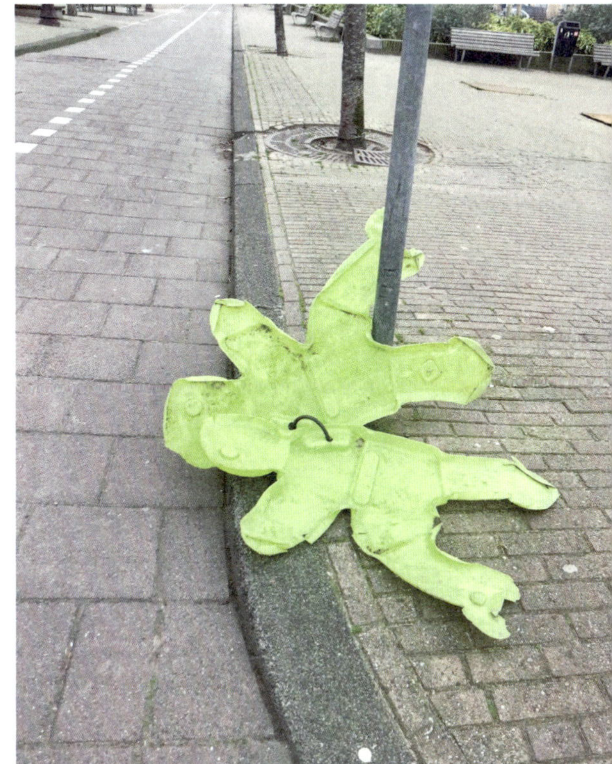

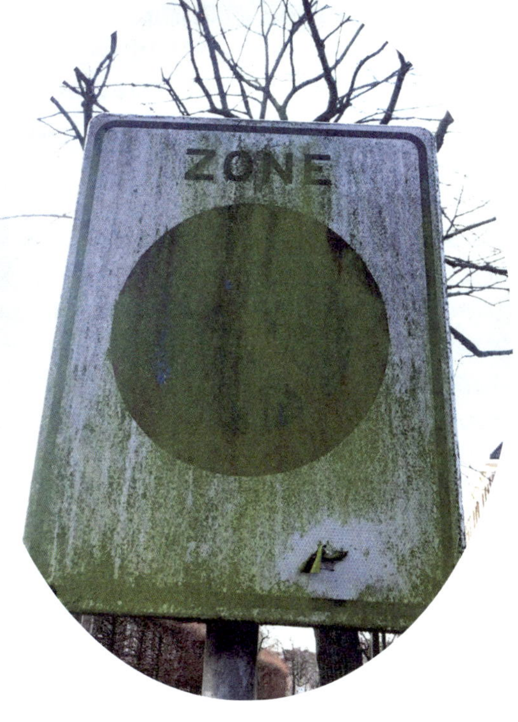

Accidental Art, 2019,
photos: Oskar Maarleveld

Accidental Art II

Discover 'art' in your daily travel and photograph your findings with your mobile device.

Eunji Lee
New York City, NY, USA

This was an exploratory assignment for my non-art major undergraduate students to challenge and expand their preconceptions of art. Moreover, the assignment was intended for my students to pay attention to the most mundane, repetitive sceneries of their dwellings with a heightened awareness. Students shared their findings of 'art' as things or scenes that stood out 'special' to them in terms of formal qualities, or in relation to memory from previous life experiences and the (emotional) state of mind at the moment of the aesthetic encounter. Once their images were laid out and discussed with peers, students were amazed by how clearly their choices of art revealed their thinking patterns and aesthetic preferences, which eventually led to deeper self-understanding. This assignment also sparked many questions related to aesthetics such as the definition of art, the value of art, good and bad art, and the complex concept of the artist in contemporary culture. Students realized that their experience of finding art in the everyday was an embodied transaction with the environment, and that the meaning of art was amplified through processes of interpretation and dialogue. Students shared their views about how this assignment broadened their understanding of art from an object-based artwork to the experience of art.

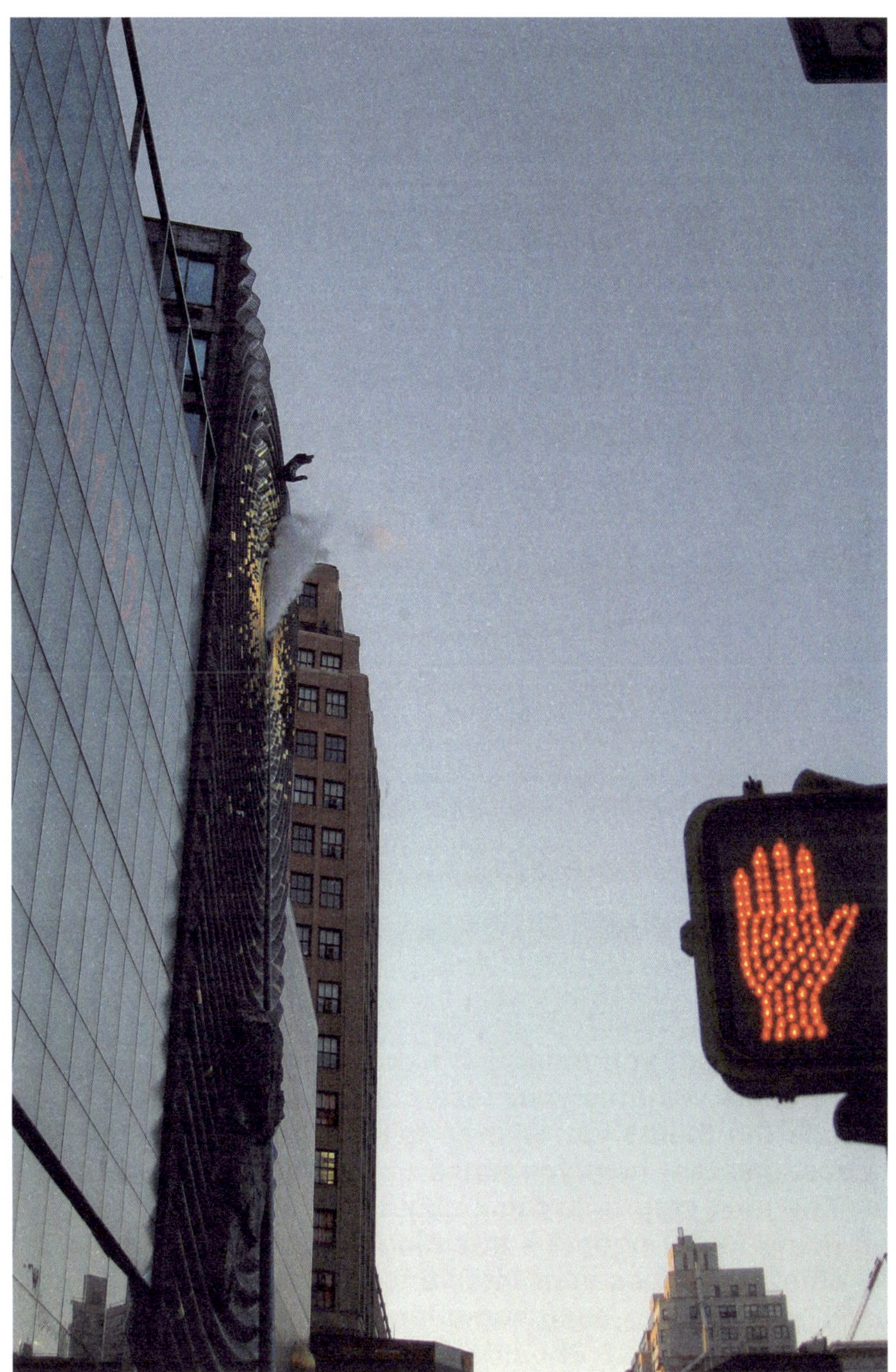

Student's work, *Art Walks: Discovering 'Art' in Daily Traveling*, New York City

Talk to a Stranger

Create an intervention in public space that invites strangers to talk to you about a specific topic.

Hanna Timmers
Amsterdam, the Netherlands

For this assignment you must first ask yourself why you wish to talk to people. What is your research object and why? Then define the theme you wish to talk about and think of initial questions that help you strike up a conversation with people. The next step is to think about the intervention: how are you going to get people's attention, so they stop to talk to you. What form does your intervention take? Think big and small: will you need to build something? Will you have to make cards with topics? Should you wear a costume? Stand in a specific place? Finally, think of how—in a simple manner—to insert the stories you collect in the moment, to make your intervention 'grow'.

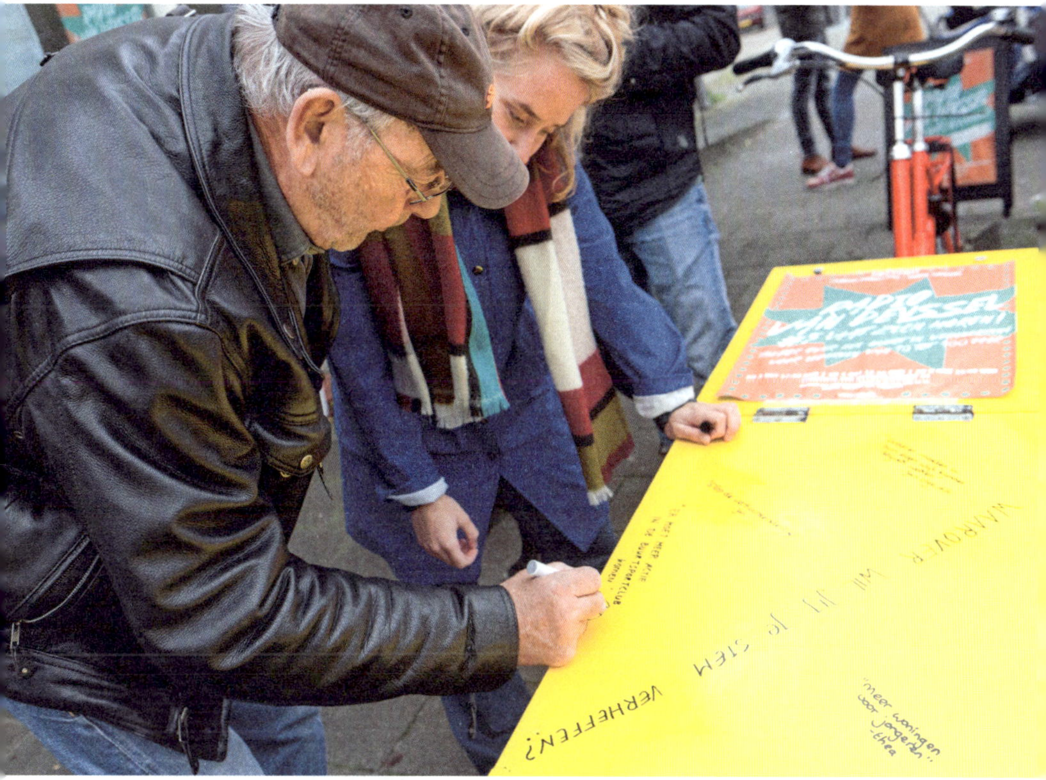

Ilon Lodewijks and Hanna Timmers / Internationaal Theater Amsterdam, *XXXjr.*, 2019, intervention as part of research for a theatre performance, photo: Jasper Groen

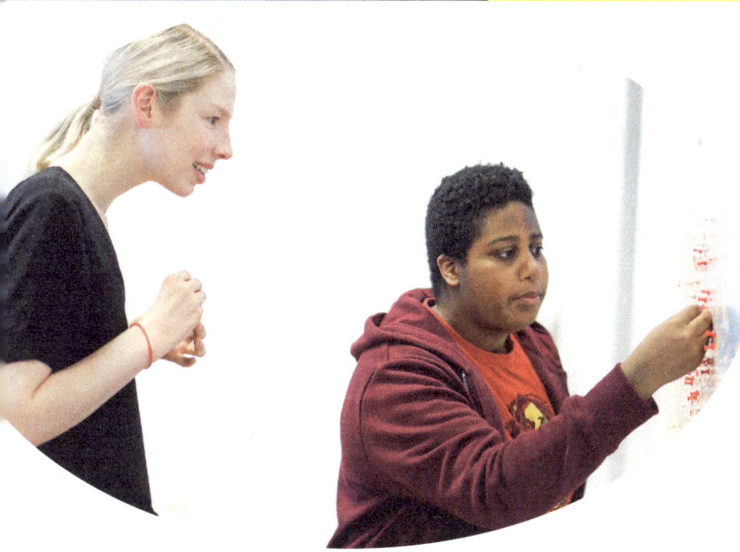

Hanna Timmers / Frascati Producties, *Radio van Deyssel #5*, 2019, intervention as part of a theatre performance, photo: Lisa Maatjens

, , ,

Nar

, , ,

, , ,

rate

, , ,

‘ ‘ ‘ ‘ ‘ ‘

Long Story Short

Write your life story in twenty three-word sentences. Translate the story into a set of twenty equally succinct drawings to display together.

’ ’ ’ ’ ’ ’

Robin Arnold
New Paltz, NY, USA

Students aim to communicate complex content through limited visual information, while maintaining pictorial dynamics. In developing an iconography for their topics, students research poetry, abstraction and symbolism, commercial signs/icons, and eccentric multi-part works by artists Ree Morton, Dieter Roth, Richard Tuttle, Margaret Kilgallen, and Louise Bourgeois. After first writing longer stories, students select their twenty most evocative sentences to translate into drawings. They make several sketches for each, exploring varied abstract and representational modes. Small group critiques probe nuance in form and meaning as each student seeks a resonant image shorthand. Results are enhanced through the creative use of multiple-panel formats (relative size and shape of the drawings) and means of display (grid, arc, accordion fold...). The three-week project is part of the college class ‘Thematic Drawing’, emphasizing in-depth investigation of content, process, and materials.

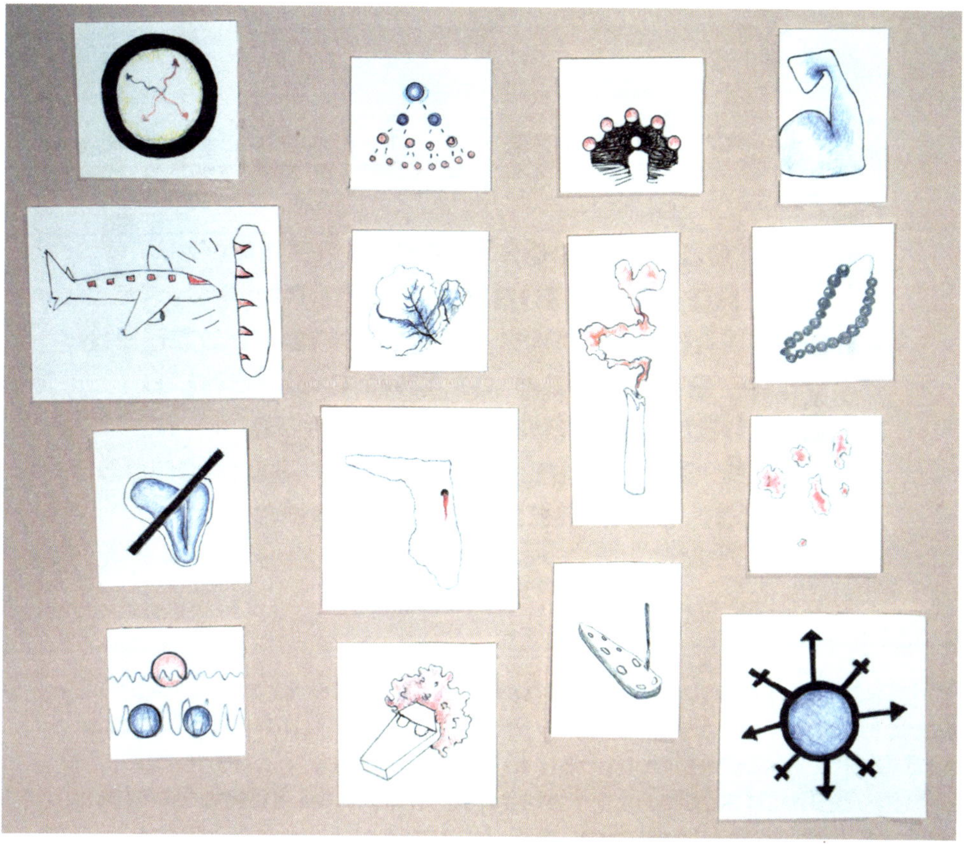

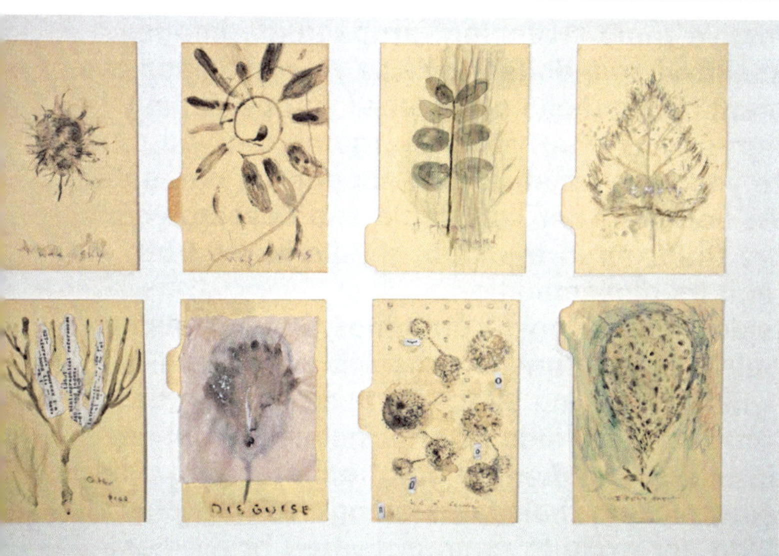

Students' work, *Long Story Short Project*, 2015,
State University of New York, New Paltz

Post-Truth Lecture

Create a post-truth lecture of no less than ten minutes. Deliver the lecture, trying to persuade your audience of the content's truthiness, and then engage in a Q&A session with your audience for another ten minutes.

Disseminart Collective
USA

This assignment uses the creative practice of the lecture performance to purposefully explore post-truth, rhetorical, and visual devices common in contemporary and less recent politics such as whataboutisms, wild interpretations of fact patterns, testimonials, false facts/news, name calling, disjunctive topic switching, propaganda images, and decontextualized soundbites to sway your audience over to your argument. Regardless of whether you personally agree or disagree with what you are arguing for, you must overcommit to your role as an expert supporting one side of an issue. As you consider your topic and develop your stance, explore the truth in the lie or the lie in the truth of any position and its dissemination.

This is inspired by our post-truth times that increasingly have us encountering truthiness, wherein we believe in an assertion without knowing all the facts so that our passionate intuition props up our side of an argument or issue. Participants in this assignment should research only their side of an issue, picking their facts along the way, cite all their sources (do not exclude rumour, twitter, or memes), consider rhetorical devices of politicians, moderate their voice (emphasis, pacing, and tone), and employ persuasive body language. 'Killer graphics' are a must.

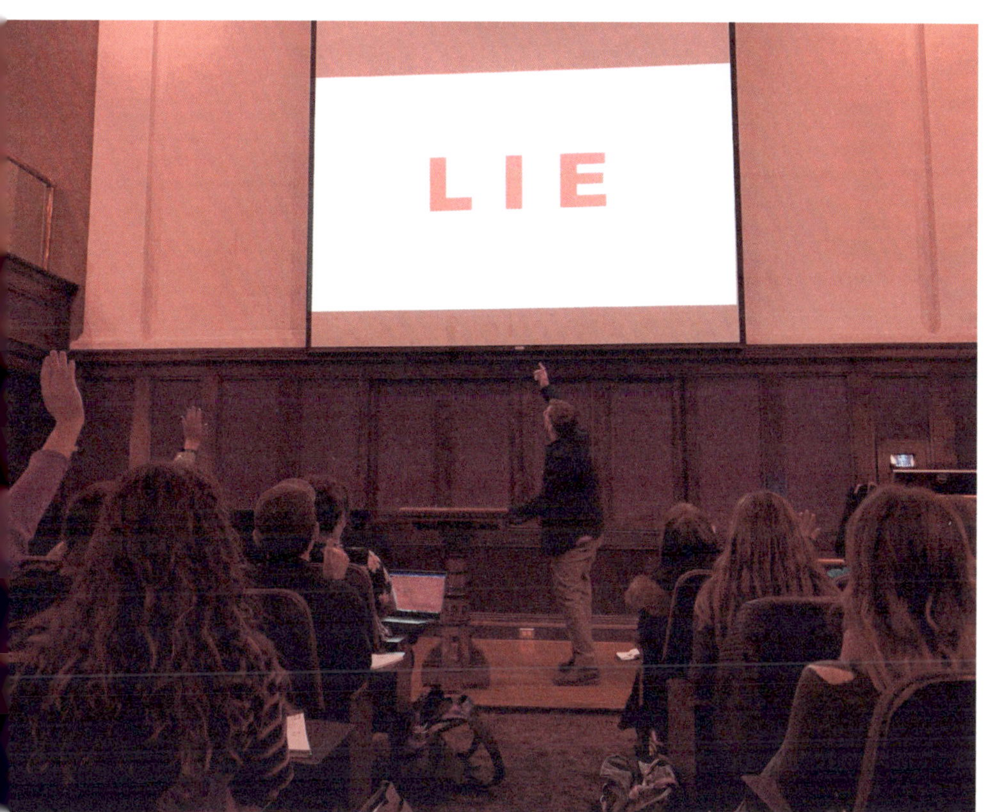

Disseminart Collective, *Lie to Me*, 2020, lecture performance

Made In X

Produce historical artefacts from a society that has never existed.

Sam de Groot
Amsterdam, the Netherlands

Each year, the Stedelijk Museum Amsterdam hosts a group exhibition called 'Rietveld Uncut', featuring new work by Rietveld students. The theme for the 2019 edition was 'fabulating alternative imaginaries'. For the graphic design department's contribution to the exhibition, I asked the students to produce a retrospective of artefacts from an imagined Republic of Amsterdam (1980–2021). The brief was to make an immersive experience that would give the viewer a strong sense of what that society would have been like, through fabricated everyday objects. The students made objects including a cookbook, street signage, a public transport map, police uniforms, currency, jenever bottles, tattoos, a phone book, and a flower-shop sign. The designs were informed by a few group sessions, in which we composed a speculative history of this Republic of Amsterdam, including its political, cultural, linguistic, and technological developments. This gave the (otherwise very distinct) projects some common ground. Of course, this assignment can easily be repurposed using a different imagined society.

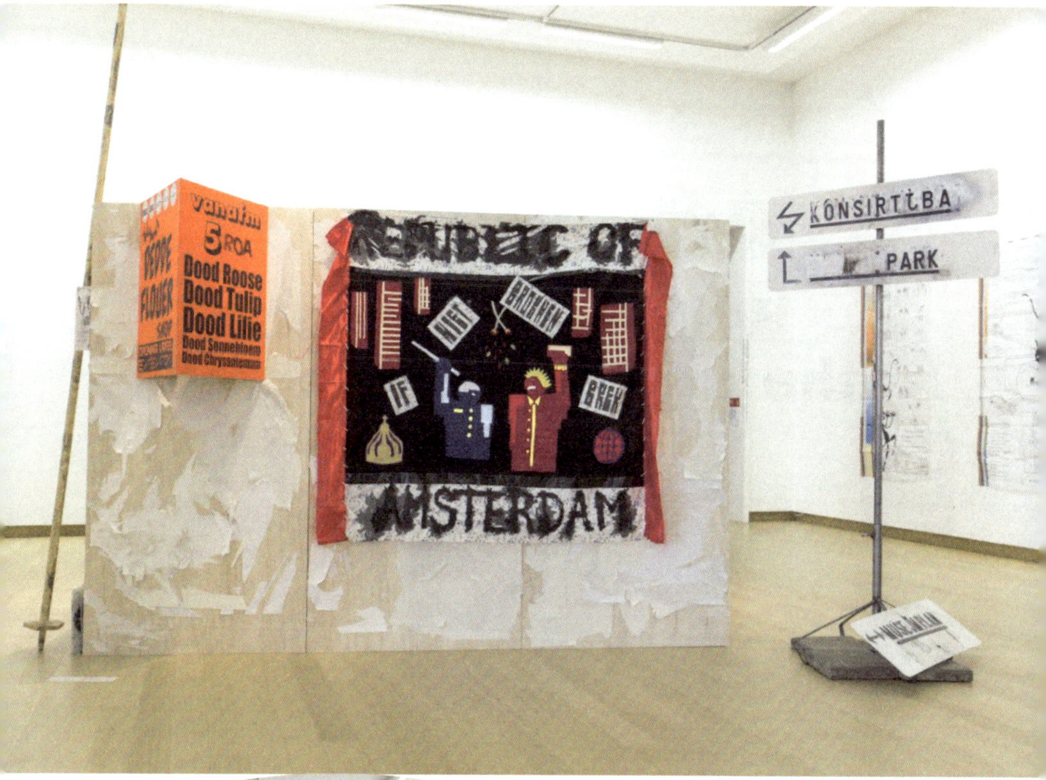

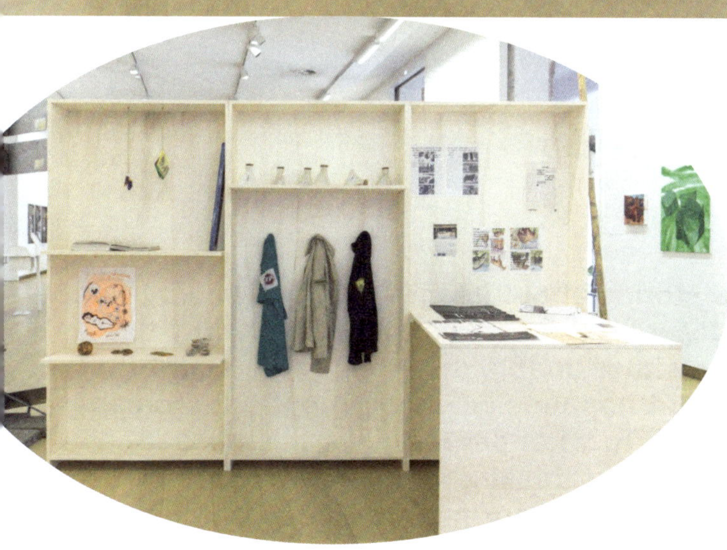

Filip Birkner, Lisa Arkhangelskaya, Étienne Clerc, Helmer Stuyt, Johannes Reisigl, *Artefacts from the Republic of Amsterdam (1980–2021)*, 2019, photo: Kateryna Snizhko, 2019

Helmer Stuyt, Chloé Delchini, Klara Eneroth, Wieke Willemsen, Eleonora Šljanda, Swani Vinton, Ossip Blits & Alex Feraday, Jim Klok, Filip Birkner, *Artefacts from the Republic of Amsterdam (1980–2021)*, 2019, photo: Kateryna Snizhko, 2019

After Images

Write a story about the untaken photograph that haunts you.

Rein Jelle Terpstra
Amsterdam, the Netherlands

After Images are stories about images that the photographer let go by. They describe the scenes and explain why the photographer was either unable or unwilling to record that specific image. What happens when an important moment cannot be recorded? To what degree does this missed opportunity influence our thinking, our imagination? How does the perceived image impact our memory? And can these fluid, never-recorded after images inspire new thoughts and stories?

After Images is about the ambivalent relationship between the image and the photographer, but also about language, image culture, and the absence of images.

The assignment is about photography, but without photos.

Dear reader,

We were in a car getting lost in one of Antwerp's old neighbourhoods, trying to find our way back to the ring road. We pulled over for a bit and there I saw them, slowly moving by on the pavement: two young girls, identical twins, walking side by side, their nanny right behind them. The girls each had one eye taped over, the left girl's right eye and the right girl's left eye. Together they saw with one pair of eyes, as if to complement each other's eyesight, as if together they could see with full depth of field. How would they see, and what were they, simultaneously, looking at? Probably not at me, who kept on staring at the girls while the car started moving again, the camera sitting on the dashboard.

Many of us carry a photo in our memory: an event or a moment that we saw but failed to capture in a photograph. Perhaps the battery was empty, or perhaps the moment was simply too important. Sometimes such perceived moments haunt you like persistent after-images. These images are fluid, because never recorded. Perhaps these kinds of afterimages will lead you to new thoughts and new stories.

With these considerations I invite you to write a story about your untaken photographs. The story might be better than the photograph could ever have been.

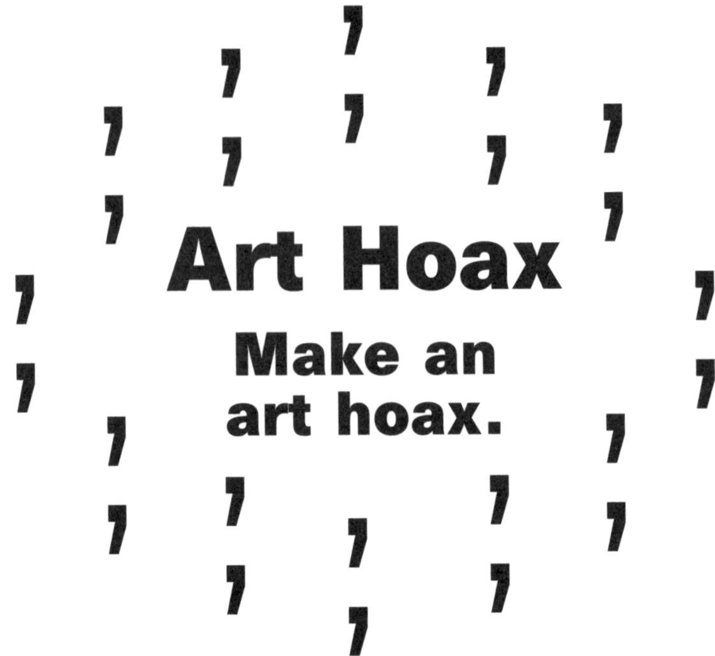

Art Hoax

Make an art hoax.

Anja Brand-Heemskerk and Margreeth Eringa
Rotterdam, the Netherlands

A hoax is often quickly associated with fake news. However, there are also artists who have created exciting hoaxes, such as the beached fake whale in the Seine River by Captain Boomer Collective and Floris Kaayk's convincing 'Human Bird Wings'. Their motives are much more about idealism, humour, fantasy, or dreams. We use these 'art hoaxes' as inspiration at the start of the assignment and then the students go to work on creating and executing their own hoax. The goal of the assignment is to make students more media savvy by challenging them. The assignment encourages the conversation about what is fake and what is real and whether there are limits to what can and may be done (for instance on the Internet). Finally, this assignment encourages taking a critical view (image analysis) and researching (checking sources).

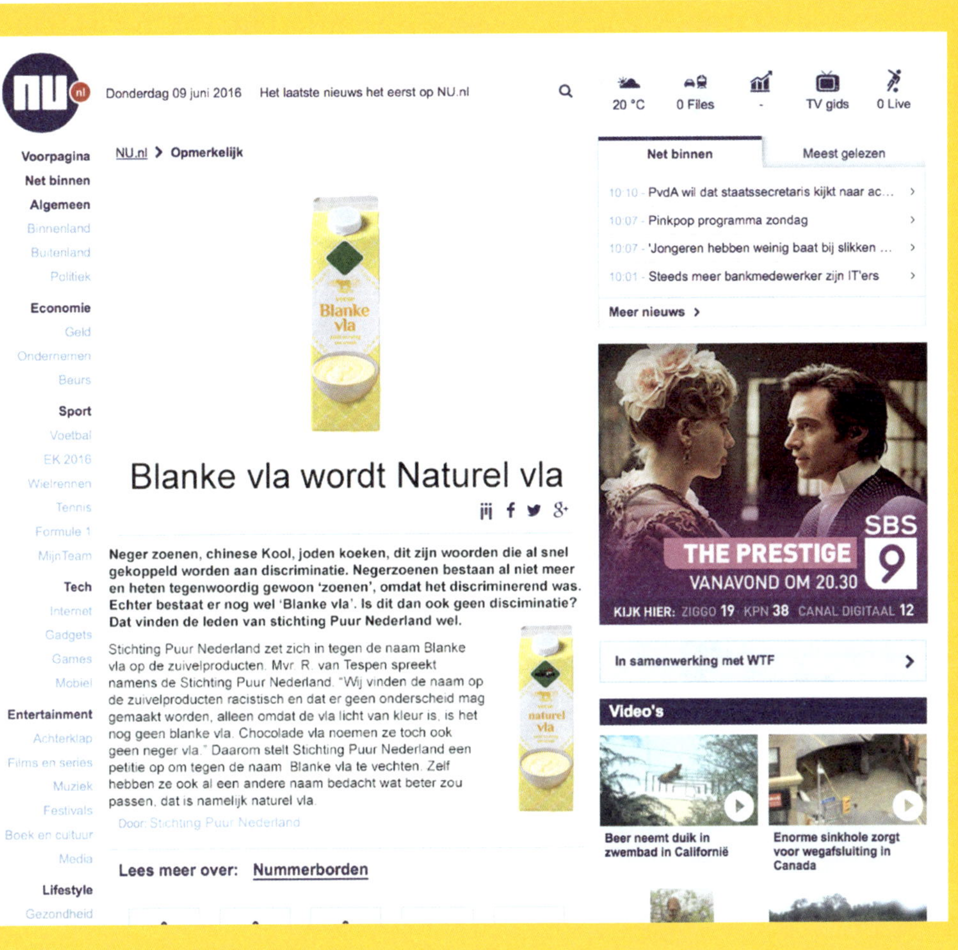

nu.nl

Donderdag 09 juni 2016 Het laatste nieuws het eerst op NU.nl

20 °C 0 Files - TV gids 0 Live

Voorpagina
Net binnen
Algemeen
Binnenland
Buitenland
Politiek
Economie
Geld
Ondernemen
Beurs
Sport
Voetbal
EK 2016
Wielrennen
Tennis
Formule 1
MijnTeam
Tech
Internet
Gadgets
Games
Mobiel
Entertainment
Achterklap
Films en series
Muziek
Festivals
Boek en cultuur
Media
Lifestyle
Gezondheid

NU.nl > Opmerkelijk

Blanke vla wordt Naturel vla

Neger zoenen, chinese Kool, joden koeken, dit zijn woorden die al snel gekoppeld worden aan discriminatie. Negerzoenen bestaan al niet meer en heten tegenwoordig gewoon 'zoenen', omdat het discriminerend was. Echter bestaat er nog wel 'Blanke vla'. Is dit dan ook geen disciminatie? Dat vinden de leden van stichting Puur Nederland wel.

Stichting Puur Nederland zet zich in tegen de naam Blanke vla op de zuivelproducten. Mvr. R. van Tespen spreekt namens de Stichting Puur Nederland. "Wij vinden de naam op de zuivelproducten racistisch en dat er geen onderscheid mag gemaakt worden, alleen omdat de vla licht van kleur is, is het nog geen blanke vla. Chocolade vla noemen ze toch ook geen neger vla." Daarom stelt Stichting Puur Nederland een petitie op om tegen de naam Blanke vla te vechten. Zelf hebben ze ook al een andere naam bedacht wat beter zou passen, dat is namelijk naturel vla.

Door: Stichting Puur Nederland

Lees meer over: Nummerborden

Net binnen | Meest gelezen

10:10 - PvdA wil dat staatssecretaris kijkt naar ac...
10:07 - Pinkpop programma zondag
10:07 - 'Jongeren hebben weinig baat bij slikken ...
10:01 - Steeds meer bankmedewerker zijn IT'ers

Meer nieuws >

SBS 9 THE PRESTIGE VANAVOND OM 20.30
KIJK HIER: ZIGGO 19 KPN 38 CANAL DIGITAAL 12

In samenwerking met WTF >

Video's

Beer neemt duik in zwembad in Californië

Enorme sinkhole zorgt voor wegafsluiting in Canada

Student's work, *'White custard' will be 'Natural custard'*, 2016

Change the Fairy Tale

Do an intervention in a traditional fairy tale, thereby causing an unexpected turn of events.

Petra Drost
Assen, the Netherlands

We all know the tales of Snow White and her seven dwarves, of Cinderella, and Sleeping Beauty. Bittersweet tales of fair ladies, brave knights, and evil wrongdoers. Everything and everyone in its place; enemies are ugly and vicious through and through, while the heroes are handsome, noble-minded, and brave, and all ends well. However, most fairy tales contain hidden truths and messages that are either contested nowadays, or have become very topical.

You will alter the traditional fairy tale into a contemporary version of it. Think of an intervention in the classic story to cause a completely different turn of events halfway through it and raise new questions. Represent both the intervention and the new ending of the fairy tale in a visual work (a drawing, painting, or animation).

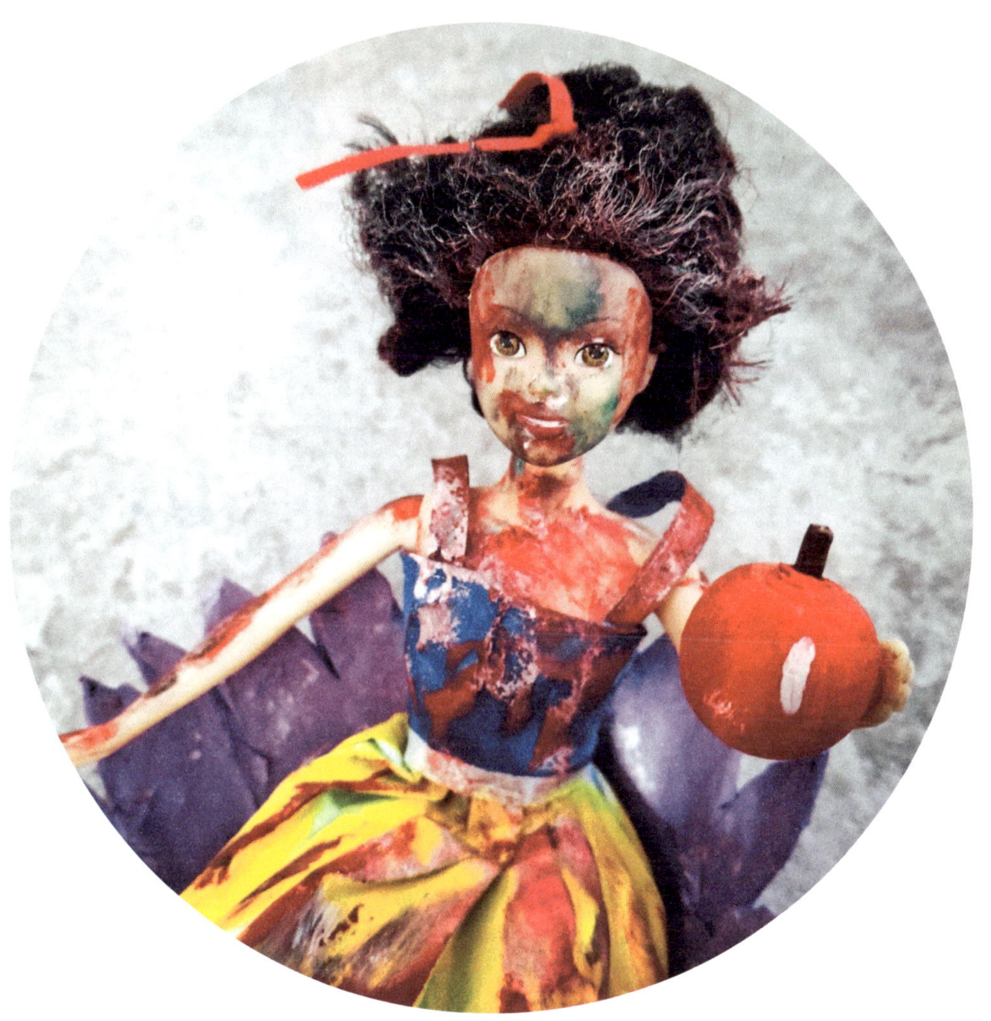

Student's work, *What Happened to Snow White?*, 2016,
Esdal College Emmen, photo: Petra Drost

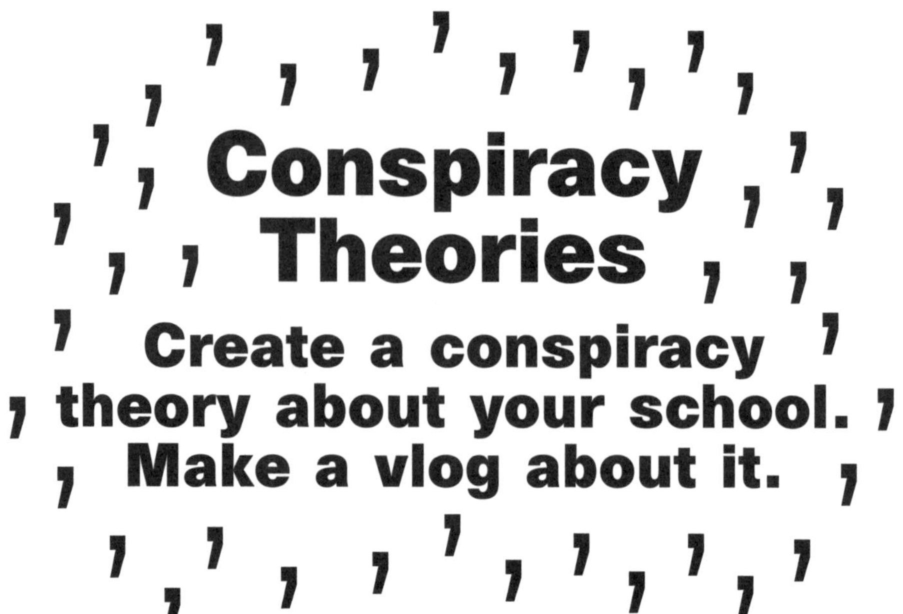

Conspiracy Theories

Create a conspiracy theory about your school. Make a vlog about it.

Geke Buis
Hengelo, the Netherlands

Conspiracy theories are phenomena we cannot ignore. Whether it's the 'flat earth movement', '9/11 was an inside job' or the 'fake moon landing', you don't have to be on the internet or social media for long before you catch something from these often far-fetched (or true?) ideas. Somehow these theories are very appealing and convincing, otherwise they wouldn't have such a following.

A conspiracy theory is a belief that some covert but influential organization is responsible for a hard to explain event. It involves a secret plot by usually powerful conspirators and masters of manipulation and disguise.

With this in mind, the assignment is as follows. With a few fellow students and the cunning use of your imagination, create a conspiracy theory about your school and make a vlog about it. Be elaborate and convincing. Anything is possible. There are no rules for this assignment, only a lot of secrets.

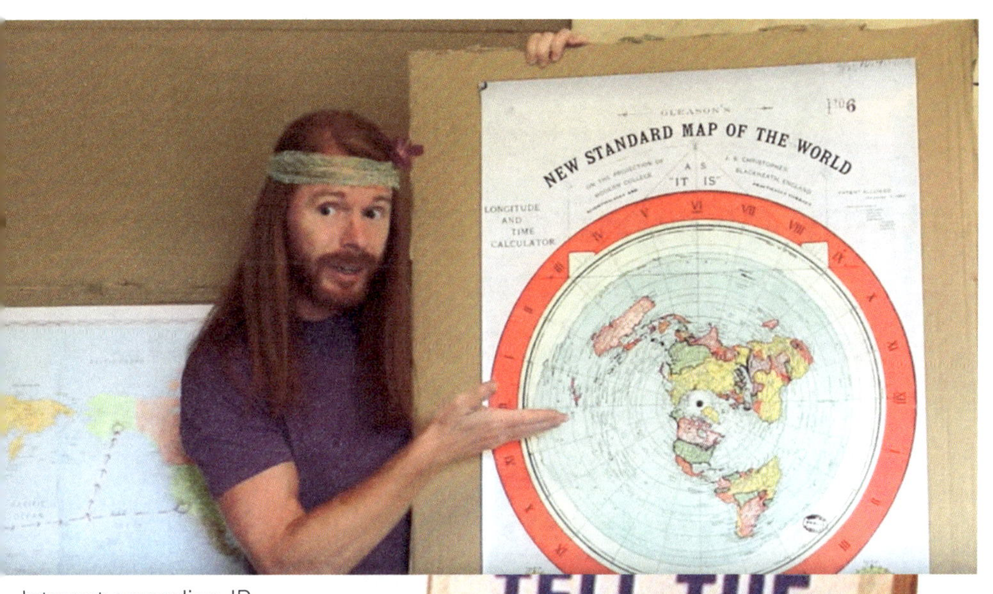

Internet comedian JP Sears explains the Flat Earth Theory in an episode of his YouTube-series *Ultra Spiritual Life*, 2016

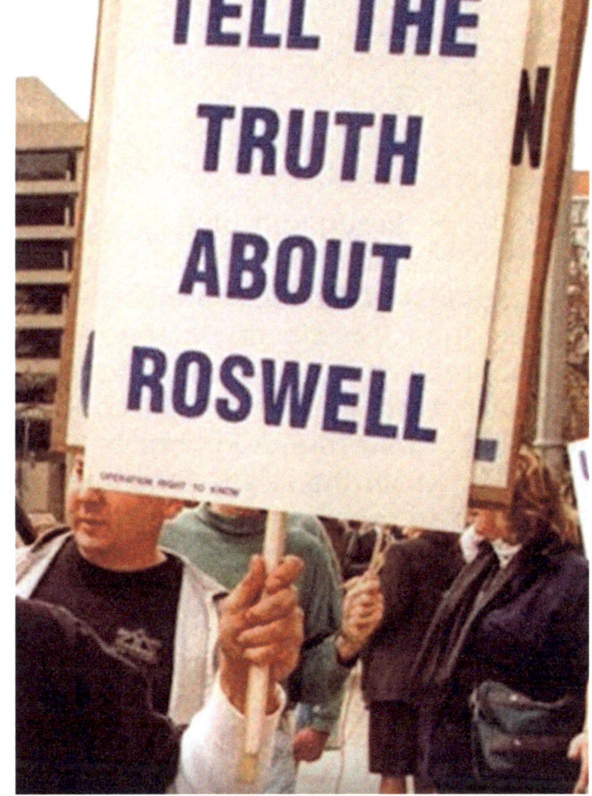

Vloggers Govert Sweep and Ties Granzier made headlines in 2019 when they tried to enter Area 51 (Groom Lake Test Site, Nevada) and got themselves arrested. Of course they vlogged about it.

“Hoax II”

Use computer manipulation or cleverly staged, performed, constructed, and photographed in-real-life scenarios to formulate an image hoax.

Riley Harmon
Amsterdam, the Netherlands

As we've seen throughout history, the line between reality and fantasy/truth and fiction/myth and certainty can be easily manipulated. For this project, you will use computer manipulation and/or cleverly staged, performed, constructed, and photographed in-real-life scenarios to formulate an image hoax. It will be extremely important for you to consider the NARRATIVE surrounding your image, the scope of the CONTEXT in which the image functions, and the DISTRIBUTION method used to relay your image to others (and hopefully spur debate/conversation). You may use any imaging device for this project (e.g. cell phone, dslr, trail camera, feed from security camera) and digital manipulation is not mandatory. However, the use of manipulation and/or your chosen imaging device should be conceptually solid and relate to the narrative, context, and distribution of your hoax. You will receive a bonus if your work is re-blogged significantly, makes a headline, or can sufficiently integrate into the visual landscape outside of the University.

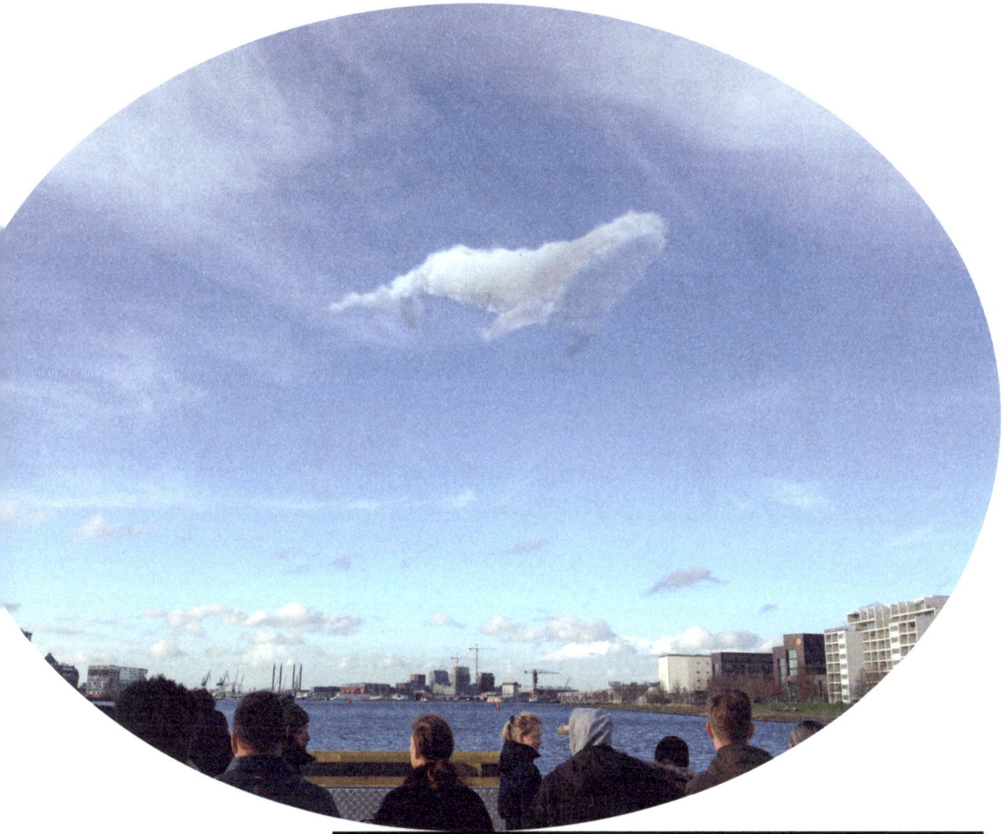

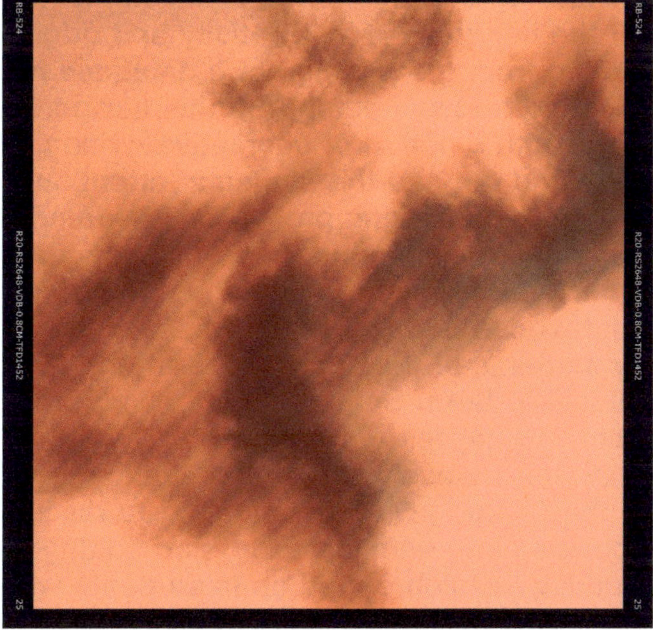

Riley Harmon, *Untitled Pareidolia Clouds*, 2016–2020, generative video and synthetic photographic process, partly supported by the Creative Industries Fund NL and Amsterdams Fonds voor de Kunst

Copy-Paste Writing

Write a dialogue between two characters relying on found material on the internet only.

Joachim Robbrecht
Brussels, Belgium

For this assignment students pick a topic of their interest (love, death, global warming, botany, whatever) and surf the internet to find citations, quotes, short comments related to that theme. Then they create two characters 'X' and 'Y' and copy and paste their quotes as if the two are discussing the topic. This exercise invites students to throw off the imperatives of creativity and originality and approach writing from the position of a database miner and sampler of found text snippets. With this assignment, inspired by K. Goldsmith's notion of uncreative writing, writing becomes easy and fun and the students' attention is directed towards the decision-making processes in writing. Questions around authorship, ownership, and originality can be addressed and other possible modes of writing in the contemporary digital context can be discussed. This assignment was carried out by students of the acting department at the Hochschule der Künste in Bern. Some students, who previously shied away from writing, felt empowered to engage in writing performance texts for themselves. Others, already using similar techniques in their writing were encouraged to discuss their modes of copy-pasting, administering, and editing found materials. Our working session ended up in students working at and editing each other's texts, acting as a collective body of writers.

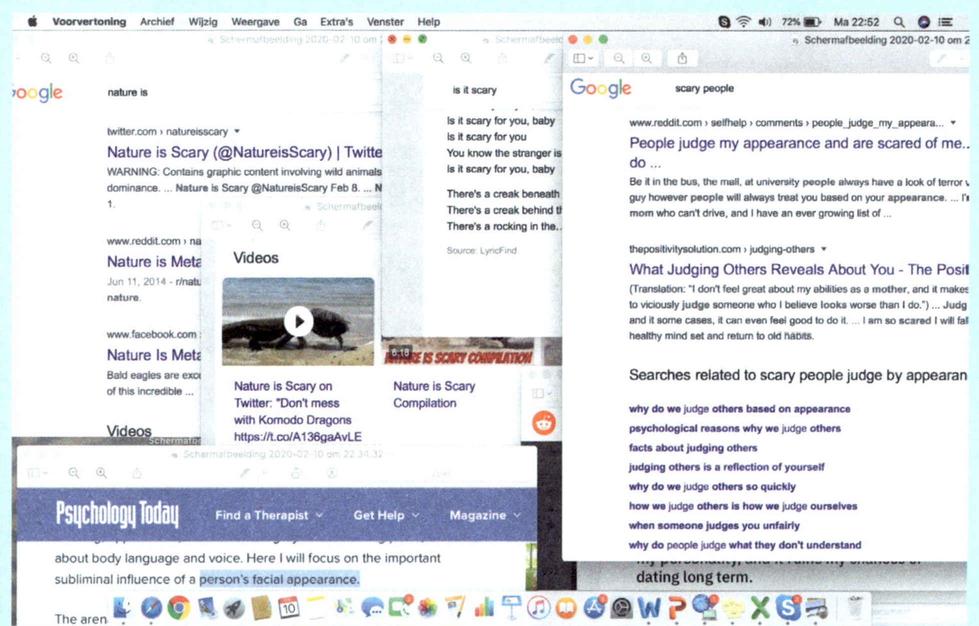

Joachim Robbrecht, *Nature is Scary*, 2020,
collage of screenshots simulating copy-paste exercise

Fake Your Social Media

Fake everything on your social-media account for a week.

Catherine Willemse
Arnhem, the Netherlands

Fake your life on a social media platform of choice: act like you are on holiday, pretend you are a very rich person, or create a super fancy alter ego. You can be anyone and anywhere you want to be...

There are many influencers and vloggers on all kinds of social media platforms and many people believe what they show and say. It seems like they created the perfect life with perfect bodies and perfect friends. But how much of this is real? How many photos were made before that one perfect shot? With this assignment I want to create awareness about the reality of social media. In addition to the assignment, I give examples of influencers and artists already creating awareness about this subject:

- **Influencer Rianne Meijer places Instagram and reality side by side by showing the 'Instagram perfect photo' of a photo shoot and a 'blooper photo' of that same shoot.**
- **Artist duo Frank & Michiel created the Cameo Series, which invites visitors to be part of a movie or well-known commercial like Dolce and Gabbana.**
- **Artist Merel Brugman faked a whole journey abroad on social media in her work 'Same same but different', by using photoshop.**

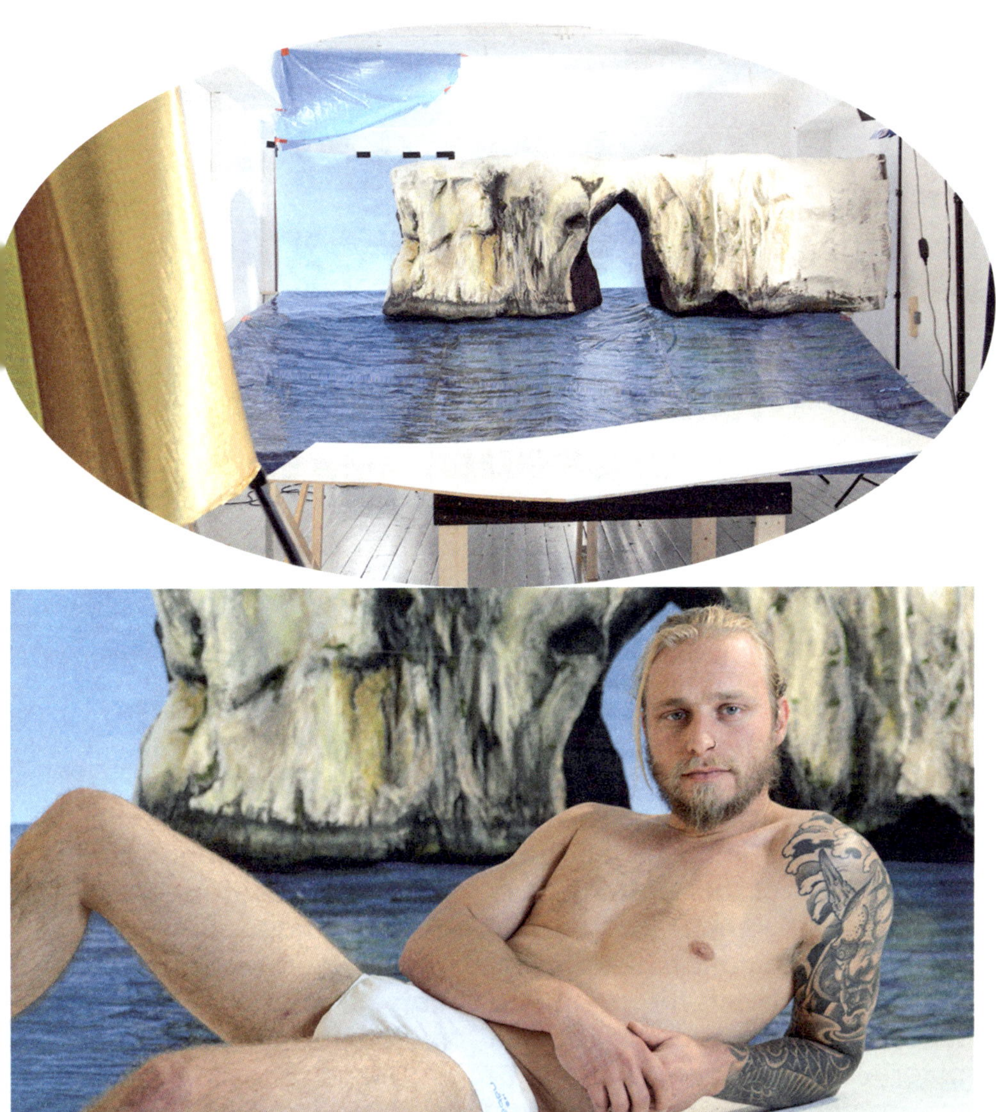

Frank and Michiel, *The Cameo Series, Episode #1–Dolce & Gabbana*, 2015

Text to Art—Art of Text

Make the artwork that is described by a museum text.

Lili Liane van Doorninck
Amsterdam, the Netherlands

Each participant will receive a description of a different artwork found in an exhibition or on the website of an artist. Among the descriptions of artworks, descriptions of words taken from dictionaries will be found. Students will not be made aware of this until the assignment is executed.

This assignment was carried out with students in secondary education. The first lesson focused on how to interpret or sketch the themes or subjects mentioned in the texts. Then students focused on visualizing their text in material of their own choosing, e.g. collage, charcoal, film, performance, photography, etc. During the last lesson, the results made by the participants were compared to the actual artworks that the texts described. Students found out that some of the descriptions did not belong to an acknowledged artwork but to a word copied from a dictionary. During the comparison, we discussed the use of written explanations of art. Afterwards, the teacher provided the students with theoretical information about how the connection between text and visual art has developed through history. This was followed by a final discussion in which this topic is reviewed from the various angles that were used.

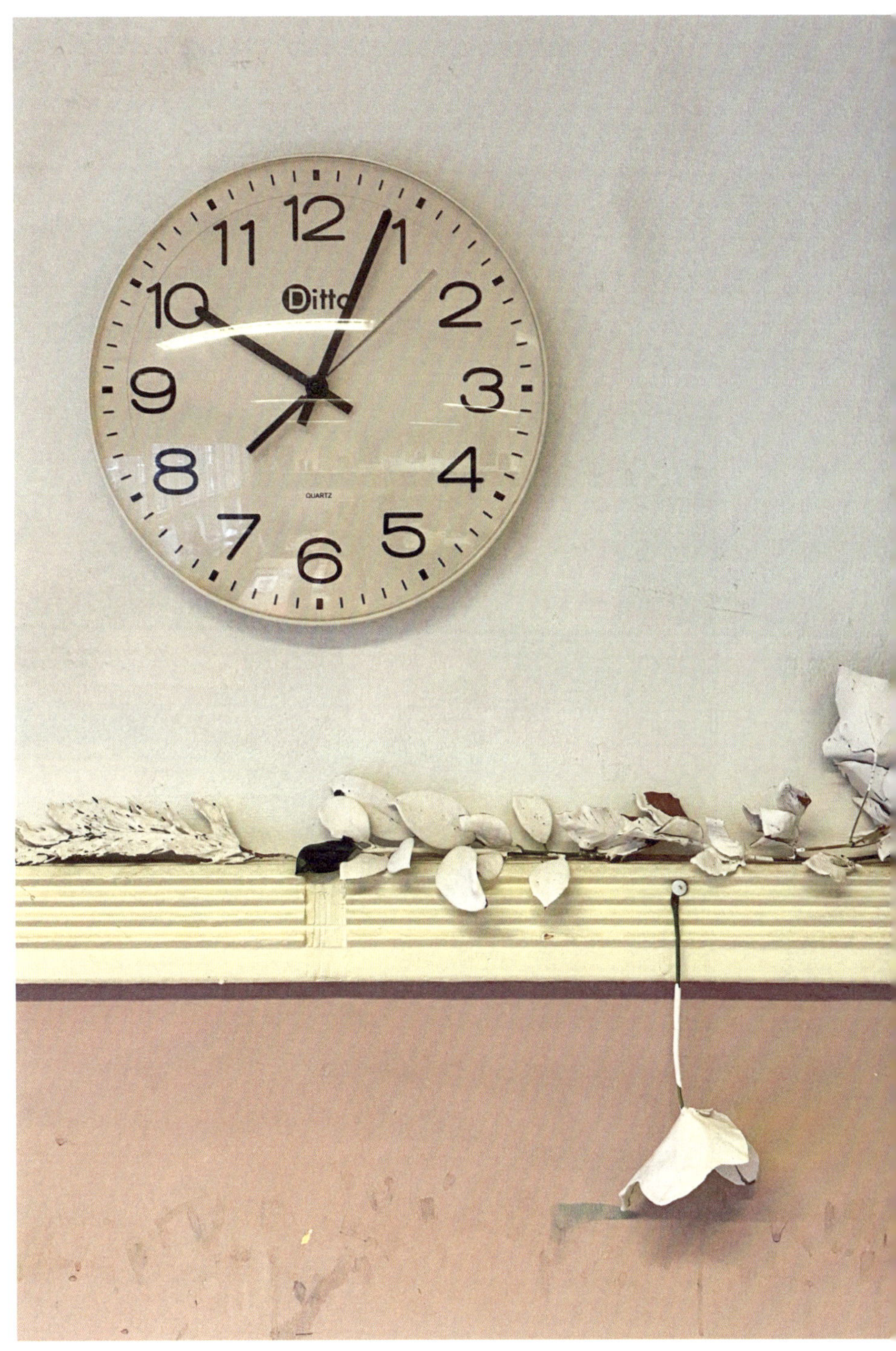

Bebel Gravendaal, *#airflowers*, 2020, photograph

Re

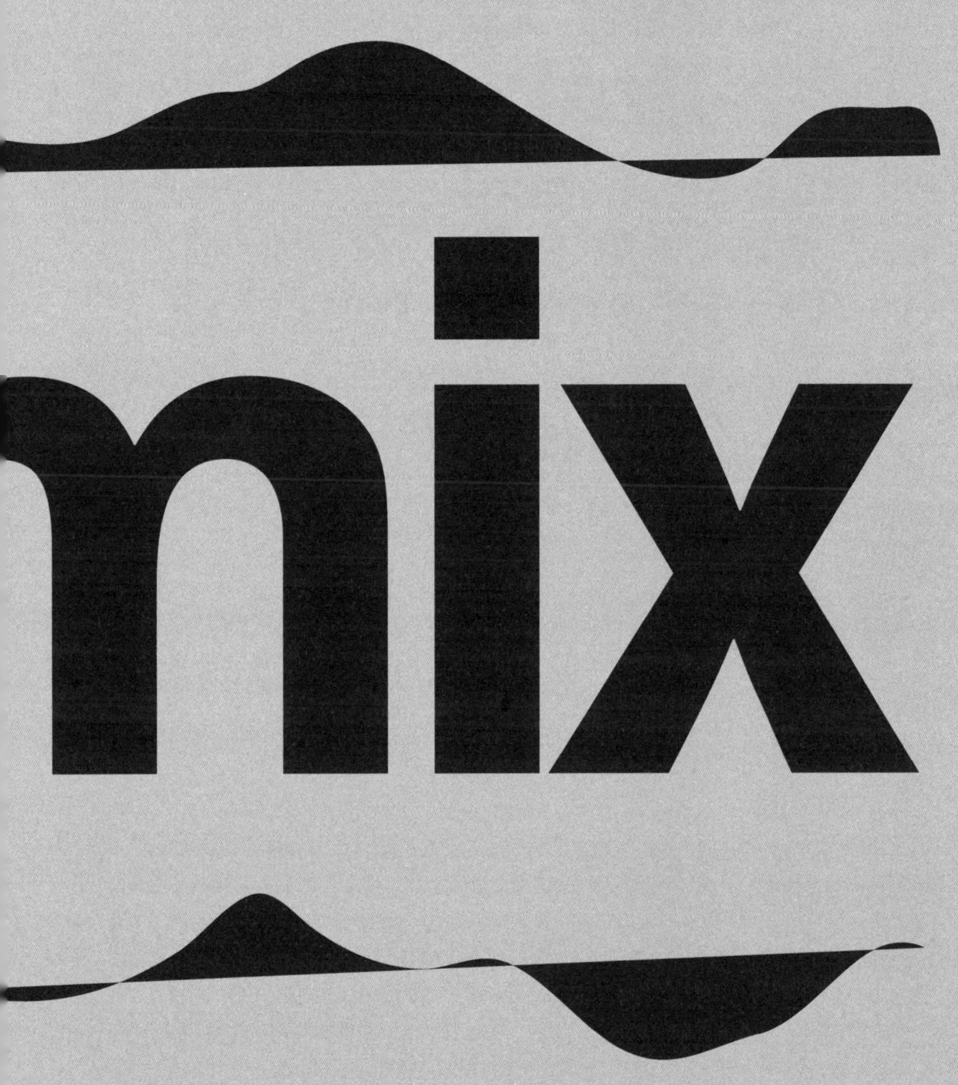
mix

Save the Life of a Broken Object

Repair a broken object, changing its original shape and/or function.

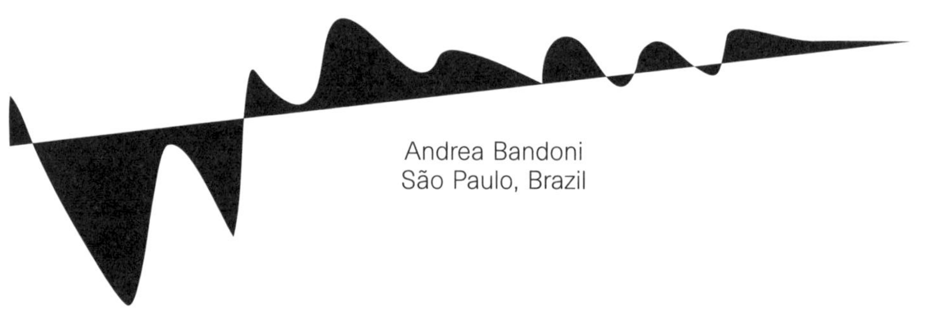

Andrea Bandoni
São Paulo, Brazil

This assignment proposes that the broken objects that surround us are re-evaluated and brought to further use. To that end, a 'transformative' repair can be practiced so that the object has its shape and/or function highly modified. A big change is expected in the final object. This kind of repair can possibly highlight specific features of broken objects and add value to them. Some questions may arise: is the past of the object still visible in the final outcome? What kind of stories can this object tell? Is functionality preserved? What is the value of the final outcome? Many different designers and artists have approached broken objects, so it can be interesting to check out inspiring references before starting the work.

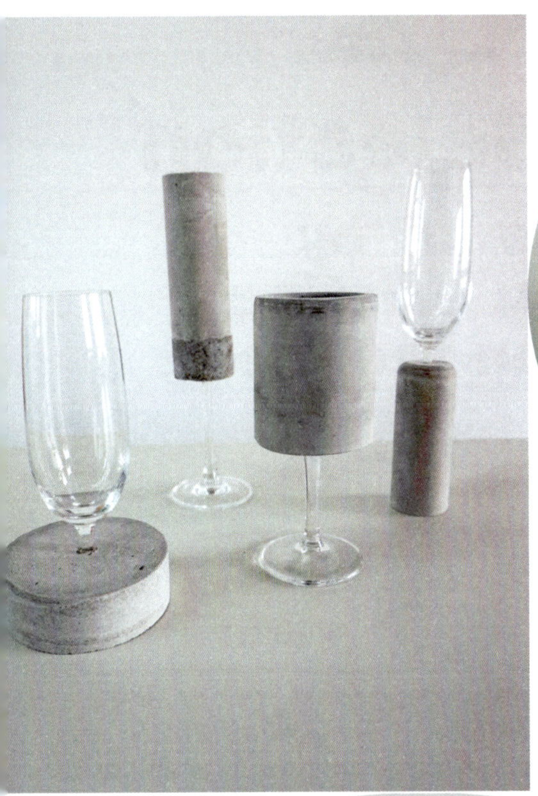

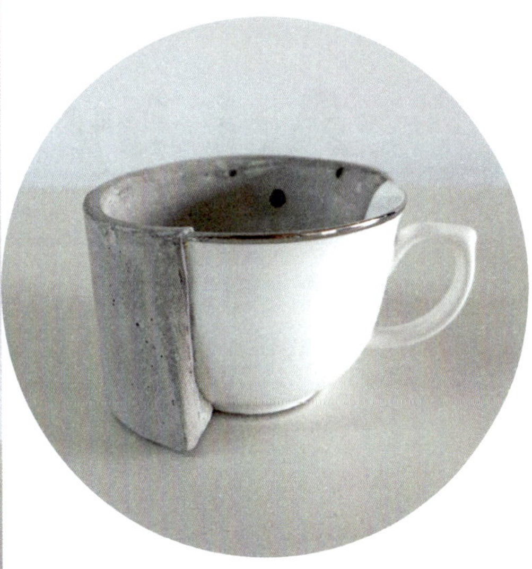

Andrea Bandoni for Projeto Garagem, *Interrupted Cup*, 2017, concrete, broken ceramics

Andrea Bandoni for Projeto Garagem, *Reconstructed Glasses*, 2017, concrete, broken ceramics

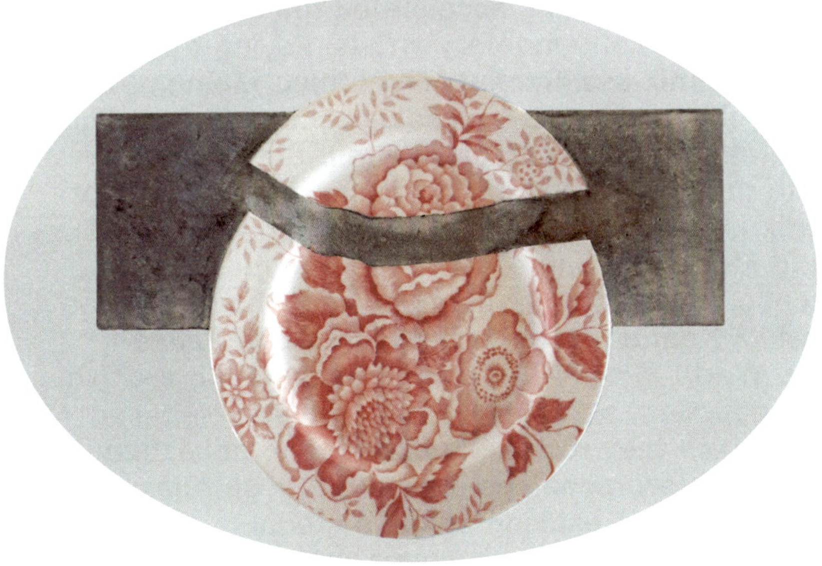

Andrea Bandoni for Projeto Garagem, *Interrupted Plate*, 2017, concrete, broken ceramics

All pieces were made in São Paulo, Brazil

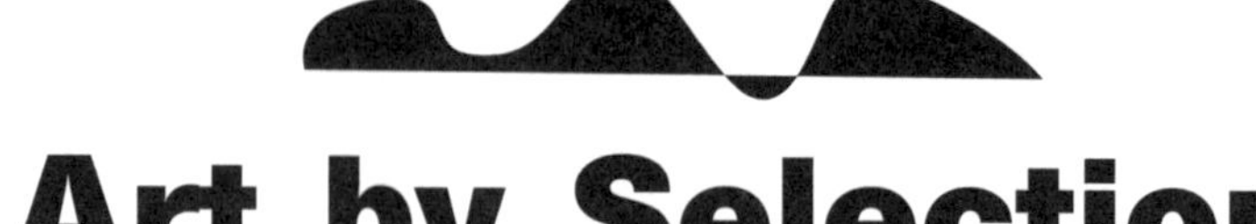

Art by Selection

Create art by sampling existing material on the Web.

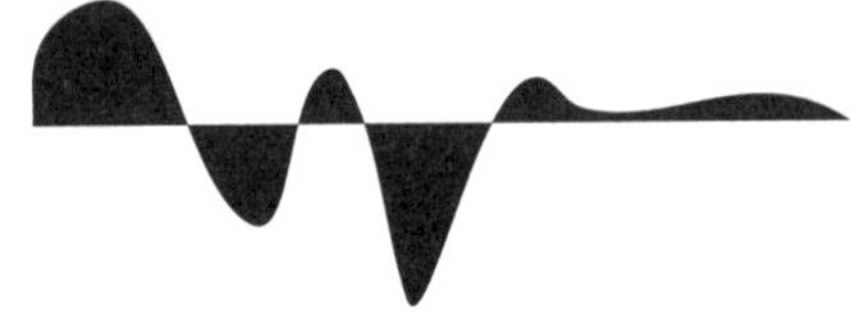

Emiel Heijnen
Amsterdam, the Netherlands

'We build new files from existing components, rather than creating from scratch.' In her article in *Art Forum* (2012), art critic Claire Bishop argued that the sheer infinite availability of resources on the internet has accelerated the use of *selection* as a key strategy for contemporary artists. Paying tribute to Astrid Hermes' remix assignment 'The Stolen Moment' in my PhD study, this assignment takes selection (or sampling) as a single method for artistic production. Students are introduced to the art of sampling by discussing the work of artists Sherrie Levine, Peter Bogers, Richard Prince, Christian Marclay, and Musique Concrète and hip hop musicians. Special attention is given to 'photographers without cameras', such as Mishka Henner, Doug Rickard, and John Rafman, who use the World Wide Web as an inexhaustible archive. After this introduction, students develop a research-based art project in which they recontextualize online published sources, creating new meanings, based on these rules:

- **You may only use existing online material**
- **Selection and sampling are your sole artistic weapons**
- **Remixing and other methods that 'distort' or alter the original sources are taboo.**
- **Give your work a title**

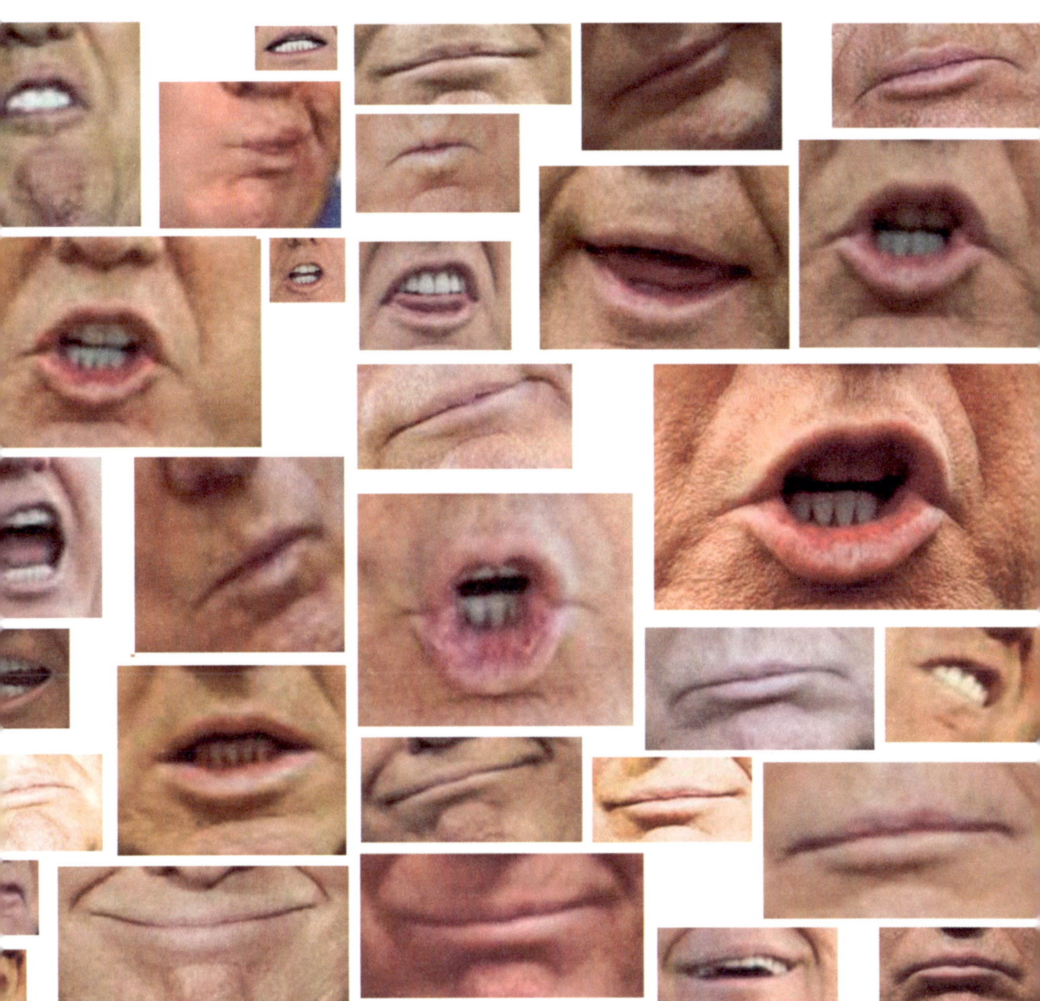

Student's work, *Lips Don't Lie*, 2017

Old Language–New Images

Take a page from an old book and make an image to go with it.

Hans Belleman
Amsterdam, the Netherlands

We salvaged some old books from the refuge container. Students pick a page from one of these old books that appeals to them or evokes a certain emotion in them. They underline one or more sentences and make an image of the emotion contained in the page. Without having to read the entire book students are touch by words or short dialogues that make them curious and trigger their imagination. The pages have flown out, have been torn out or cut up to serve in a new life as a print, a linocut, a collage, or yet another page in a book designed by the students.

Students' work, Zaanlands Lyceum, Zaandam, school year 2019-2020, photos: Hans Belleman

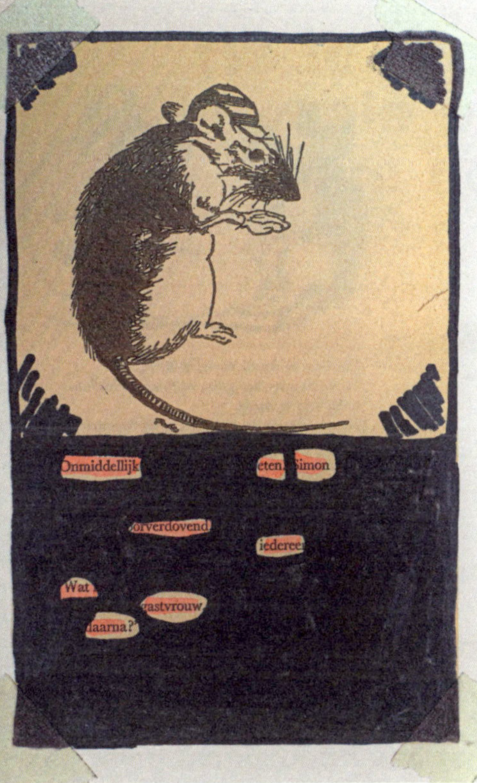

Student's work, *Incredibly loud*

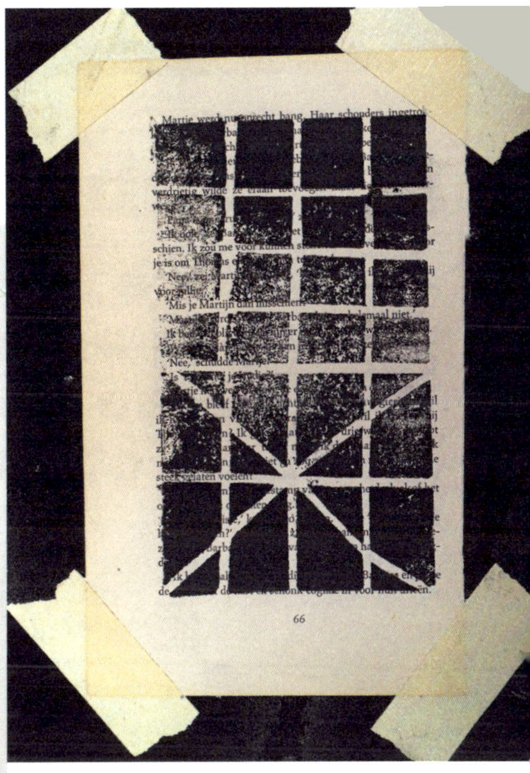

Student's work, *I could imagine...*

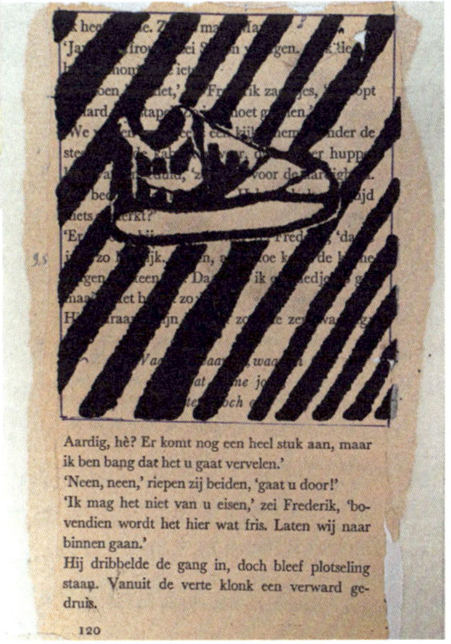

Student's work, *Nice, isn't it? There's more to come, but I'm afraid you will be bored*

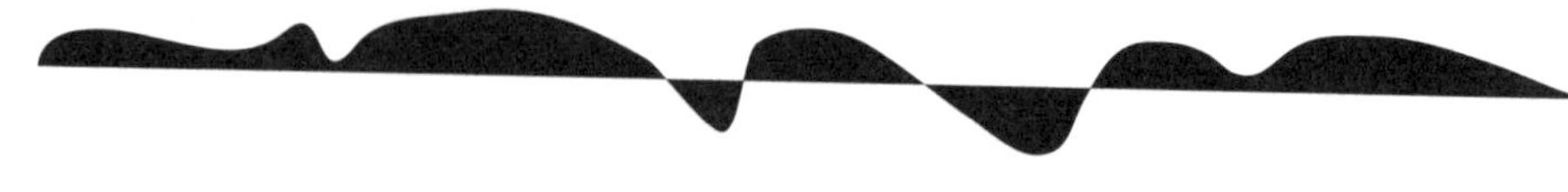

Collaborative Art

Make a work of art where all the elements have been made by other people.

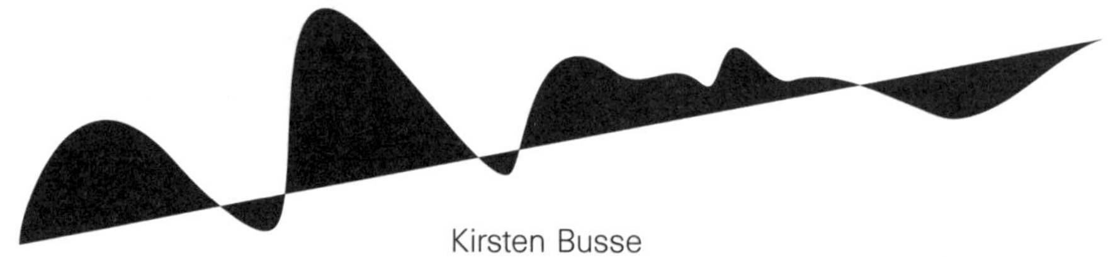

Kirsten Busse
Provo, UT, United States

I do a lot of work in theatre, which is a very collaborative environment. Everyone on a production team has a different role, but they are all important to making a good show happen. You also have to trust that other people are going to do their jobs. I applied this idea of not having control to my art practice and decided to do a project where all the pieces were made by other people. I had my friends trace their hands on pieces of printer paper and then cover, dip, or drag them in different substances. One friend smashed fruit snacks on hers while another spread peanut butter on theirs. Then, I took all these pieces and arranged them in different ways. I only had a say in what the final arrangement of the pieces was, but not of what colour, size, or texture all the traced hands would be. Oftentimes we are limited by our own minds and it is amazing to see what happens when we allow other people to take over the creative process. Art is seeing what happens when we learn how to let go.

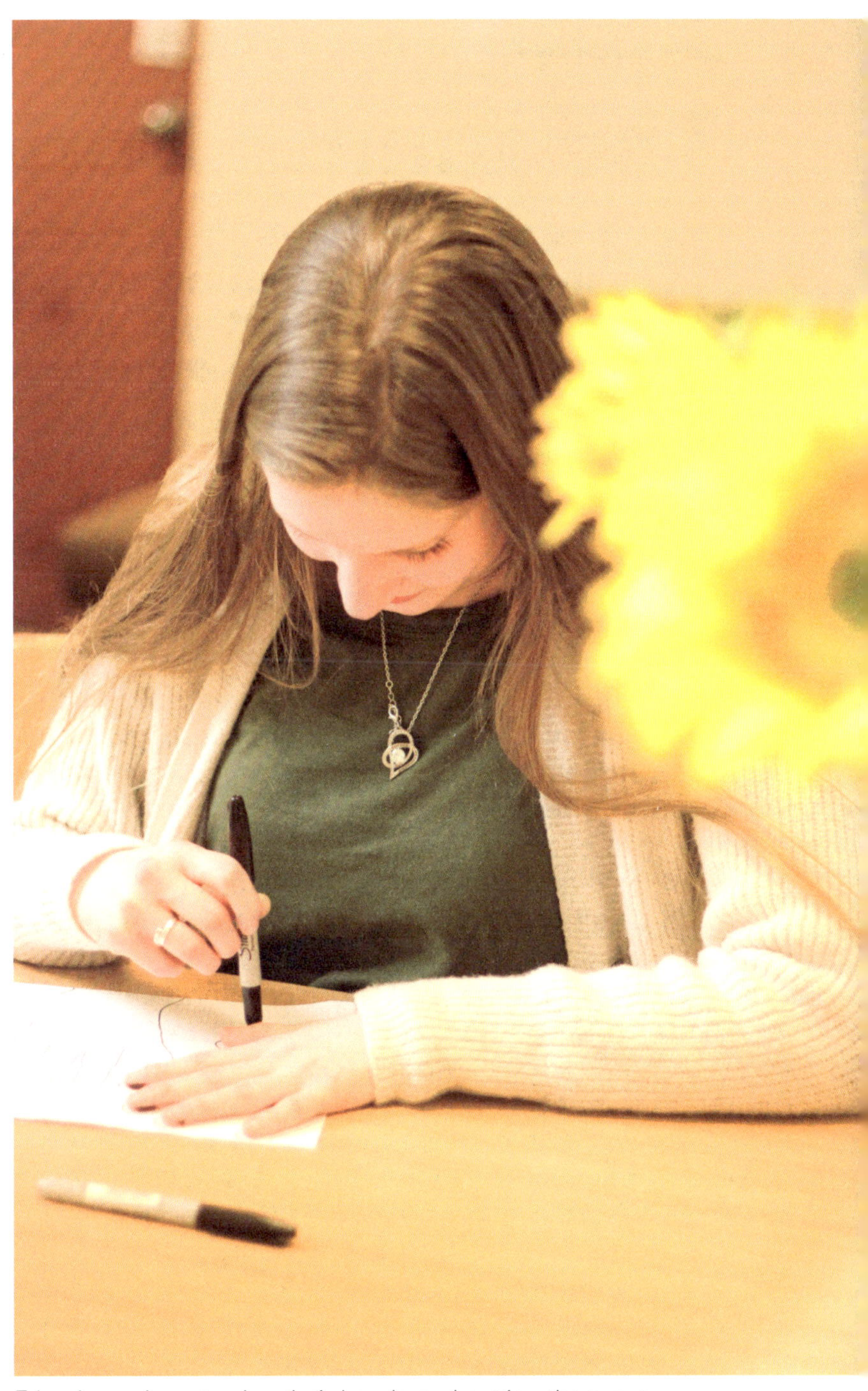

Friends work on tracing their hands and cutting them out to contribute to this project, in Provo, UT, USA, 2019

The Dinner Series

Cook a dish and design a matching setting including eating utensils. Consider what we eat but also how we eat and what we experience.

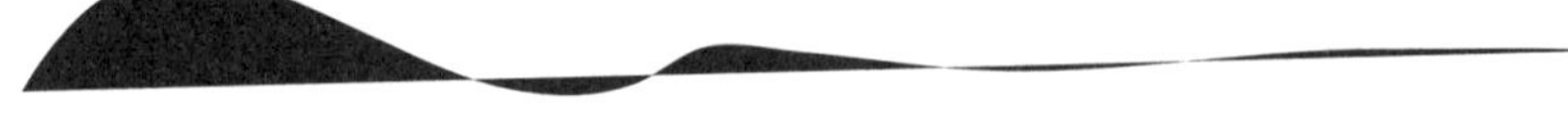

Liesbet Bussche
Amsterdam, the Netherlands

As a jewellery designer, I wanted to respond to the long-standing relation between the dinner table and its objects because I noticed a growing awareness among students of the social and ecological aspects of food and tableware. This resulted in a series of evening classes in the form of three consecutive dinners with different starting points. Six students prepared a full dinner, each student being responsible for the food and accompanying tableware of a course.

The first one, entitled ‘The Homeland Dinner’, started from a personal perspective and had a memory or remarkable event of the student’s home country as input. ‘The Newspaper Dinner’ was based on an article in which the students related their table objects and courses to the political role of food in today’s society. In ‘The Gesture Dinner’, a repetitive body movement from a profession outside the art field, such as science, sports, or music, was leading.

The seemingly mundane act of eating together combined with the unusual time of the classes made students dare to execute the assignment experimentally. Witnessing the interaction of these creative and social aspects culminated in several spontaneous department dinners such as ‘The Nuts Dinner’ and ‘The Dinner in Red’.

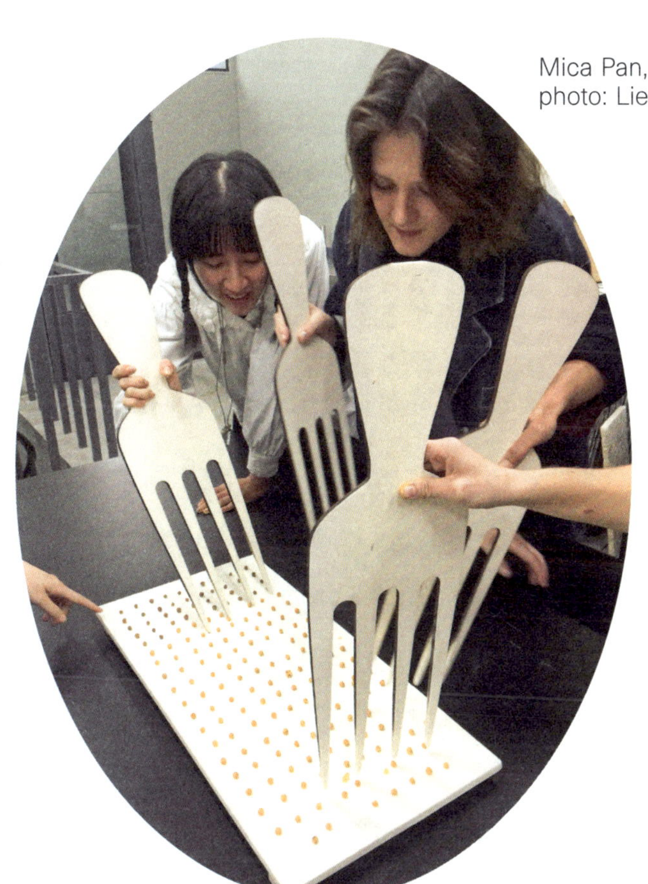

Mica Pan, *The Dinner Series*, 2018, photo: Liesbet Bussche (teacher)

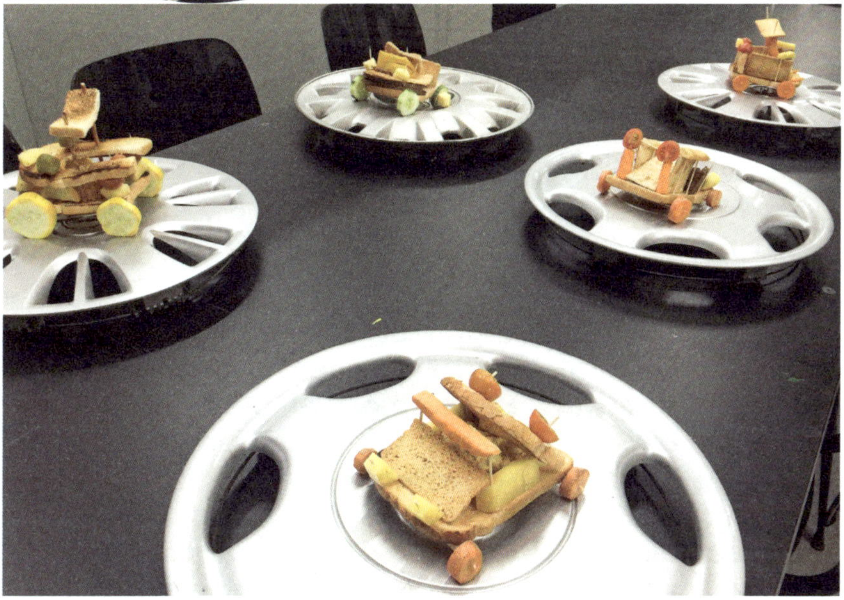

Lucas Cero, *The Dinner Series*, 2018, photo: Liesbet Bussche (teacher)

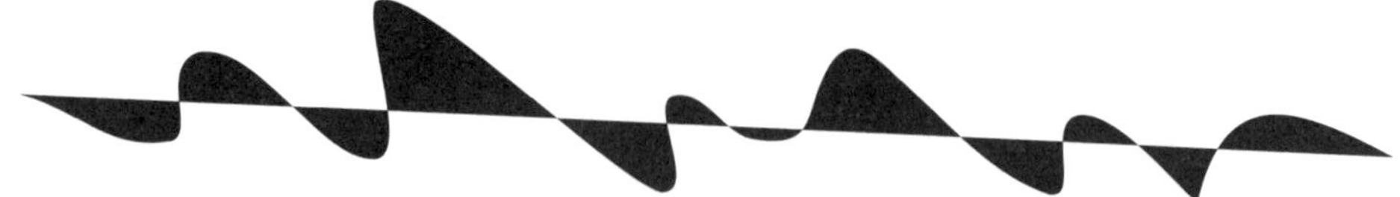

Going Dutch Salad (By Chance)

Make a group salad through chance operations. Eat the salad as in regular life, but also as an artwork.

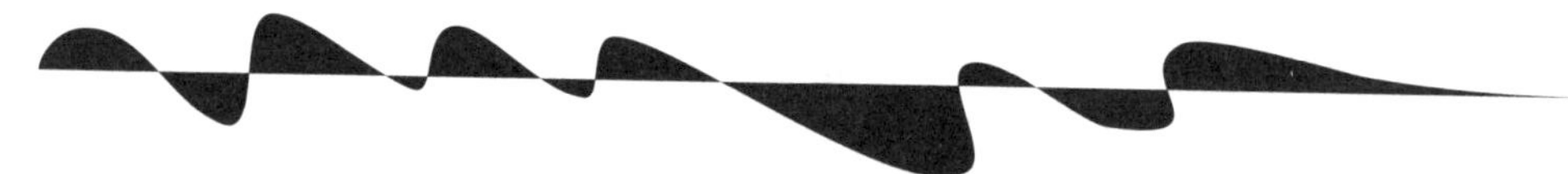

Jorge Lucero
Urbana and Chicago, IL, USA

At the beginning of the project 'Teacher as conceptual artist', a collaborative artist/teacher residency, the students were sent on a walk. Before the walk they were each given one of the directives from a list. Directives were assigned by chance. When everyone returned from their walk, after having completed their directive, the group cooked, chopped, and assembled a salad buffet. The event occurred in the communal kitchen of the Amsterdam University of the Arts. The salad was then enjoyed by all.

1. For the next hour each one of you will go out and buy no more than €7,50-worth* of certain *salad* ingredients. You'll notice here that the word salad has been put into italics indicating that the idea of what can make a salad can and should be reimagined.

2. Before you leave you will be assigned a number.
— If that number is 1 or 2 you are assigned to buy only ingredients that are green in color, but not leaves of any kind. Please select more than one ingredient, and have the things you choose contrast in texture.
— If your number is 3 or 4 bring items that are wet and items that are by contrast dry. Consider the potential smell of the ingredients when making your decisions.
— If your number is 5 or 6 bring ingredients that you would designate as being a warm color on the color wheel. Bring more than one ingredient that fits this description insuring that the items you bring contrast especially in size.
— If your number is 7 bring ingredients that are liquids and one or two accompanying ingredients that need to be eaten fast before the liquids you are buying destroy their integrity.
— If your number is either 8 or 9 you need to bring ingredients that are grown or originate from another country you have visited. Only some of these things should have seeds or pits.
— If your number is 10 you need to bring ingredients you would describe as white or translucent. In addition look for contrast in flavors (e.g. sour v. sweet, bland v. salty, spicy v. bitter etc.)
— If your number is 11 or 12 you need to bring two thing that need to be cooked before they are added to a salad. Create contrast in those ingredients by thinking about their point-of-origin. When you select your first ingredient, ask yourself, 'where did this come from?', at that point find something you would consider its opposite and bring that ingredient too.
— If your number is 13 bring two ingredient that had human interference in them somehow. That 'interference' should not involve death (however you want to define that term). Also consider the names of these ingredients. Select at least one with a short name and one with a long name.
— If your number is 14 bring two things that are traditionally Dutch. One that you've seen in a salad before and something you never seen in a salad but you would dare to try.
— If your number is 15 go wherever you've decided to go, and when you get there make conversation with someone who is also shopping or selling. Ask them what their favorite thing is to put on a salad. Bring us that. Do this two times unless both people tell you the same thing, then do it a third time.
— Additionally, you have been split into two groups. If you're in group A you need to buy leaves of some kind. If you're in group B you need to by one other thing that needs to be sliced, but that isn't already in your category.
— In terms of quantity, buy what you would consider enough for eight people, but stay within budget. It is better you buy less within budget than to go over budget to buy enough for eight people.

3. As you make your way to and from your destination, do these three things: 1. Even though you and your colleagues may be going to the same site, go separately. 2. Go quietly. 3. Go slowly, but not artificially. There is no rush. Come back when you are done, but don't get 'distracted'. 4. Make five documents of things that are special to this particular trek. Let it be something you've never noticed before. This doesn't mean that you've never come across it before, rather it means that this time you're purposely giving it your attention. In this case, 'documents' can mean any type of capturing (e.g. your camera, a drawing, an audio recording, a small piece of prose or poetry that captures what you noticed, etc.)

When everyone returns we will arrange our ingredients on one large table. We will then make and document our salads. We will eat our salads. While we eat our salads, we will talk about what was witnessed during the trek.

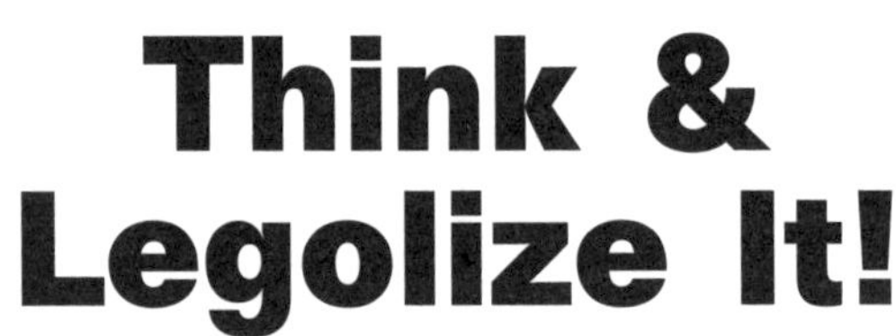

Think & Legolize It!

Choose your favourite painting and recreate it with Lego.

David Serra Navarro (alias Kenneth Russo)
Girona, Spain

The strategy of reproducing reality has always been an academic learning resource. If we combine this idea with the methodology of Lego Serious Play (Its goal is improving creative thinking and communication. People build three-dimensional models of their ideas with Lego bricks and tell stories about their models), we open up new perceptions of spatiality. Thinking, analyzing, and understanding a pictorial composition in this way 'of doing' shows us a new point of view, which can be shared, creating a dialogue between the interpretations of diverse participants. The assignment is very flexible and is designed for different educational levels, mainly students in secondary education, but also students of higher artistic education. Even with design students, sessions have been carried out through the Minecraft platform, using virtual blocks (as Lego blocks) and the 'Redstone', to recreate interactive interpretations. Personal artistic production and collective exploration of the resulting art works are the assignment's foci.

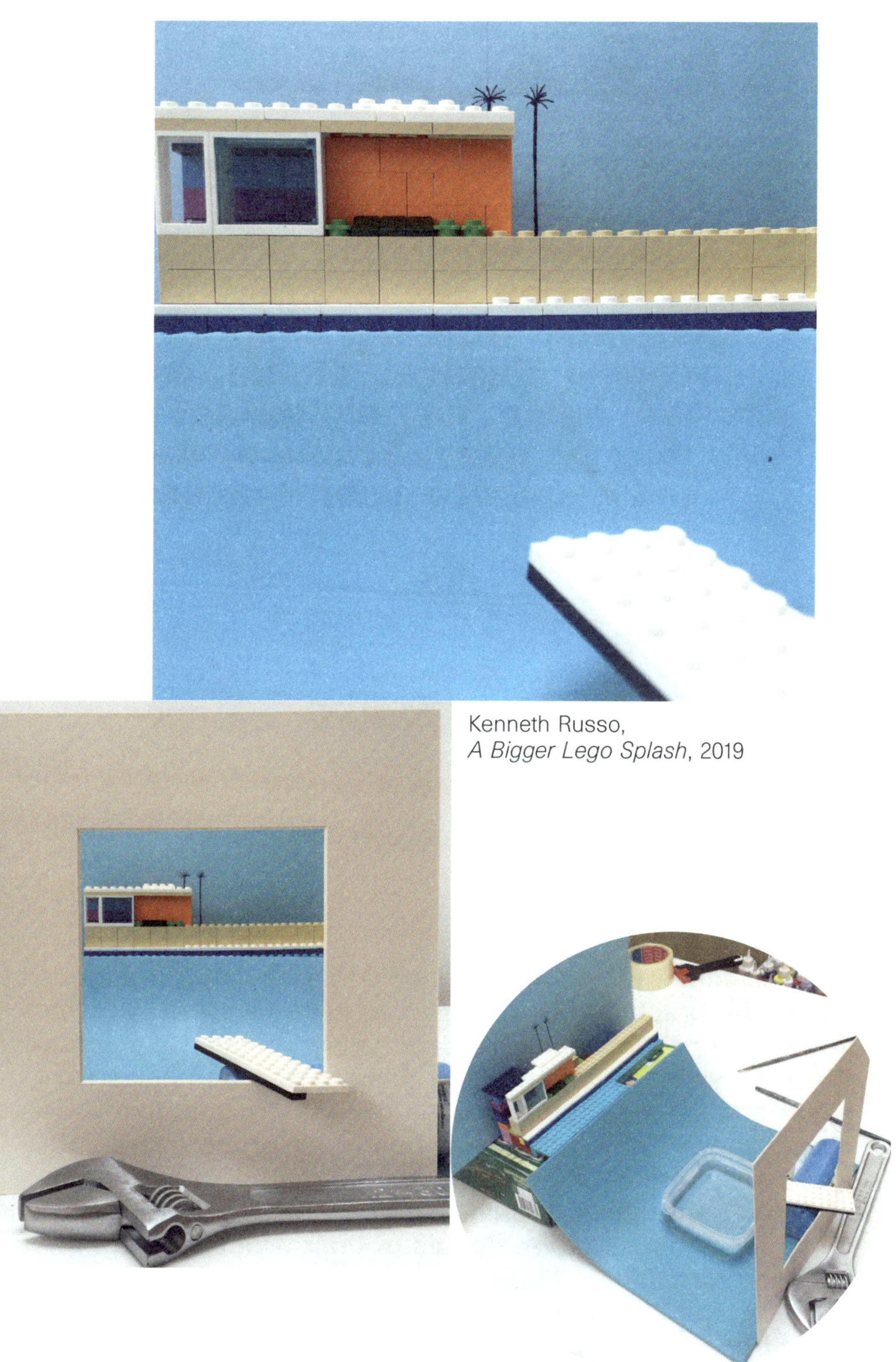

Kenneth Russo,
A Bigger Lego Splash, 2019

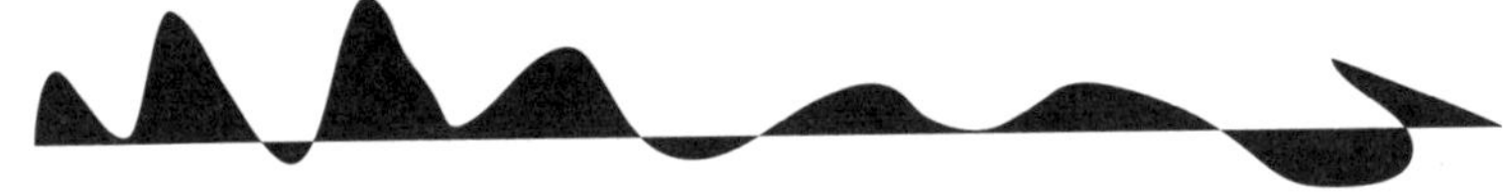

Translations

Using an oscillating process of translation, explore how forms generated from the digital can become physical, digital, and physical again: any digital/analogue tool may be used. Produce, curate, and sequence your images.

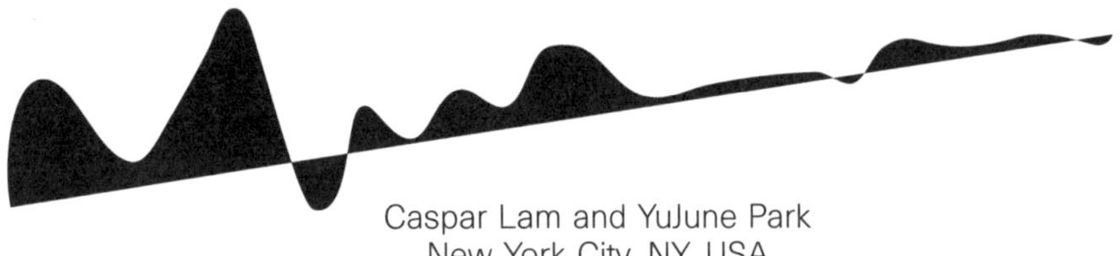

Caspar Lam and YuJune Park
New York City, NY, USA

The assignment is closely aligned with the design methods of our studio practice, Synoptic Office, where we are interested in the idea of translation between forms, media, and cultures. Our brief was developed out of this practice and given to junior and senior communication design students as the basis of an experimental form-making class. Over the course of a semester, students had to learn abstract form-making by making and remaking visual artefacts processed with different tools, techniques, and materials of their own choosing. The resulting forms were curated into a sequenced set of images and published in three volumes: *Currents: Translations*; *Currents: Translations 2*; and *Currents: Translations 3*.

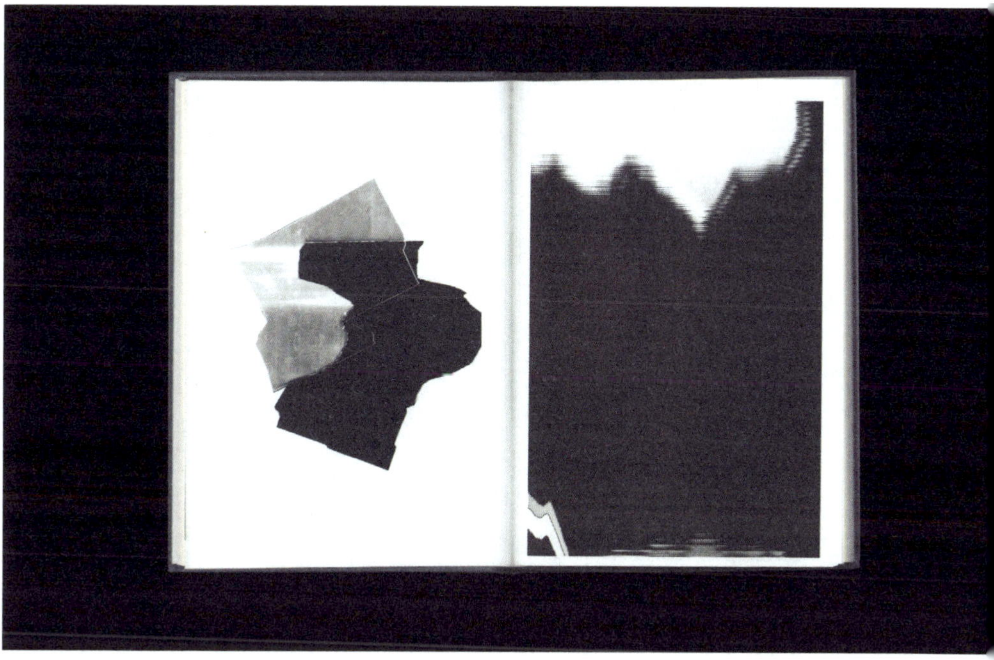

Elaine Il Ji Choi, Emilio Sanchez, Mary Scahill, *Currents: Translations*, 2013, double-page spread from book

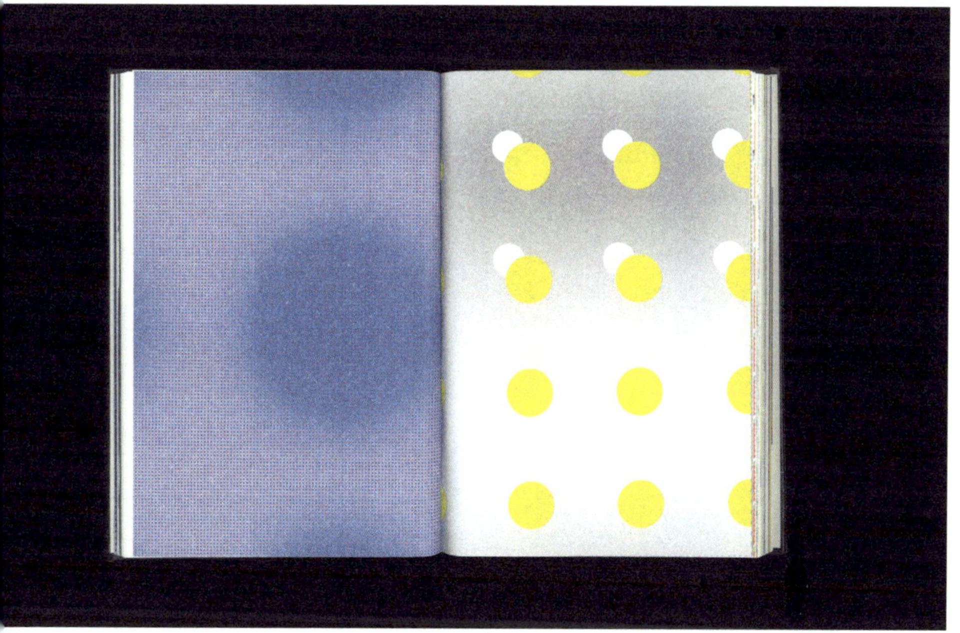

Em Grey, *Currents: Translations 3*, 2015, double-page spread from book

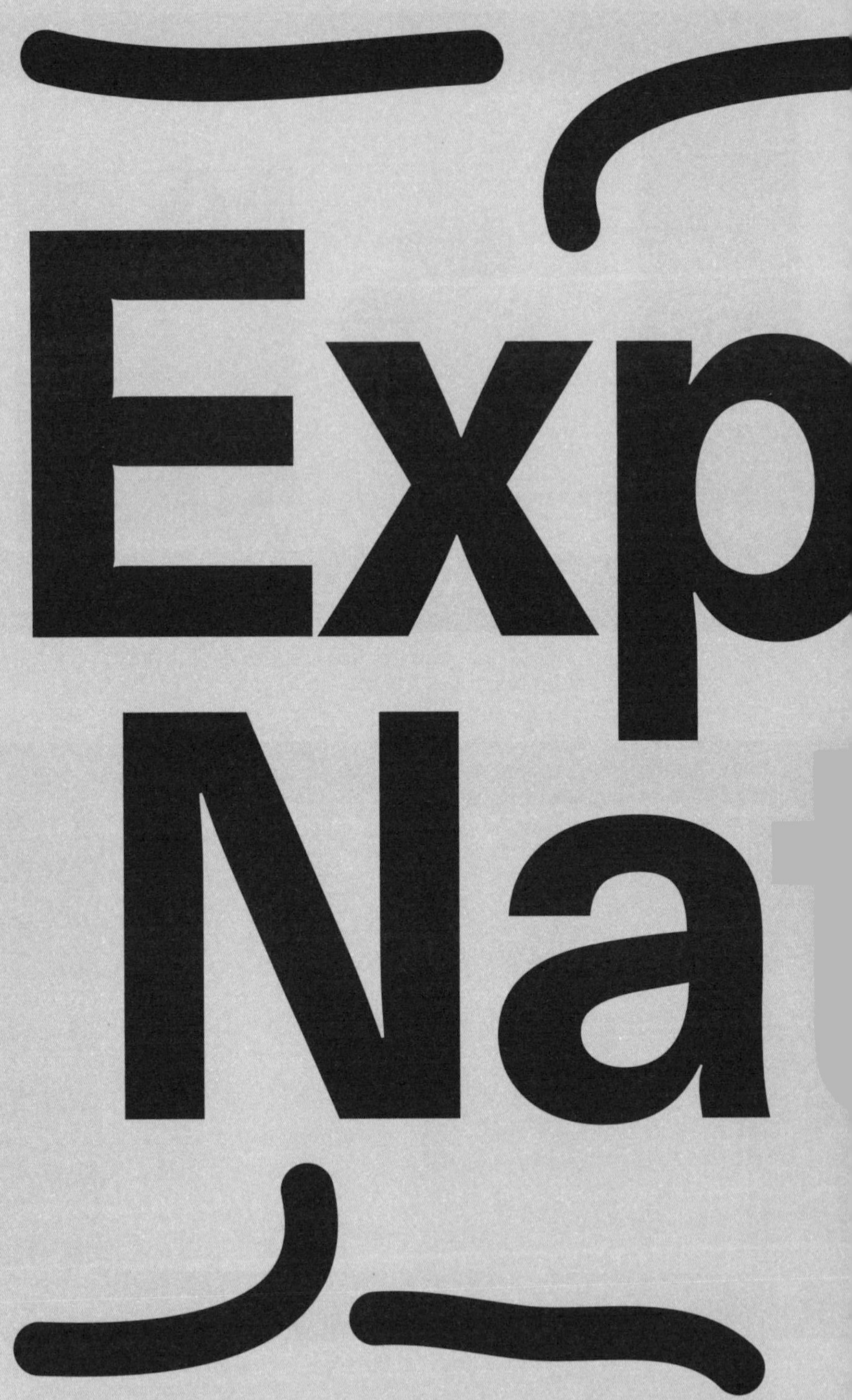
Exp
Na

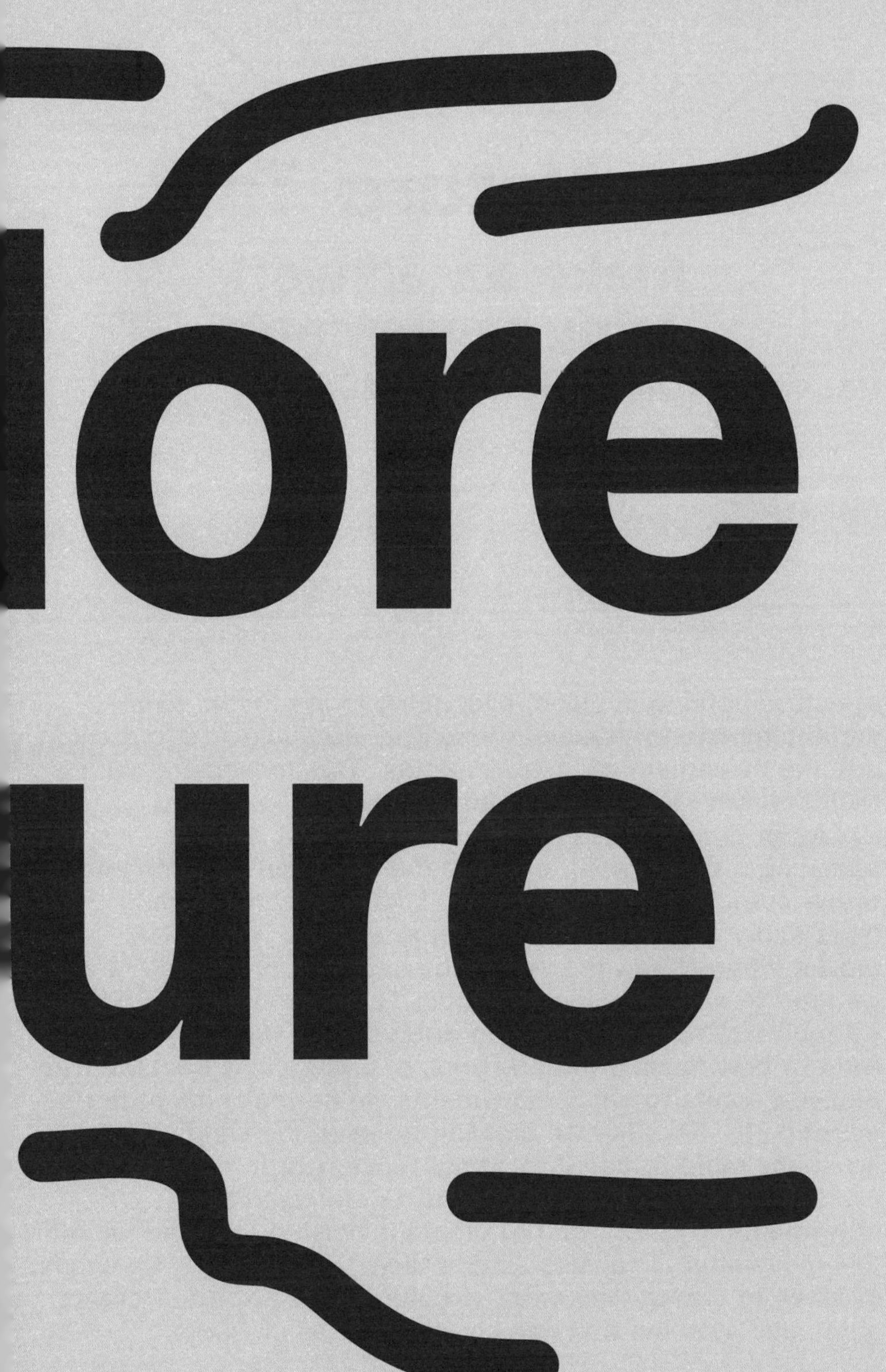
lore
ure

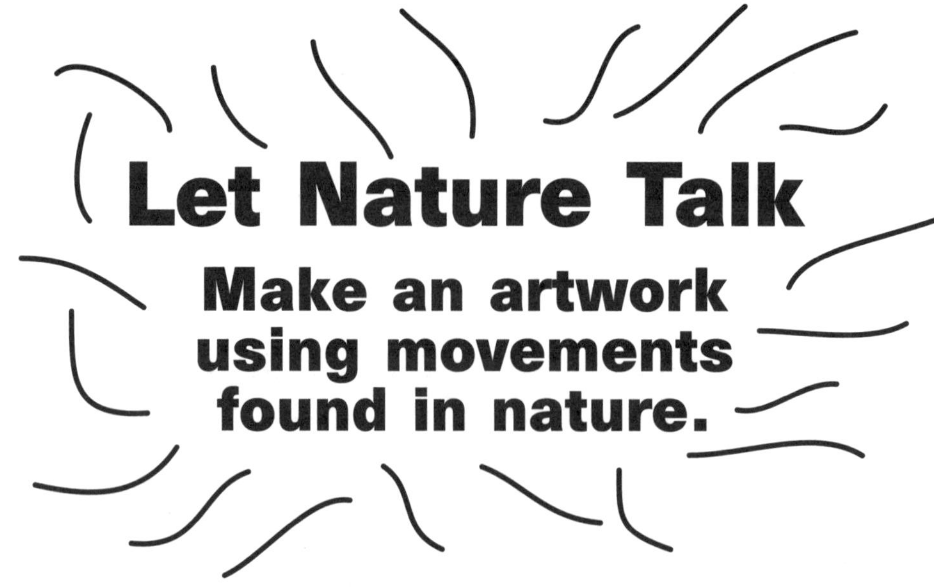

Let Nature Talk

Make an artwork using movements found in nature.

Michiel Koelink
Leeuwarden, the Netherlands

In nature nothing is static, everything is in motion. Even mountains are not frozen in time and are subjected to erosion and the movement of tectonic plates. This movement can be found on both a global and small scale.

Artist Tim Knowles has made a series of drawings by attaching a pen, pencil, or other drawing utensil to the ends of the branches of various trees. Like a signature, these trees show their own identity, because each type of tree moves differently in the wind. The series of drawings are also referred to as automatic drawings. The drawings are made without external influence; the artist has no influence on the wind or how flexible the branches of a particular tree are. Tim Knowles wants to show movements we normally might not pay attention to. For the tree drawing he used the wind, but there are many more forces that create movement in nature.

Students are asked to go outside and search for movements in nature and to create a work of art together with this movement. They use simple tools such as tape, tie wraps, or wires to create temporary structures that are art or create automatic systems that can create a series of works.

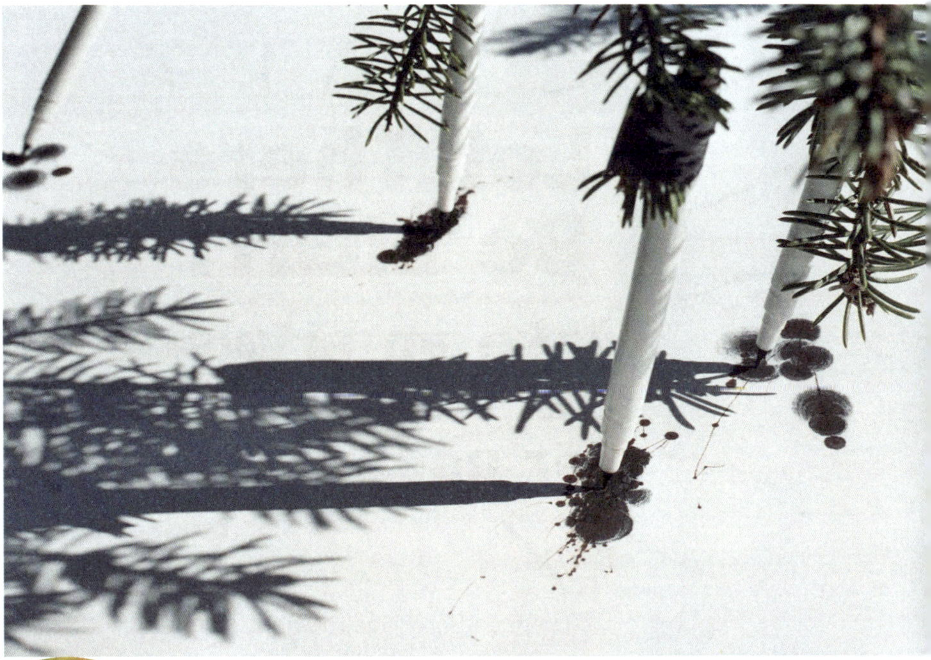

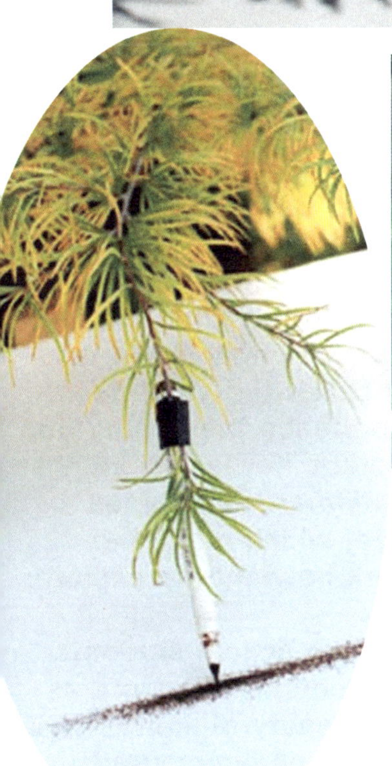

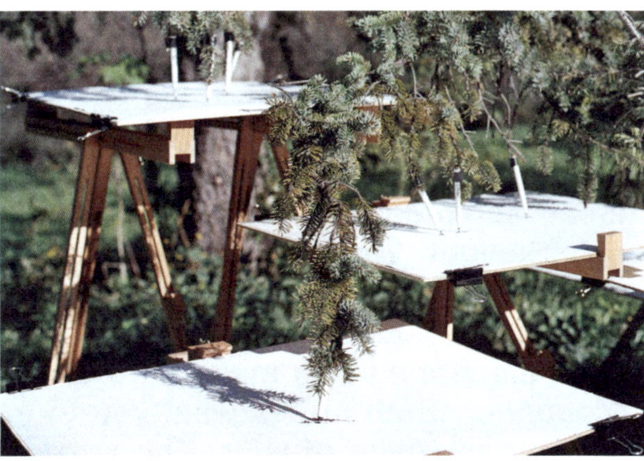

Tim Knowles, *Tree Drawings*, 2012

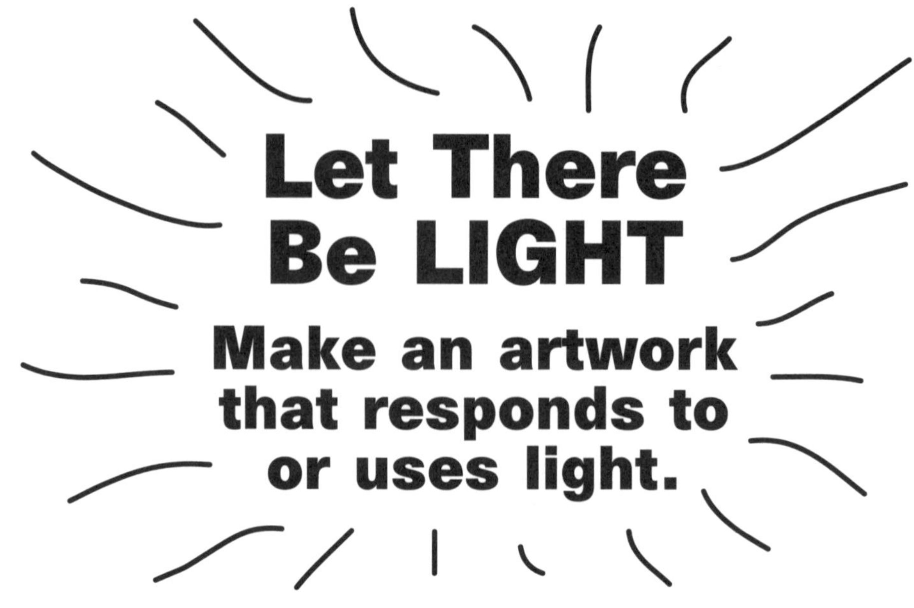

Let There Be LIGHT

Make an artwork that responds to or uses light.

Arida Bandringa-Hendriks
Hilversum, the Netherlands

In life we need daylight. If we don't have enough light, we become depressed or ill. Light also helps plants grow or generates energy. In this assignment, students use light as an artistic medium. This can be natural light, like the sun, or electric light. Works that may inspire the students are those of Olafur Eliasson, who mimics the sun with the *Weather Project*, or of earlier artists such as László Moholy-Nagy, who used electric light to make a 3D object called the *Licht-Raum-Modulator*. Both artists want you to experience the beauty but also the meaning of light. The artist Markus Keyser uses light to 3D-print Sahara sand with his *Solar Sinther*. Sun shines through a magnifying glass, creating heat which melts the sand into shapes of glass. With this work he wants to explore the use of sand as a building material.

The assignment was carried out by high school students, over the course of three weeks. The students had to work as a duo and examine the different uses or beauty of light. The results were very varied, from sticking differently coloured lights to a van and see how they merge into one colour to growing flowers by illuminating them with black light.

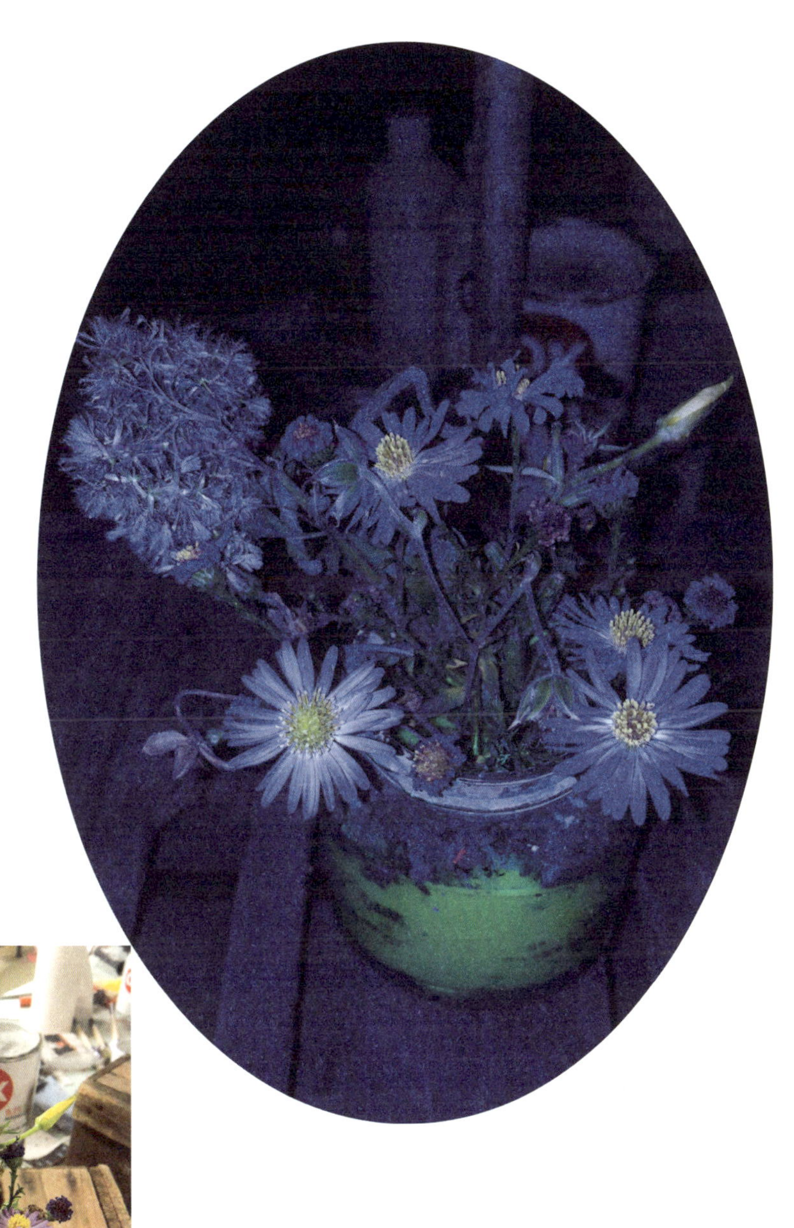

Madelief Schut and Rozemarijn de Bruijn, *Black Light Flowers*, 2018, installation view, photographs

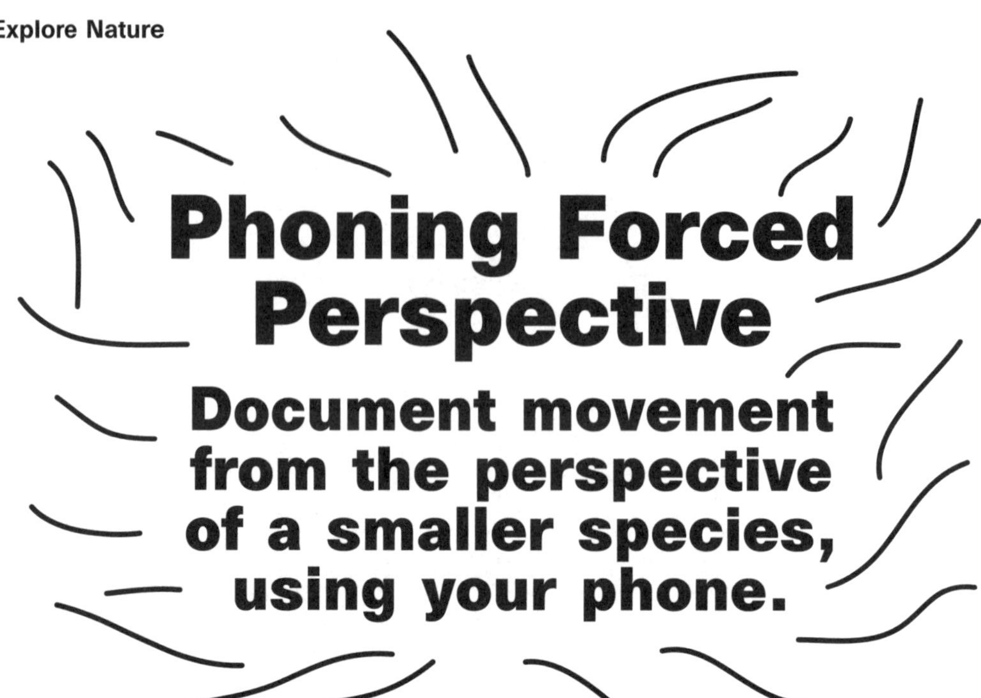

Phoning Forced Perspective

Document movement from the perspective of a smaller species, using your phone.

Angela Inez Baldus
Vancouver, BC, Canada

This assignment is originally based on the documentation of a hike at Mount Washington shared between graduate students in Art Education at the University of Illinois. What started out in the familiarity of a silly conversation between friends (a prompt to follow the movement of a leader up the mountain), later became interesting as a direct result of how the movement was filmed. Ordinary experiences and everyday objects become opportunities to subtly shift our understanding of things. This assignment considers opening up spaces to include the perspective of many species as means of telling and retelling stories that are important to the process of remembering both a simple bit of fun and the complexity of bodies moving through familiar ideas in unfamiliar places.

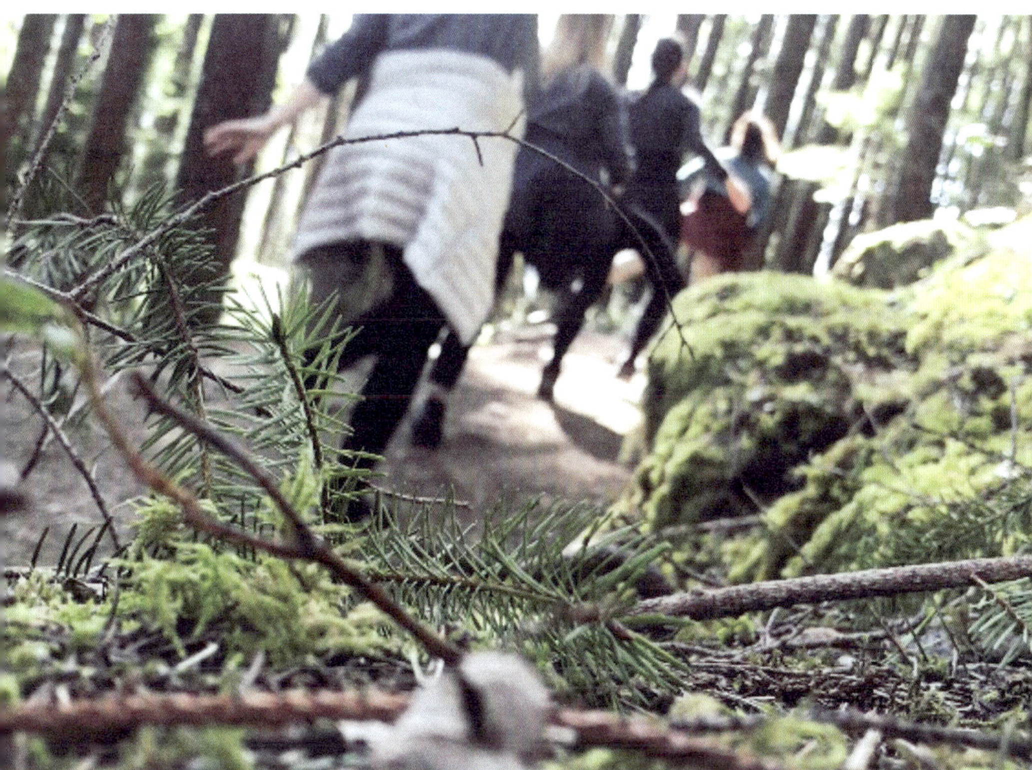

Angela Inez Baldus, Catalina Hernández-Cabal, Ahu Yolac, Hannah Ayers, *Somewhat Synchronized Walking Up Mount Washington*, 2018, film still

Art for Your Pet

Make an artwork in which you attempt to communicate your feelings for or thoughts about your pet. Show the work to the animal and make a two-minute video about its reaction.

Ronald Nijhof
De Bilt, the Netherlands

This assignment is loosely based on my relationship with my cat. We don't really seem to understand each other very well and the only moment of real contact is when I pet her on the head. Despite this lack of mutual understanding I talk to her, which for me is quite comforting. I once deliberately showed her some drawings, in which she wasn't interested at all, which I found rather funny.

Hence the assignment is to make an artwork for someone (in this case an animal) who is 100 percent sure to know nothing of art and is not part of the art world. The relationship between maker, artwork, and public remains a source of inspiration. You can make it your subject matter and see what it brings you.

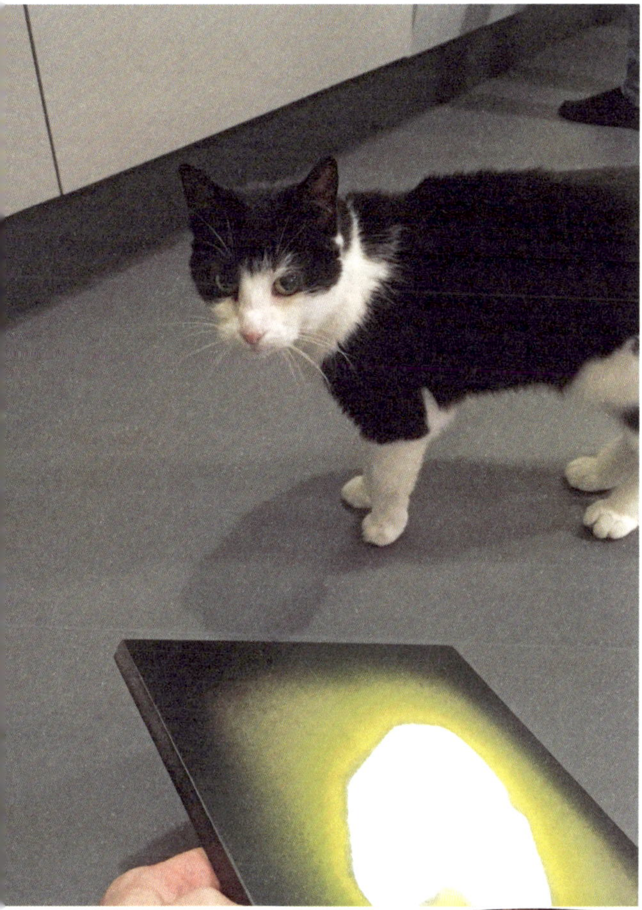

Ronald Nijhof, *Emmie with painting, not really caring*, 2020

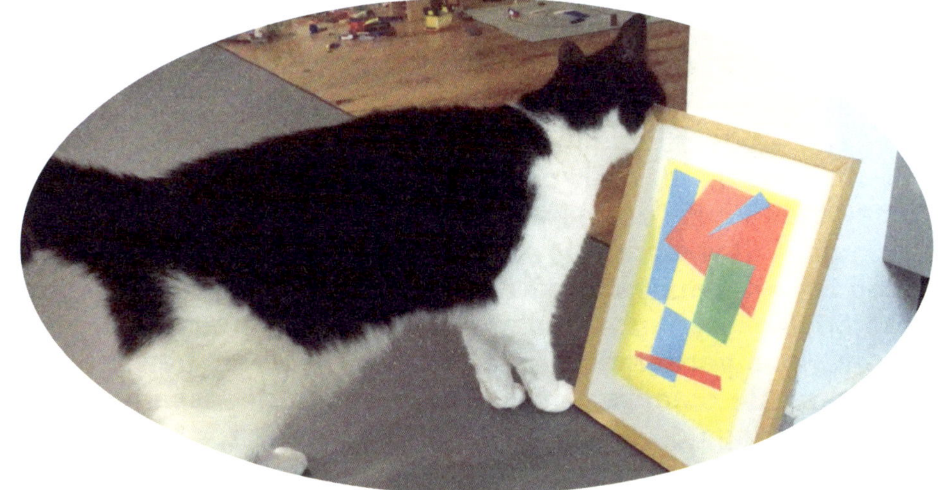

Ronald Nijhof, *Emmie head bumping a framed collage*, film still, 2019

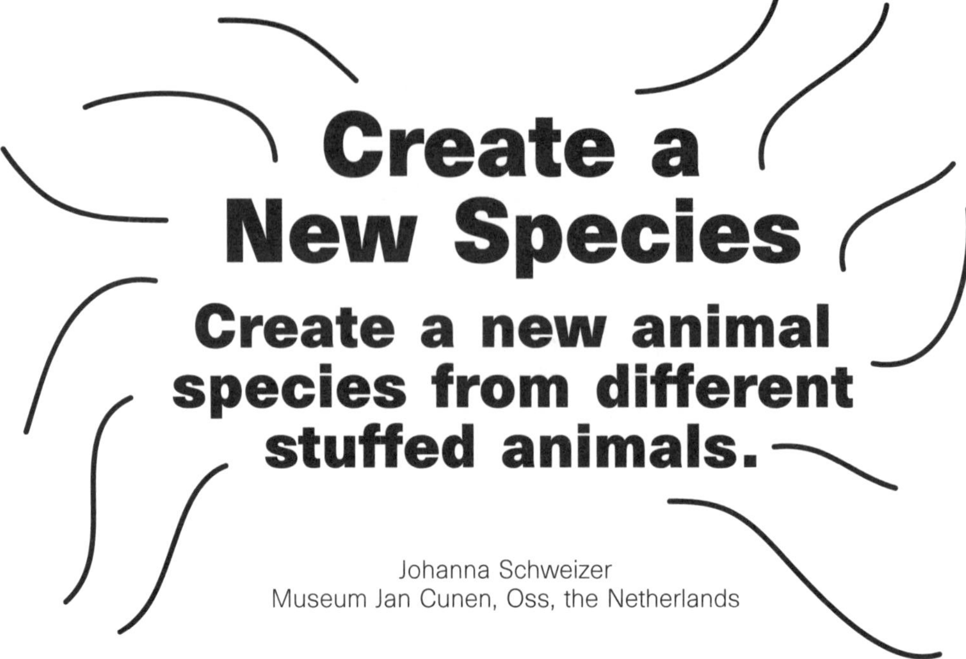

Create a New Species

Create a new animal species from different stuffed animals.

Johanna Schweizer
Museum Jan Cunen, Oss, the Netherlands

Due to pollution and climate change, many animal species are becoming extinct. In this assignment, students work to do the opposite in a playful way: they create a new species out of used stuffed animals. In 2014 and 2015, several high school students from Oss worked together with visual artists to create the exhibition 'We Proudly Present' in Museum Jan Cunen.

The students choose a few stuffed animals that speak to them, because of their colour or the way their body looks. They then figure out how they want to assemble their new animal. If they want, they can make a sketch first. The next step is to carefully cut off the pieces they want to use from the original stuffed animals. After that, the students will stitch the various parts together to create an entirely new kind of creature. Be creative: an animal does not necessarily need to have four legs or one head! The last step is to think of a name for the new creature, and other background information. What does the animal eat? When or where was it born? Write all this on a label, add it to the creature and voilà, a new animal!

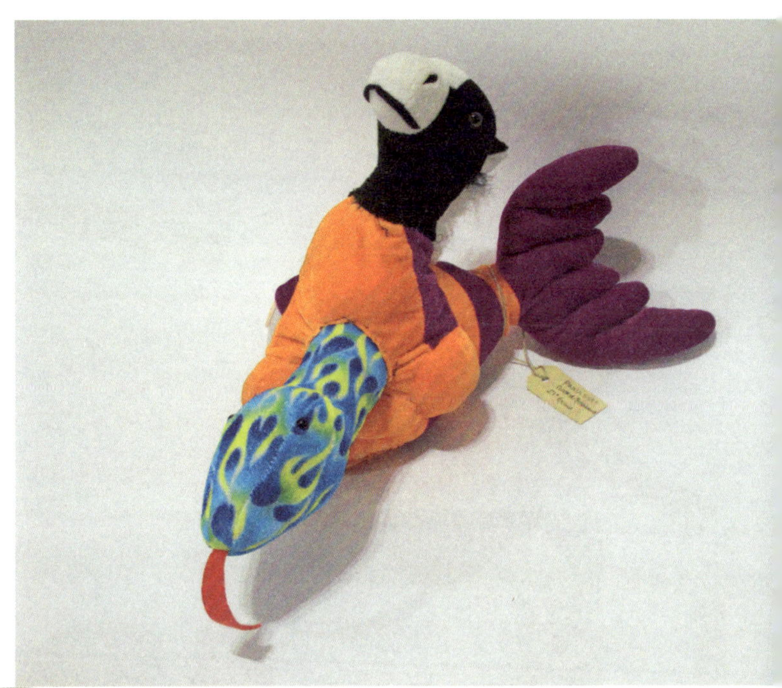

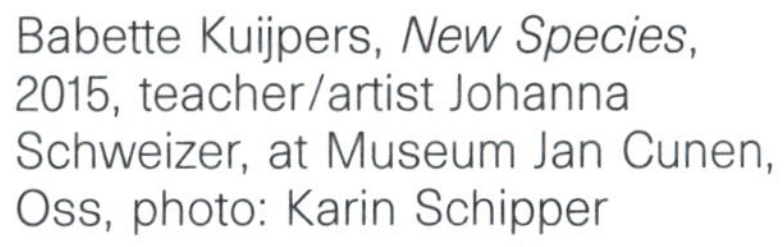

Babette Kuijpers, *New Species*, 2015, teacher/artist Johanna Schweizer, at Museum Jan Cunen, Oss, photo: Karin Schipper

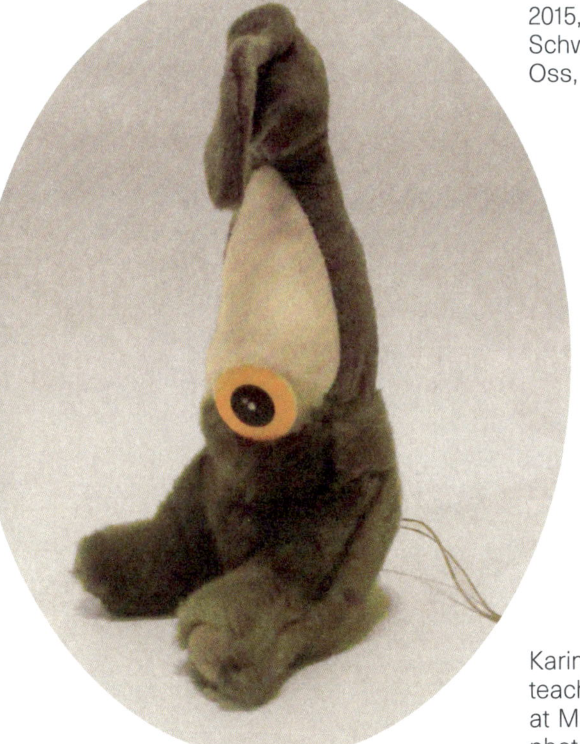

Karin Schipper, *New Species*, 2015, teacher/artist Johanna Schweizer, at Museum Jan Cunen, Oss, photo: Karin Schipper

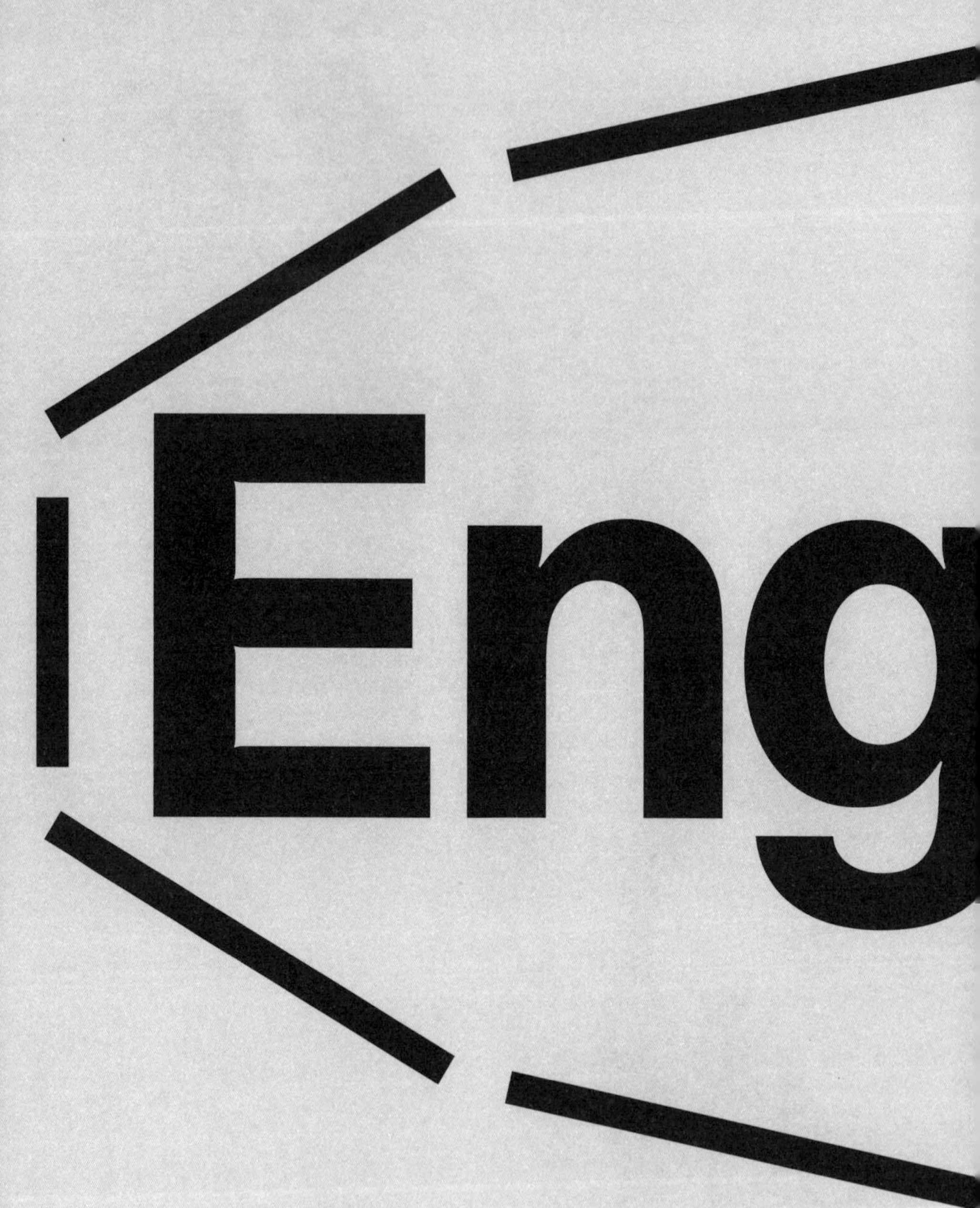
Eng

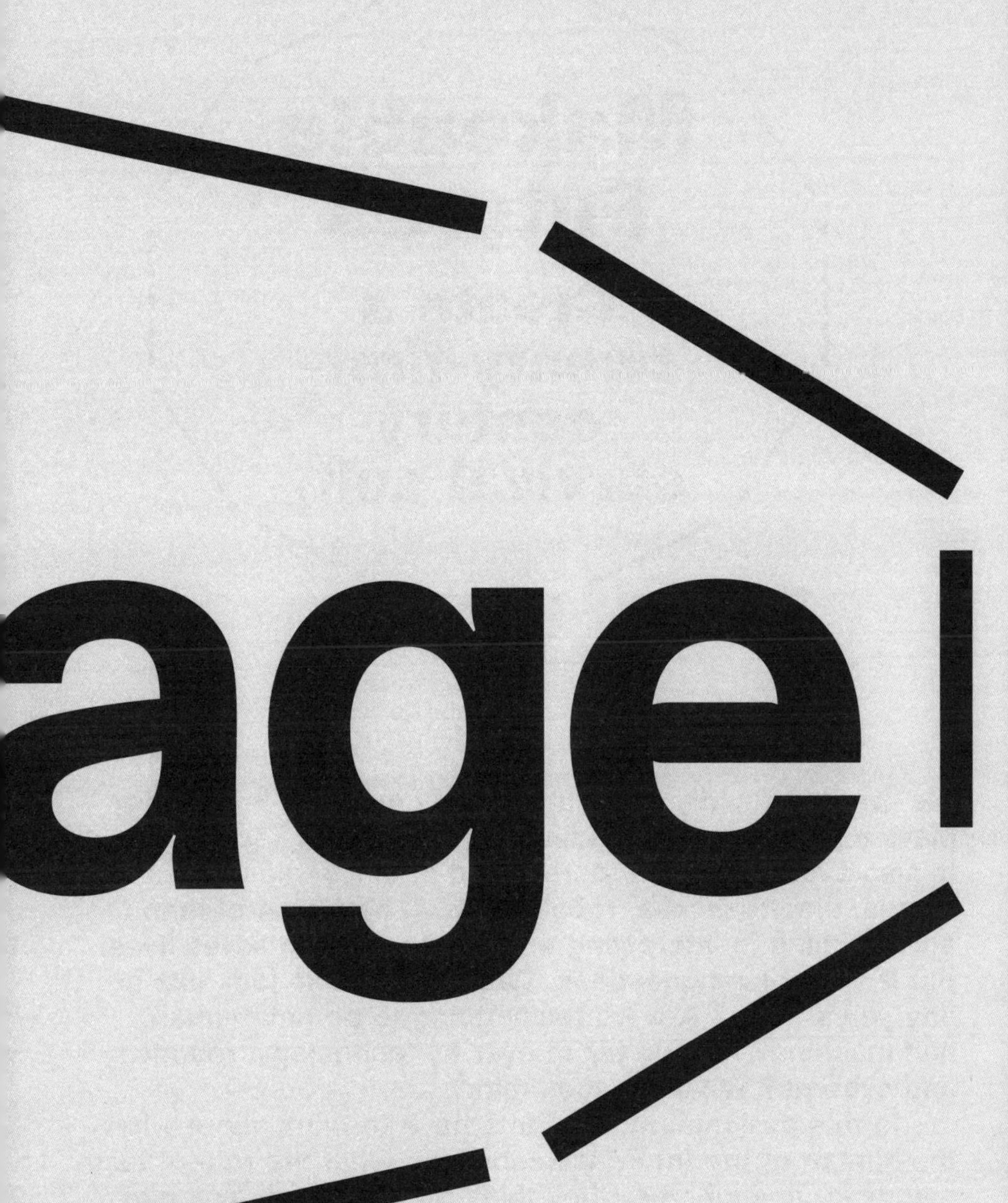
age

Makeable Futures

Create a twenty-first-century survival suit.

Gabriela Acosta Camacho, Amsterdam
Tamar Clasquin, Amsterdam
Marja Reniers, Breda, the Netherlands

We live in a rapidly changing society in which technology plays a major role, pervading our daily lives. Technology is also even more and more found in our bodies. Think of clones, electroshocks, robot arms... The fusion of man and machine is interesting and useful. It even saves lives... But it also raises questions. What will people look like in fifty years' time? Are we really going to be half-human, half-machine? Are we taken over by technology, robotics, and cyborgs? What are the limits?

In this assignment, students have to think about what the human of the future will look like, what the role of technology is, and whether they think that's a good or a bad thing. The students think about the ethical consequences of man as a machine and express their vision in a wearable body object or suit. This is an interdisciplinary art assignment. Through lessons in dance and movement and working with a green screen, a film of the designed suit will be the end product.

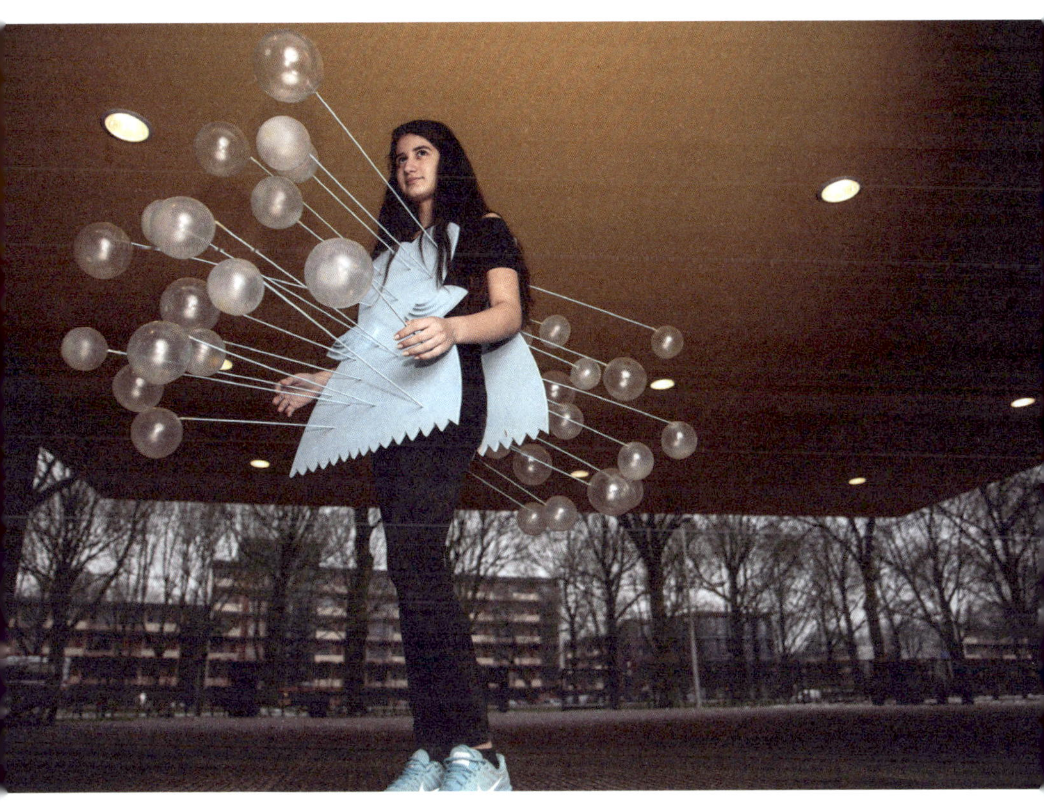

Meriné Shrininyan (14 years old, pupil Revius Lyceum, Wijk bij Duurstede) showing her work, 2019, photo: Frank Auperlé

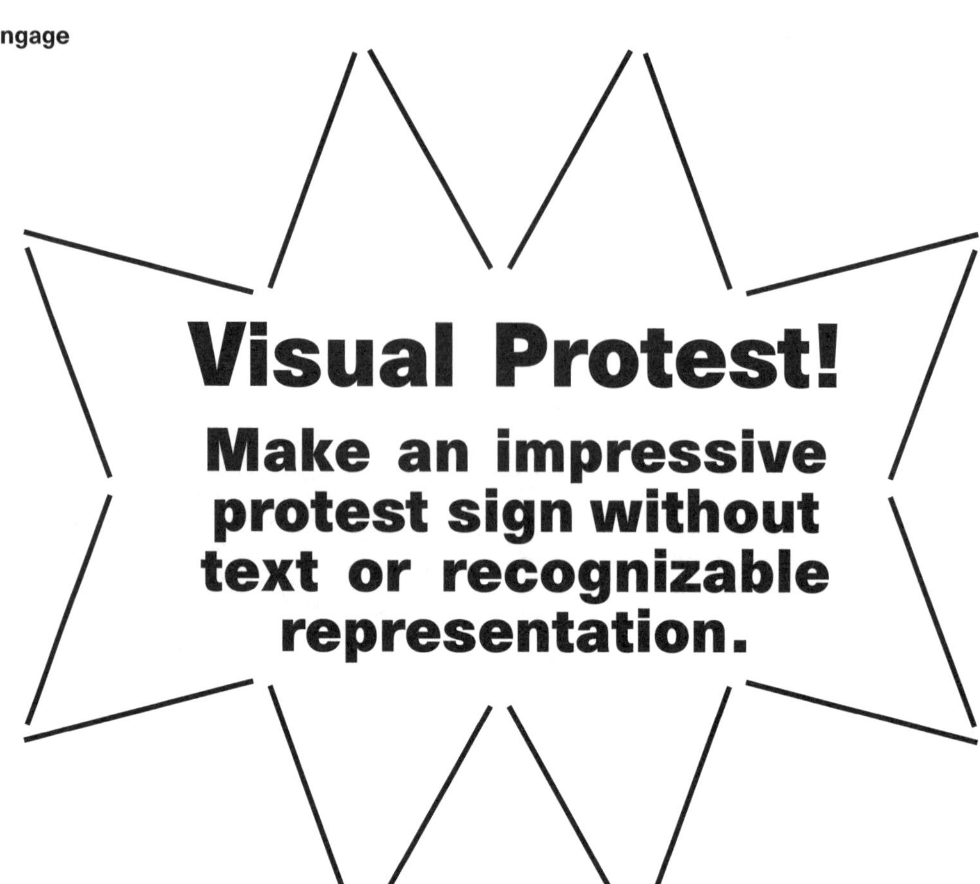

Visual Protest!

Make an impressive protest sign without text or recognizable representation.

Oskar Maarleveld
Amsterdam, the Netherlands

What needs to change in the world? Protest wordlessly in a public space and take a photo.

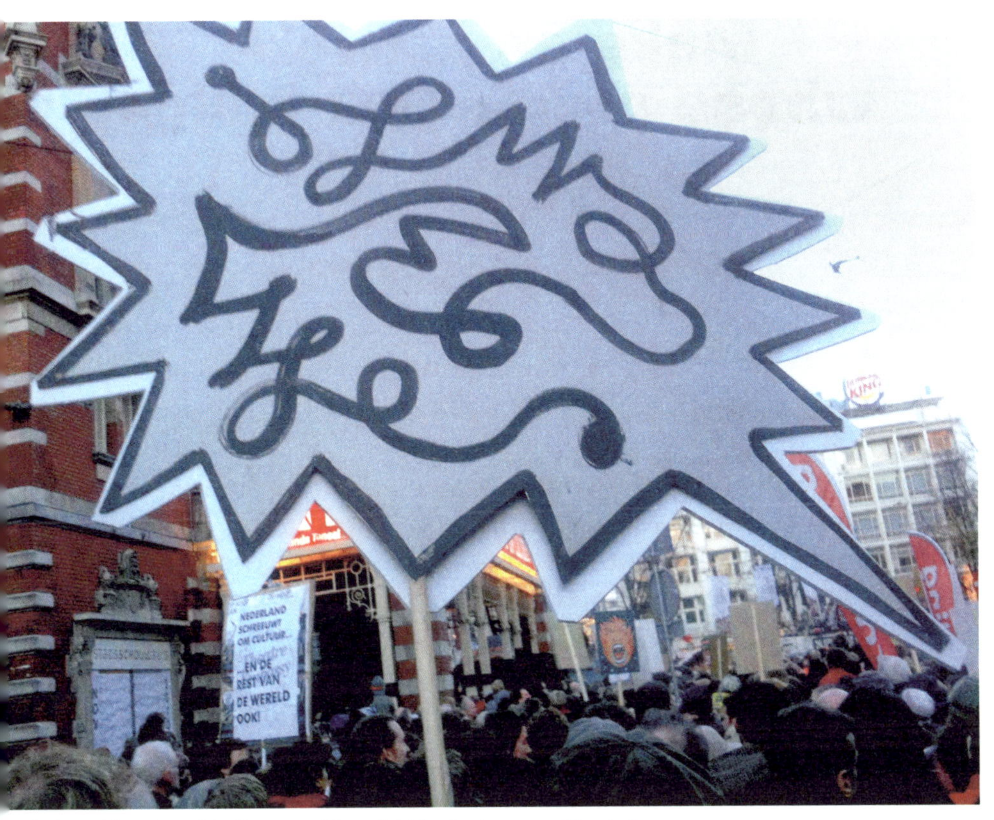

Oskar Maarleveld, *Protest Sign*, 2010, during manifestation
'Schreeuw voor cultuur' [Cry for Culture], 2010

€6 Budget

Make an artwork whose production budget is exactly €6.

Cabello/Carceller (Helena Cabello and Ana Carceller)
Madrid, Spain

€6 is the equivalent of the old Spanish 1,000 pesetas, which used to be a very common sum. Producing an artwork that is limited to this small budget is oriented to critically addressing the power and sophistication of creative/conceptual significance, and to not favouring over-expensive productions that have no content.

The project can be produced in any discipline. Using technical equipment (cameras, computers, etc.) provided by the school is allowed; also recycling found materials. This way, art production in the art school context becomes somehow more democratic, and the focus of the results are more centred on ideas. Critical approaches to art production issues are welcome. A receipt for the expenses must be included when presenting the work.

The assignment wants to reflect on aspects such as local economy, global art markets, and neoliberalism. Some of the main topics addressed during the implementation were precariousness, dematerialization, social/economic class, ecology, popular culture, unconventional and alternative practices, and low cost/no cost art. In 2010, the proposal was also activated as an open call for an exhibition in an alternative space in Madrid (Off Limits Art Space), mixing works by students and emerging artists.

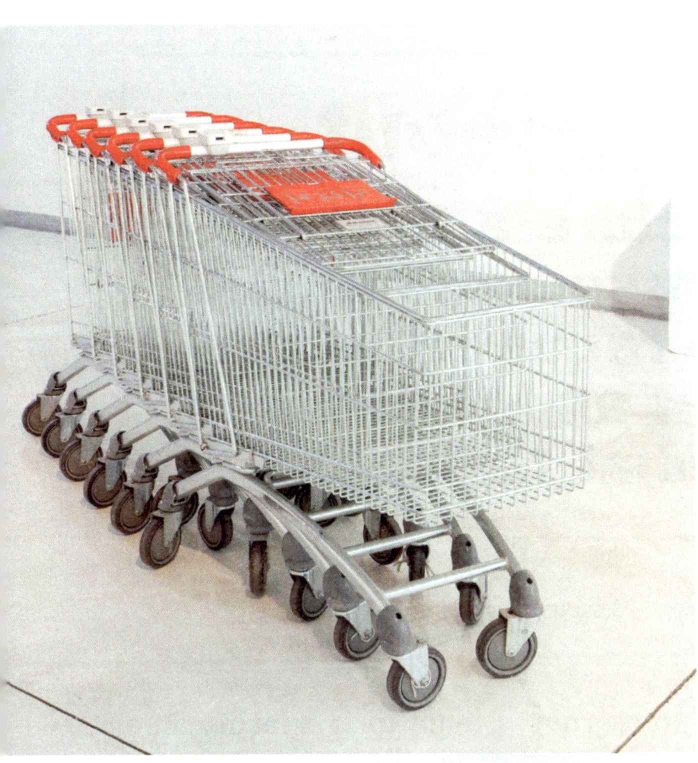

Mikel Tellería, *Art, Art Market, Consumer Society*, 2010, 6 supermarket trolleys, installation view, 'Off Limits', Madrid, photo: Pedro Laguna

Angela Cuadra, *All That Is Solid Melts Into Air*, 2010, installation view with 5 eurocent coins, 'Off Limits', Madrid, photo: Pedro Laguna

Timeout

Declare a timeout from something you are required to do. Do it and document what happens.

Disseminart Collective
USA

A timeout is called to regroup a team for a specific time period during a sporting event or used as a punitive device to cease inappropriate behaviour, again for a set amount of time. What if a timeline was used as a performative undertaking? This assignment requires people to declare a timeout from something they are expected to do within any social context with rules in place, such as a school, worksite, home, etc. where they are expected to be productive. The one rule to be followed is to not tell any individual in this context about the nature of this assignment beforehand. Consideration should be taken to how this break from productivity will be indicated within the context, what will be performed instead, what risks might be faced, time parameters for the timeout, how documentation of reactions will be undertaken, and how or if the people in the chosen context will be notified at the conclusion of the assignment.

The Disseminart Collective has asked this of differing participants such as art teachers at conferences and students, to varied responses. This purposeful suspension strikes at how we gauge time, value, productivity, and labour in our interactions with others.

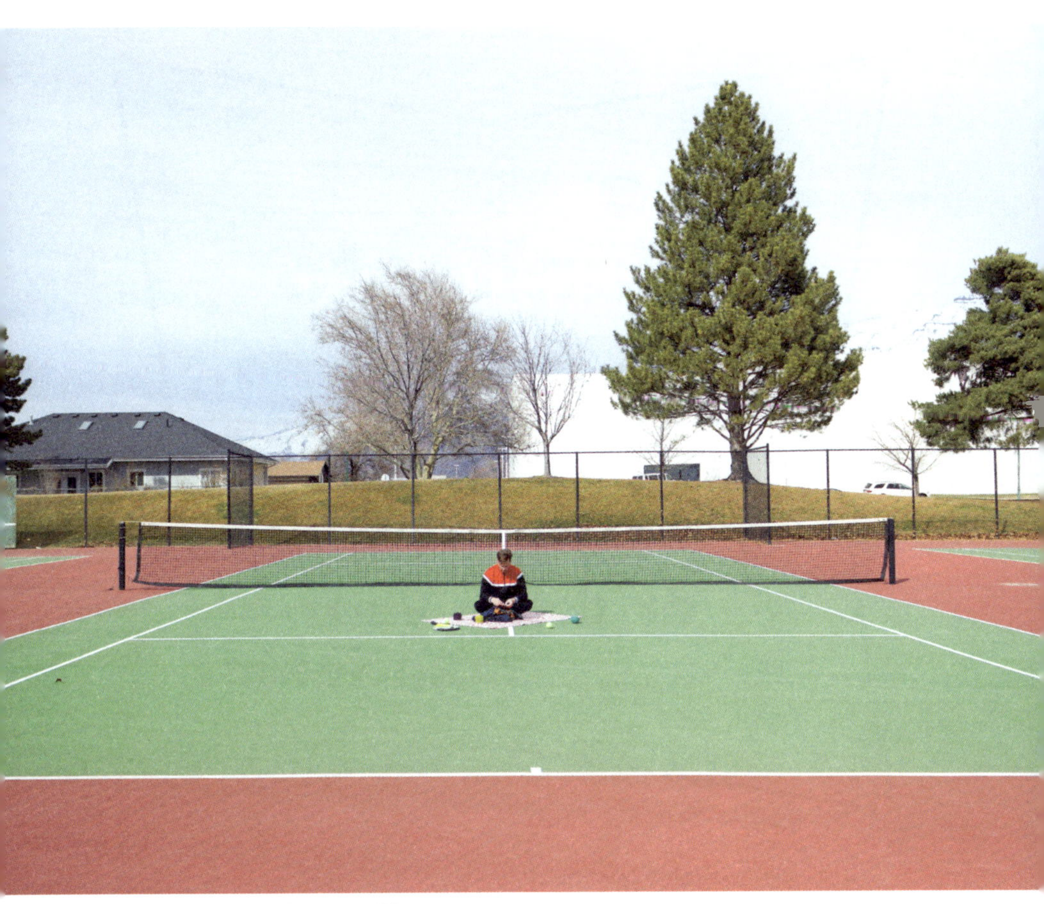

Disseminart Collective, *Taking a Time Out from Sports to Knit a Sweater*, 2020, interventionalist performance

The ________ Manifesto

Make a manifesto. Write, sing, dance, shout, whisper, perform, record, or draw your ________ manifesto.

Gila Kolb
Berne, Switzerland, Kassel, Germany

This assignment was developed in classes and workshops on art education at art schools and museums. I do this assignment some weeks after students have done some reading and discussing. When students have been listening to, reading about, and discussing art educational positions for some time, the assignment gives them the opportunity to change their perspective. It gives them an opportunity to formulate their wishes, ideas, and visions—without getting too concrete at first. Manifestos, especially nonverbal ones, can be polemic. Still, they can show a vision of an art education that may never happen, but lead to serious questions that can contribute to an ongoing individual understanding of being an art educator. This assignment can also work for art educators who want to improve or reflect on their everyday practice.

Manifesto of the air guitar art education

Air guitar art education is free.
Air guitar art education is live. Air guitar art pedagogy is transparent, obvious for everyone. Air guitar art education is real and in situ improvised, at the same time it is carefully planned and staged.
Air guitar art education has no tangible result or end. The focus is on the process. Air guitar art educators do not always know what will come out of the process.
But anyone can play a little bit of air guitar. Air guitar art education means: Not everybody should have to do the same. There is also air percussion. We want to jam. Let's be a band.
Air guitar art education requires good air guitar art educators. Air guitar players are art educators. Art teachers are air guitar players.
We must go in a new direction. The direction still has to be determined. Air guitar art education could be, that we operate with terms, which are not defined yet.
Air guitar playing is art is art education.

Art Eyes Shut

Make an artwork for the senses other than the sight.

Sabina Enéa Téari
Berlin, Germany

Many people live in a very visual culture. Other senses just aren't used enough to stay fit, and in worst cases almost risk becoming atrophied. Yet we exist as multi-sensory and multi-intelligent beings, and keeping all senses at work is the way to develop what makes us more alive and smarter—our capacity for attention.

The invitation of this assignment is to decolonize ourselves from the dominance of visuality, by creating an artwork that reintegrates the body into the act of looking and invites the whole organic experience to be part of it. It offers opportunities to play with and explore non-visual senses—to make edible artworks, paintings that smell and sound and can be touched, and so on.

With Foresta Collective we like to play with this in the context of a multi-sensory lab; a space where participants can work with various media: food ingredients, textiles, materials with inspiring texture, sound-creating objects, smells and perfumes, separately or in a vivid combination. The artworks can then be appreciated in a format of participatory performance, involving movement, touch, barefooted, smelling, tasting, listening or engaging senses like body balance.

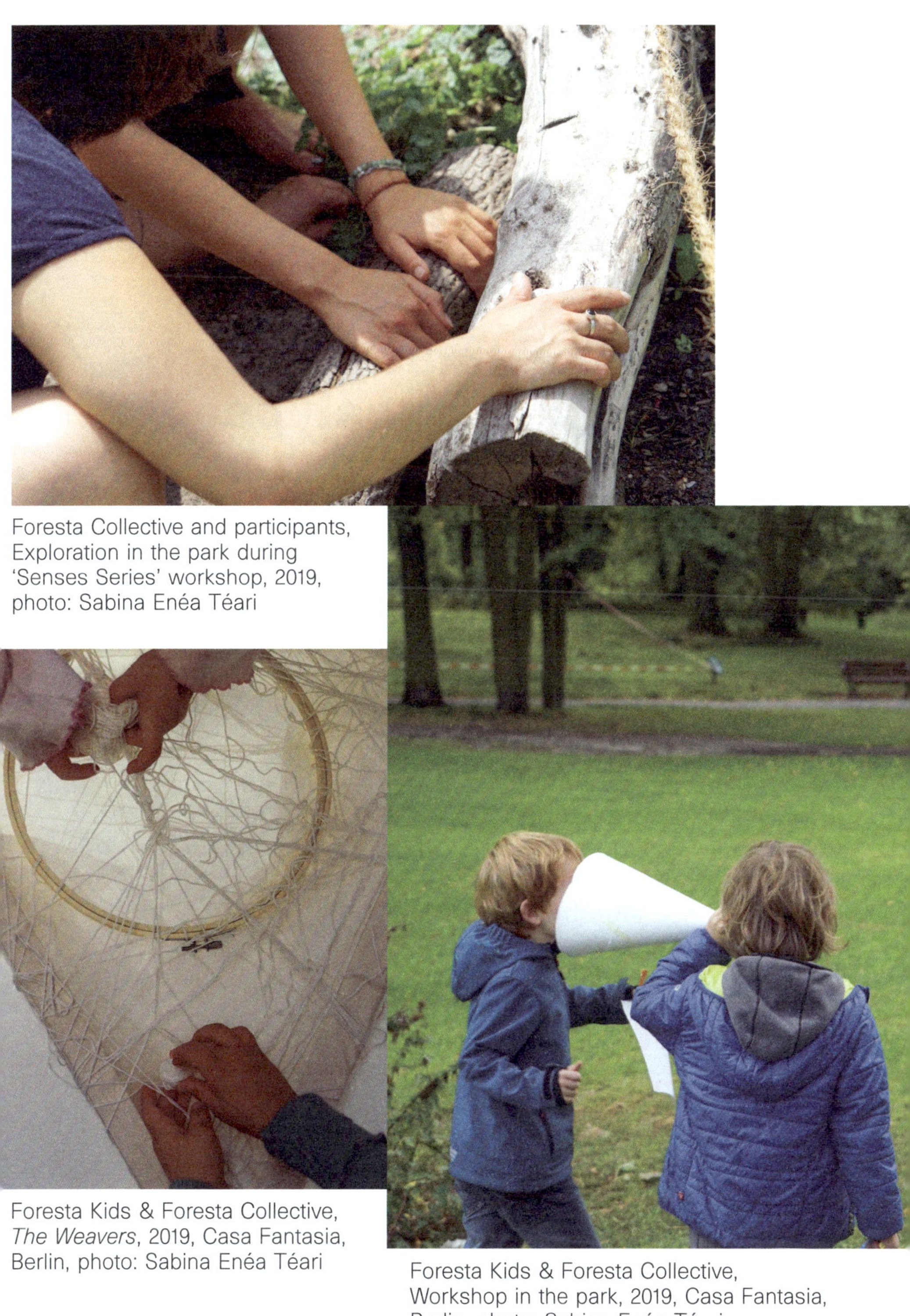

Foresta Collective and participants, Exploration in the park during 'Senses Series' workshop, 2019, photo: Sabina Enéa Téari

Foresta Kids & Foresta Collective, *The Weavers*, 2019, Casa Fantasia, Berlin, photo: Sabina Enéa Téari

Foresta Kids & Foresta Collective, Workshop in the park, 2019, Casa Fantasia, Berlin, photo: Sabina Enéa Téari

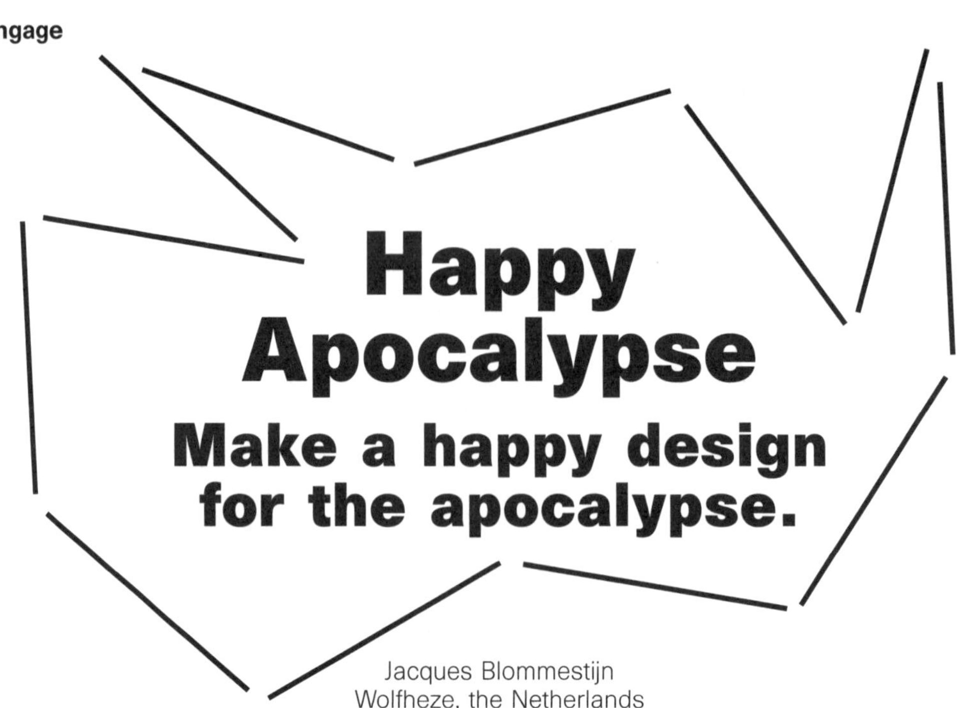

Happy Apocalypse

Make a happy design for the apocalypse.

Jacques Blommestijn
Wolfheze, the Netherlands

In order to prevent us all having to go into therapy so we won't immediately succumb to a climate-related depression or other ailments of our day and age, I want to give students the opportunity to confront problems with optimism. Certainly not in an attempt to deny these problems. On the contrary, this is an exercise in the artful shifting of perspectives. In art, misery is often portrayed in a highly dramatized form. This is taking it one step further: portraying misery in a happy, poetic manner.

The work *Plastic Soup* by Iva Bakker, a final-year student in secondary education, clearly reflects this approach. Her theme is the environmental problem of plastic waste that she observed in many countries. Also, plastic appealed to her as a material. In her work the plastic falls down from the sky like rain and new life grows from the condensed plastic soup: plastic flowers. That she was able to execute her work on this scale is thanks to a housing corporation that made an empty floor in an office building available to us. So there was SPACE. Which is ideal for students: space to work. And mental space!

Iva Bakker, *Plastic Soup*, 2019, photo: Jacques Blommestijn

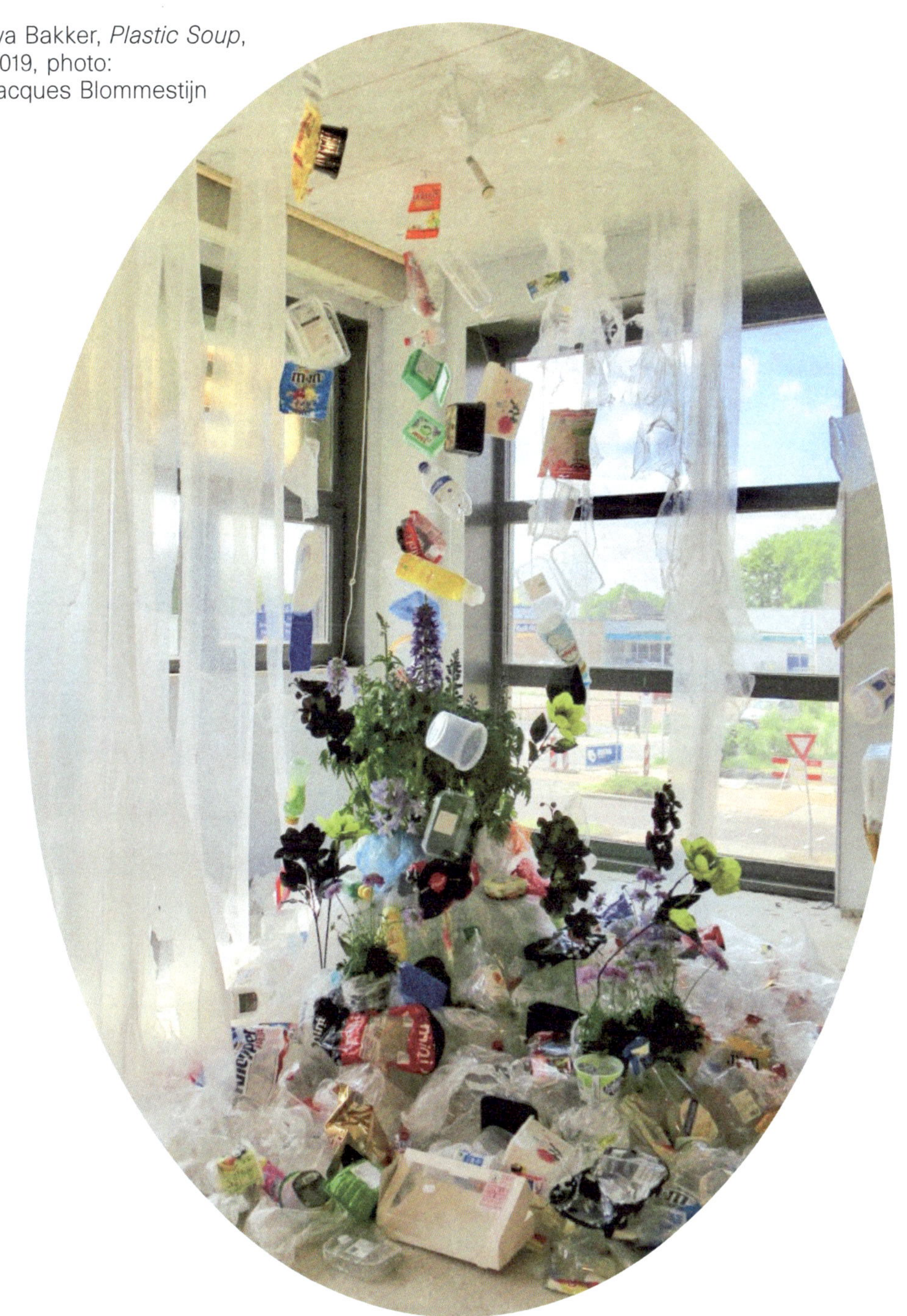

The students of the Rietveld Lyceum carried out the assignment in a new office building in Doetinchem that was not yet in use and was made available for the exhibition by housing corporation Site.

Bucket List for Humanity

Imagine all earthlings as one and create a bucket list for them—present it beautifully.

Erin Tapley
Cullowhee, NC, USA

There are many things we wish for individually but what might be some of the things we'd wish for collectively. Be more specific than merely the vague concept of PEACE. Consider things such as 'water free of plastic particles' or 'weekly love letters between countries'. Then, illustrate how these might look or be accomplished.

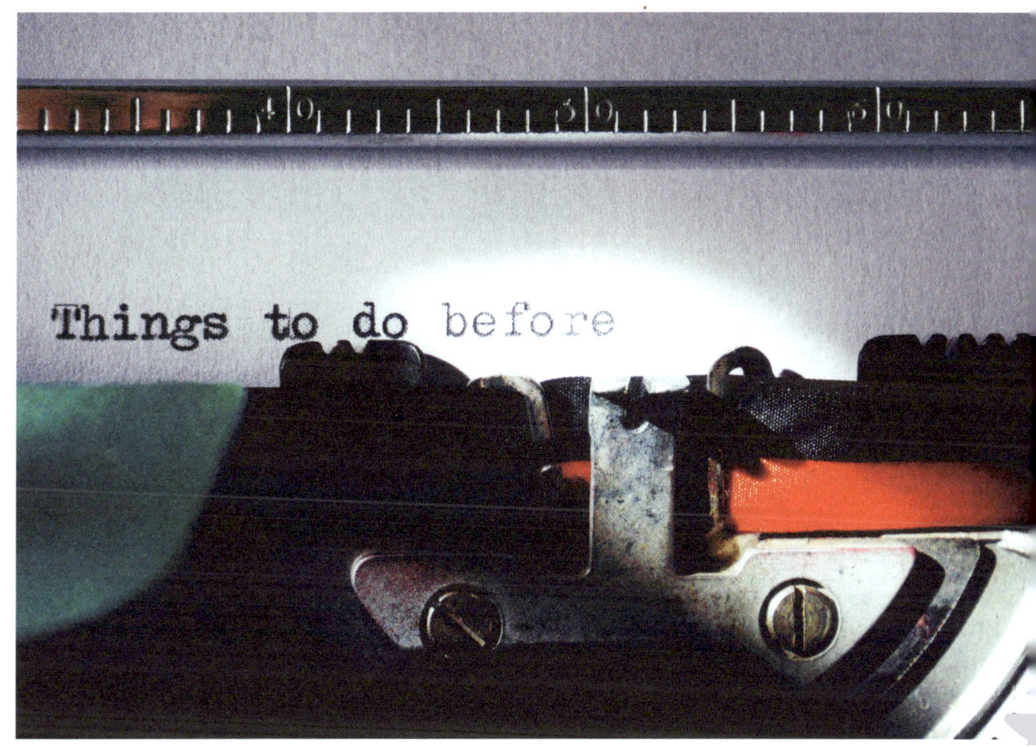

Photo: Suzy Hazelwood

Sc

Sear

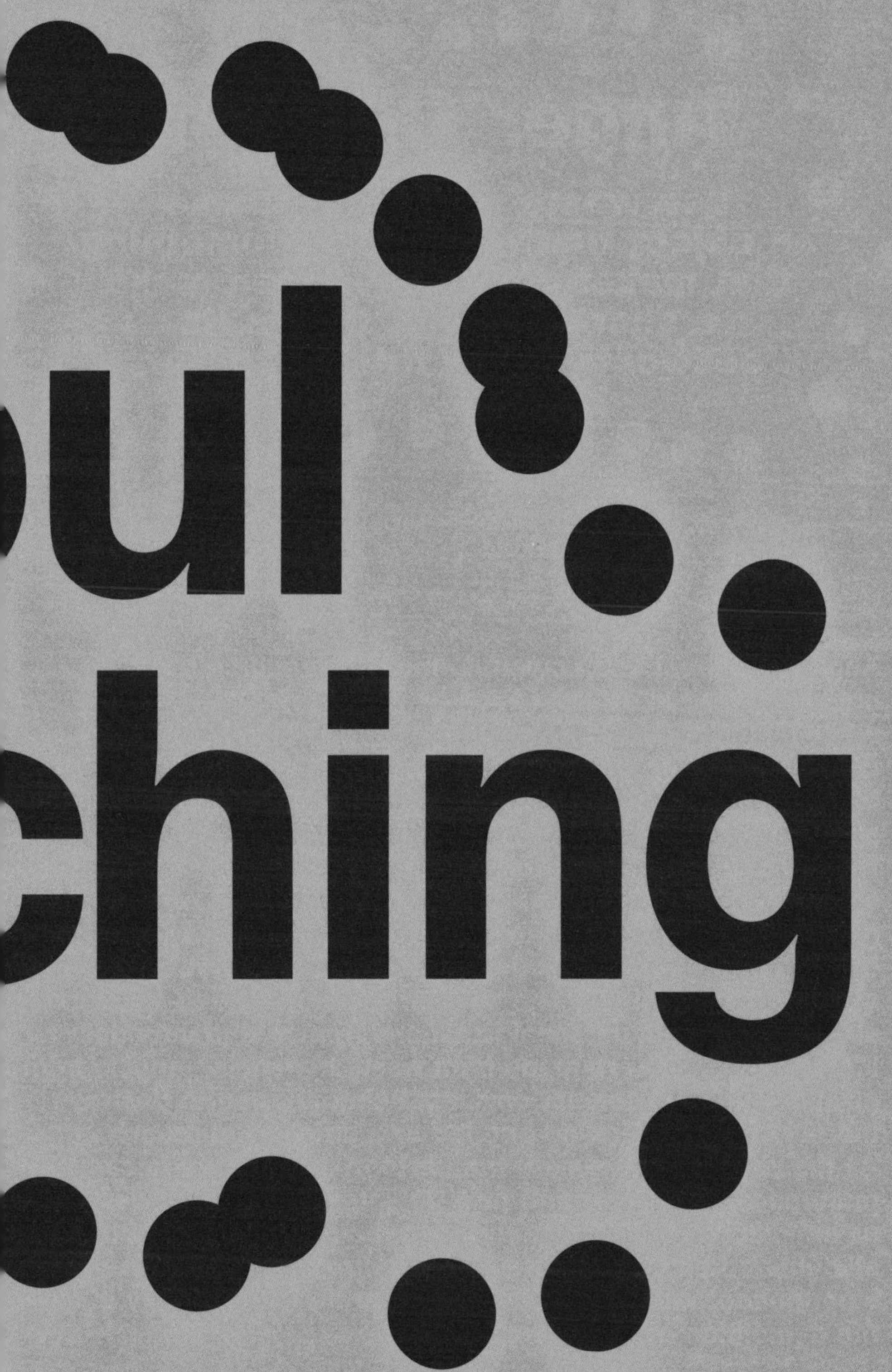
ul
ching

Anger Control

Use waste material to make an object that represents something that makes you angry. Then make a short film that shows its destruction in a fitting manner.

Sterre Boerkamp
Amsterdam, the Netherlands

Anger is a direct and powerful emotion, a source that is not yet tapped in art education as a matter of course. This assignment is inspired by Doug Aitken's work *The Living Garden*, in which visitors were sent into a room carrying a baseball bat. The classes also featured other destructive art projects, such as Banksy's shredding of *Girl with Balloon* and Marco Evaristti, who exhibited living fish in blenders. This spurred debates about liability, the expression of anger and how art can be used as activism. The assignment is carried out with a group of second-year pupils with special needs in secondary education. The chosen subjects varied from hefty social criticism to personal irritations from a student's daily life. The objects were made from waste materials, ranging from plastic bottles to defunct devices. Being allowed to destroy the object was liberating and led to a different approach. As the project progressed, the performative aspect became more and more important: how do you use body language as an instrument, how do you record a performance? Some students opted to work in a more controlled medium like stop motion, whereas others could vent a lot of energy in the demolition and performing.

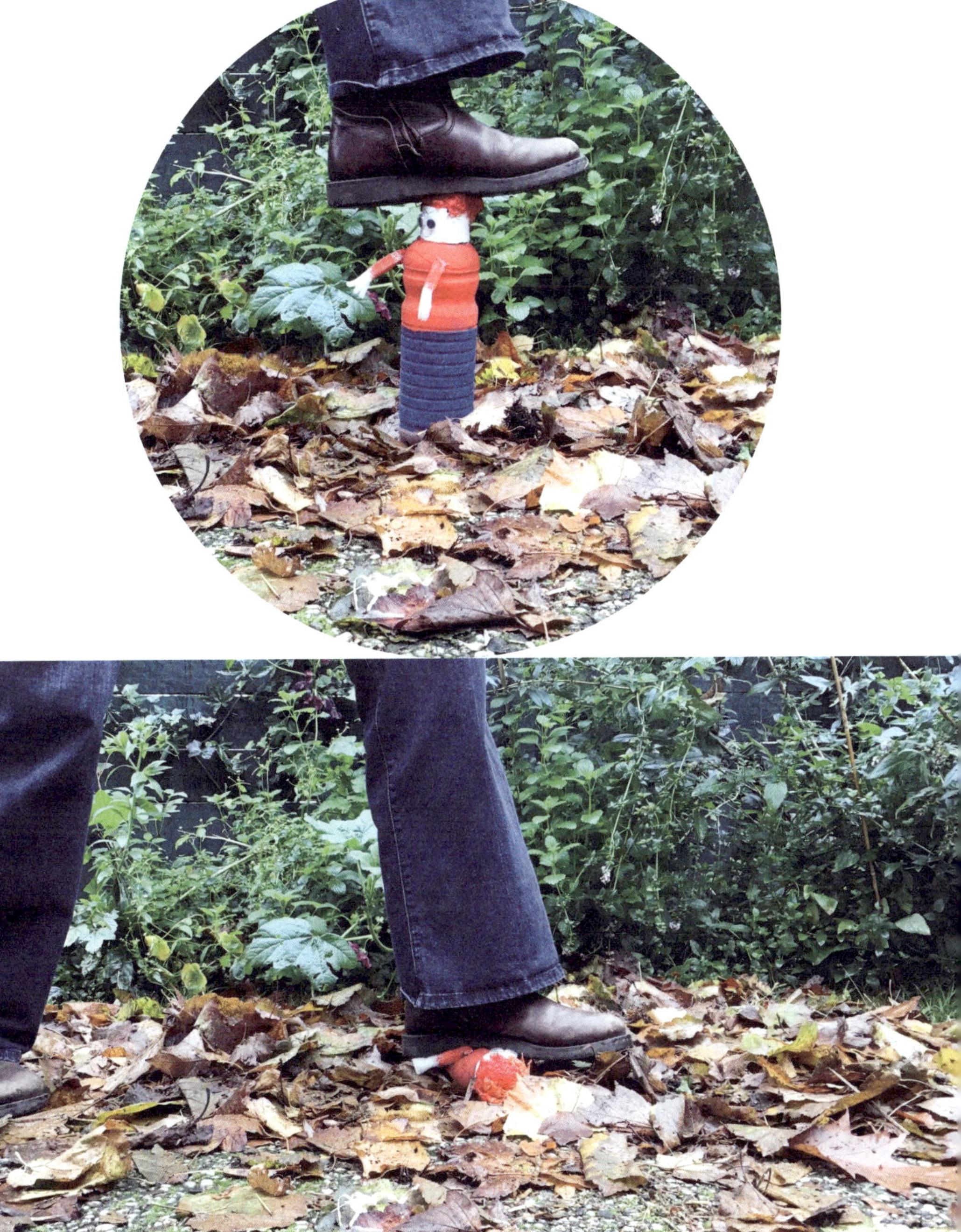

Linde van Driesten, *Against Animal Abuse*, 2019, stills of stop motion film, Berg en Bosch College, Bilthoven

Anti-Self-Portrait

Photograph Your Opposite.

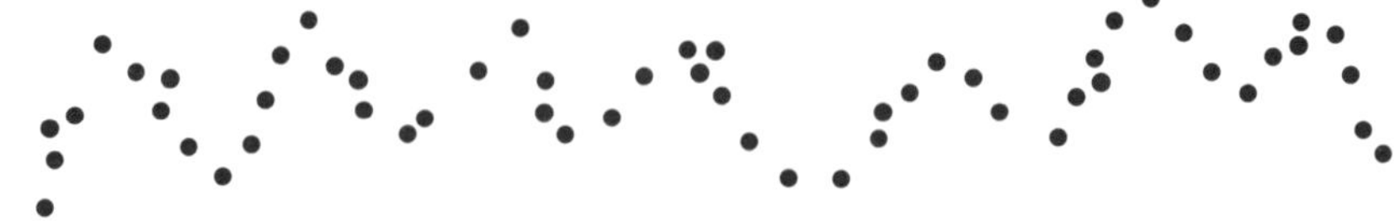

Ber van de Rijdt
Montfoort, the Netherlands

You are the director, the initiator, and take care of the mise en scène: you select the place where you will make the photograph, you provide the props and wardrobe, you decide the framing and composition, and you select the photo you will eventually submit. Preferably, don't use knives, ketchup, masks, weapons in general: less is almost always more. Try to convey as much as you can in as simple a manner as possible. The little that remains will then have *much more to say*.

The Opposite assignment started almost twenty years ago as one in a series of graduation assignments in which I wanted to do *something* with photography. Back then we still used film rolls and photographic paper. From the very first, the assignment was a success and it became part of my permanent repertoire. Students born after the year 2000 grew up with image technology and technically speaking the assignment has only become easier for them to do. It fits in with their world: self-reflection, functioning in peer groups, being aware of your social position. Some students, in order to form an image, a notion of themselves (*what am I really like*) conduct a 'poll' among their friends and/or classmates. I have follow-up discussions with the students in which I discuss what made them select a particular photo.

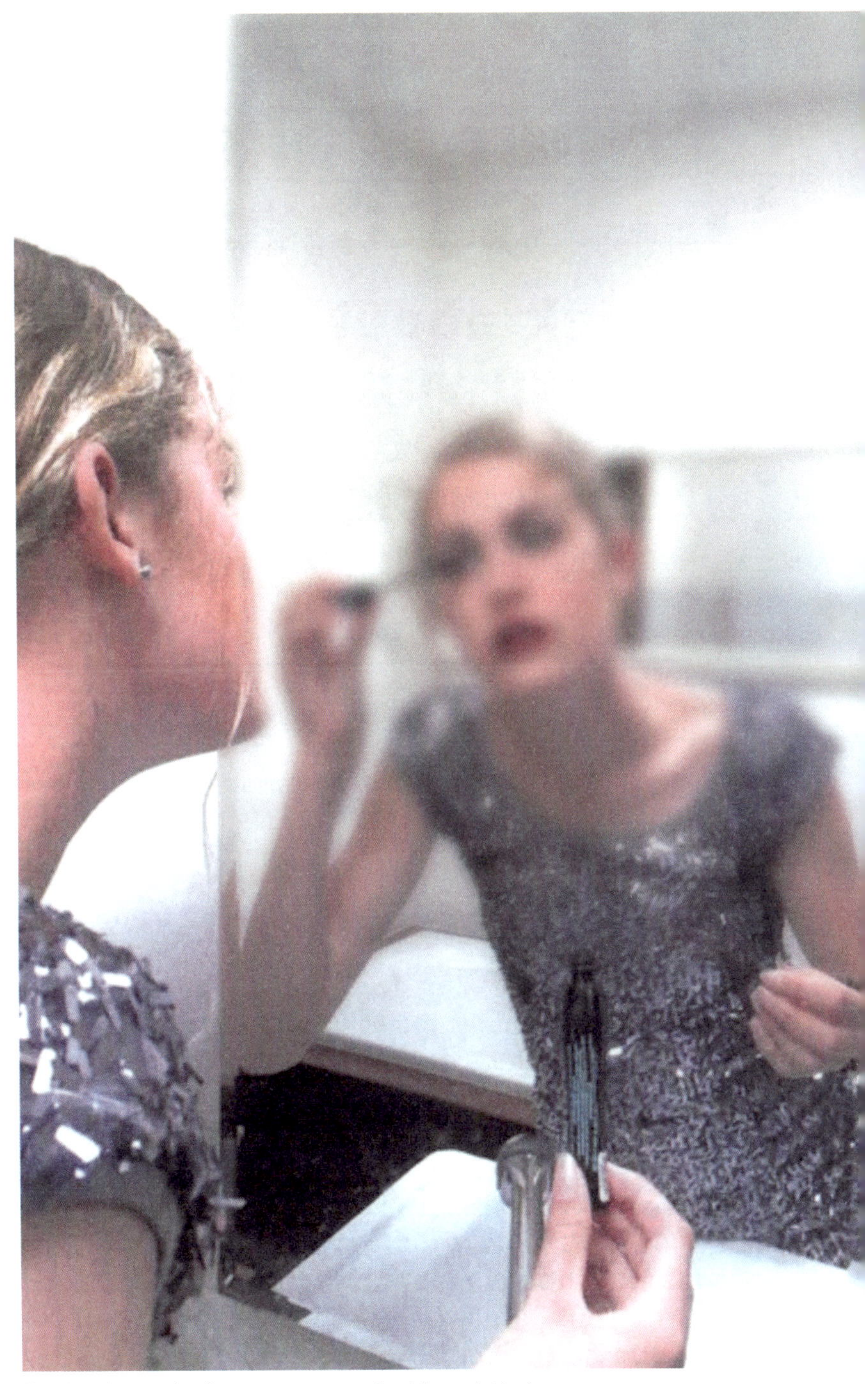

Student's work, *'I am not some fashion victim'*

What Makes You Go Crazy?

Think about the moment when you went crazy. Describe the moment very precisely, in terms of all your senses.

Karlijn Benthem
Groningen, the Netherlands

The assignment is a start for a performance. It is a way to connect to your reason for telling a story. Not the anecdote, but the message underneath the moment is the material to work with. Going crazy in a positive or negative way is an inspiration for making beautiful things. Think of all the meanings of 'going crazy': getting mad, being too much in love, or sad like it will never go away, the moment you thought you lost someone, or the night in your tent with mosquitos everywhere. When working in a group, and everybody has thought of a moment, you can first share the moment as if it happens all over again. Try to use all your senses when reliving the moment. After sharing, you can make a theatre piece about it, a performance that captures the feeling you just described.

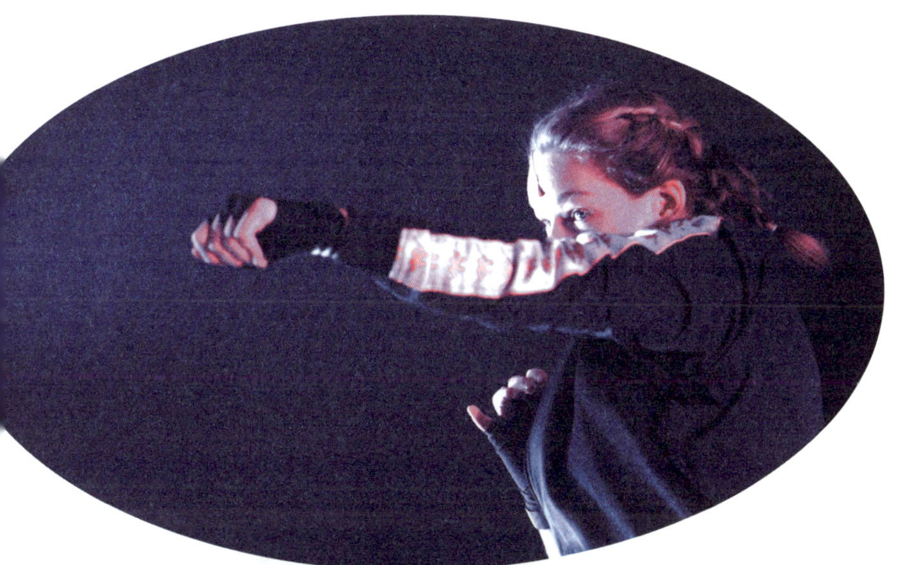

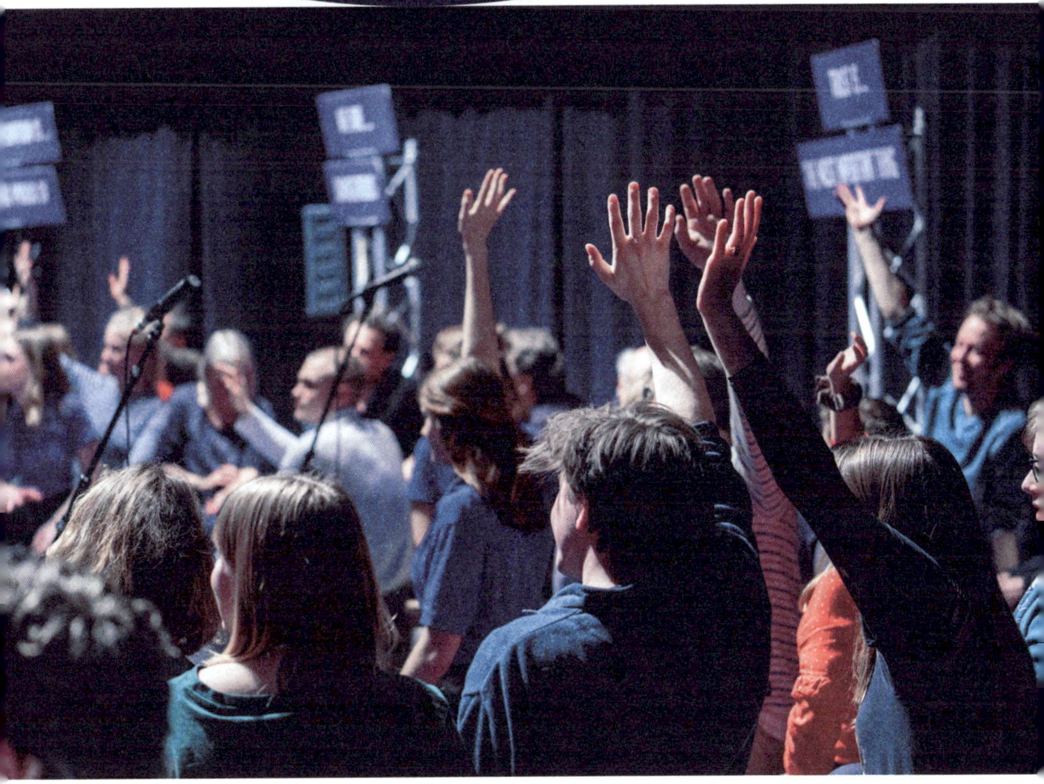

Project Occident, 2019, photo: Bas de Brouwer

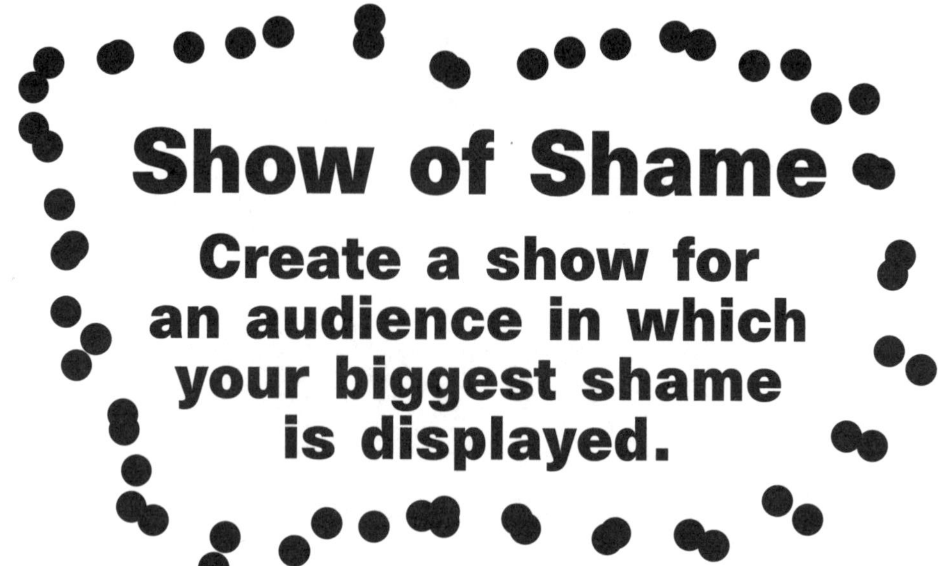

Show of Shame

Create a show for an audience in which your biggest shame is displayed.

Nadieh Graumans-Tigchelaar
Almelo, the Netherlands

Students individually think about something they are ashamed of. This may be anything: a part of the body, something they cannot do, do not dare to do, or an embarrassing moment. The shameful stories can vary from being too shy to call an unknown person to daring to talk about your small penis. The attendees work in groups of four to five people and discuss the stories behind their shame. Together they choose which shameful stories will be the subject of their show and they think about how the show takes place. It can be a musical, a talk show, a dating show: as long as the form is highly exaggerated and absurd. Students can pull out all the stops in terms of text, music, movement, technology, and costumes. Play the Show of Shame. To be carried out with students of twelve years and older.

In the show *Shame on You* (Theatermakerij Enschede, 2018) for the Kunstbaken Festival, shame of the players and director was combined with shameful stories people submitted via Instagram. This resulted in a colourful show about shame, love, and sexuality with flashy clothing, music, and dance.

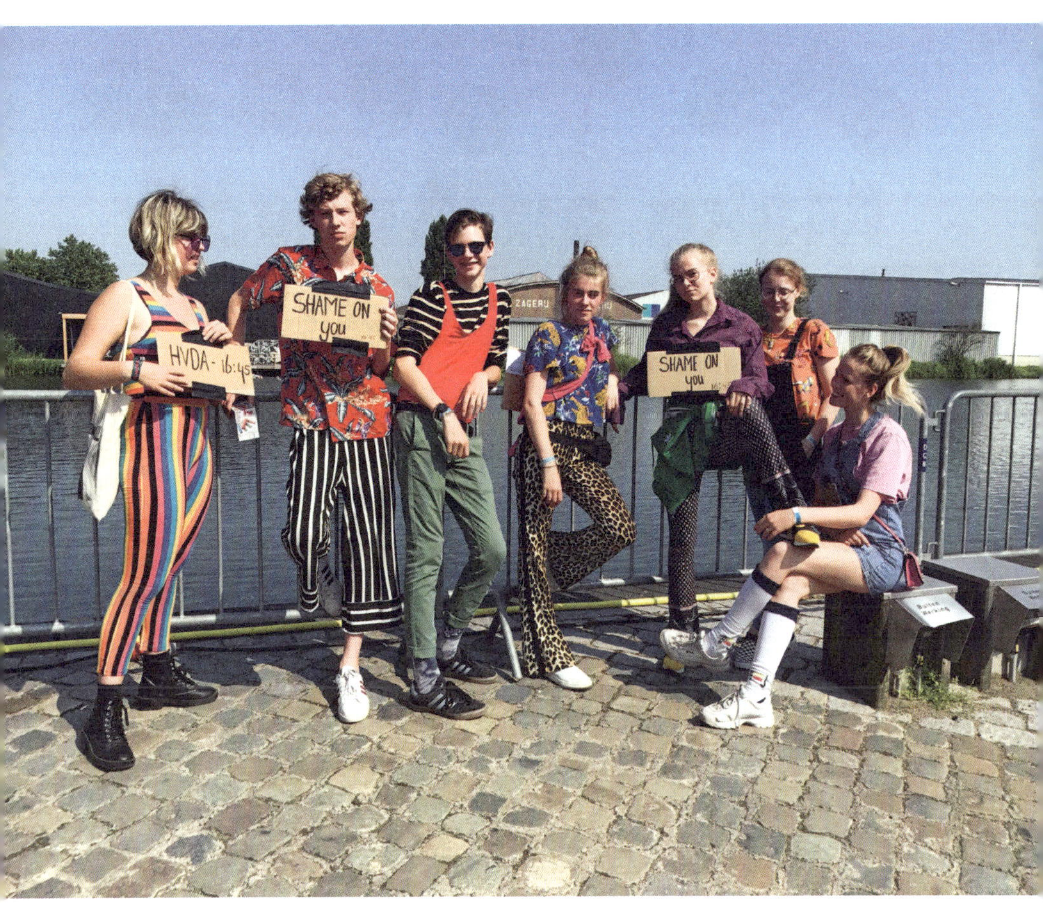

Nadieh Graumans-Tigchelaar, *Shame on You*, 2018, photo: Theatermakerij Enschede

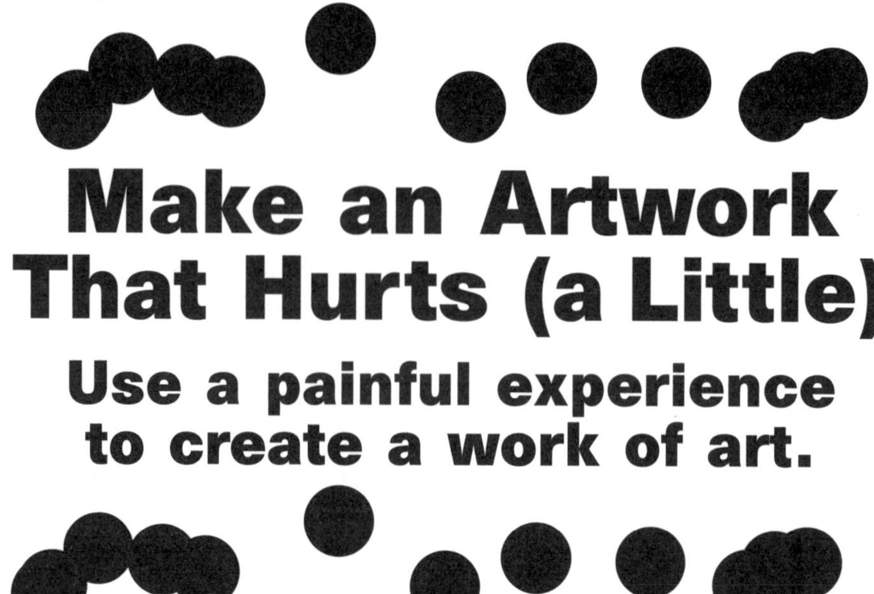

Make an Artwork That Hurts (a Little)

Use a painful experience to create a work of art.

Lisette de Hooge
Arnhem, the Netherlands

By doing a little thought experiment, students reminisce about a painful experience in their lives. First, they look at this pain in an analytical way: was the pain they felt physical or emotional, concrete or abstract, funny or really painful, and did it last long or was it short? Maybe your father has died or you once ran into a cactus? Any kind of pain can be used in this assignment. Students discuss contemporary artists who have used pain in their visual work and are then asked to think about representing this pain through sketches. What does pain actually look like? What colour does it have an what does it feel like if you could touch it? The students enter into a process in which they can work with any material or technique to express their painful experience until this results in a final work that dares to look pain straight in the eye. The aim is an artwork that preferably hurts (a little) too. Ouch!

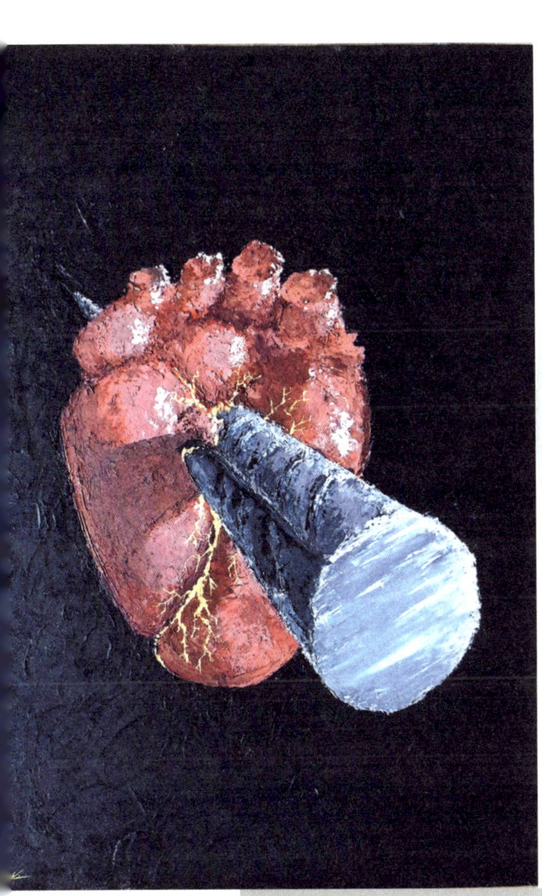

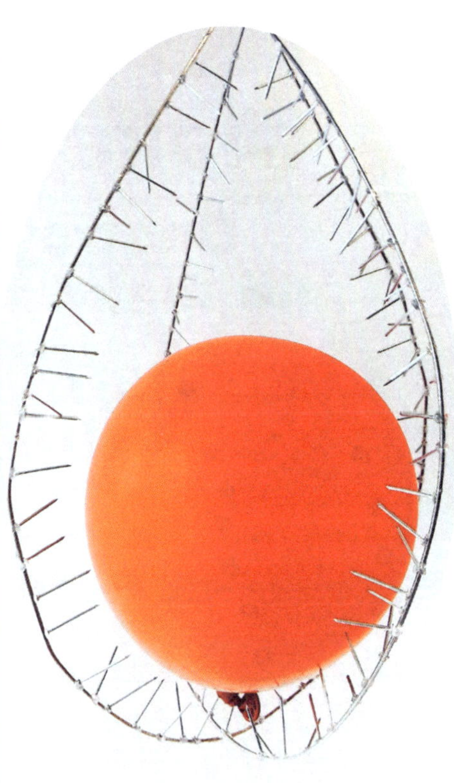

Enzo Smink, 2020, mixed materials

Lucas Willemsen, 2020, oil painting

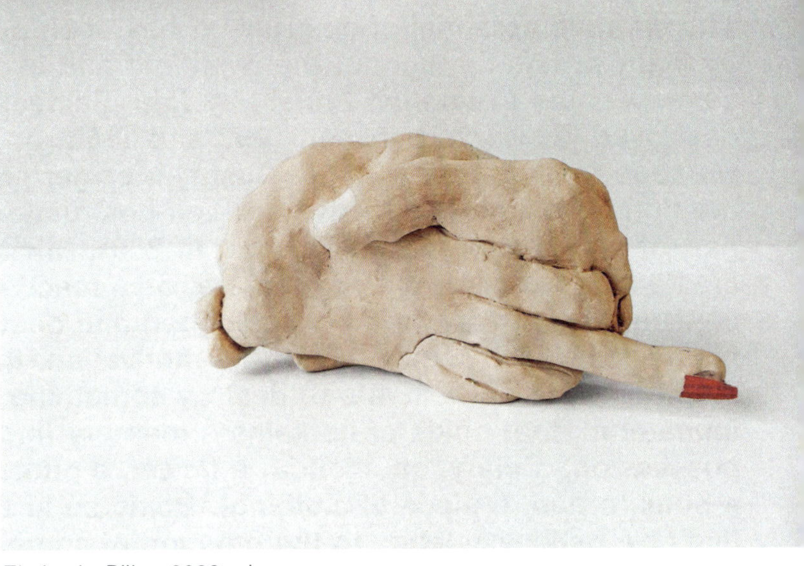

Elwin de Rijke, 2020, clay

Make & Destroy

Destroy a memory and make it an art piece.

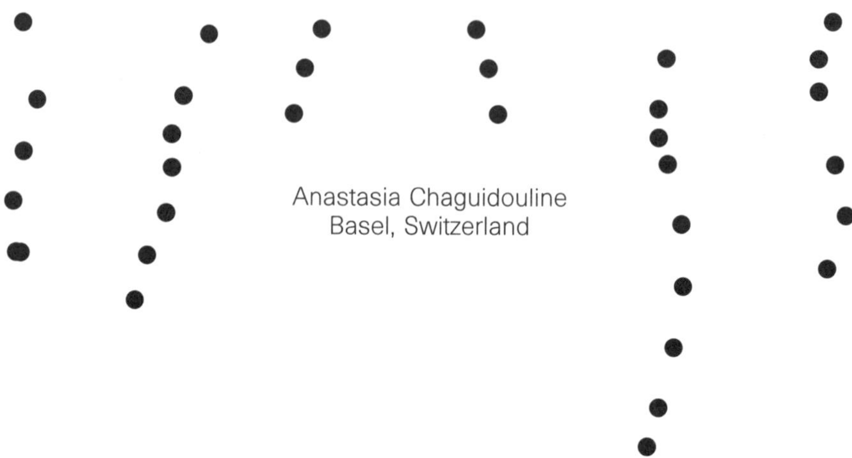

Anastasia Chaguidouline
Basel, Switzerland

The creative potential of destruction has been outlined by many artists throughout the twentieth and twenty-first centuries: the *Cremation Project* by John Baldessari, who destroyed his works between 1953 and 1966, or Tinguely's *Homage to New York* in 1960. Gustav Metzger proposed the notion of auto-destructive art: self-destruction as a vital part of the creation of the artwork. In 2001, Michael Landy created his work *Break Down*, where, as a reaction to today's consumerist society, he has catalogued and destroyed all his possessions. Regardless of the motivation, this assignment asks the participants to destroy something, material or immaterial, that holds or contains a memory (e.g. a personal possession, a diary, an agenda, a flower, a photograph, a book, a pen, a piece of clothing). Doing so in a performative or artistic way leads to the creation of something new, a new art piece, a new memory.

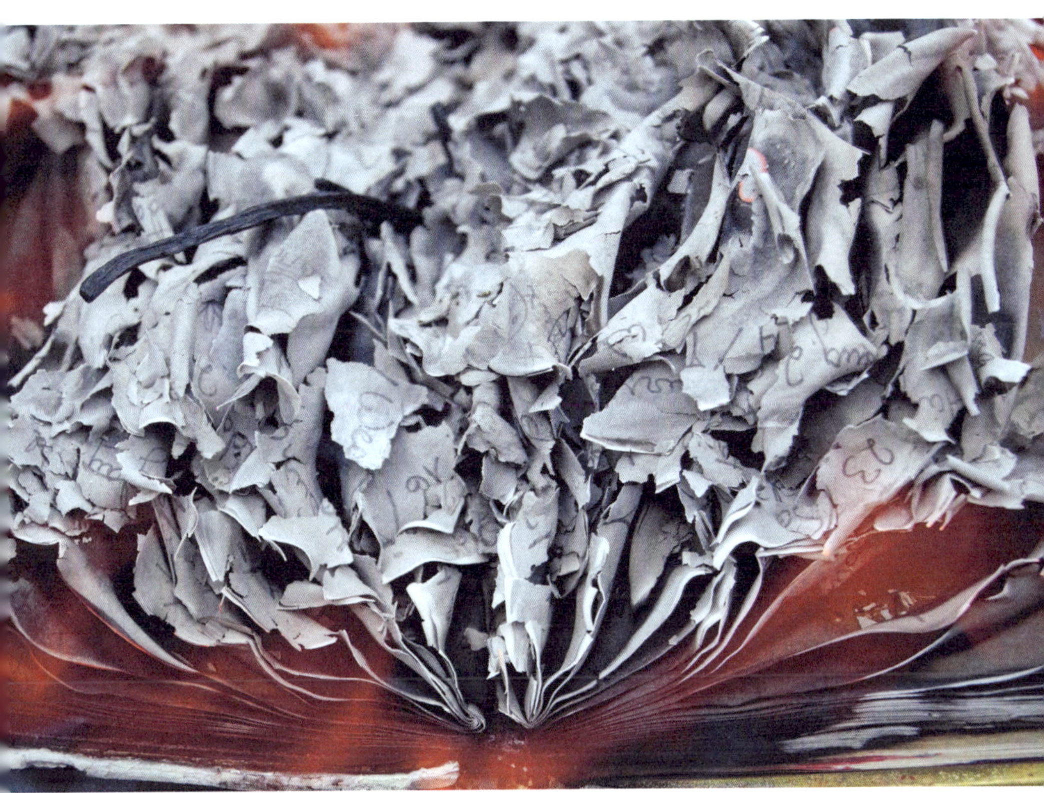

Anastasia Chaguidouline, *Destroy a Memory*, 2015, performance Royal Academy of Art, The Hague

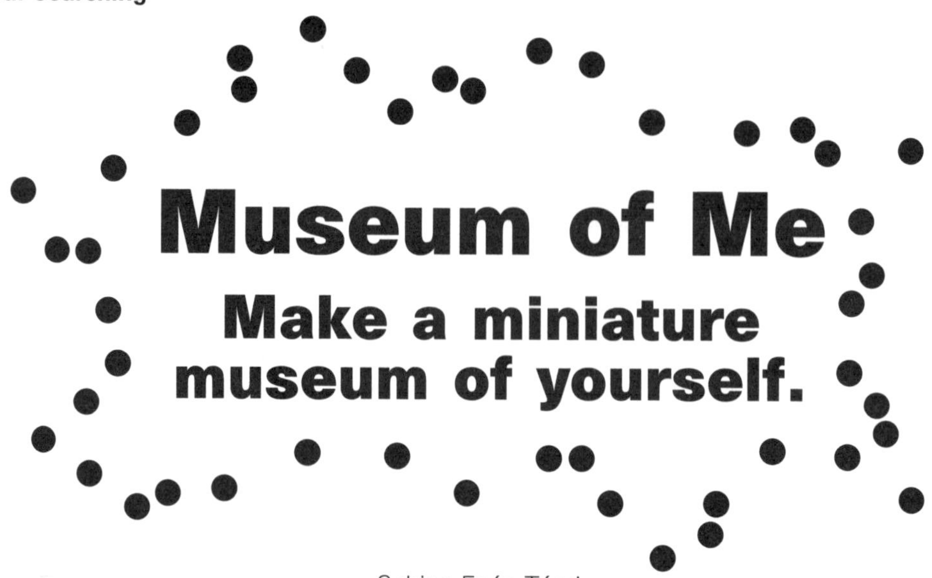

Museum of Me

Make a miniature museum of yourself.

Sabina Enéa Téari,
Berlin, Germany

Humans exist in and through togetherness. Being together can become tricky, though, as we sometimes see our own inner characters in other people and treat others as if they were those characters. The assignment invites these kinds of projections or interpretations to be expressed and made into artworks of an imaginary museum instead of infiltrating a person's relationships in real life. Merging inner and outer worlds, being and becoming with, honesty and playfulness. Participants are getting to know the inhabitants of their inner forest who are being released by the presence of others. The result is a miniature museum of their own perception. It can contain works in multiple media: sculptures, paintings, poems, memory stories, videos, drawings, magic objects... The assignment is suitable for teenagers and from there all the way up the age scale. We discovered it's important, when introducing this exercise to participants, to find lightness and sincerity in ourselves, so that it doesn't become embarrassing and heavy. It's also good to permeate the instructions with small and personal every-day life examples.

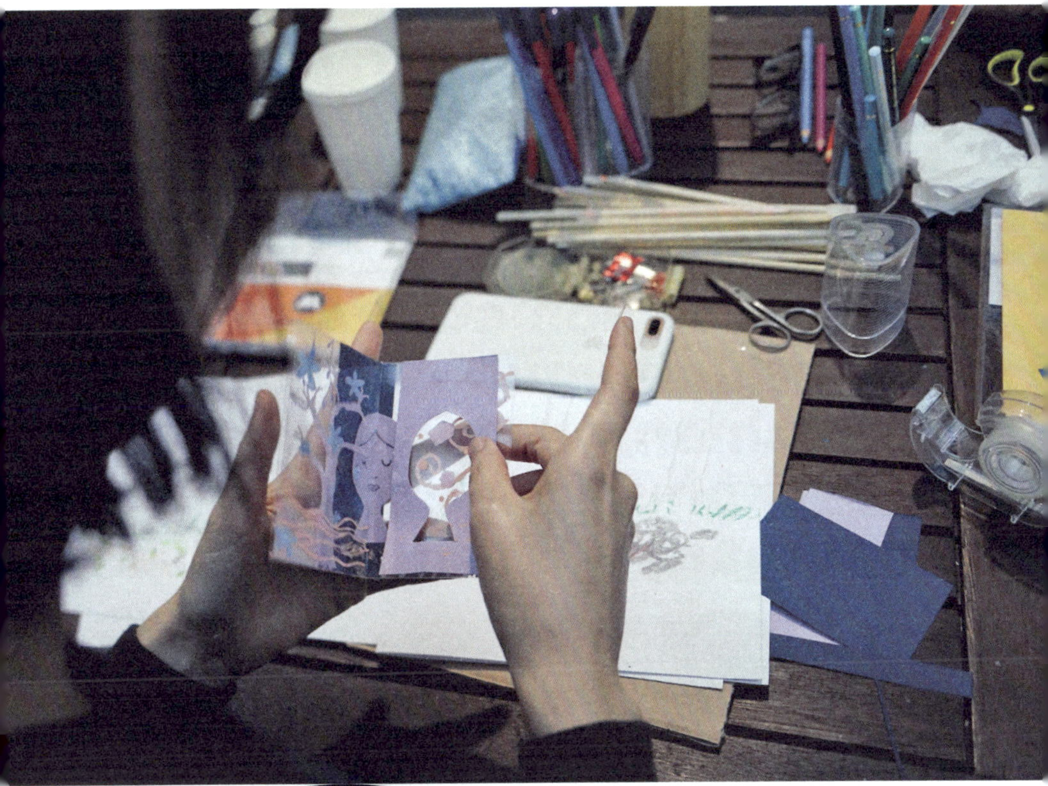

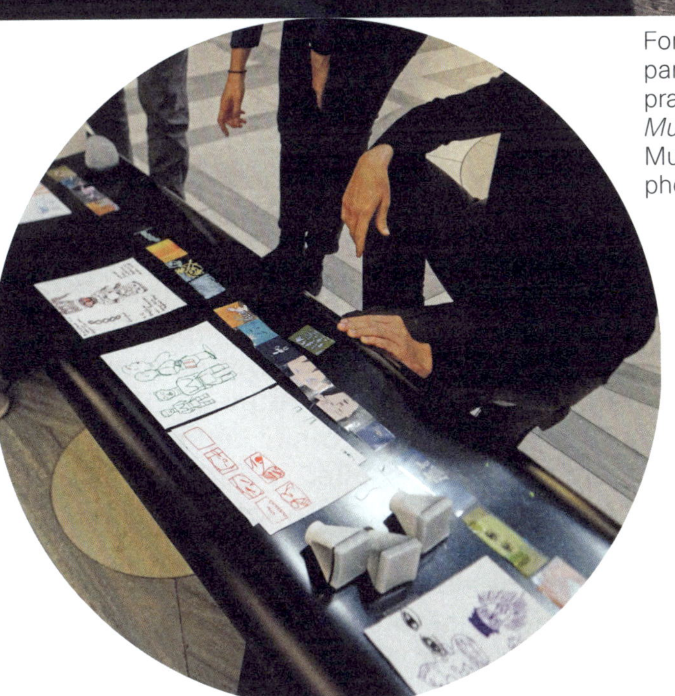

Foresta Collective and participants, collective practice during *Personal Museum* project at Bode-Museum, Berlin, 2019, photo: Sabina Enéa Téari

Apologize Monumentally

Find something for which you are sorry. Fashion an apology that is monumental in scale, intensity, and/or breadth.

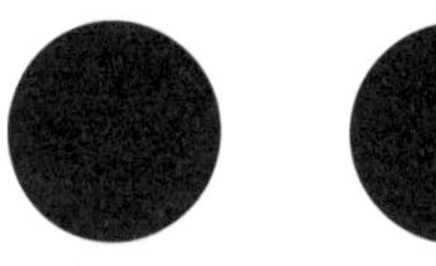

Christopher Lynn
Salt Lake City, UT, USA

The Topaz Internment Camp near Delta, Utah, was one of ten concentration camps in the United States where Japanese-Americans were sequestered during World War II. When visiting what remains of the site, I saw that a previous visitor had moved handfuls of gravel from the parking area and used those rocks to spell out a phrase on nearby concrete slabs: 'WE ARE SORRY / NEVER AGAIN.' It was an honest response to the paranoid and prejudiced existence of the Topaz Camp. However, I saw it as being too localized. Appropriating satellite imagery of hillside letters that are strewn throughout Utah to celebrate high schools, universities, and other institutions, I recreated the same sentiment, but spelled it out as a state-wide, monumental apology. I turned public pride into public shame. Students may find events that fill them with regret, and fashion an apology that speaks loudly or to many—thinking beyond small gestures. What constitutes an ample apology for an enduring wrong, and how can one person's voice be amplified?

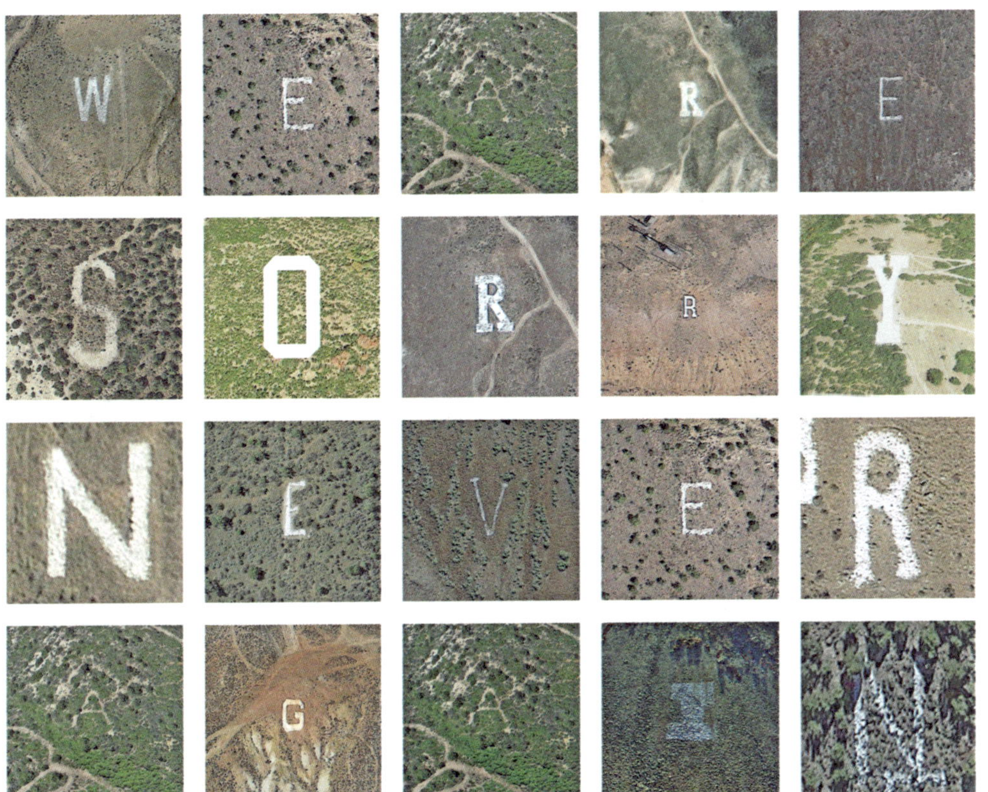

Christopher Lynn, *Appropriated Monuments for Topaz Internment Camp*, 2019, satellite imagery

An Ode to Pitfalls

Design and build a monument to your own pitfall.

Pavèl van Houten
Amsterdam, the Netherlands

This assignment was created specifically for students of the art academy to reflect on their own development in a non-lingual manner. They look back on the past year and reflect on the researches and projects they did. They articulate the pitfalls they encountered in the process. How did they handle this experience and what have they learned from it? How did they overcome it and what developments did it bring?

Based on this theme, they individually develop a cultural monument, as an ode to their pitfall(s). It can be looked upon as something that gives them heart for the years to come. They are free to choose the material. From polystyrene foam to wood, from glass to metal, as long as the result is a physical object. The students also choose a location where they feel their monument should be placed. During the project the pitfalls are discussed in class, while looking for metaphors for the oftentimes abstract themes. For this project students often make scale models of their monuments, which they can then place in their rooms as a reminder of the lessons they learned while making them.

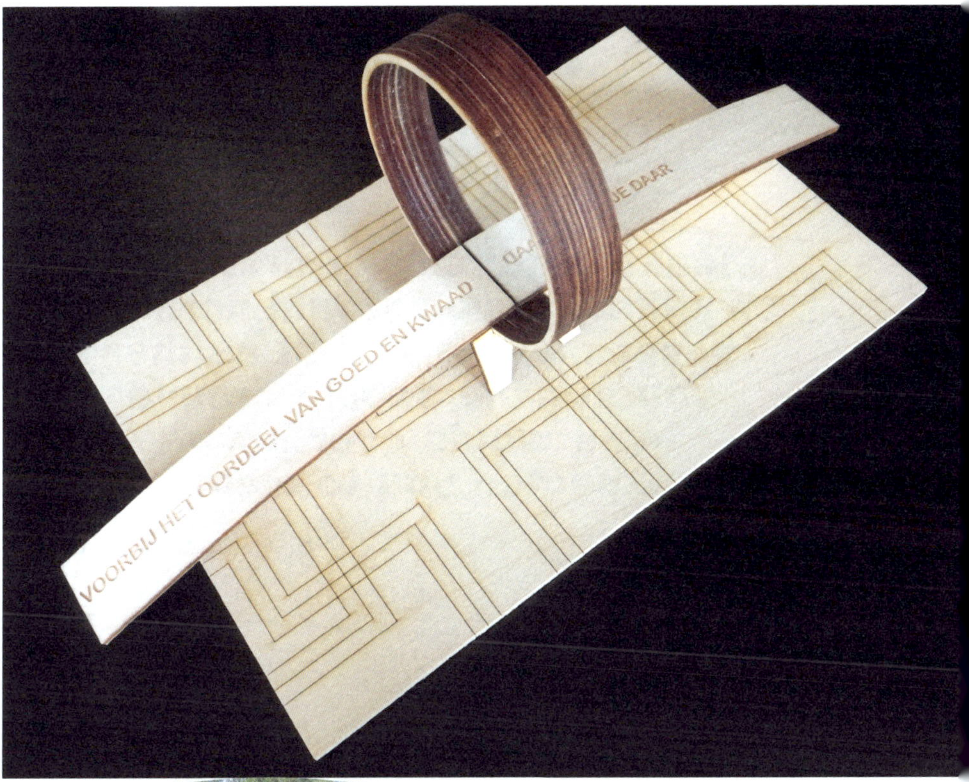

Froukje Doodkorte, *Ont-Moeten*, 2017, student's work, 'The work expresses a personal theme: less self-pressure, less looking at what others are doing and feeling confident in choosing your own path'

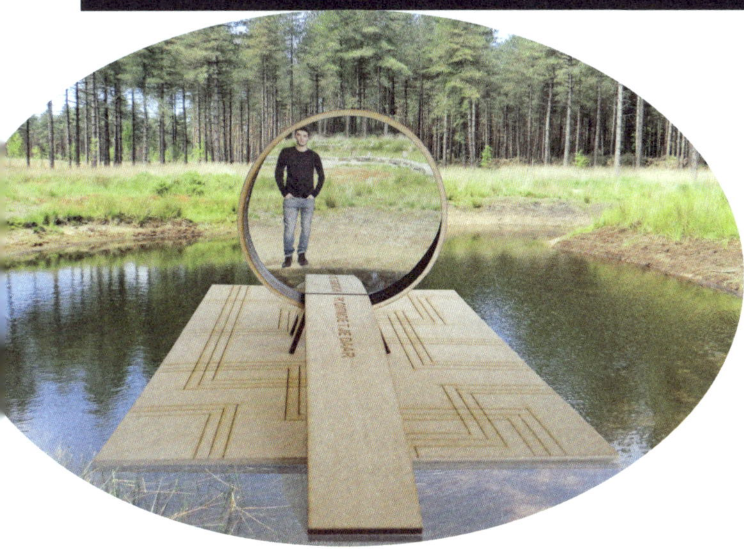

Froukje Doodkorte, *Ont-Moeten*, 2017, student's work, visualization at nature cemetery 'De Utrecht'

Unrelated

Make a number of drawings or paintings you would normally never make and that neither you nor the people around you would ever have expected you to make.

Ronald Nijhof
De Bilt, the Netherlands

Most of us will recognize this: you are watching a TV programme about deep-sea animals or insects and you see creatures that you can hardly believe exist. A wealth of shapes and colours you've never seen before. It's totally new to you and you never even imagined something this weird. It just goes to show how limited our frame of reference is.

Likewise, in retro-futurism (how we envisioned the future in the past) one can see in the designs for the spaceships of the future the design concepts of those days. A UFO from the 1960s looks like a car from that decade. And a spaceship conceived in the 1970s is truly the design concept from those days.

It is interesting in this regard to try and make something that is outside your frame of reference, something that is completely new to you and is unrelated to anything you have ever made.

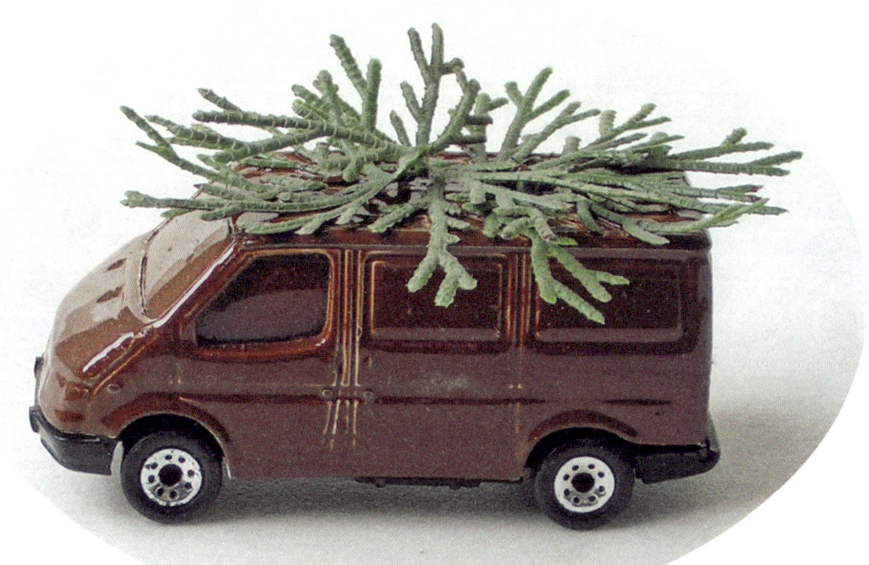

Ronald Nijhof, *Van camouflaged as a tree*, 2004, steel, paint, plastics

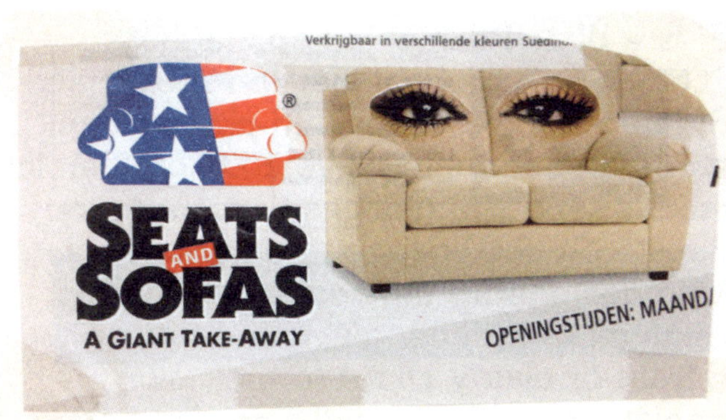

Ronald Nijhof, *Couch with eyes*, 2016, collage

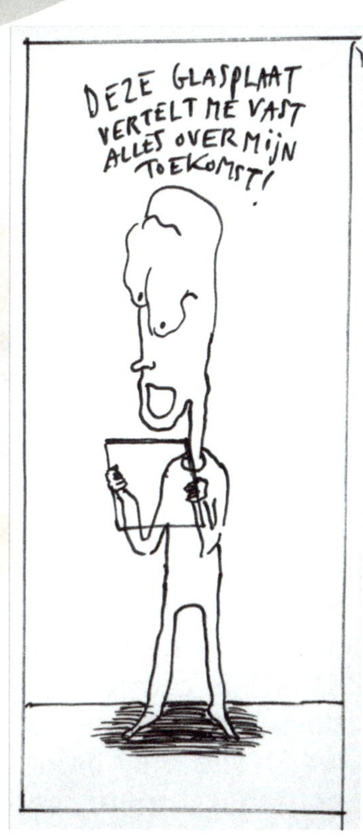

Ronald Nijhof, *Prospect*, 2013, pen on paper ('this sheet of glass surely will tell me all about my future!')

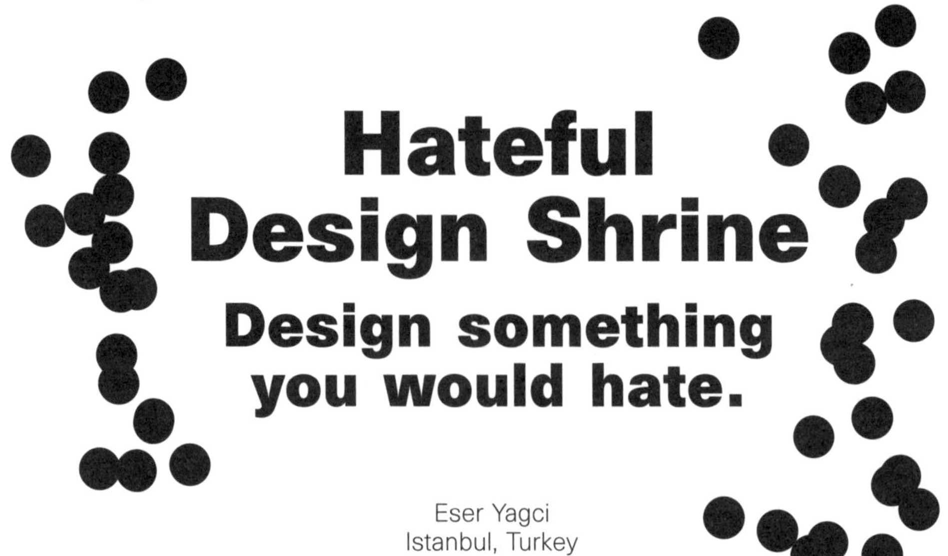

Hateful Design Shrine

Design something you would hate.

Eser Yagci
Istanbul, Turkey

Designers and design students tend to think about the best design solutions aiming to catch the pulse of contemporary culture. Accordingly, unpleasant forms and imperfection are not seen by designers who mostly love their own designs. 'Hateful Design Shrine' is a digital exhibition space that invites everyone who intends to be a designer to make peace with stylelessness and defects and blesses anti-professional, pragmatic productions. It's a both competitive and commercial space to imagine, assemble, and sell designs that are found hateful, especially by their own designers and others. It's a design therapy to liberate designers from conditions, norms, biased concepts, and high expectations, giving them the opportunity to alienate from or overly adopt to their own designs by facing off egoistic processes of design. Designers from different ages can participate with their submissions and auctions to digest and commodify disinterested designs. Take this chance to engage in such a non-critical and informal design community to express and quiz aesthetic tolerances in which the only limitations to avoid are violent, fascist, sexist contents, nature, and animal damage. Take your part and invest in this cultural experiment whereby you can reflect your anti-aesthetic likes, challenge fashionable pattens, and alter hot topics in art and design culture.

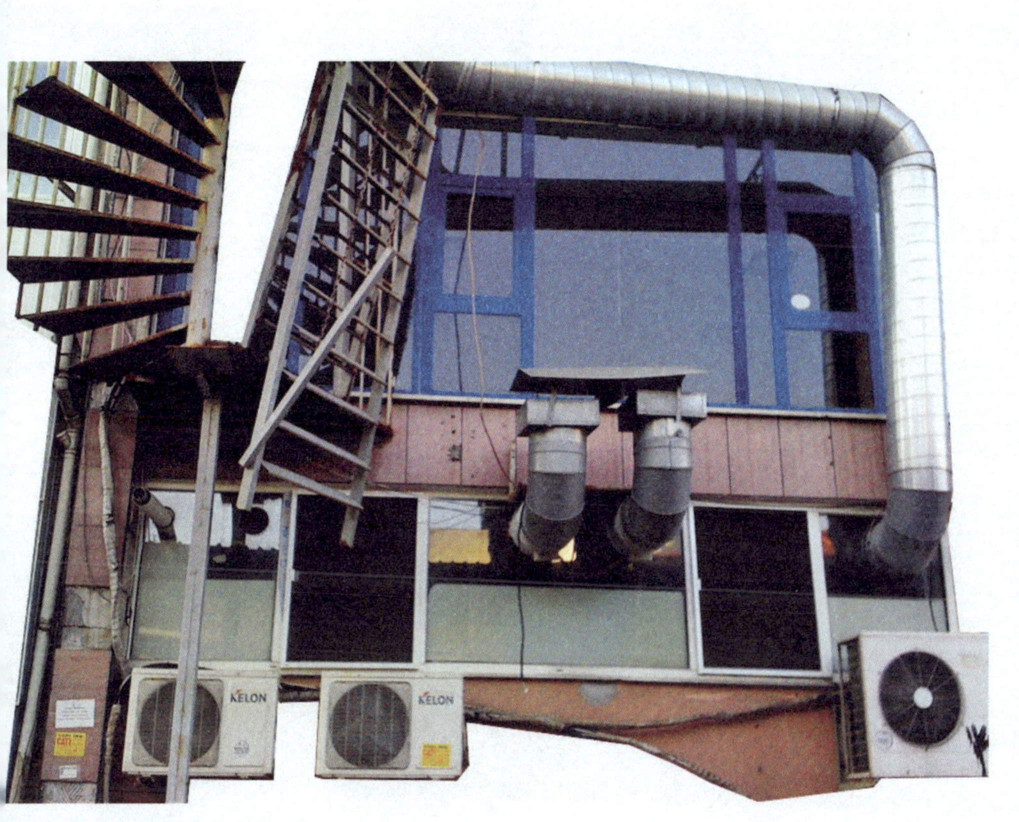

Eser Yagci, *Hateful Design Shrine*, 2011

Ma
So
No

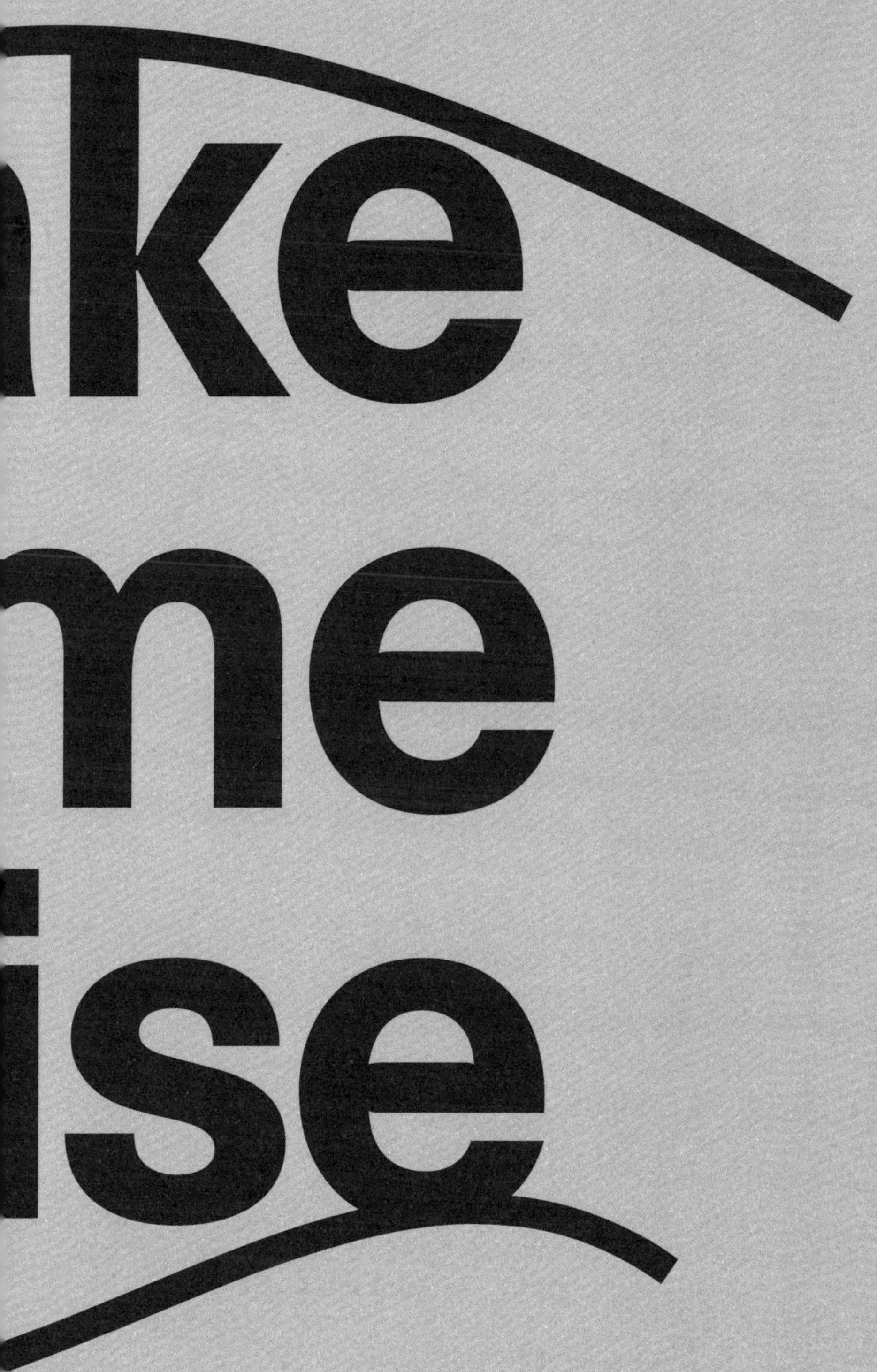
ke
me
ise

First-KISS-Music

Write a score for a first-kiss scene.

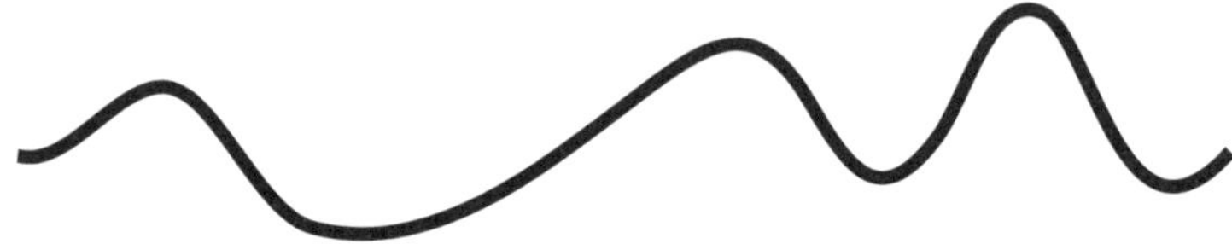

Erik Schrooten
Pelt, Belgium

This assignment challenges students to write their own music for a film sequence: a score for a first-kiss scene. In preparation they could watch and listen to a number of film sequences. The students will then discover that quite often the same ingredients are used: a slow pace, sensual violins and gently modulating melodic lines without too many jumps. So, here's an extra tip for this assignment: KISS—Keep It Simple and Slow.

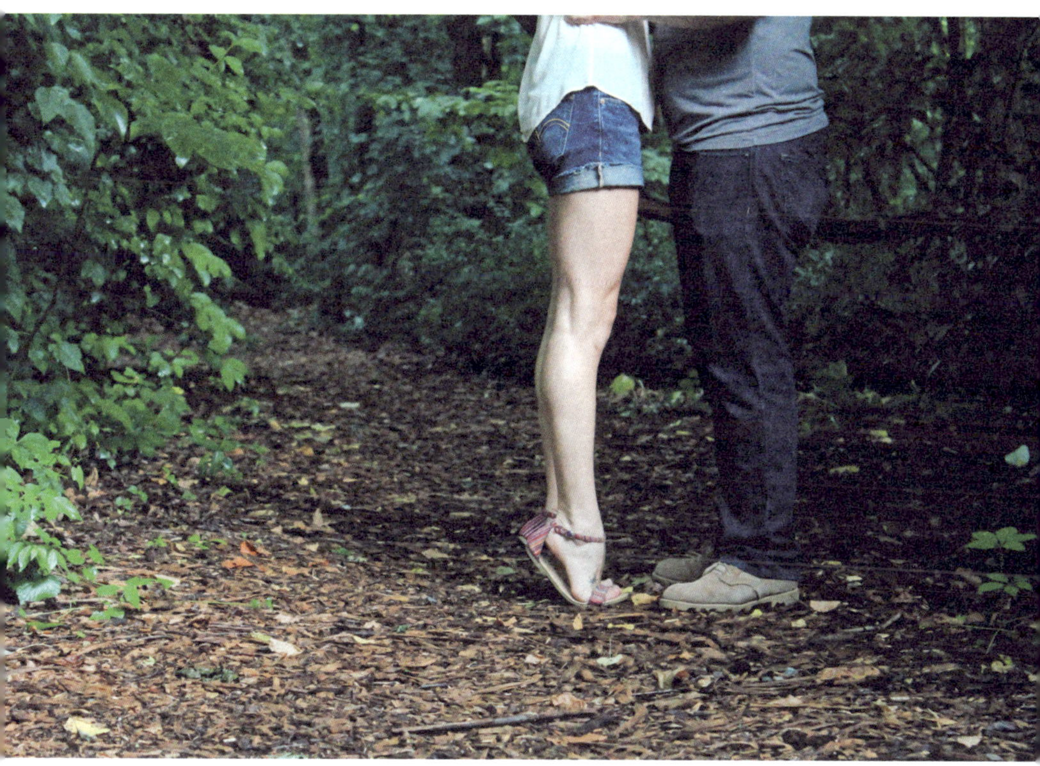

Photo: Katie Salerno, Pexels

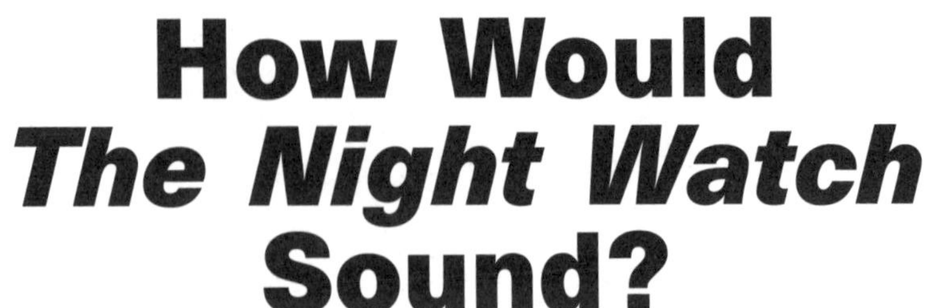

How Would *The Night Watch* Sound?

Perform a graphic music score that is based on an art piece.

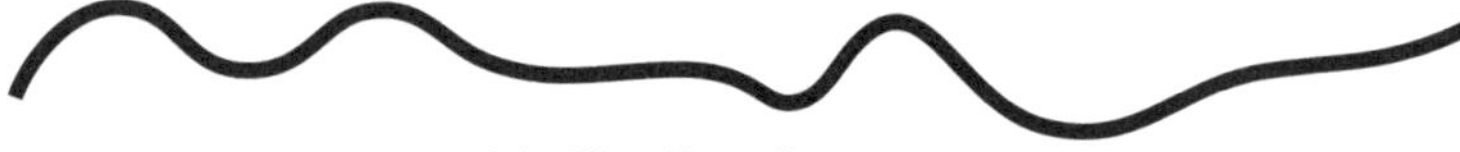

Marijke Smedema
Amsterdam, the Netherlands

In this assignment we bring a 2D- or 3D-artwork to life by adding sound. The students fantasize about what it would be like to step into an artwork and what sounds they would then hear. With any means available (voice, instruments, or other materials) the imagined sounds are imitated. Together, the students make a graphic core of the sounds and perform it.

The assignment was carried out by children with special needs between the ages of nine and twelve, around the theme of Rembrandt's *The Night Watch*. They explored the story behind the painting, got to know the people in it, and learned about the context in which it was made. In groups they brainstormed about sounds that might suit the painting: a barking dog, a swaying banner, or the clanging of lances. They also imagined what the people in the painting may have said while sitting for it: 'How much did you pay for your spot?' These sounds and texts were then transposed into a graphic score. During the presentation the artwork was projected on a large screen and the score was performed as a radio play. With the combination of image and sound it was as if the painting came to life.

Pupils of Olivijn performing
The Night Watch, 2019

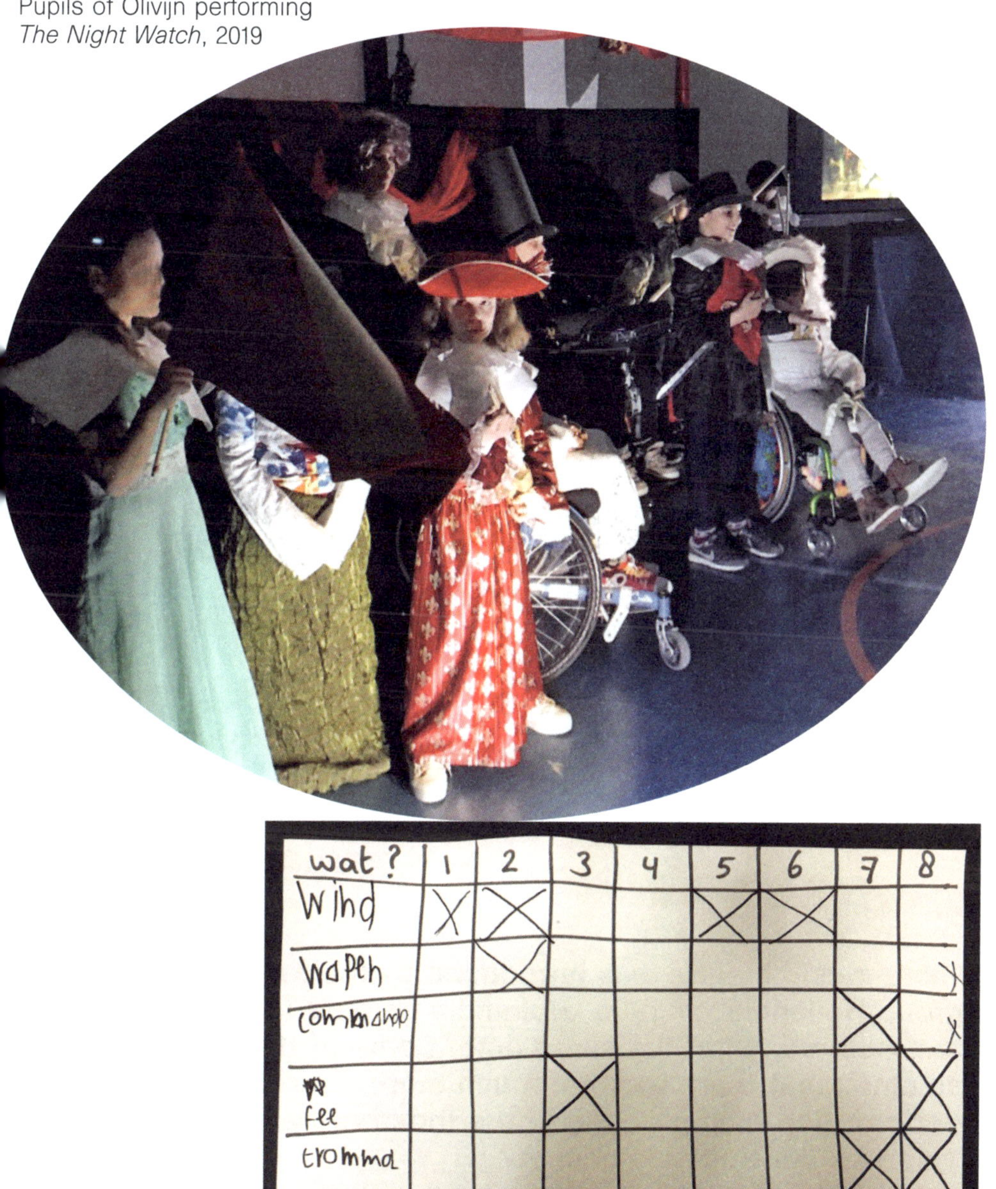

wat?	1	2	3	4	5	6	7	8
wind	X	X			X	X		
wapen		X						X
commandant							X	X
fee			X					X
tromma							X	X
lans			X					X
hond				X				X

Pupils' score that links to visual elements
of *The Night Watch*, 2019

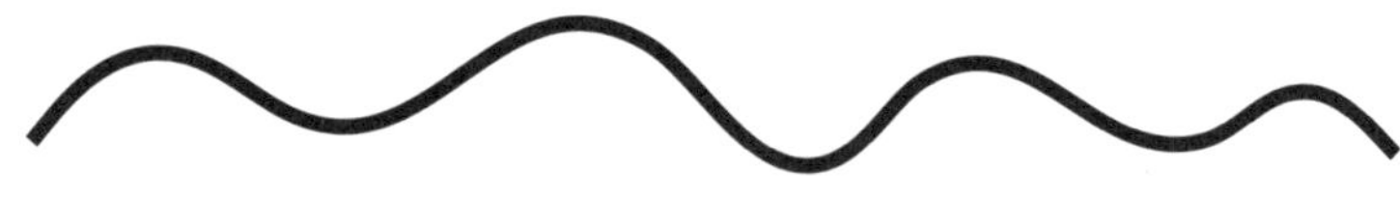

Table Music Theatre

Buy a newspaper and create a music theatre performance on a table, using all necessary ingredients, such as duration, form, harmony, rhythm, pace, tone-colour, pitch, and the text of one of the newspaper articles.

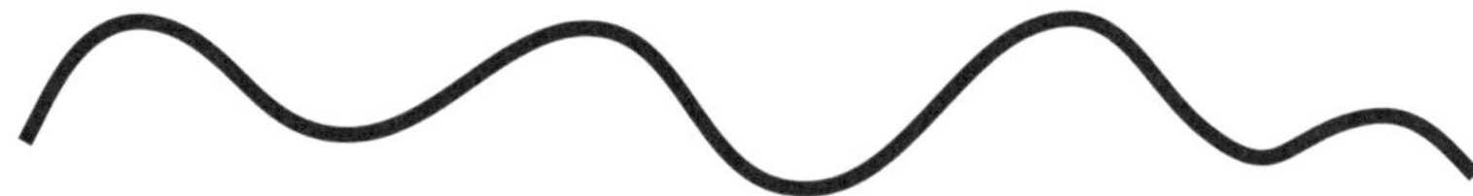

Paul Koek
Roelofarendsveen, the Netherlands

Table music theatre was introduced by the music theatre group Hollandia, in 1990. Hollandia created ten premieres in ten theatres, all at the same time. Some of the theatres were so small that there was not much more room than a table to perform (for example, one of the theatres was inside a boat). This was the original concept.

In 2010, it became part of the audition procedure for T.I.M.E., a two-year Master's programme in Music Theatre at the Royal Conservatory in The Hague. Aspiring students were asked to look at the Monday paper of the audition week and pick an article that appealed to them and then, by using the ingredients of music theatre (duration, form, harmony, rhythm, pace, tone-colour, pitch, and text) 'musicalize' the article and present a music theatre performance based on current events.

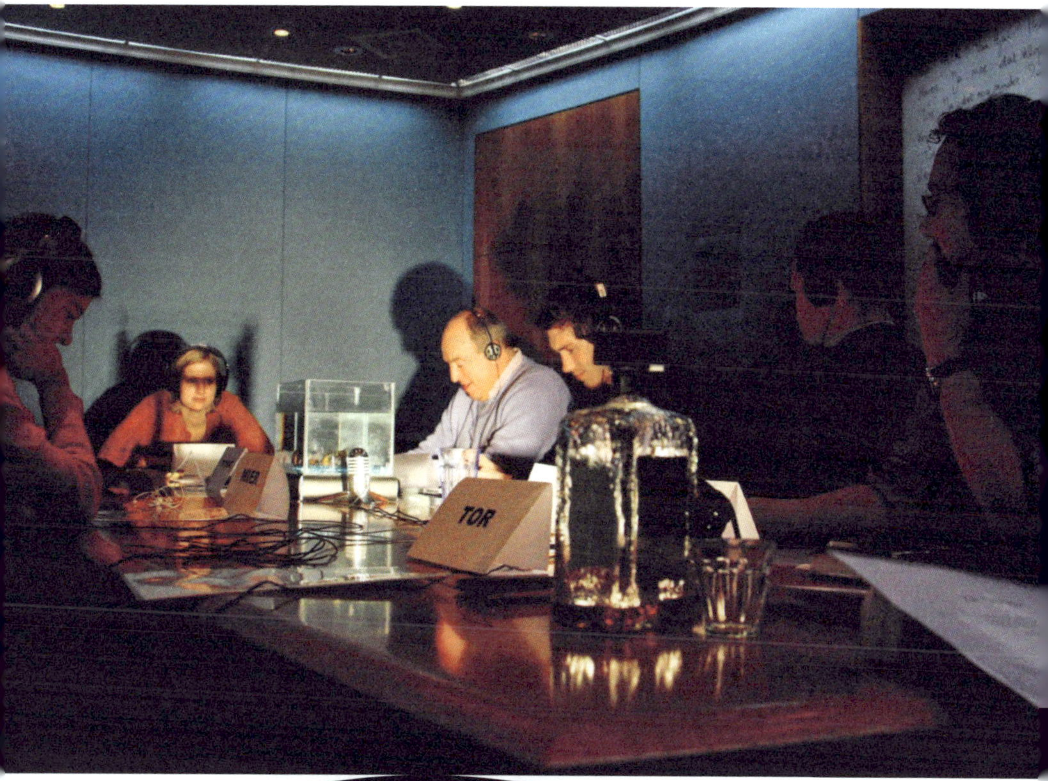

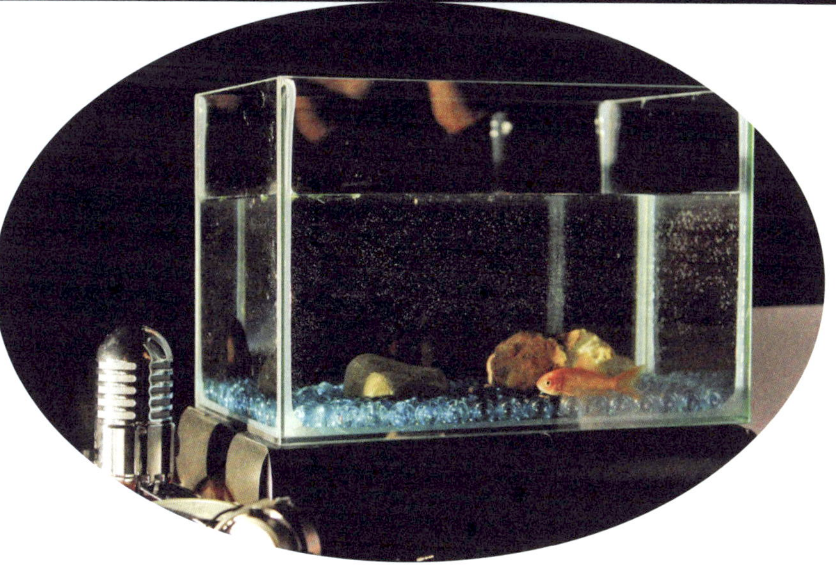

Tijs Huys, *The Goldfish Speaks*, 2010-2012, project *Tafeltheater*, performance, assignment of T.I.M.E. Master, Royal Conservatory, The Hague, photo: Ines van der Scheer

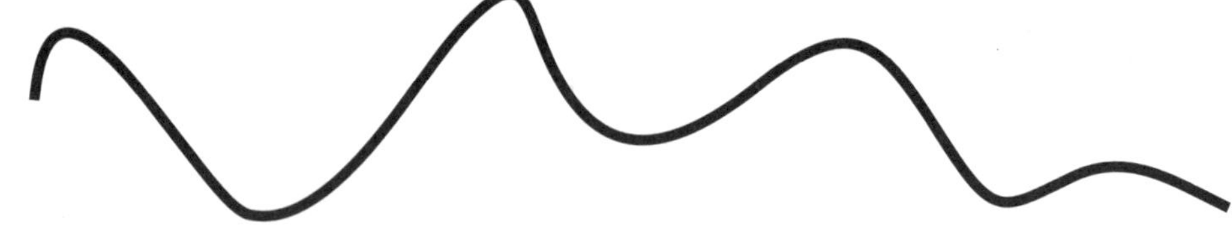

We Are a Band

Make groups of 3–4 students and form a band.

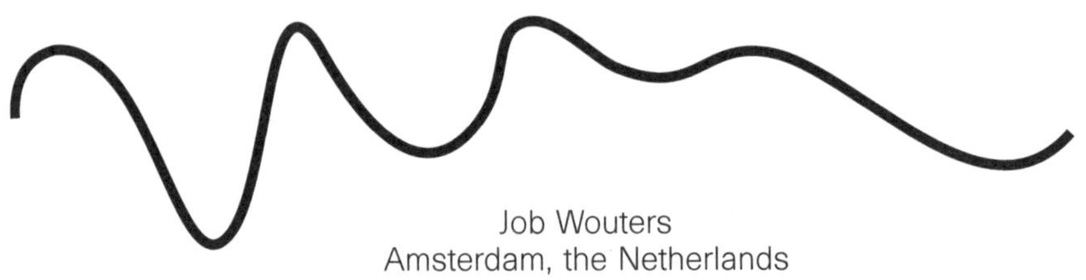

Job Wouters
Amsterdam, the Netherlands

As a designer you have to collaborate a lot: with other designers, writers, artists, photographers, printers, publishers, clients, etc. *We are a band* is an exercise in collaboration.

Make groups of 3–4 students and form a band. Decide what kind of music your band makes, what your band's name is and where you come from.

- make a band picture
- make a record cover
- make merchandize
- for the diehards: play some music and record it.

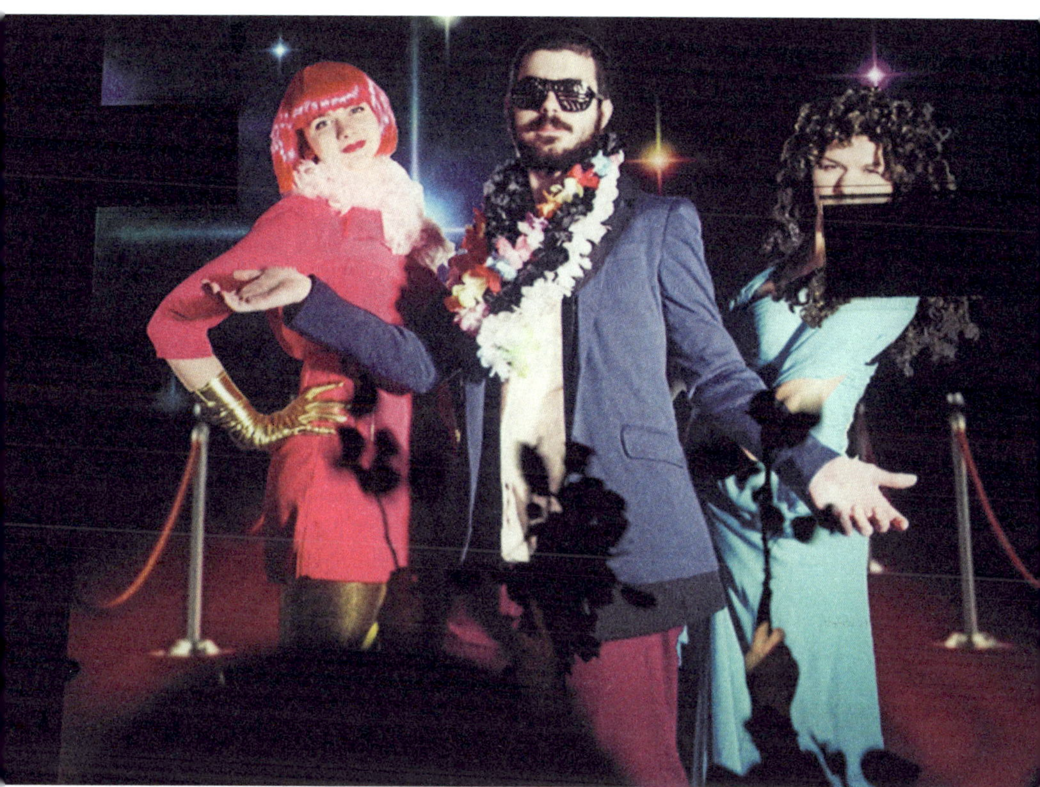

The Eddy the Eagle Museum (artists' collective) organized a band night in 2015, where students displayed their merchandise and performed with their bands, photo: Raymond van Mil

Machines as Performers

Make a sound sculpture, using self-designed machines as performers.

Marloes Nieuweboer, Amsterdam, the Netherlands
Hanna Salonen, Amersfoort, the Netherlands
Annelies den Boon, Amersfoort, the Netherlands

This assignment is based on the machines of Jean Tinguely. His art and various sources from popular culture, such as the video *This Too Shall Pass* by OK Go and the work of Simone Giertz, were used to explore the theme of the useless machine and the technologization of society. A theme that fits within the demand for more technology lessons in education. This assignment was carried out by students in their second year of the Pabo (Teacher Education for Primary Schools). Not only were they instructed to build a machine, but to have it make a sound so that it could be used in an orchestra of sorts, to perform in a soundscape. In order to do this, the students were provided with small DC motors on battery packs and all kinds of materials like cardboard, plastic, glass, wood, wires, hot glue and little bits and bobs. These unconventional materials were challenging for the students, as they were not used to working with them, but they also invited them to experiment. This way of just trial and error was very enjoyable for the students. In the end several machines were created and exhibited in the hall for a visual and auditory performance.

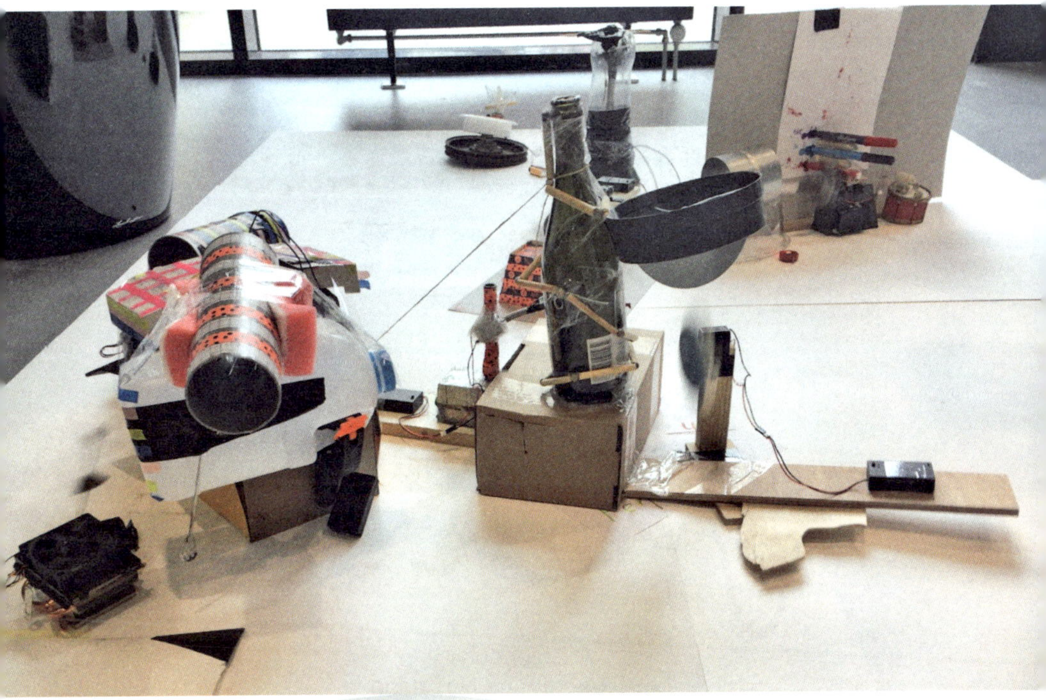

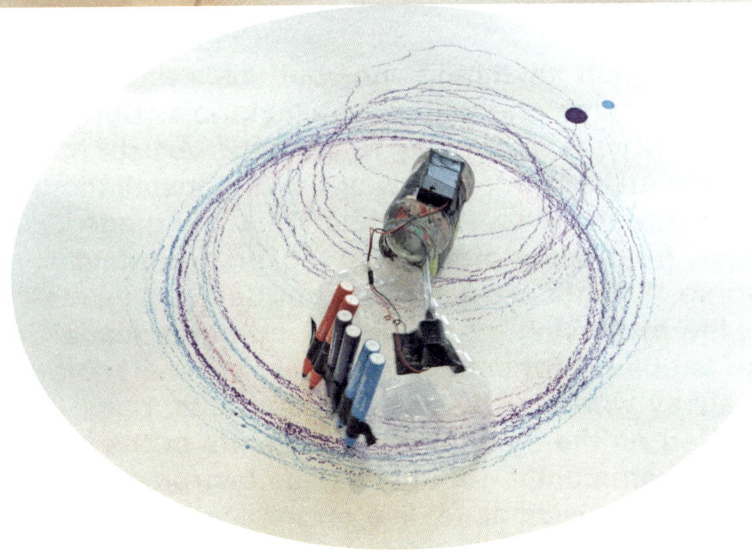

Student's work, *Machines as Performers*, 2017

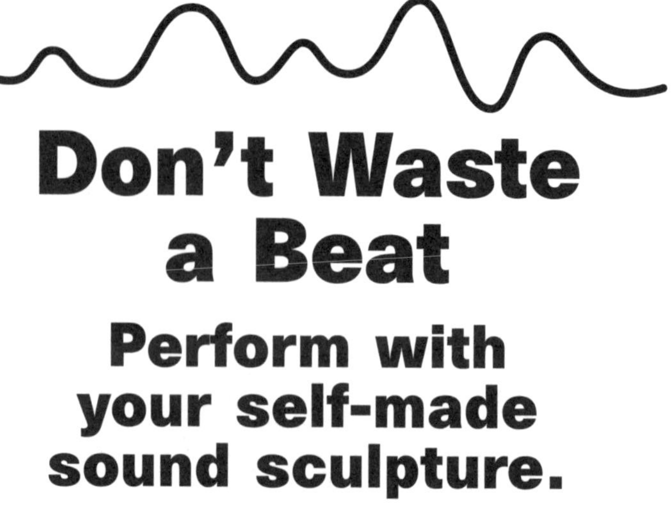

Don't Waste a Beat

Perform with your self-made sound sculpture.

Michiel Koelink
Leeuwarden, the Netherlands

You can make music with anything, with your voice and your hand, with a concert piano and with waste materials. Humans love music and will always find a way to create it. Artists have been inventing new instruments and weird sound installations from all kind of materials, even trash. Jean Tinguely made huge installations, from scrap metal, that looked great and sounded awesome. Trashbeatz, a group from Belgium, gives trash a second life by playing music with instruments made from trash. The Landfill Harmonic Orchestra is a remarkable group from Paraguay who play classical instruments made from trash collected on the landfills by inhabitants of the slums on top. The community not only makes instruments from trash, the young musicians all live on the landfill.

During this assignment, which lasted a day, we asked a recycling plant for materials. Groups of students did material research, sound research, construction research, and form research. They made a first prototype and/or test set-ups and gave each other feedback. Then the groups built their sound sculptures and planned their performance. At the end of the day every group performed for about two minutes.

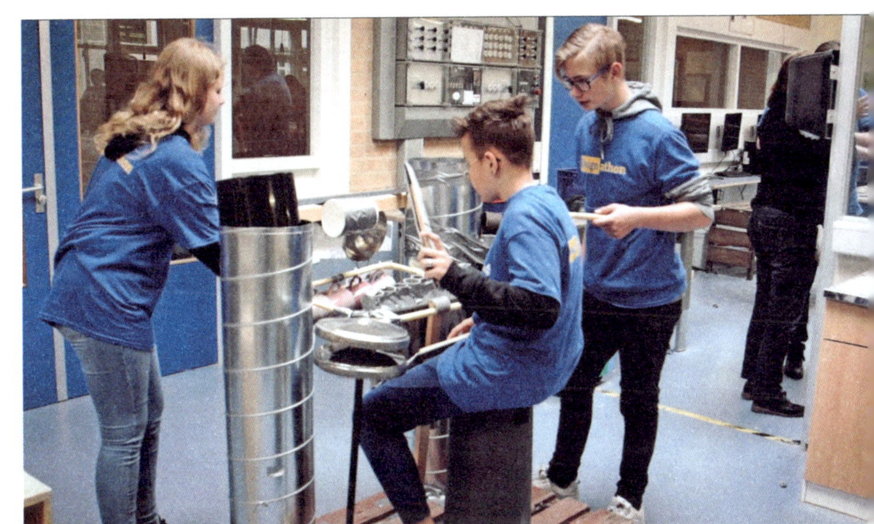

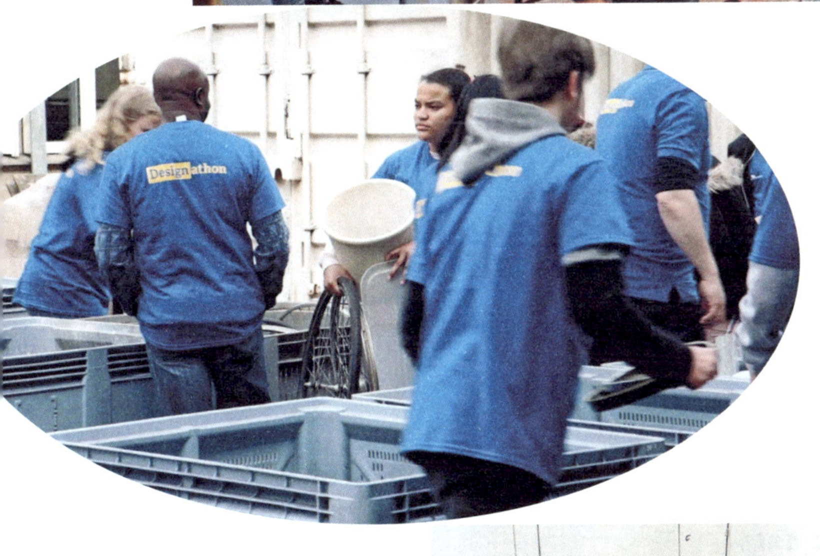

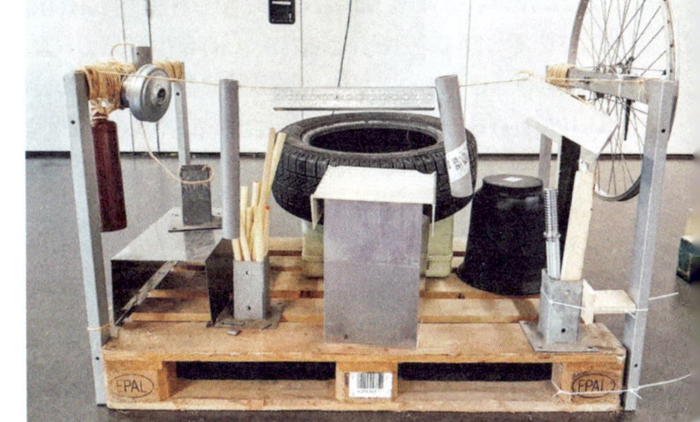

Pupils of Baken Stad College, Almere, 2019, photo: Bart Voorbergen

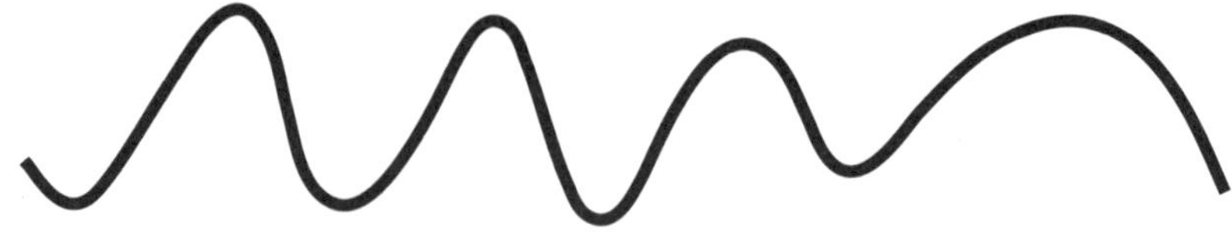

Auto Music

Write a signature tune for the new electric car of your favourite brand.

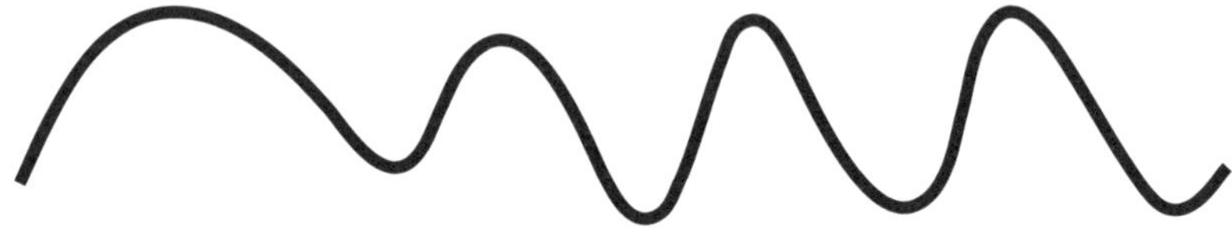

Erik Schrooten
Pelt, Belgium

Electric cars are silent, which is a blessing but also entails danger, especially for vulnerable people in traffic. In 2020, the EU therefore intends to make an audio signal mandatory for electric cars.

BMW took a professional stance and have asked film score composer Hans Zimmer to develop sounds that enable people to hear electric BMW's approach. Classic cars, stylish music. Unfortunately, other car brands are not yet as far. Did anyone say 'market opportunity'? Well, here's a sound assignment:

Write a signature tune for the new electric car of your favourite brand. What would that sound like for your favourite car?
Or for a Ferrari?
Or a Toyota?

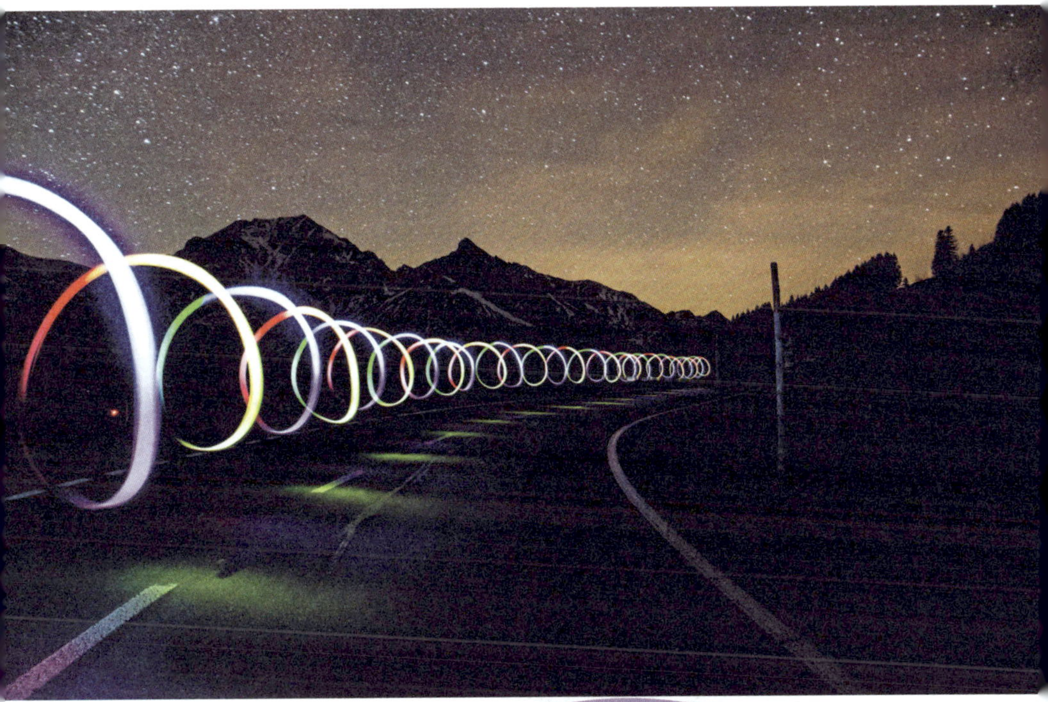

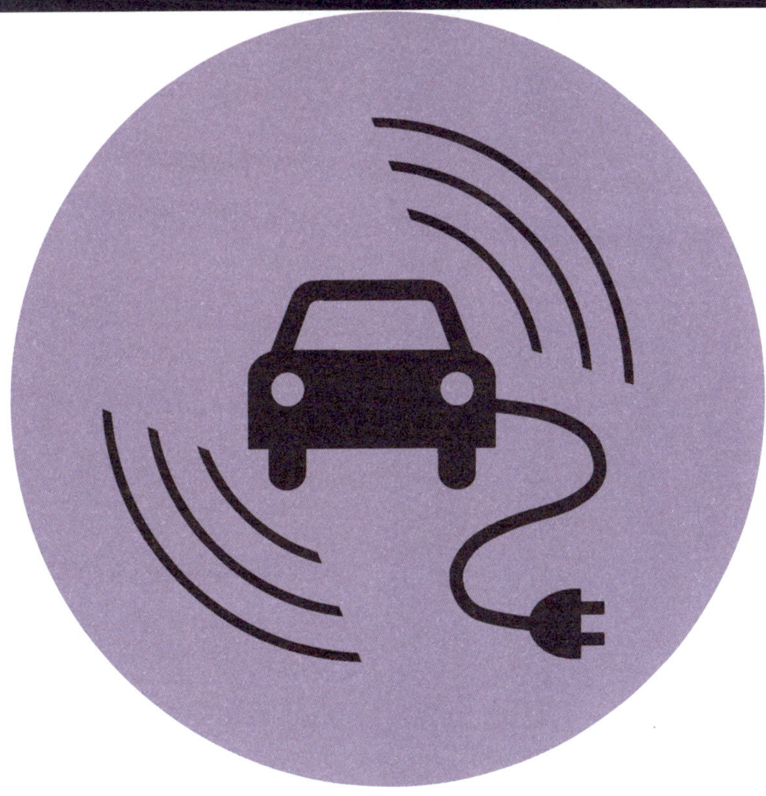

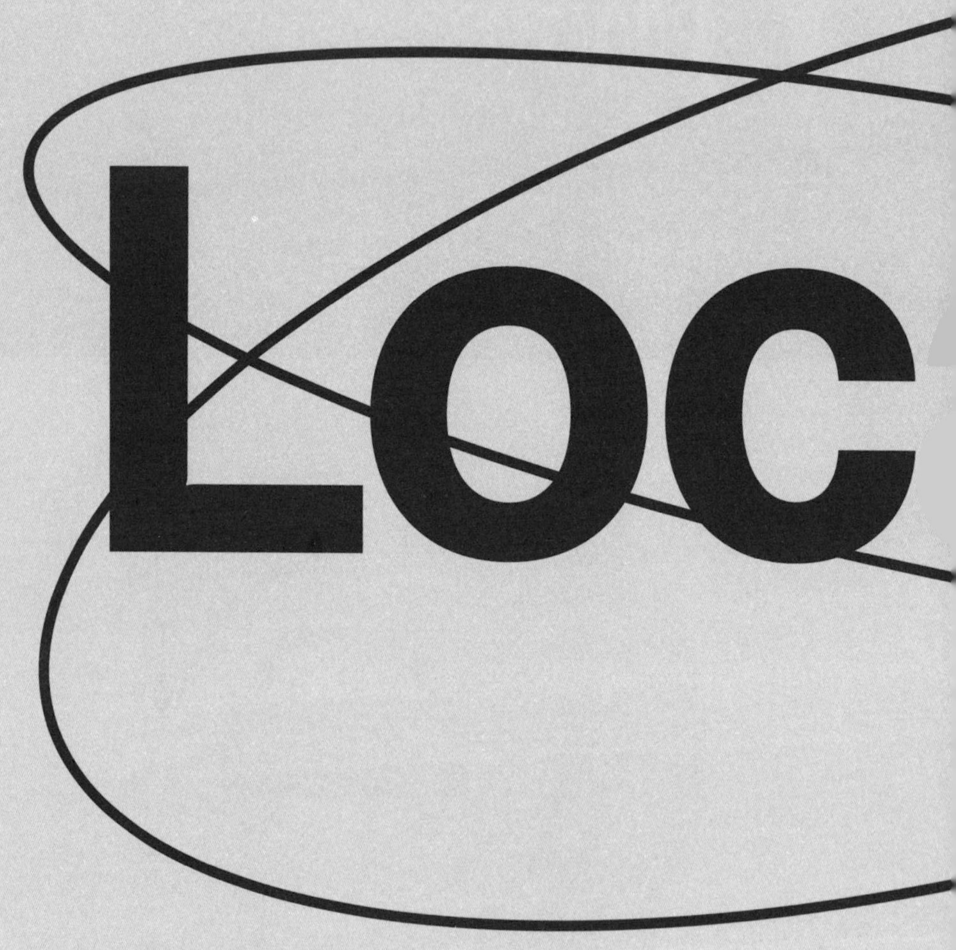
Loc

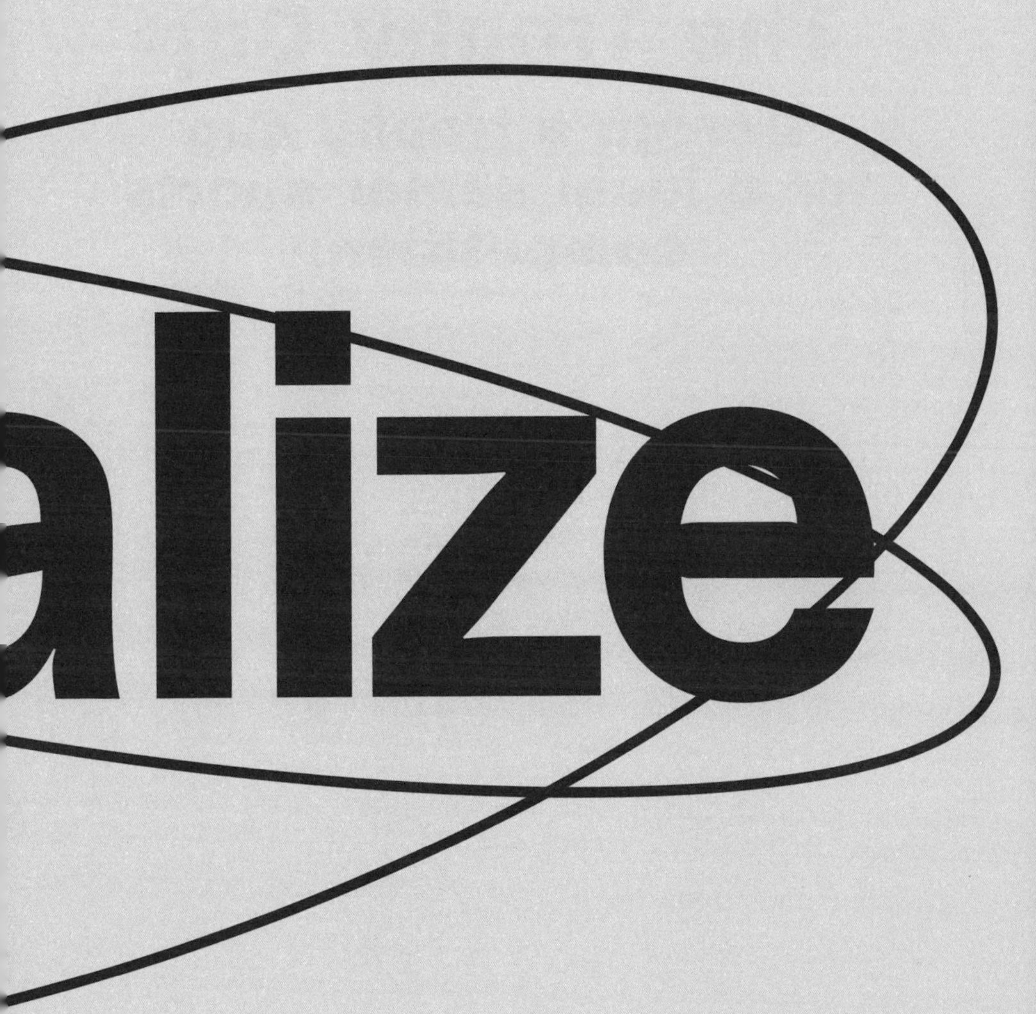
alize

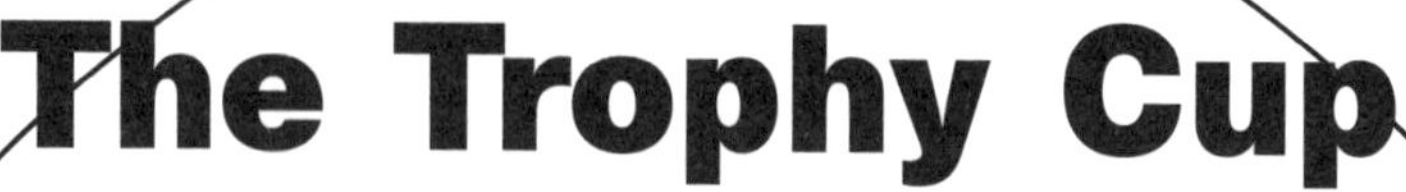

The Trophy Cup

Design a trophy cup for a local senior sports competition.

Andrea Palašti
Novi Sad, Serbia

Thinking about the pensioners / retirees in sport activities, the idea of the assignment is to get in touch with the local elderly community and develop a trophy cup for a specific sports tournament. It can be delivered from recyclable materials, ready-mades, 3D-prints, or as ephemeral objects.

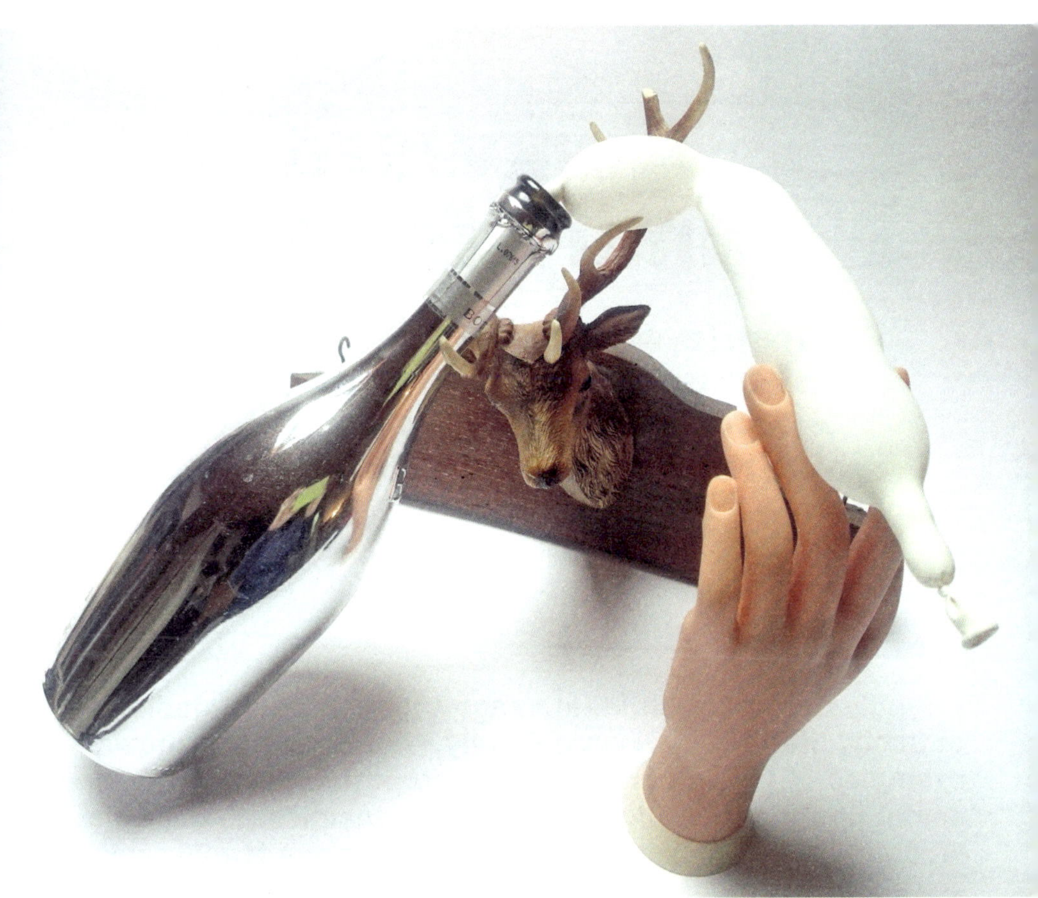

Monika Sigeti, *The Trophy Cup*, documentation

Awkward Family Photos

Create a photographic portrait of your family using members of your class, inspired by the website awkwardfamilyphotos.com.

Ross Coulter
Melbourne, Australia

A family portrait is an ideal image that can be an outlier of family life. The Awkward Family Photos website shows examples of family portraits that disrupt the ideal and present something more telling about family dynamics. Engage the students in a discussion of family. How is the family represented in the media, film, television, and cartoons, in art or discussed politically? Show students examples of the Awkward Family Photos website. These imperfect, often-humorous photographs have the potential to tell a more complex or interesting narrative about family. Ask your students to draw their family portrait. This portrait can be from an actual image or an imaginary one, a biological, blended, or chosen family. Encourage the students to think about the composition. Have the students write down five characteristics of each family member. Use a photography lighting studio or alternately whatever space you can find. Each student takes a turn photographing their family portraits by casting fellow students as the different family members. Ensure the students direct the subjects in terms of posture, expression, and motivation. It is best to have a variety of photographs to select from. Display the photographs; discuss the process and project with the students.

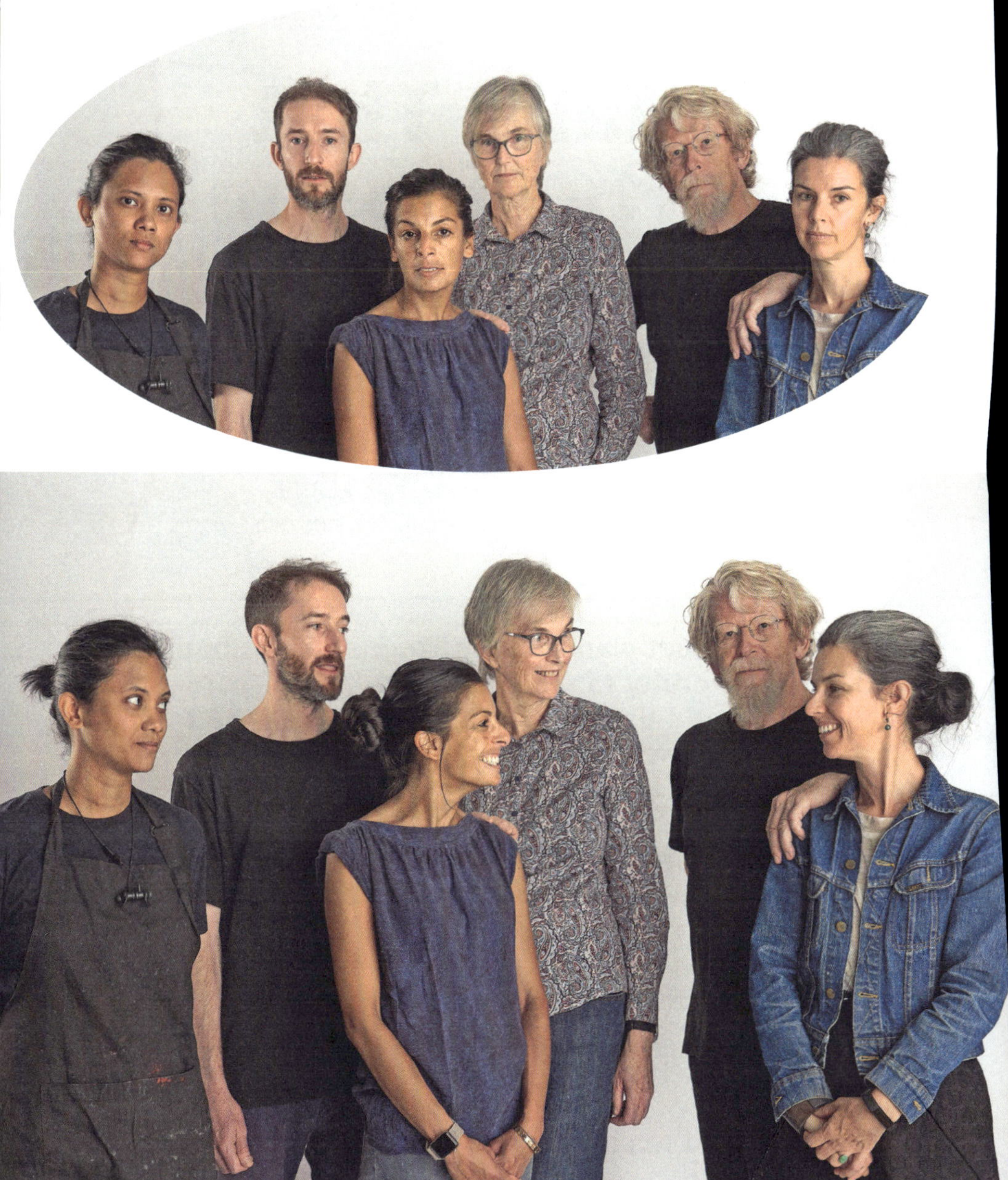

Ross Coulter, *Awkward Family Photo*, 2020, photograph

Make That Party Happen!

Design a new kind of party.

Anne Graswinckel, Leeuwarden, the Netherlands
Jeffrey Deelman, Groningen, the Netherlands

Sometimes you just want to lose yourself in a good party. By now we are pretty familiar with the kind of parties we usually have. Let's design a new party with all the trappings! With fresh, brand-new rituals. Be inspired by other parties, rituals and forms of greetings all over the world. Use, borrow, and steal whatever you need. Pull out all the stops to make the party even more fun and better. Take the party seriously!

What do we need for our own party? Does it have a name? Is there a theme? What special rituals will we think of? And how often do you have to do a ritual before it really becomes one? Are we going to make a party song? What shall we eat and drink? Or wear? Do we need a special dance? Have a test party. Is everything working the way we thought it would?

If you want to make your party more meaningful, then use restrictions:

- **have the party in silence, so no one at school will find out;**
- **have the girls make a party for the boys, and vice versa;**
- **let the new party replace an existing one. Why can we dispense with the old party?**
- **for older groups: 'Make a Festival.'**

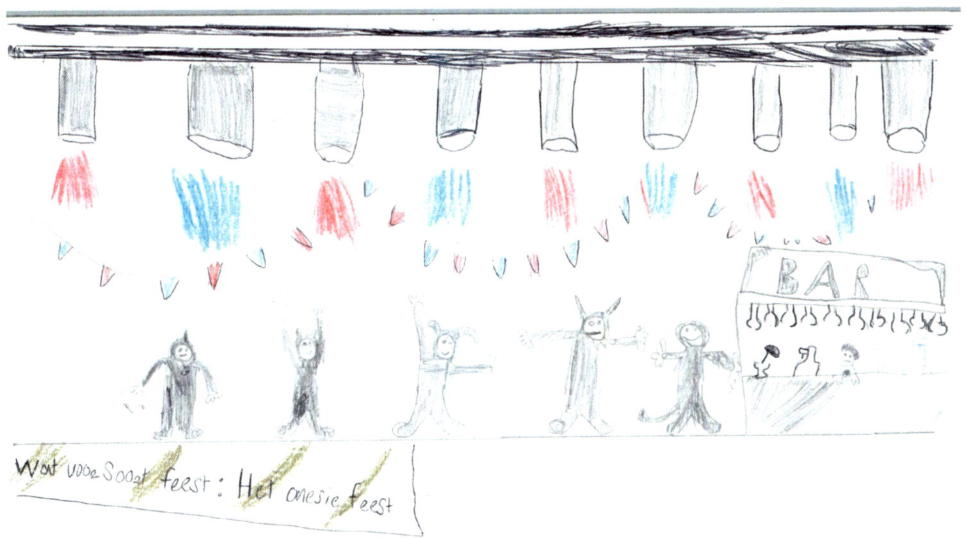

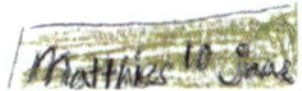

Matthies Bollen, *Het onesie feest* [The onesie party], 2020

Moving the City

Find new ways to move through the city or re-think one that already exist. Try to go from one place to another using different strategies and/or devices.

Natalia Espinel
Bogotá, Colombia

This assignment emerged from two particular situations related to young people's rights and their capacity of moving through and occupying public space. The first one is the massive youth-led public protests that have taken place in the past two years in Colombia, where students took over the streets in a collective gesture of expression and recognition. The second is an episode where police officers on motorcycles violently, and without any reason, attacked a group of young skaters parading through a main avenue in Bogotá. These situations reveal students' intent of reclaiming public space as a site of encounter and circulation of their ideas. It also shows the police's determination of violently removing their bodies from the streets, thereby neutralizing their political agency. Witnessing these two angles of political struggle over public space motivated me to propose this assignment to my students. Their challenge is to find new ways to move through the city, thinking about their bodies' possibilities of becoming more fluid and expansive in space. I invited a *parkour* teacher who, from his vision of the city, proposes other ways of moving in it. As a theoretical frame, we read 'The affective politics of fear' from the book *The Cultural Politics of Emotion* by Sara Ahmed.

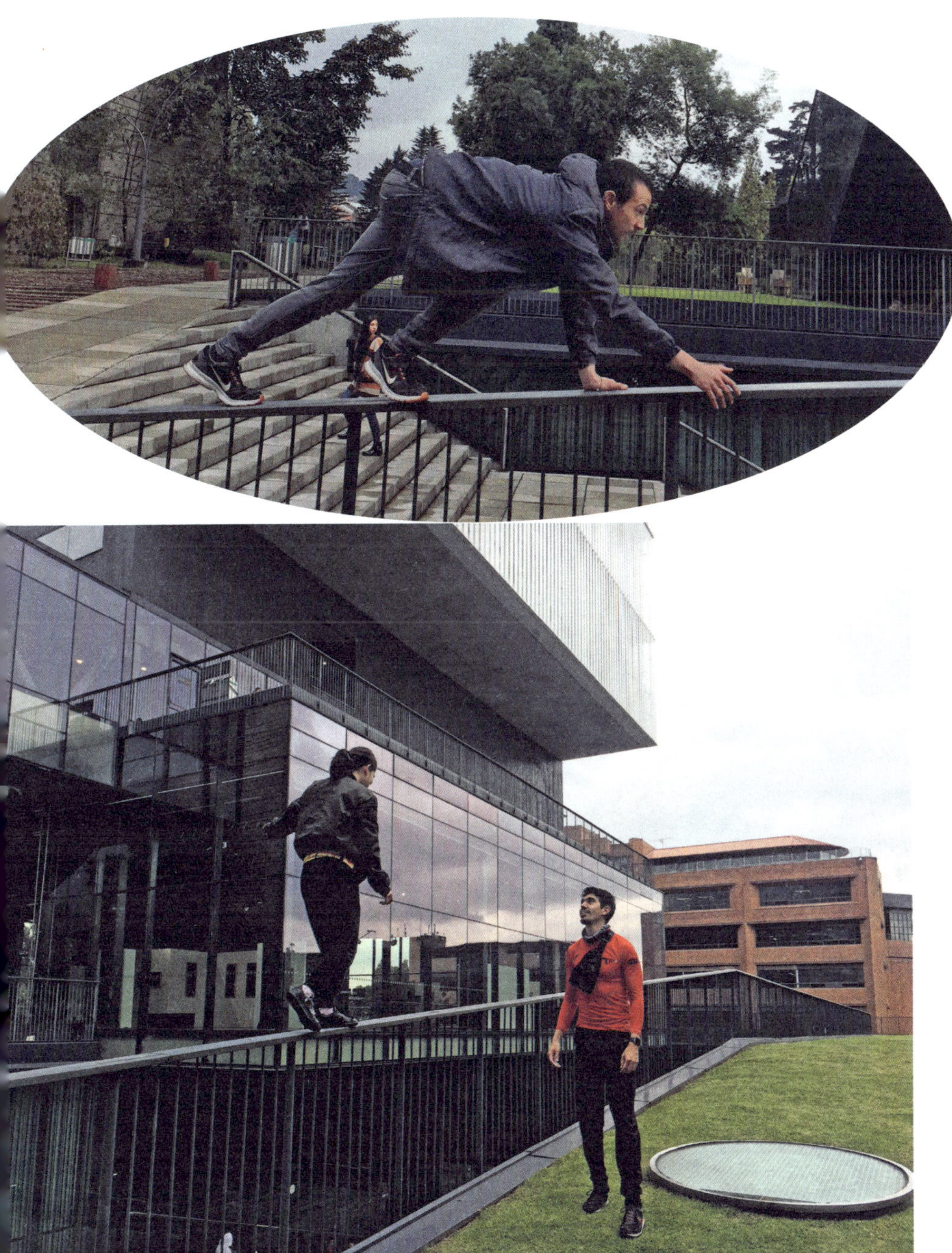

Natalia Espinel, *Moving the City*, 2019, students of the class of Practices of Space and Place/Visual Arts at the Pontificia Universidad Javeriana, Bogotá, and invited Parkour teacher, Sebastián Ruiz Jiménez.

Family Dinner

Create a critical work around the theme 'Family Dinner'.

Patrick Earl Hammie
Champaign, IL, USA

Food and its occasions represent our heritage, home, and current place in the world. It's an excuse that brings family together and potentially prompts tense interactions. Using these ideas, students examine our dynamic relationships with family and cultural identity through imaginings of family, food, gatherings, and rituals. By accomplishing this assignment students question how we identify, connect, and tell stories through food and the systems that they support. They research how class, faith, sex, consumerism, and culture have been presented, evolved, and critiqued in art. Students may work in any liquid or photographic medium, including food, on substrates such as mylar, metal, glass, and ceramic.

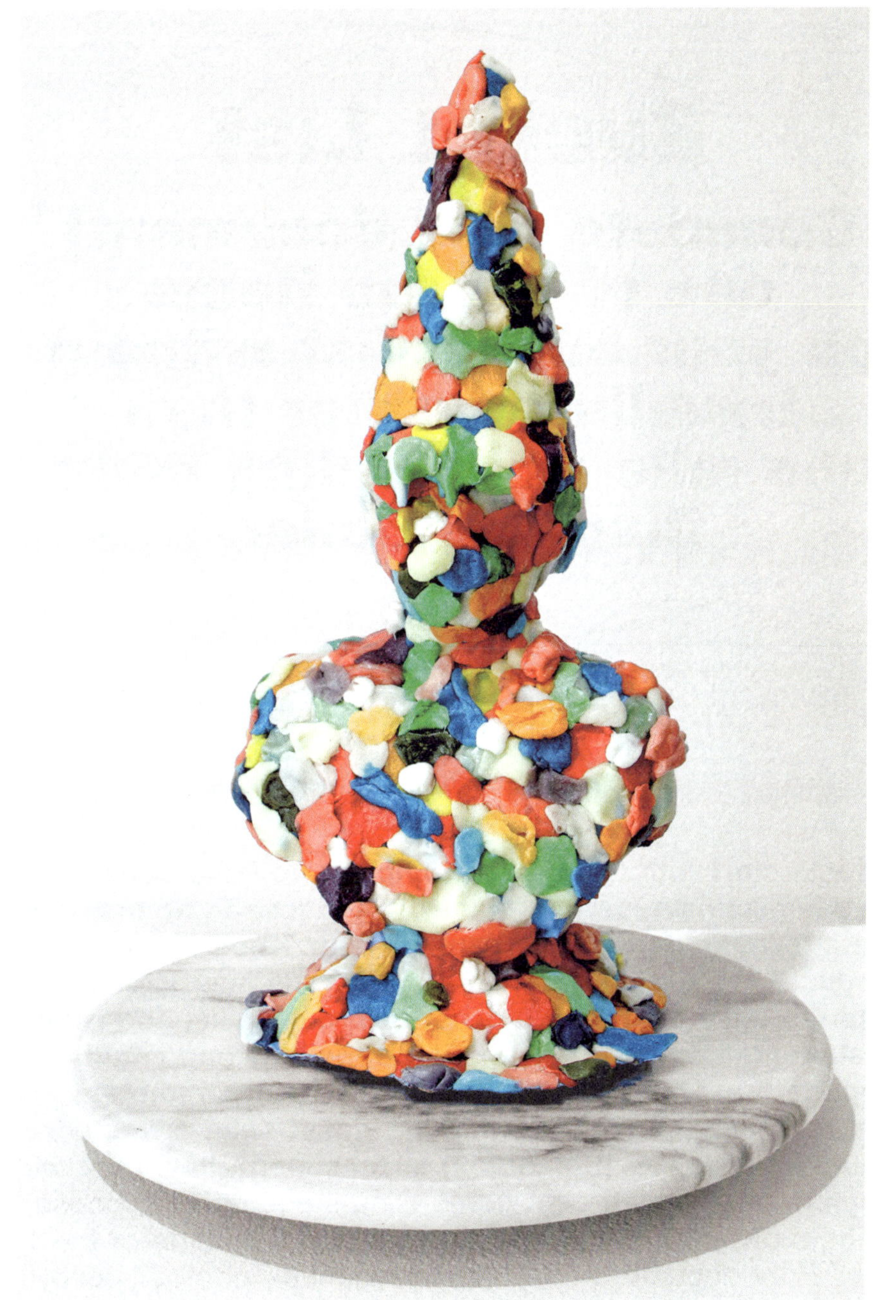

Paul Kenneth, *Idle Worship*, 2019

Bucket List

Complete (and document) one of the top items on your bucket list without travelling further than one mile or spending more than one dollar.

Kira Jo Baldwin
American Fork, UT, USA

Students start with taking a few minutes to write down five to ten bucket-list-type things they would love to do one day; have a few students share there #1 item. Then the instructor introduces the assignment. To practice, the instructor will present a few items from his/her own bucket list and have the students brainstorm in small groups how one might complete these items within the assignment parameters; have each group share one of their ideas. Then give students a chunk of time (10–15 minutes) to brainstorm how they might complete one of their own items. The students will choose one item on their bucket list and execute it outside of the class. They document their experience with photos/video, write a paragraph or two about what happened and what they learned and come prepared to share their documentation and reflection with the class. On the due date, each student will present and discuss their experience with their documentation and reflection.

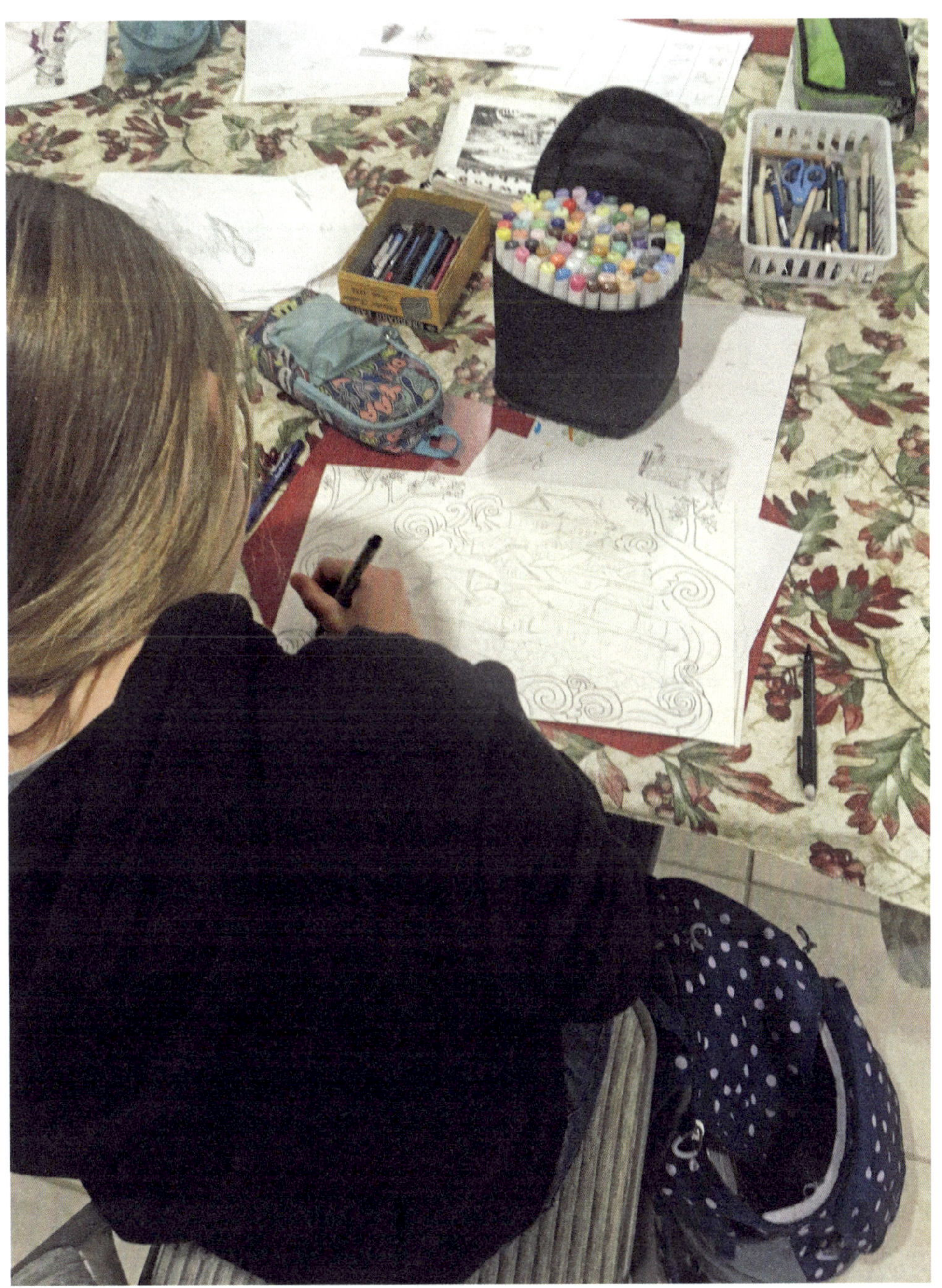

A student who has always wanted to visit Japan learned more about their culture, a couple of Japanese words, and even made some of her own Japanese-style artwork, 2020, Mountain Ridge Junior High School, Utah, USA

Speed-Teaching

Teach something useful to a number of individuals in short intervals.

Oliver Klimpel
Berlin, Germany

Learning as teaching—Teaching as learning.

This is an alternative set-up to the conventions of institutional knowledge distribution. We turn the tables and we all become teachers—and students—and borrow the setting of speed dating. Think of something really useful to know for your fellow students. Something you can explain or demonstrate within a time slot of five minutes to someone sitting opposite you. And then the next one...

What would you have liked to have known earlier? Students accumulate a lot of specific knowledge during their years at the college, including things about the college itself and its inner workings. After graduation this collected knowledge leaves with them.

This is to share knowledge in a fun, non-hierarchical, social, and emancipatory way. It could be something very particular and specialized. It could be even unofficial, insider knowledge about things in college only students know! Think of appropriate tools, objects, or handouts for your five-minute teaching format. Prepare it well and test things beforehand: what works within that little time you have available?

There will be a sound indicating when the five minutes have elapsed and it is time for the 'students' to move one seat further to the next 'teacher'.

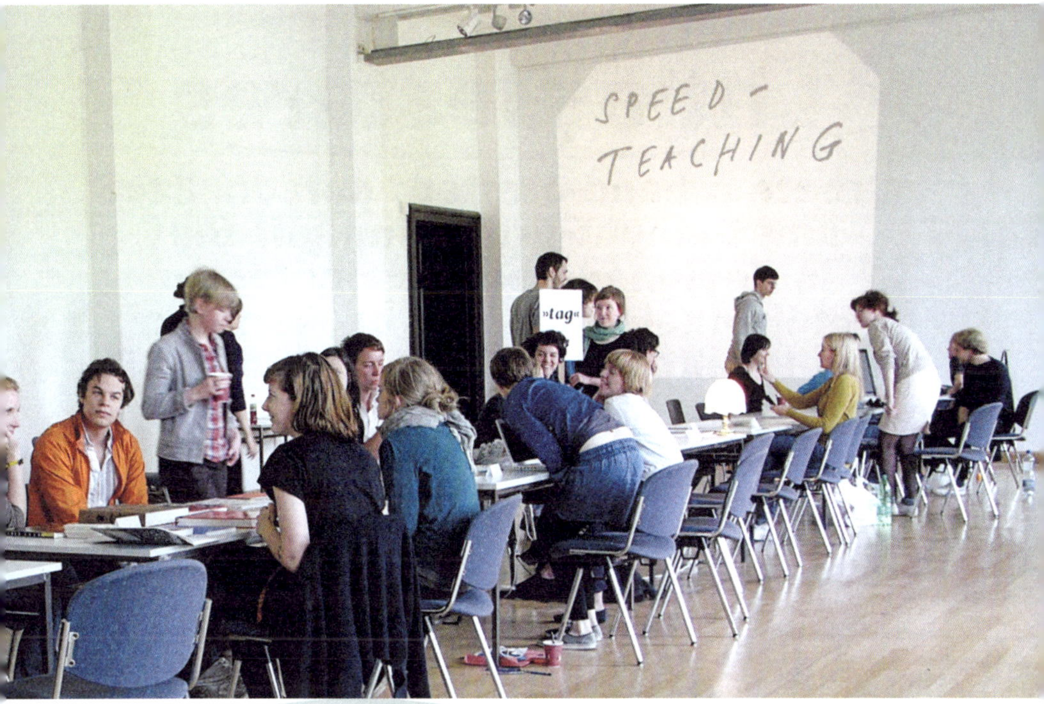

Oliver Klimpel, *Speed-Teaching*, session at the Academy of Visual Arts Leipzig, 2008, photo: Oliver Klimpel, 2009

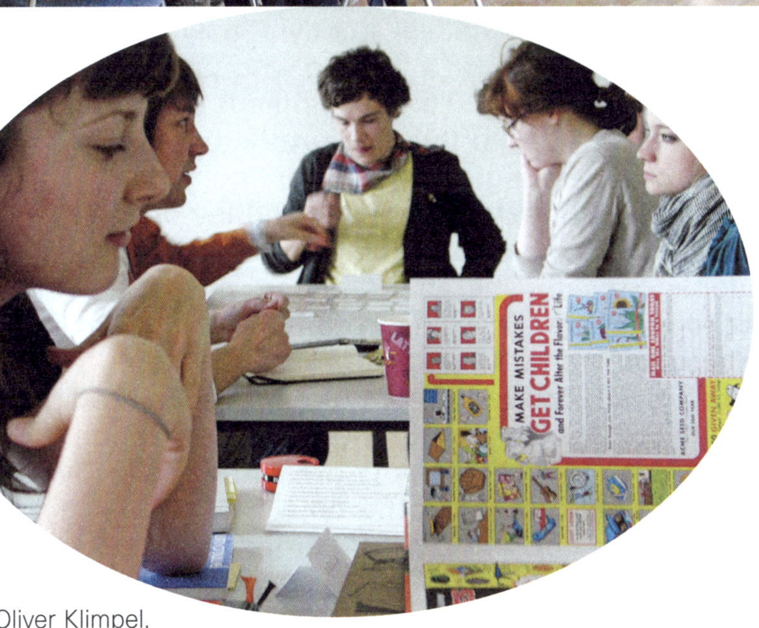

Oliver Klimpel, *Speed-Teaching*, session at the Academy of Visual Arts Leipzig, 2008, photo: Anna-Lena von Helldorf, 2009

Little Gestures

Create a hand-crafted, personalized and thought-provoking gift that is designed specifically for an individual who lives or works in the locality. Consider the material, concept, meaning, and message. Deliver the gift anonymously.

Matt Lee, London, UK
Ramesh Kalkur, Bengaluru, India

In this assignment, students create hand-crafted and personalized gifts, which they deliver anonymously to an acquaintance who lives locally or a person who provides a service within the community. The assignment encourages both the sender and receiver to think about the other. The challenge is to create meaningful objects that consider the lives and personal contexts of individuals they do not have personal relationships with. In developing their concepts, students consider the affect, action, or response they would like to instigate, provoking the recipient to think about themselves, the world around them, or who sent the gift. By working with the restriction of anonymity, they develop a strategy for the delivery of their art intervention and an important part of the process is presenting reflective documentation, from the making of the object to its delivery. The assignment was carried out with undergraduate design students at the Srishti Institute of Art, Design and Technology in Bengaluru. The gifts they created included a personalized paper kite for a local street food vendor, a puzzle of an Assamese rural landscape for a security guard, a hand-decorated journal for the college librarian, and a set of care dolls for the wellness team.

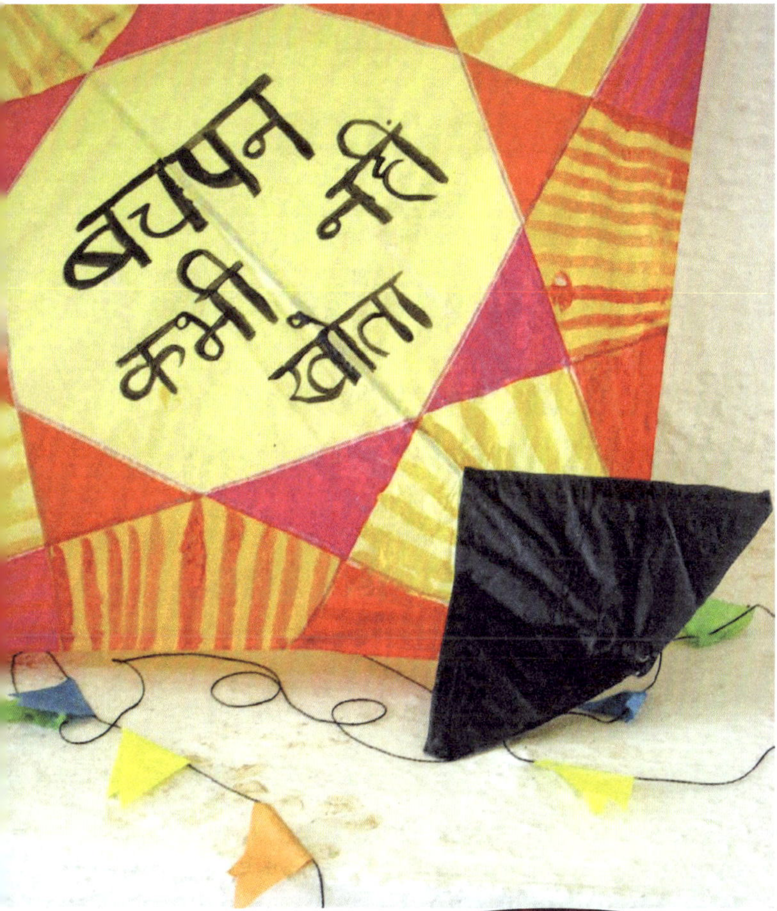

Urmila Shastry, *A gift for the pani puri man*, 2009. The title is based on the Hindi text that Urmila has written on the bag. The 'pani puri man' is a street food vendor.

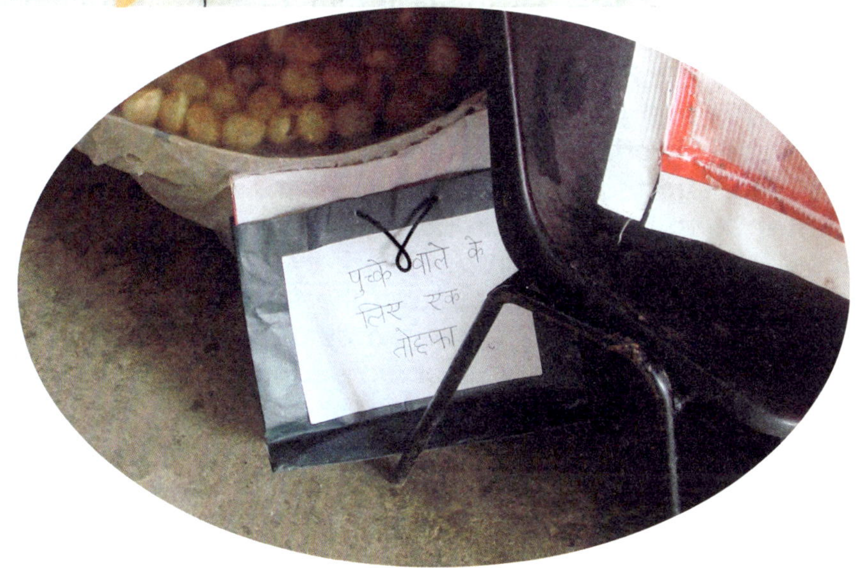

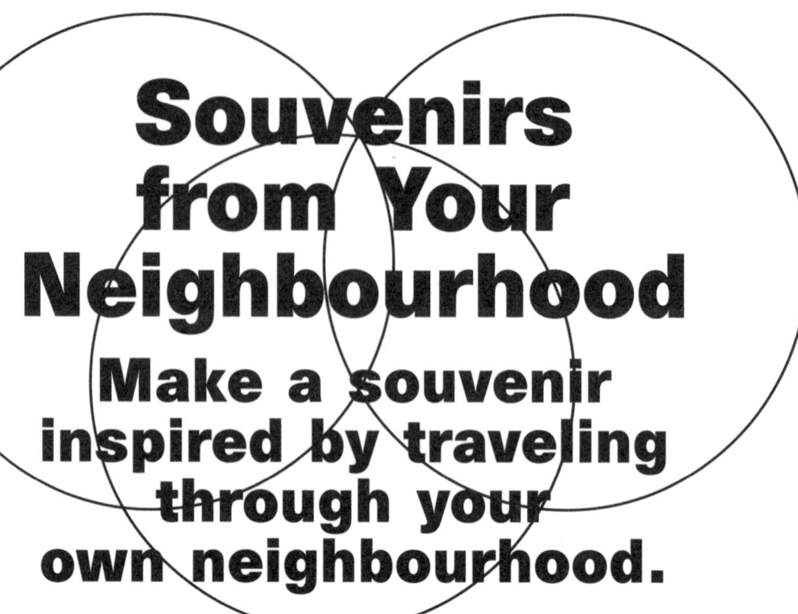

Souvenirs from Your Neighbourhood

Make a souvenir inspired by traveling through your own neighbourhood.

Susanne Venbrux
Nijmegen, the Netherlands

What does a souvenir brought back from a holiday mean to you? Often, it reminds you of the good times you had. In this assignment, students will make a journey through their own neighbourhood. For example, their bedroom, their living room, their garden or the street they live on. Or, maybe the kitchen of their grandparents' house? They collect souvenirs by making illustrations and taking photographs. And this becomes the inspiration for designing their own souvenir. Beforehand, I show them three contemporary artists who work with this theme: *By Nature Inspired*, a work by Herman de Vries who collects all kinds of pieces from the forest and combines them into a collaged artwork; *Inspired by the City* by Raubdruckerin who makes prints of unobserved parts of the city, such as manhole covers, grids, technical objects, other surfaces of the urban landscape; and the third artist Michael Hughes, who puts cheap souvenirs in front of famous landmarks, and blends both in a photograph. His work is meant to be funny but also critical of society.

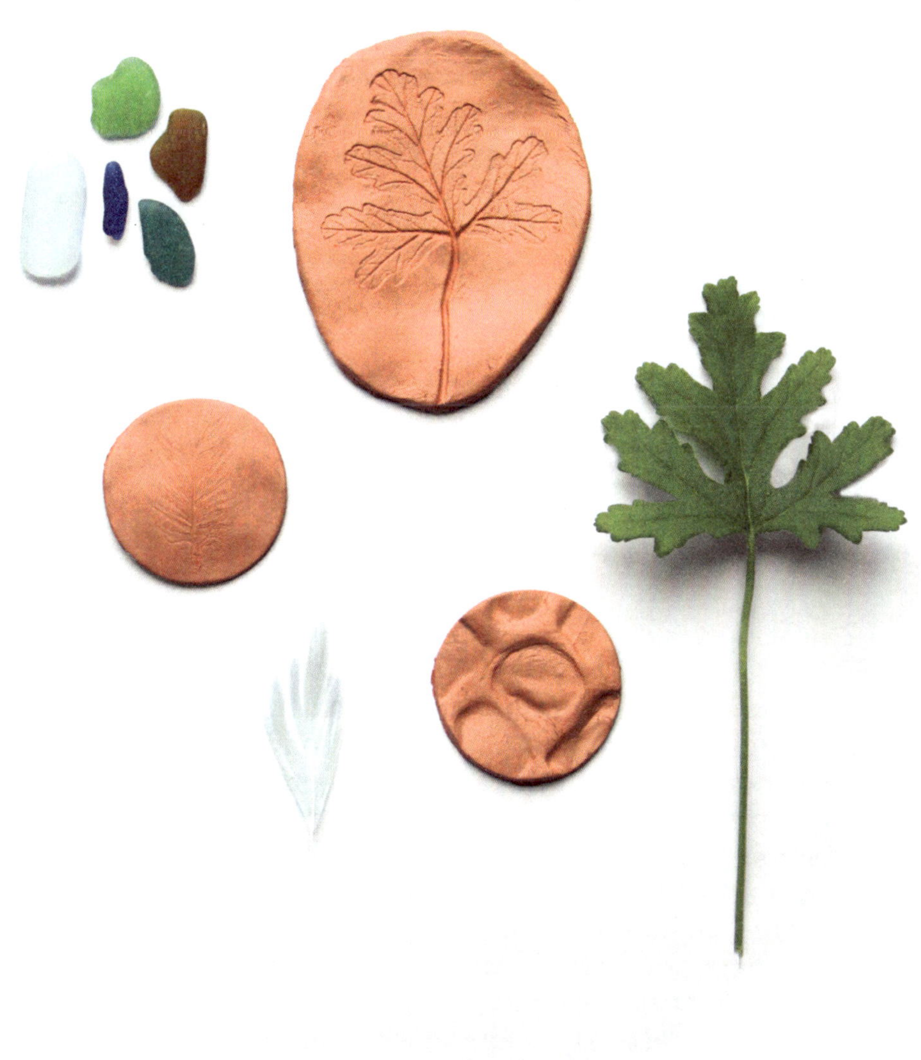

My souvenirs, 2020,
photo: Susanne Venbrux

How to Treat Me Well

Design a book to help your parents understand more about you.

Linda Mekkes
Alkmaar, the Netherlands

You are born without written instructions. Lucky for you; since you have grown up and learned how to read and write, you can write them yourself! Make your parents finally understand you! Explain to them who you actually are. Because pictures speak louder than words: the cover of the book is the most important part of the assignment. Give it a suitable title and a fitting font (typeface) to contribute to the feeling of your book.

Perhaps a book just makes you think about paper and words, but this is not always the case. You don't have to fill the book with words. The focus of this assignment is the design of the book and the message you wish to bring across.

Don't forget that books come in different shapes and sizes. So feel free to create any 'book' you like, as long as the viewer understands that there is a connection between your artwork and a book.

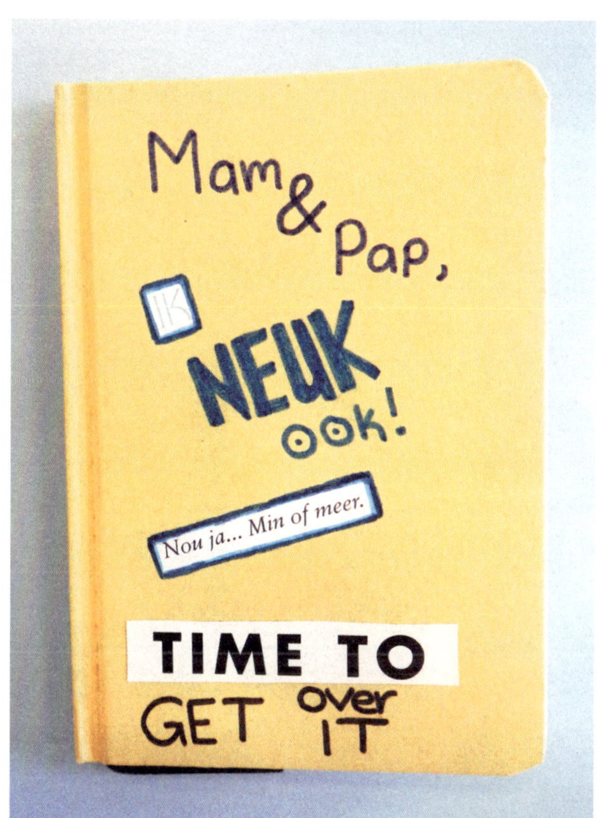

Dani Krijt, *Mam & Pap, Ik NEUK ook!* [Mum & Dad, I also fuck], 2020, Breitner Academie, Amsterdam

Hannah van der Eng, *AFRUIMEN* [Clear up], 2020, Breitner Academie, Amsterdam

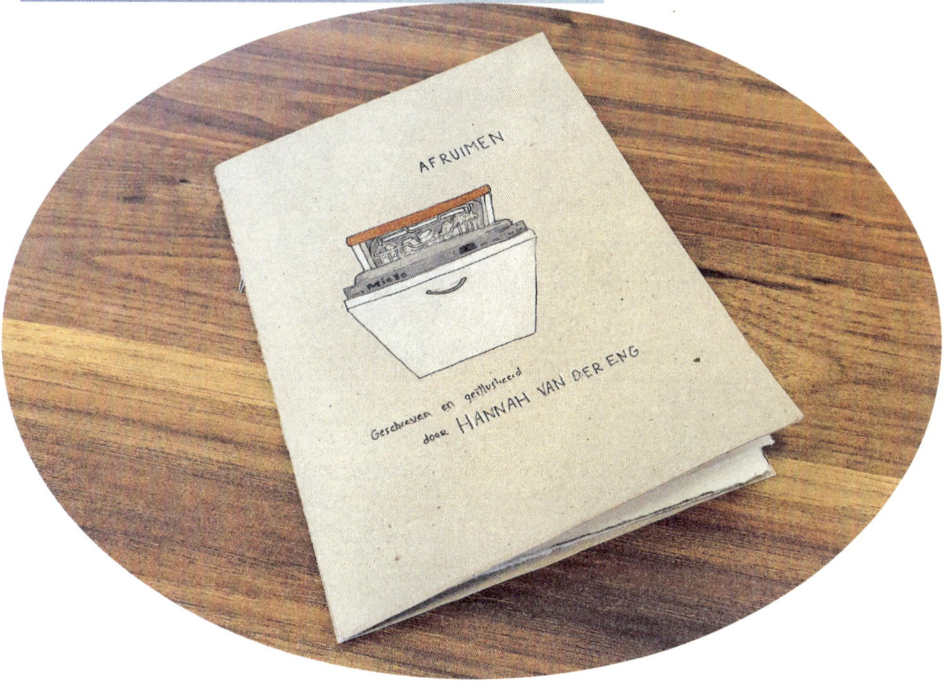

Bui
M

d &

ove

Water Travel

Build a boat that can carry a group of people over water.

Wolf Brinkman
Schiedam, the Netherlands

In this experiment, eighth-graders in primary school investigated how to build a boat by making a brick float. By using simple materials, music, gravity, Archimedes, and their unimaginable imagination they discovered how to build a real boat. Where art meets language and mathematics, school is transformed into a playground where all kids find their natural place in the process and discover their true potential. Of course, at the end, an everyday event turns into a magic moment when a self-built boat floats gently on a pond and carries the explorers into an experience they will never forget.

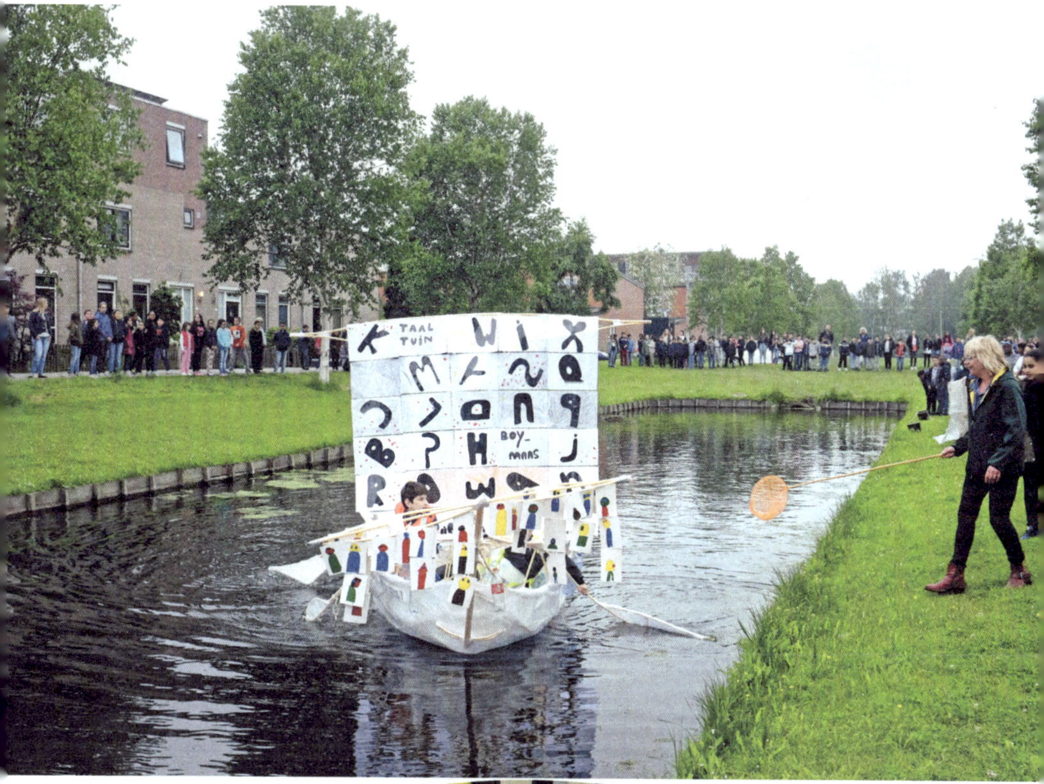

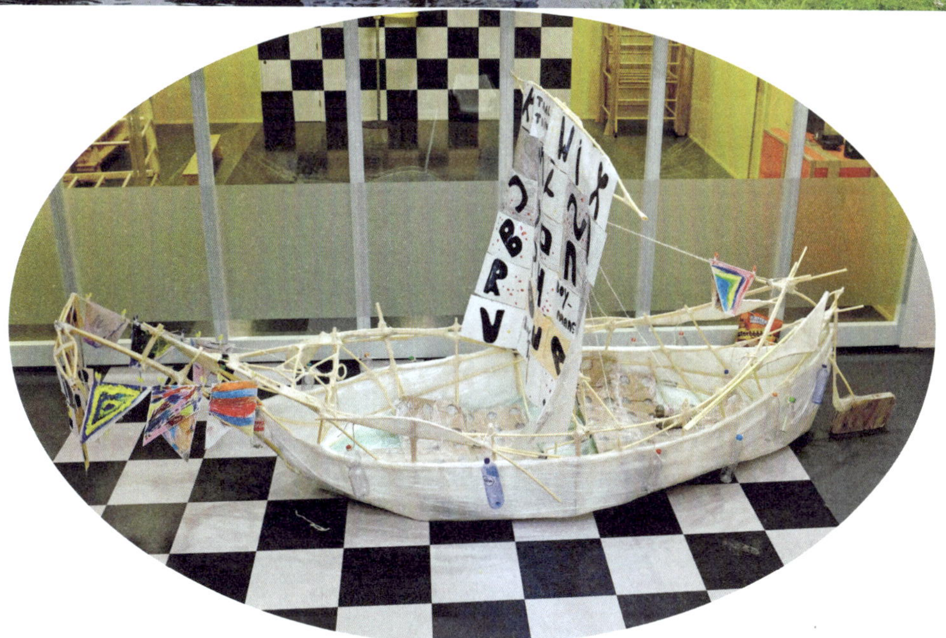

Pupils' work, *Water Travel*, 2016,
OBS De Taaltuin primary school, 8th group, Schiedam

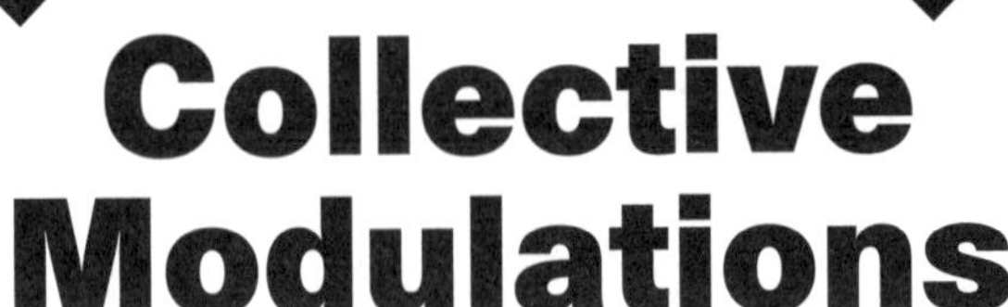

Collective Modulations

Collectively develop ways to modulate 3 tonnes of builder's sand.

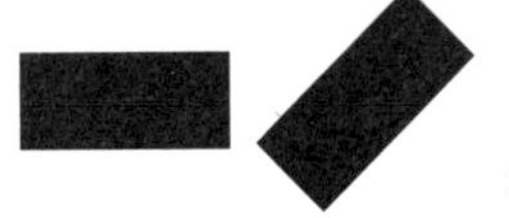

Bianca Hester
Sydney, Australia

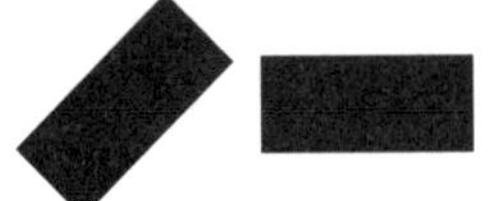

Three tonnes of fresh builder's sand were deposited at the entrance of the sculpture department at the Victorian College of the Arts, Melbourne. Students had an entire day to collectively develop ways to 'modulate' this material. Modulate is a concept borrowed from Gilbert Simondon, whereby formation is understood as a continuous process of modulation involving a dynamic movement of forces and materials in a process of emergence. Students were invited to collectively develop strategies for relocating this heap into the studios and then experiment working with the sand in a myriad of ways over the course of the day. Questions posed were: What are the possibilities that emerge in forming and reforming this material? What configurations does the sand put your individual and collective bodies into? How might the sand shape your thinking processes?

The students decided to work collectively for an exhibition. They 'pressed' twelve cubes—each 1 m³ in size—and installed them throughout the entire exhibition space. Buried inside each form was a stash of beer and as the audience arrived, one of the students kicked the corner of a cube to reveal the first can. Students then leapt upon all the cubes, destroying them in order to access the beer stash held temporarily within.

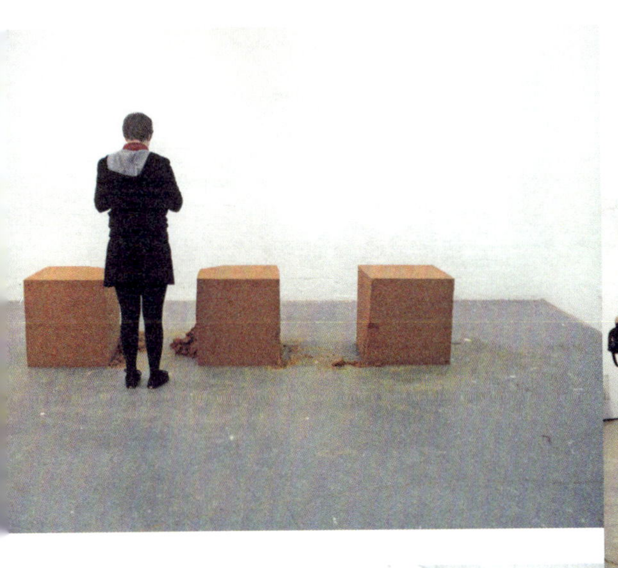

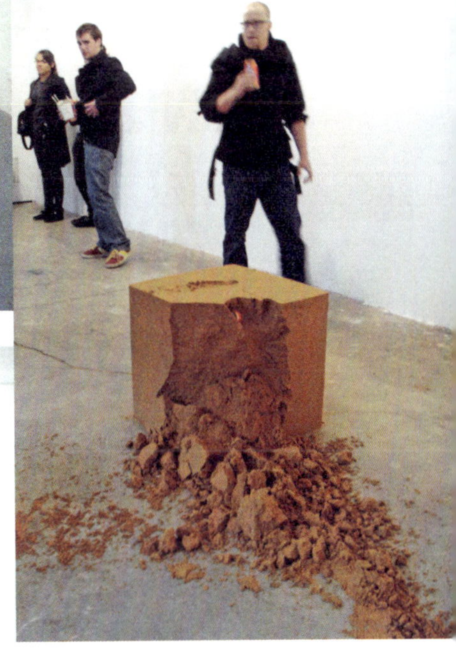

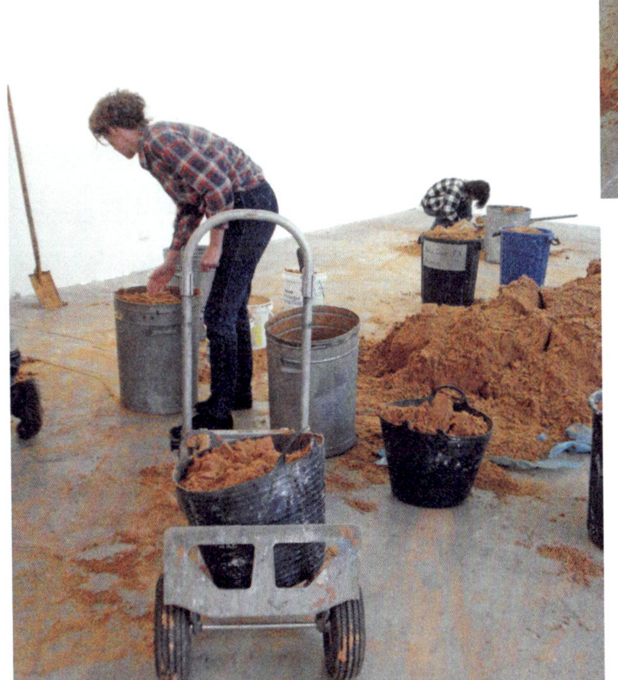

Bianca Hester and second-year students from the department of Sculpture, *Three tonnes of builder's sand*, 2010, documentation of action in the student gallery at Victorian College of the Arts, The University of Melbourne

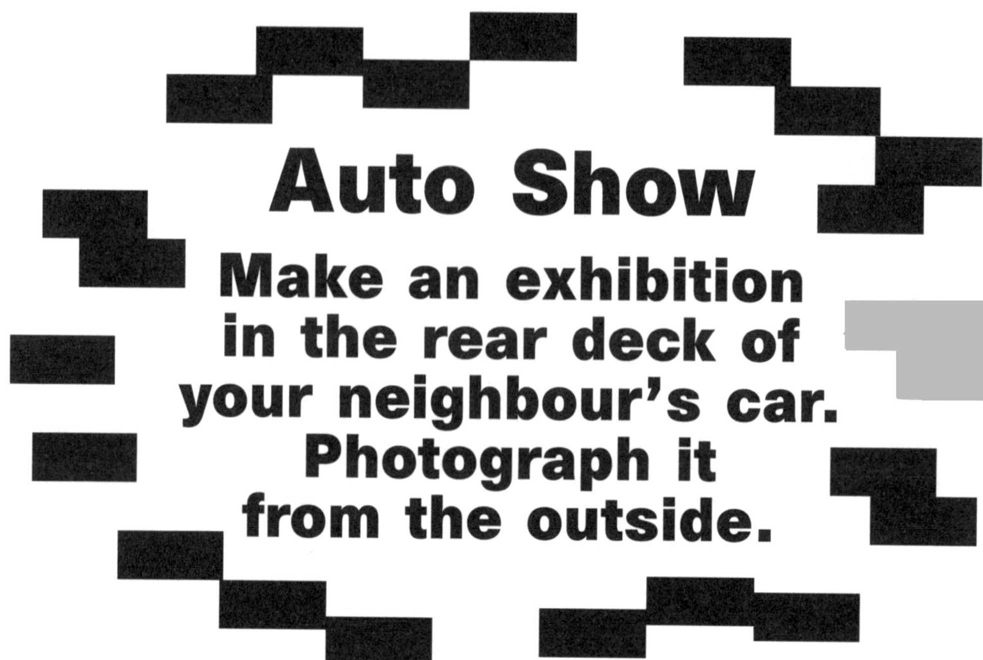

Auto Show

Make an exhibition in the rear deck of your neighbour's car. Photograph it from the outside.

Andrea Palašti
Novi Sad, Serbia

This assignment explores the meaning, function, and status of the work of art outside institutional spaces like galleries. It can be done easily, with minimal equipment and without 'conceptual pretensions'. It is a conceptual flexibility exercise, where the students rehearse ad hoc exhibition making at someone else's private 'place'.

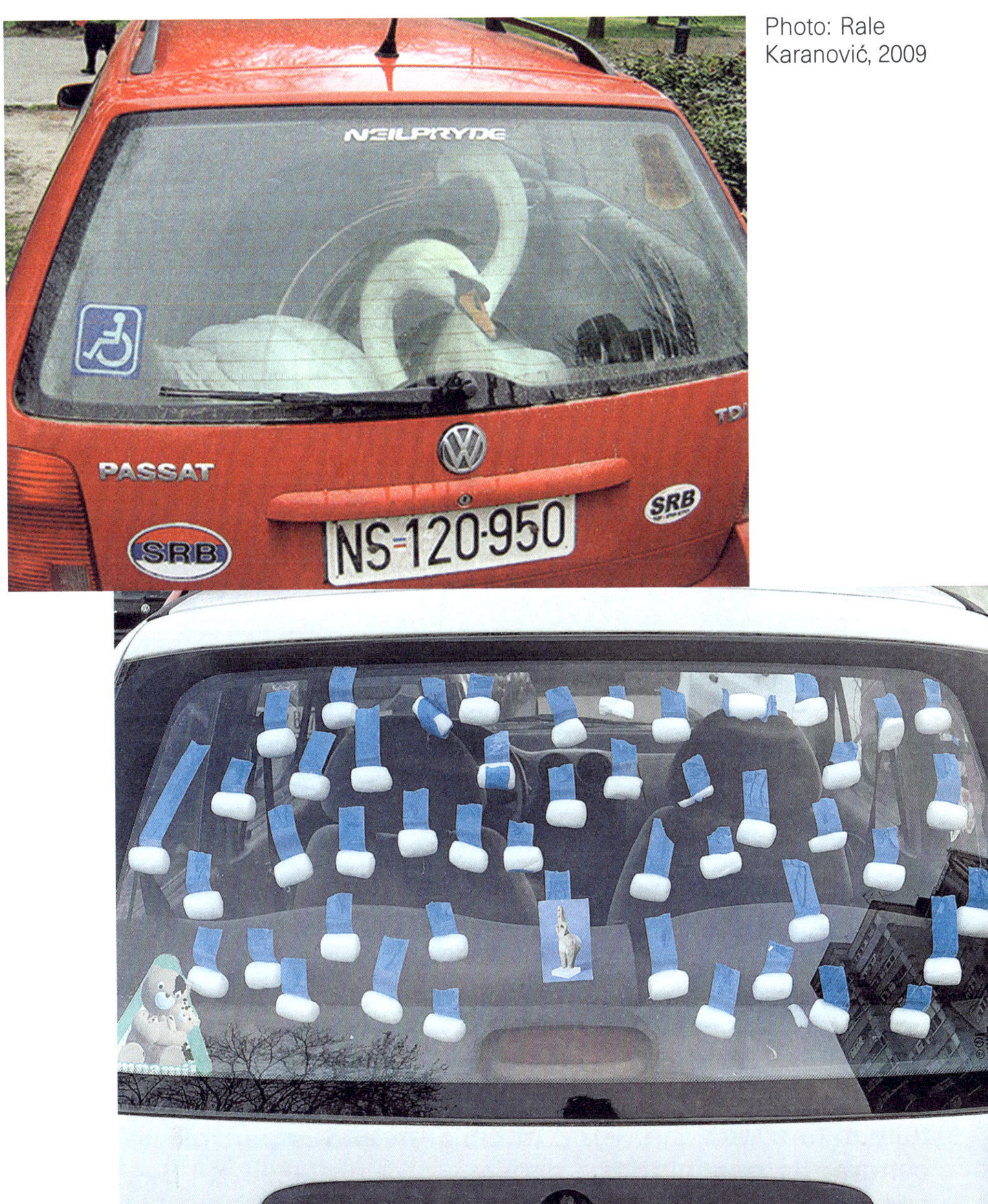

Photo: Rale Karanović, 2009

Nadja and Kristian Palašti, *Auto Show*, 2020

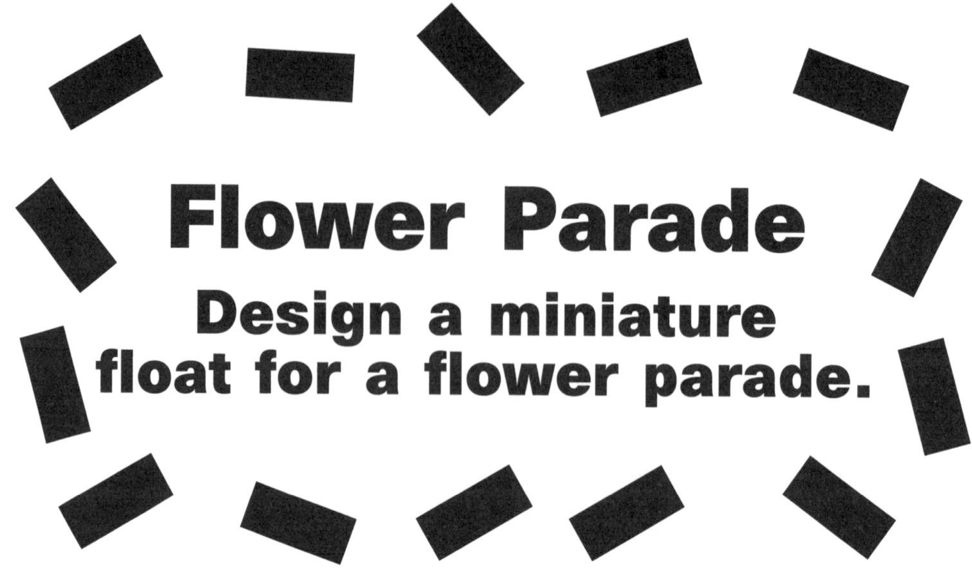

Flower Parade

Design a miniature float for a flower parade.

Rolinda Rook-Heetebrij, Sint Jansklooster, the Netherlands
Marijke Rook-Lassche, Vollenhove, the Netherlands

This project was designed in the module 'talent development' of the study programme Pedagogic Professional Children and Education (PPKE) of the University of Applied Sciences KPZ in Zwolle. We were given the assignment to design a cultural project for a specific target group. We chose to develop innovations for the traditional flower parade of primary school Eben Haëzer in Sint Jansklooster. This renewed project is fully in line with the world of children and is part of the village culture. By engaging the services of a professional designer and a graphic design teacher we were able to involve the children in thinking about what colours and materials to use and how they could imagine and create a miniature float. In addition, a student videography introduced a number of children to the world of vlogging and how to make professional photographs, so that the festive flower parade was documented in a modern, contemporary manner.

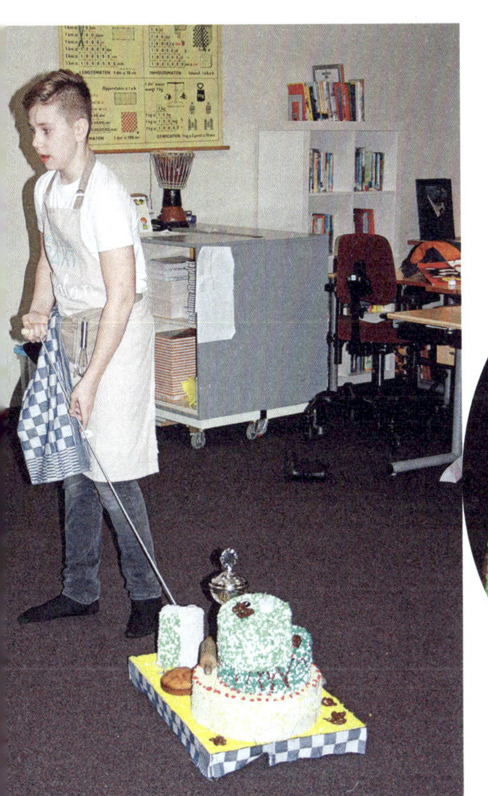

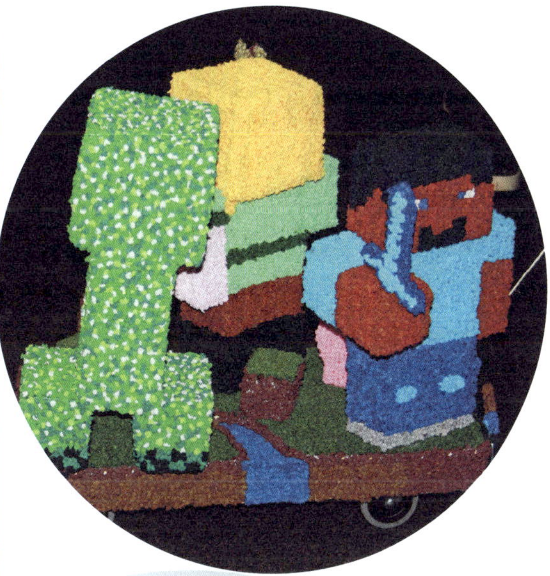

Pupils' work, *Flower Parade*, 2019, Eben Haëzer primary school, 7th and 8th group, Sint Jansklooster

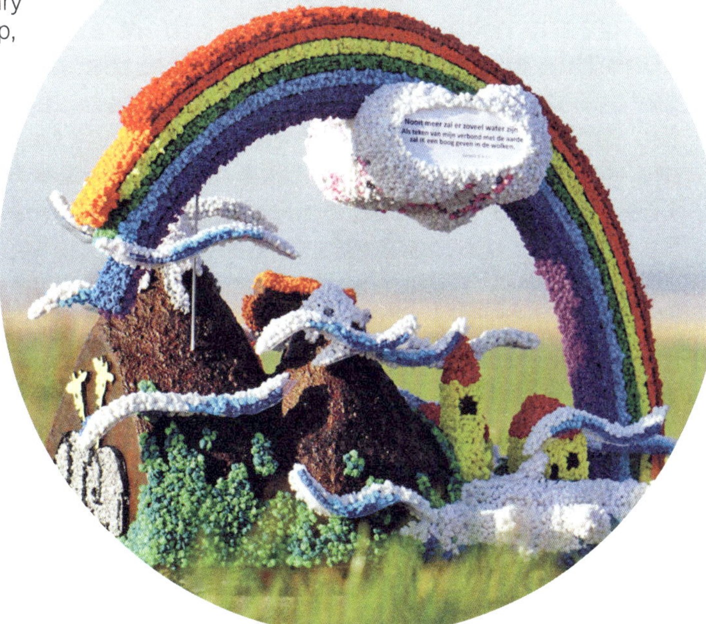

Office Memory

Make a scale model of the principal's office from memory.

Mirjam van Tilburg
Rotterdam, the Netherlands

The assignment is inspired by Mike Kelley's *Educational Complex*. Kelley made scale models of all the buildings where he studied. Because he did this from memory, some details are clearly recognizable, while others are black holes. I have done this short assignment with art teachers working in secondary education. I challenged them to make a model of the principal's office. The question I put to them was: what are you looking at if you take an imaginary tour of the school? The way you look can become worn, like an ingrained habit. By building a model you force yourself to really think about what you have seen and what you didn't see. Especially this ability to identify what you see and what you 'unsee' is to me an important quality for an art teacher. What rooms do you know well and which less well? What do you remember? What do you forget? How do you walk in different spaces? What are your blind spots in the school building? And, who is allowed to go where? What role do power and hierarchy play? Does the principal's office have the same effect on you as your classroom has on your students? What are the written or unwritten rules of the school building?

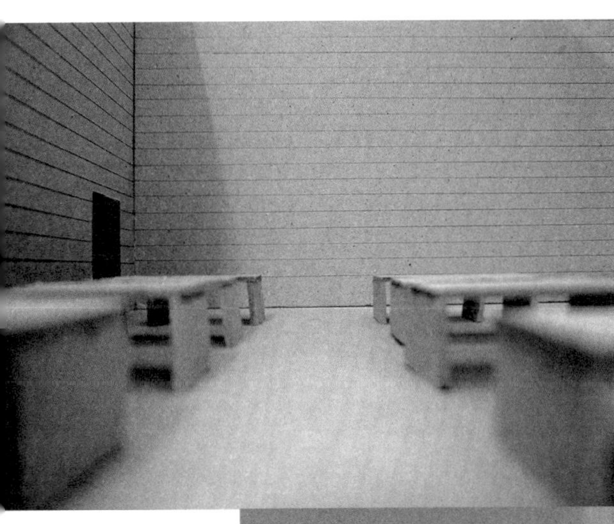

Mirjam van Tilburg,
Disciplinary Residence, 2008

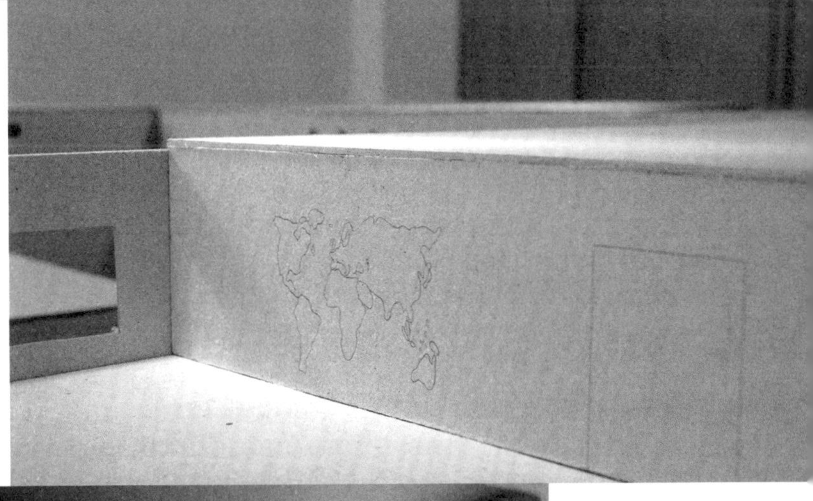

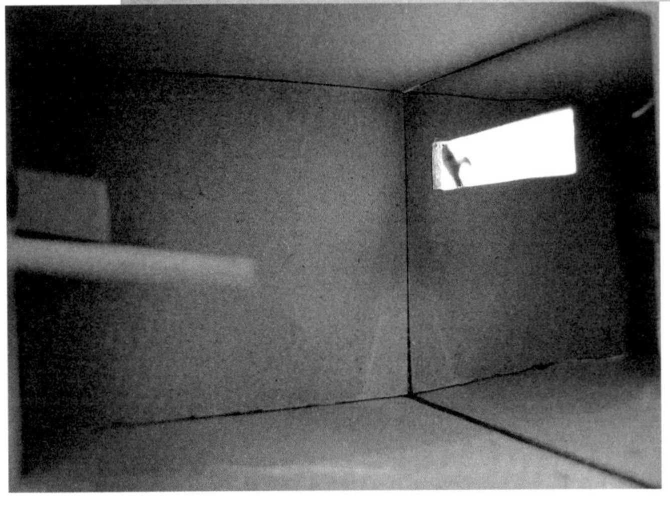

Tower of Babel

Build a tower as high as you can, using only: cardboard, newspapers, skewers, and toothpicks.

Davy Yong
Rotterdam, the Netherlands and London, UK

Legends surrounding the Tower of Babel and its rendition by Pieter Bruegel the Elder have captivated our imagination for centuries. Students are introduced to the story of the Tower of Babel and challenged to enact its build. Collaborating in groups of at least three, the class competes in building the tallest tower, using only cardboard, newspapers, skewers, and toothpicks. As they progress, tools may be 'acquired' or 'unlocked' (game terminology) for a limited time: think of scissors, glue, tape, more cardboard, a demonstration, or advice. However, not only height plays a role in the assessment of the towers. An 'aesthetic factor' plays another crucial role in their assessment, and consists of creativity, inventiveness, the construction's reliability, appearance, and the students' ability to highlight these characteristics in the presentation of their tower. So, despite having a smaller tower, a group of students could still triumph through the following grading formula: Height (m) x aesthetic factor (%)

Example

Group 1:	**2 m x 1,2 =**	**2,4**
Group 2:	**1,5 m x 1,7 =**	**2,55**

This assignment can be moulded in many ways and is the perfect team-building activity to support intimate interactions, enhance problem-solving skills and group cohesiveness.

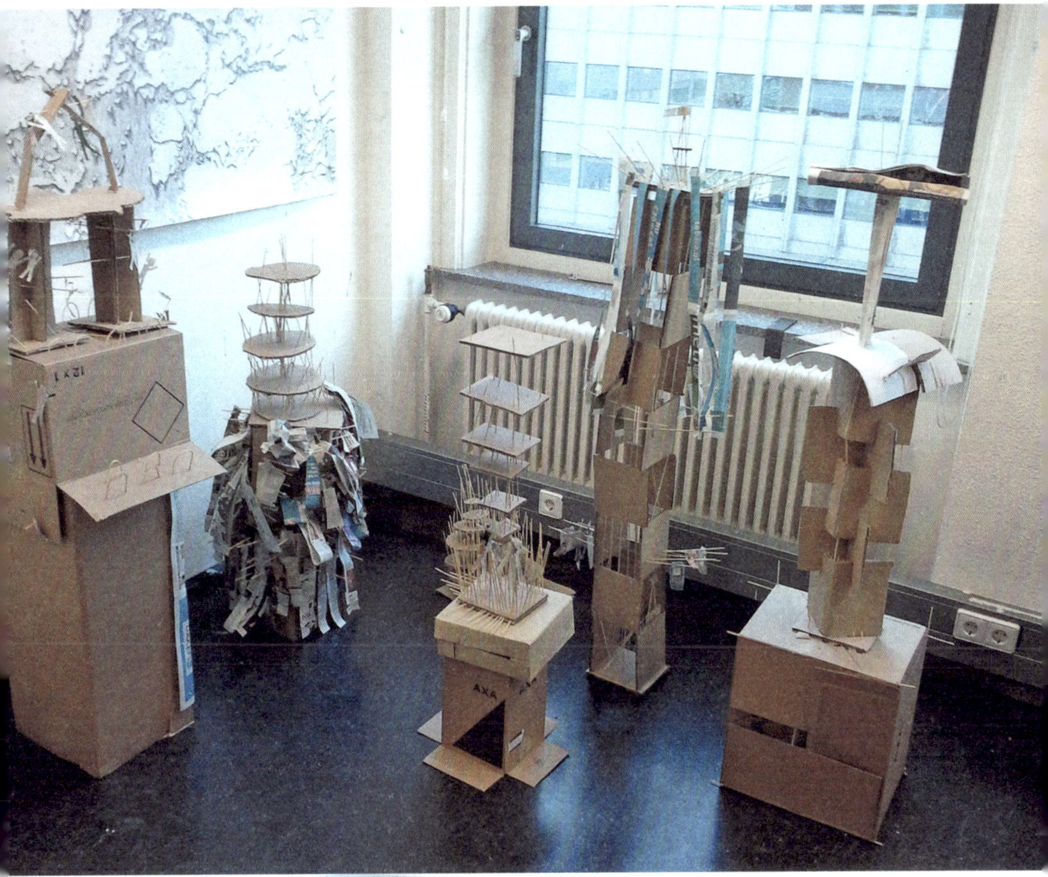

Pupils' end results of the pilot lesson, March 2012, Rotterdam, photo: Davy Yong

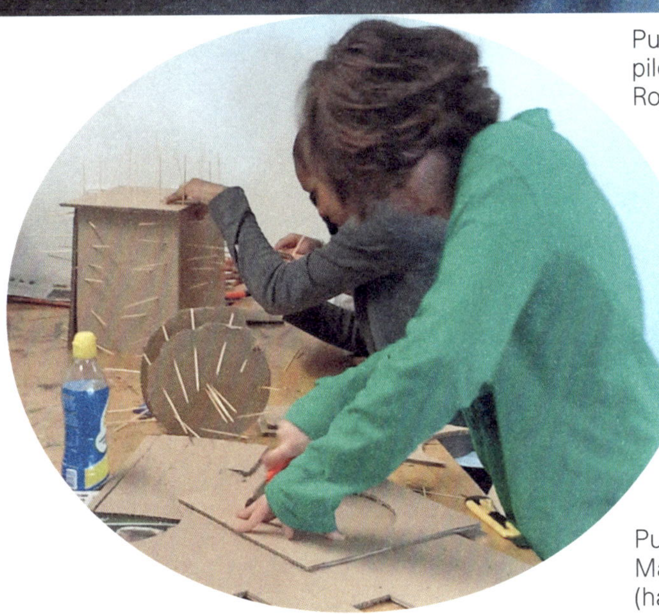

Pupils' problem-solving skills, March 2012, secondary school (havo/vwo), photo: Davy Yong

Kee
Tii

pin

ne

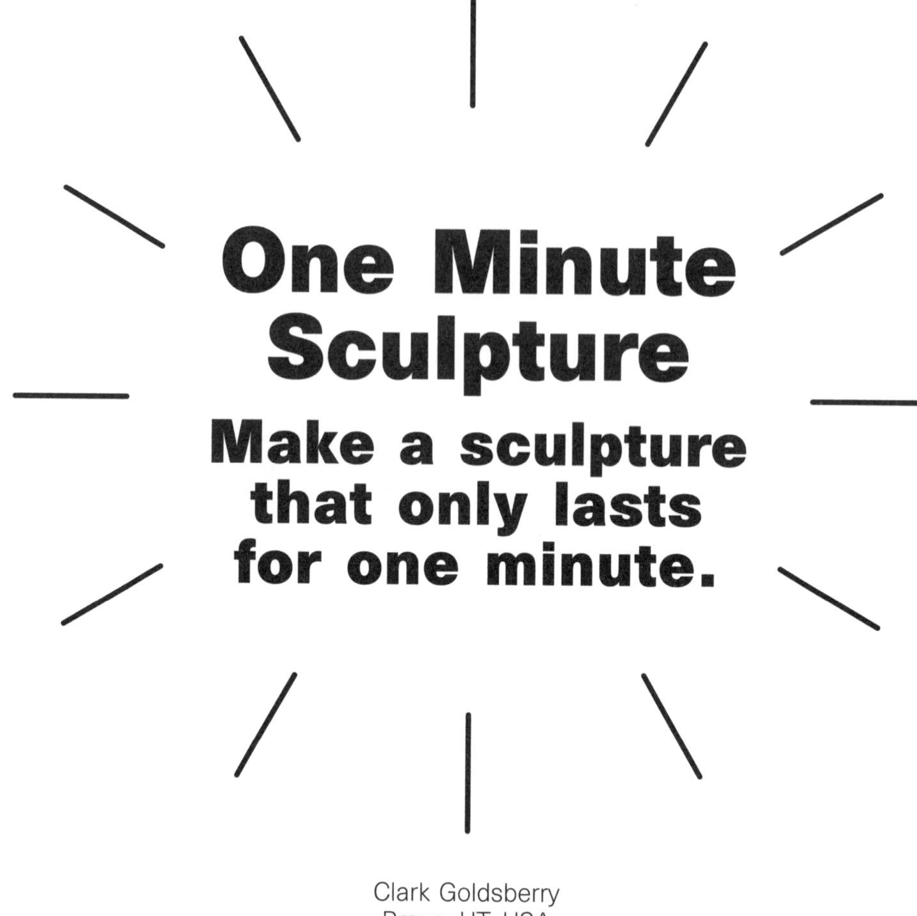

One Minute Sculpture

Make a sculpture that only lasts for one minute.

Clark Goldsberry
Provo, UT, USA

Inspired by the Austrian artist Erwin Wurm, we utilized available materials to create spontaneous sculptures that lasted for only one minute. This project was done on the first day in a high school photography class. The process invited students to play, overlap, and interact in unexpected ways.

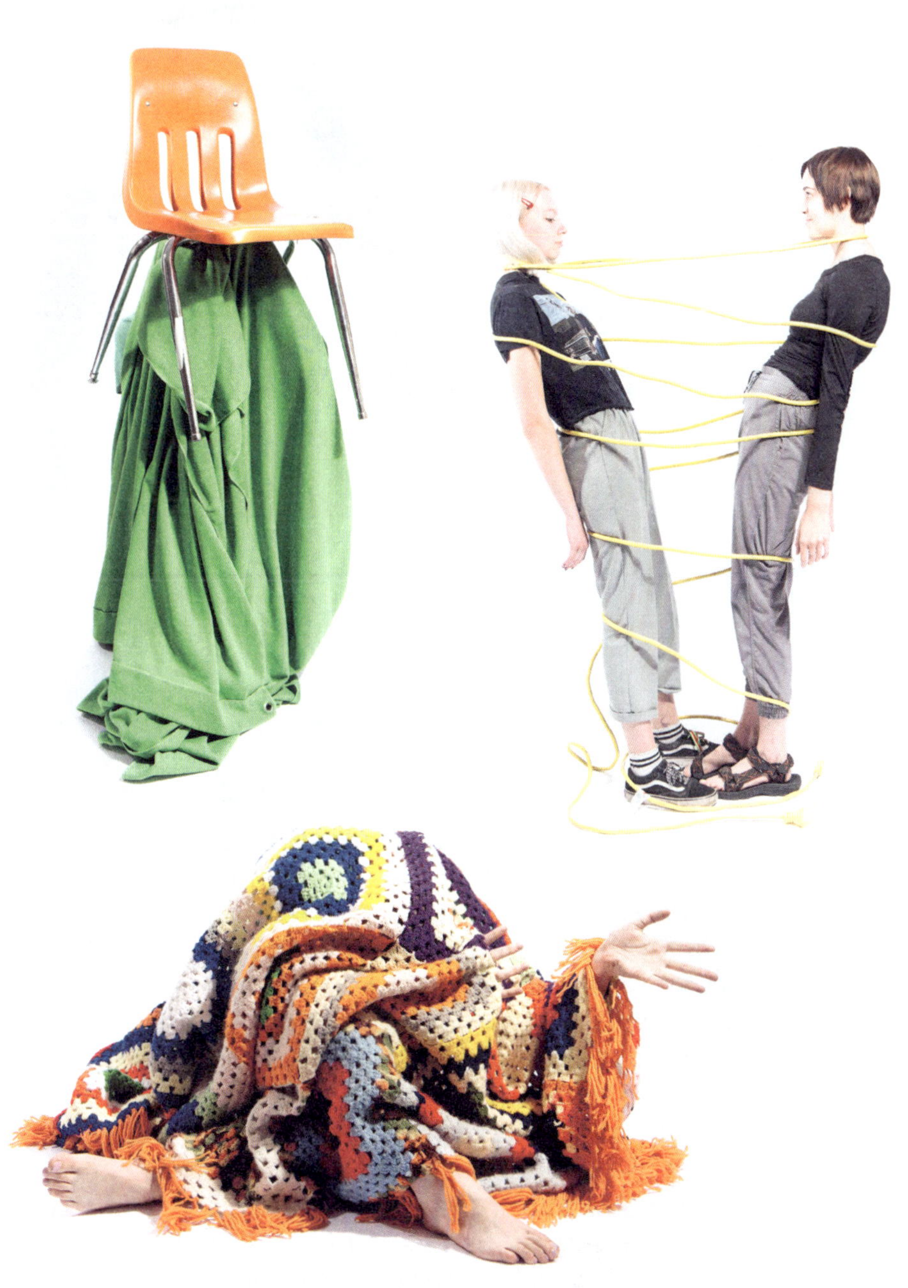

Students' work, *One Minute Sculptures*, American Fork High School, Utah, USA, 2019, photos: Clark Goldsberry

Eating, Talking, and Watching TV

Knit to mark the passing of time, watch TV, talk to others, and eat, but don't stop knitting.

Jorge Lucero
Urbana and Chicago, IL, USA

While teaching painting to a smart—but talkative—group of teenagers I became frustrated at how much extra time their projects were taking due to their excessive socializing. Their actions were harmless, but as a new teacher I was conflicted. Instead of chastising the students I decided to make all their talking into an artwork. I bought knitting supplies and had the students with knitting knowledge teach those who didn't know how to knit. I then told everybody that for the next three weeks they could talk as much as they wanted. Also (to increase the absurdity) they could watch TV and eat snacks as much as they wanted. The only rule was to 'keep knitting' all the time. No parameters were given for 'what' to knit. No specific shapes or usable objects were supposed to come from the knitting. After three weeks we installed all the knitting-gestures as a painting in the main hallway of the school. We talked about contemporary painting, performance, and conceptual art in front of this installation.

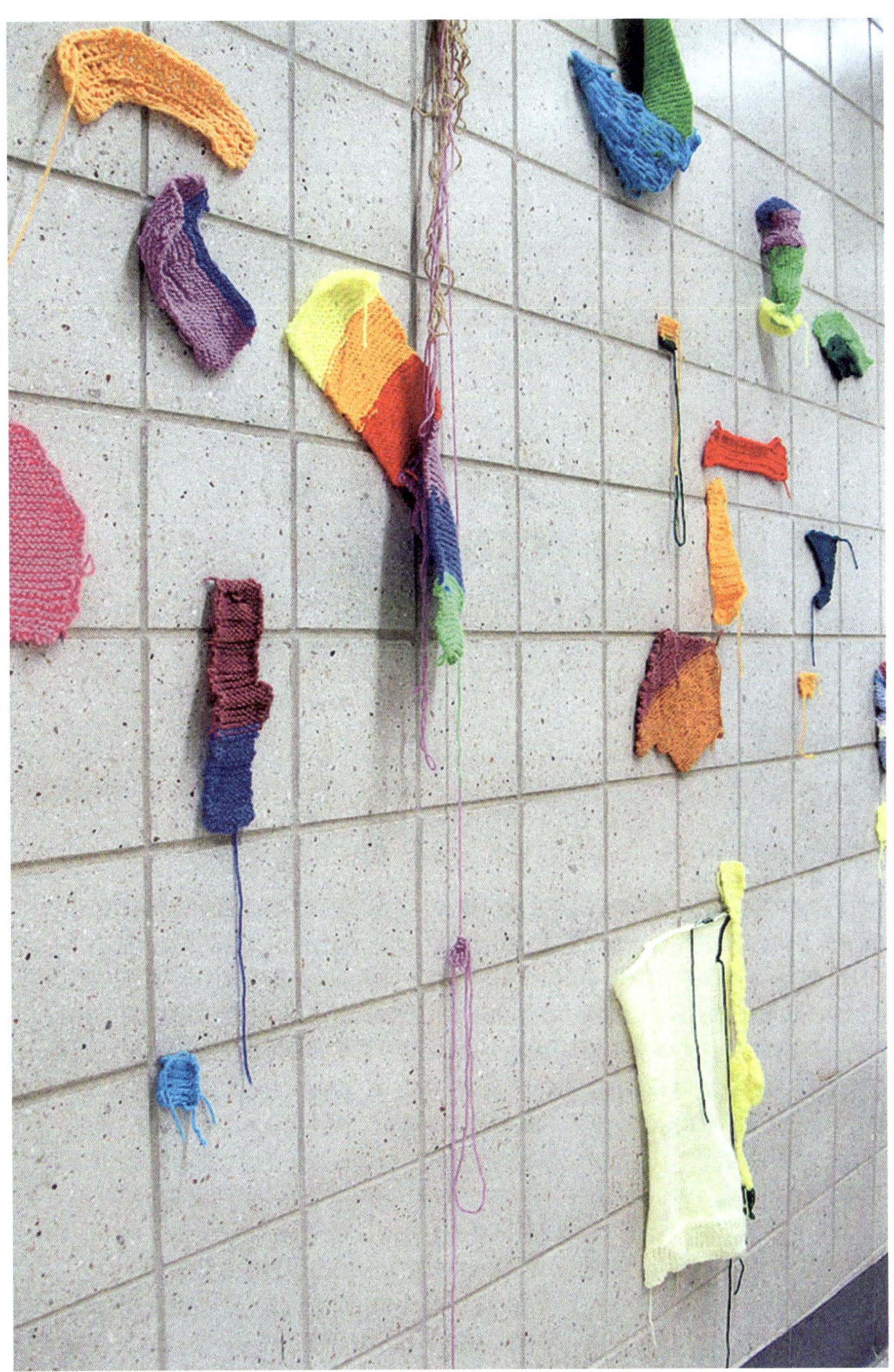

Students of Art 1-Cubed Class at Northside College Preparatory High School, *Eating, Talking, and Watching TV*, 2007, installation view, photo: Jorge Lucero

The Art of Worn Out

Make an artwork using a worn-out process.

Nicolet Bekker
Amsterdam, the Netherlands

The assignment is based on one of my graduation projects at the art academy (Gerrit Rietveld Academie, Architectural Design). It's about the fascination of what worn-out processes can contribute to the appearance of an interior or art object. If the worn-out process coincides with the shape of the object it can lead to surprising, new results. It also adds depth to the meaning of the object, because the worn-out process captures different 'time gaps' in one object. I created a worn-out floor that shows all its layers in time. The students that executed this assignment created much more diverse results: using worn-out (or broken) materials in sculptures, making stamps from a worn-out process and repeat it or speeding up the process in creating a collection of furniture. The beauty of worn-out can lead to more acceptance in using second-hand, imperfect, or leftover materials and therefore can contribute to sustainable design.

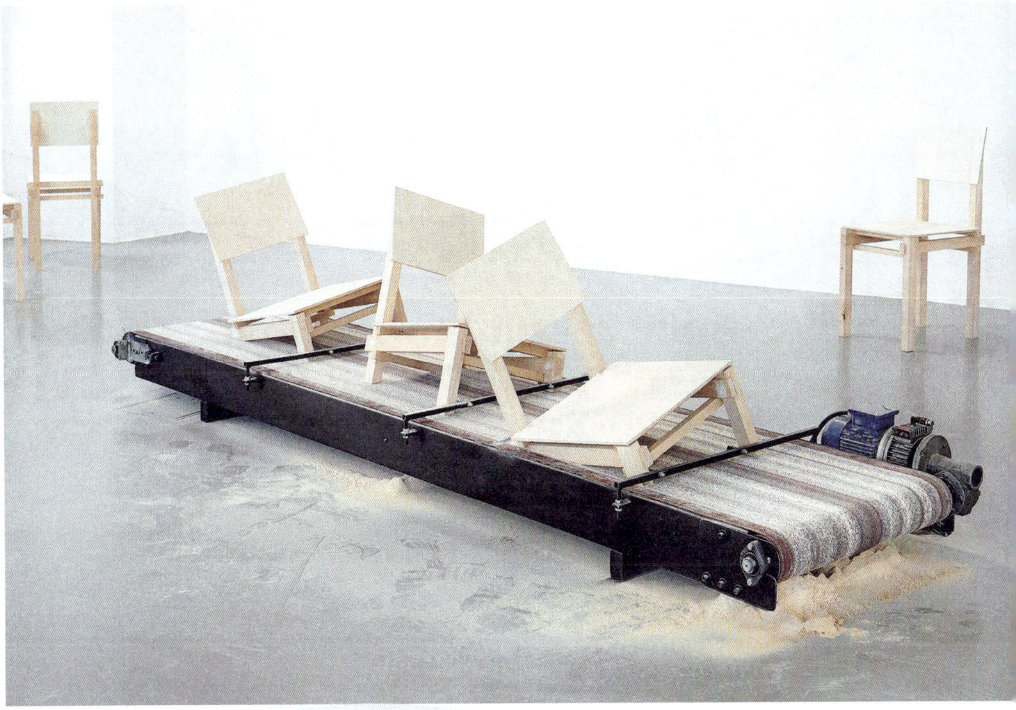

Leon de Bruijne, *Quick Sand*, 2019, solo exhibition 'Modus', Kasseler Kunstverein, photo: Nicolas Wefers

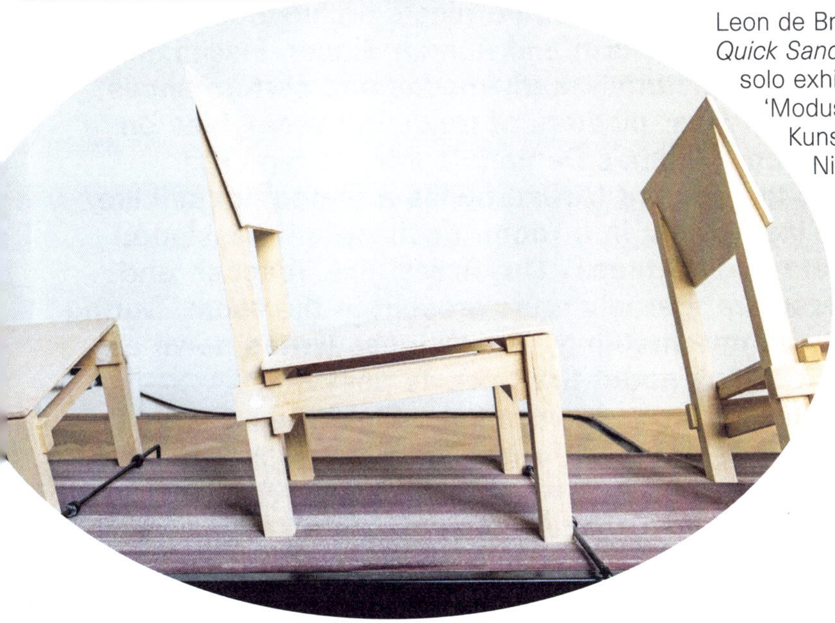

Leon de Bruijne, *Quick Sand*, 2019, group exhibition 'Night Shift', De Studio, Antwerp, photo: Leontien Allermeersch

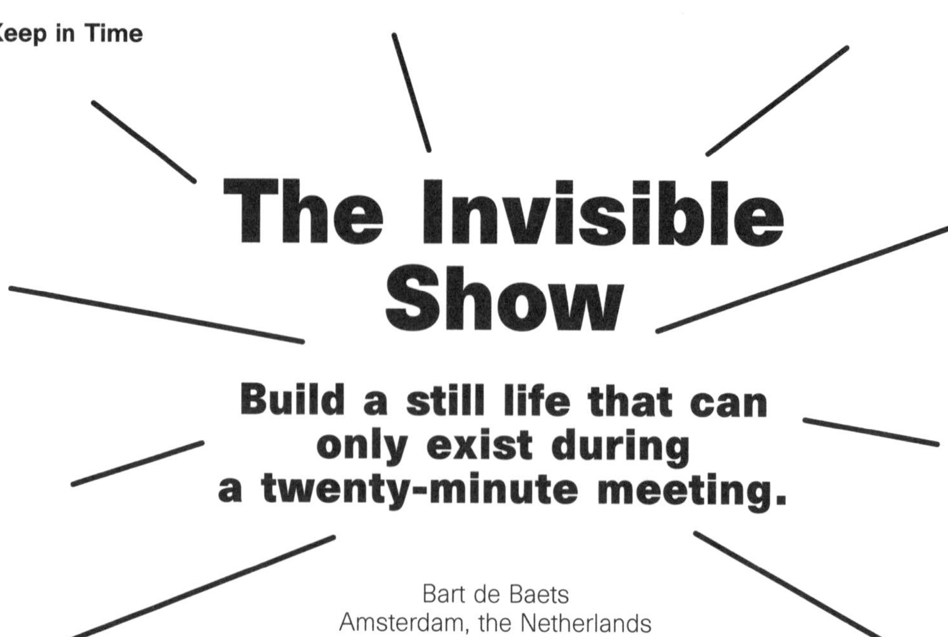

The Invisible Show

Build a still life that can only exist during a twenty-minute meeting.

Bart de Baets
Amsterdam, the Netherlands

Before: Students prepare a temporary still life/sculpture/installation. For inspiration, they study Isa Genzken's sculptured assemblages, Manfred Pernice's architectural models, tricksters like Erwin Wurm and Roman Signer, Fischli and Weiss' sausage pictures, ready-mades and performances, Wolfgang Tillmanns' pictures of fruits and vegetables on windowsills and Thomas Demand's interior remakes.

During: the student (Artist) builds a temporary still life/sculpture/installation in a room. Each Artist is assigned a classmate as a Witness. The Artist, The Teacher, and The Witness are the only ones present in the room. During the twenty-minute meeting, The Witness writes down as many impressions about the work as possible.

After: Based on the impressions, The Witness writes a text and sends it to The Artist. The Witness is asked to consider what the writer's role is: Fan? Lover? Hater? Art critic? etc. Meanwhile, The Artist produces a series of images that reflect the no longer existing work, exploring different avenues to revive the moment shared by The Artist, The Witness and The Teacher. The images should say something about the work and the reasons behind the making of it. The final presentation consists of The Witness' text together with the Artist's images, which can be accompanied by a simple pamphlet of no more than twelve pages.

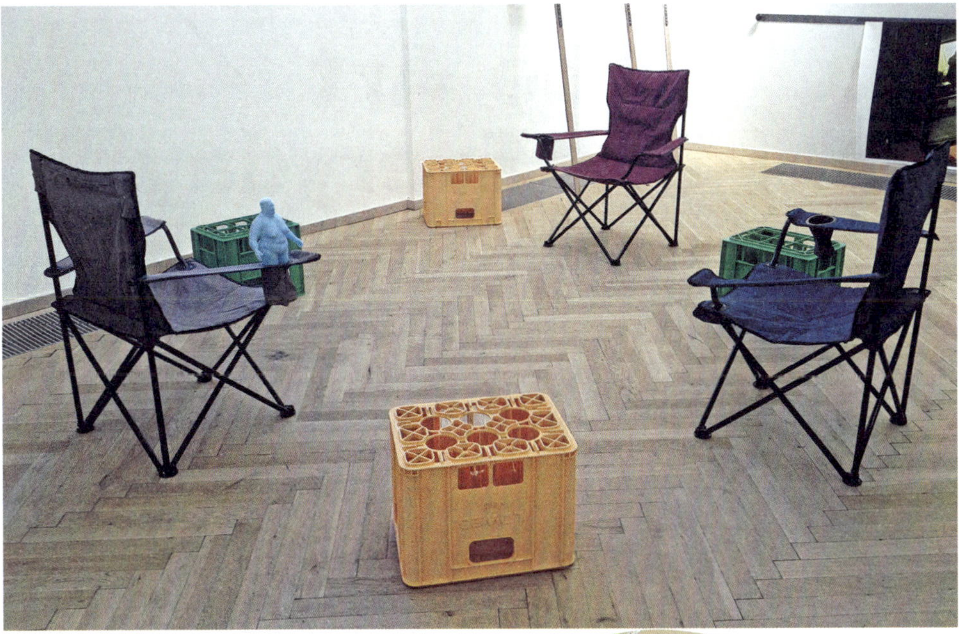

Inspiring Interiors. I stumbled upon this installation–artist unknown–at Kunsthal Charlottenborg, Copenhagen, which sparked ideas for some home renovating, May 2012, photo: Bart de Baets

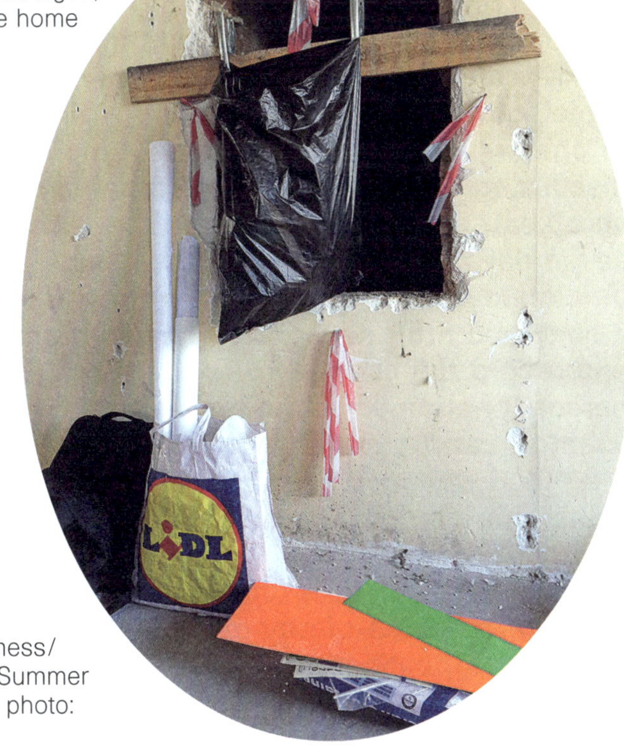

An accidental good-looking mess/ cleaning up after Boomtown Summer School, Ghent, summer 2016, photo: Bart de Baets

The Art of the Everyday

Choose an object, a place, a person or a 'thing' that you can follow for the duration of seven days. Observe the changes that your chosen object/person/thing has been going through during those seven days.

Seher Uysal, Istanbul, Turkey
Mike Bode, Tranås, Sweden

The assignment invariably starts in the same manner: a thirty-minute presentation of artworks, screen grabs from social media, film stills, installation shots, acting as inspiration to open up students' conceptual thought processes. After discussing the shown works, students are asked to choose an object, a place, person or 'thing' which they can follow for seven days. It can be what takes place in one's apartment, a neighbourhood, it could be what you carry in your bag, or a song you are attached to. The students are asked to follow and record the changes or patterns of their chosen object/person/phenomenon during seven days. The observed changes can be merely the reflections of light upon an object, the mood swings while listening to the same song, or expressions on a person's face. How can students present these changes? They are free to use any medium. Students can record sounds or take photographs, they can draw, perform, write, or combine of any of these techniques. After seven days of exploring, collecting, and recording, students return to the group and discuss what they found. When telling stories, the importance of an audience should not be underestimated.

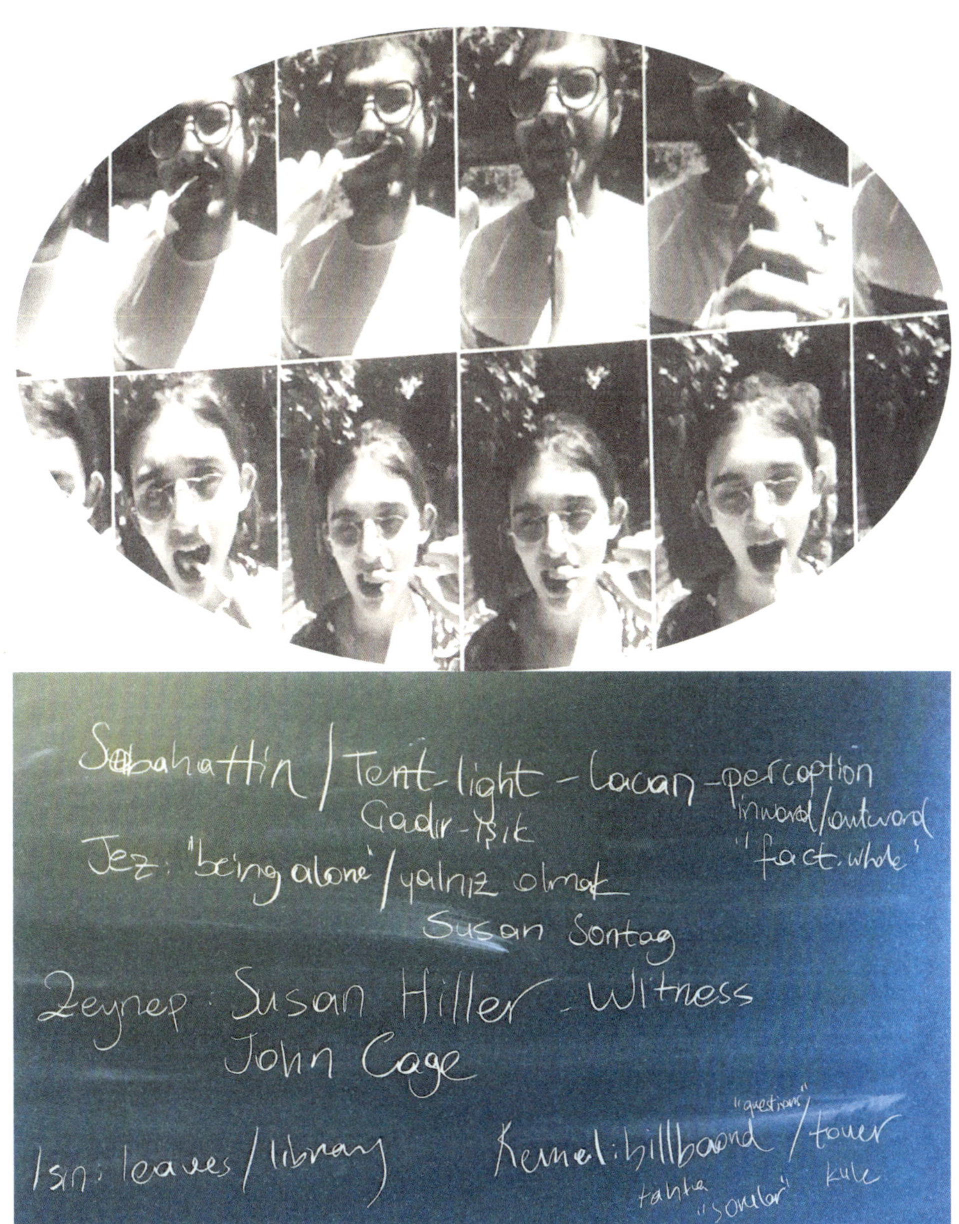

Cell phone images from the Narrative Strategies course at Nesin Art Village, Şirince (TR), 2019

Let It Grow

Make an artwork or design that grows and is ready after one year of maintenance.

Michiel Koelink
Leeuwarden, the Netherlands

In nature, growth takes place on many different timescales and varies in different environments. Artist Gavin Munro lets willow trees grow into chairs, sculptures, lamps, mirror frames, and tables. If you have a piece of his furniture in mind, you have to wait until it can be harvested. This can take a number of years. But then you have a unique piece of furniture that is produced in a radically different way.

Why would you first grow a tree, then cut it down, saw it into small pieces and have it assembled by a furniture maker? Why build furniture if you can also grow it?

Students develop a plan for a growing artwork or design. The design will have to grow for one year until completion. For their designs they have to research the growth characteristics of different plants and/or organisms and choose one that suits their design. They have to find a place for the design to grow and make a schedule for maintaining the design during growth. In the end the designs are harvested and finished and polished if required.

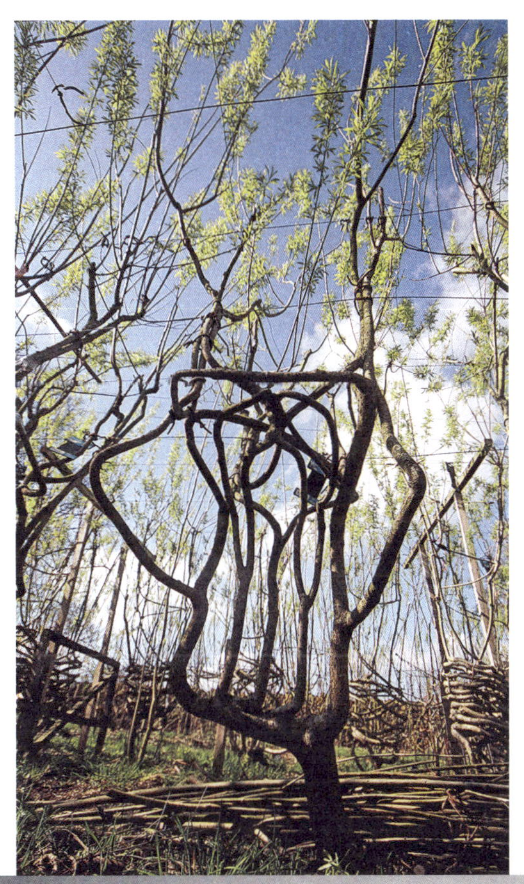

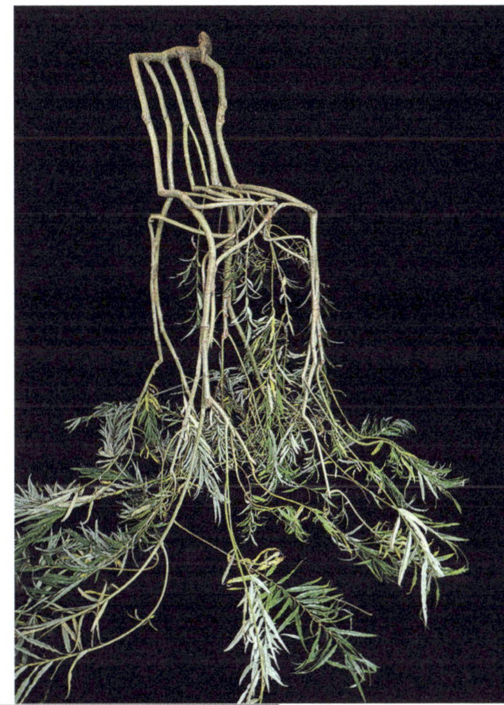

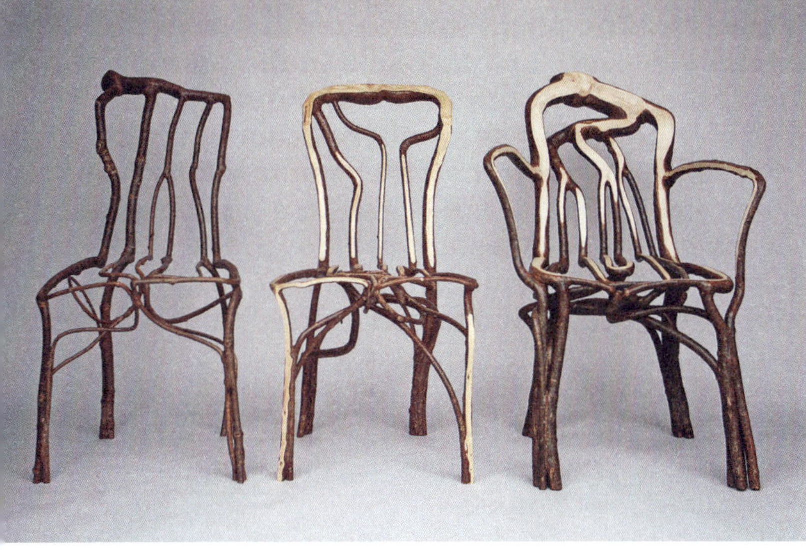

Gavin Munro,
Willow Chairs,
2015–

Empty Your BIC®

You just received a new BIC® ballpoint. Make sure that the pen is empty by next week. Document how you ran out of ink.

Hansje van Halem
Amsterdam, the Netherlands

The BIC® Cristal® pen is a part of the permanent collection of the Museum of Modern Art in New York. 'Its hexagonal shape was taken from the wooden pencil and yields an economical use of plastic along with strength and three grip points giving high writing stability. The pen's transparent polystyrene barrel shows the ink-level. ... A tiny hole in the barrel's body maintains the same air pressure inside and outside the pen. The thick ink flows down due to capillary action from the tube inside the barrel, to feed the ball bearing which spins freely within a brass tip. In 1961, the stainless-steel ball was replaced with much harder tungsten carbide. ... Since 1991 the pen's streamlined polypropylene cap has had a small hole to reduce the risk of suffocation if the cap is inhaled.'—Wikipedia

WARMING UP: You are issued with a full BIC® pen.
Leave it untouched for now. A BIC pen contains enough ink for three kilometres of writing. Reflect on this length.
What exactly is three kilometres?
START & FINISH: Make sure that the pen is empty when you come to the next class. Document how the pen was emptied.

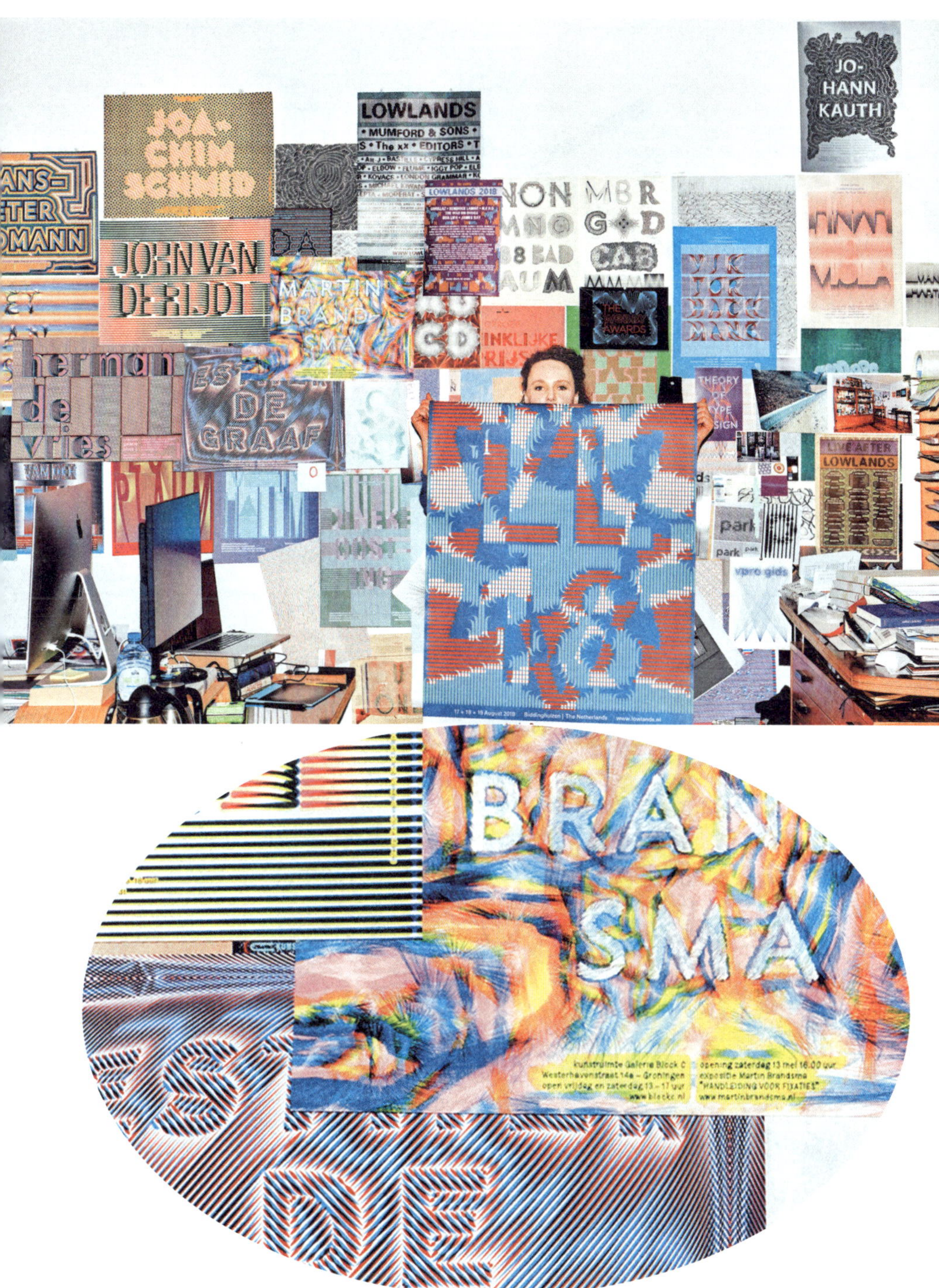

Hansje van Halem in her studio, 2010, photo: Valentina Vos

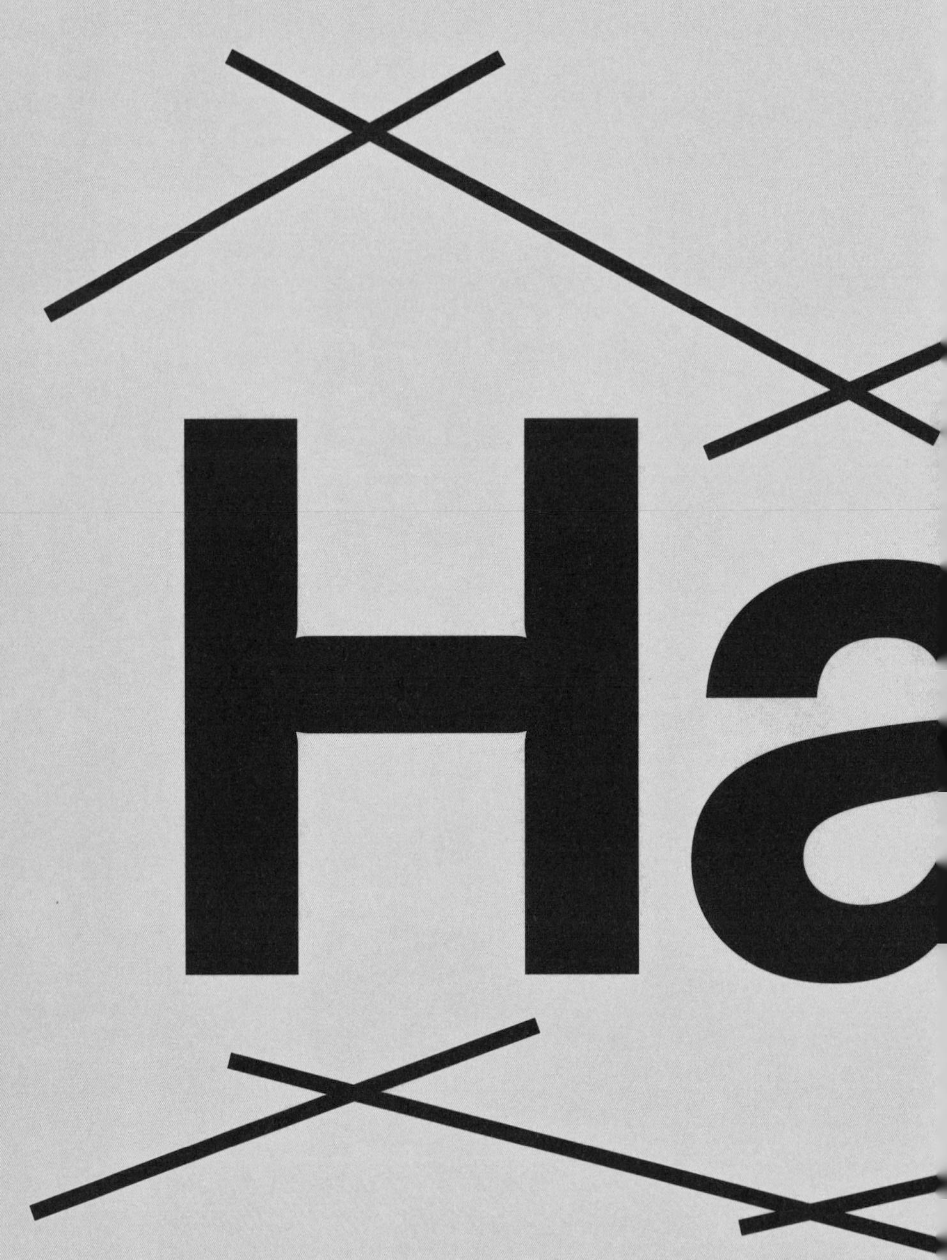

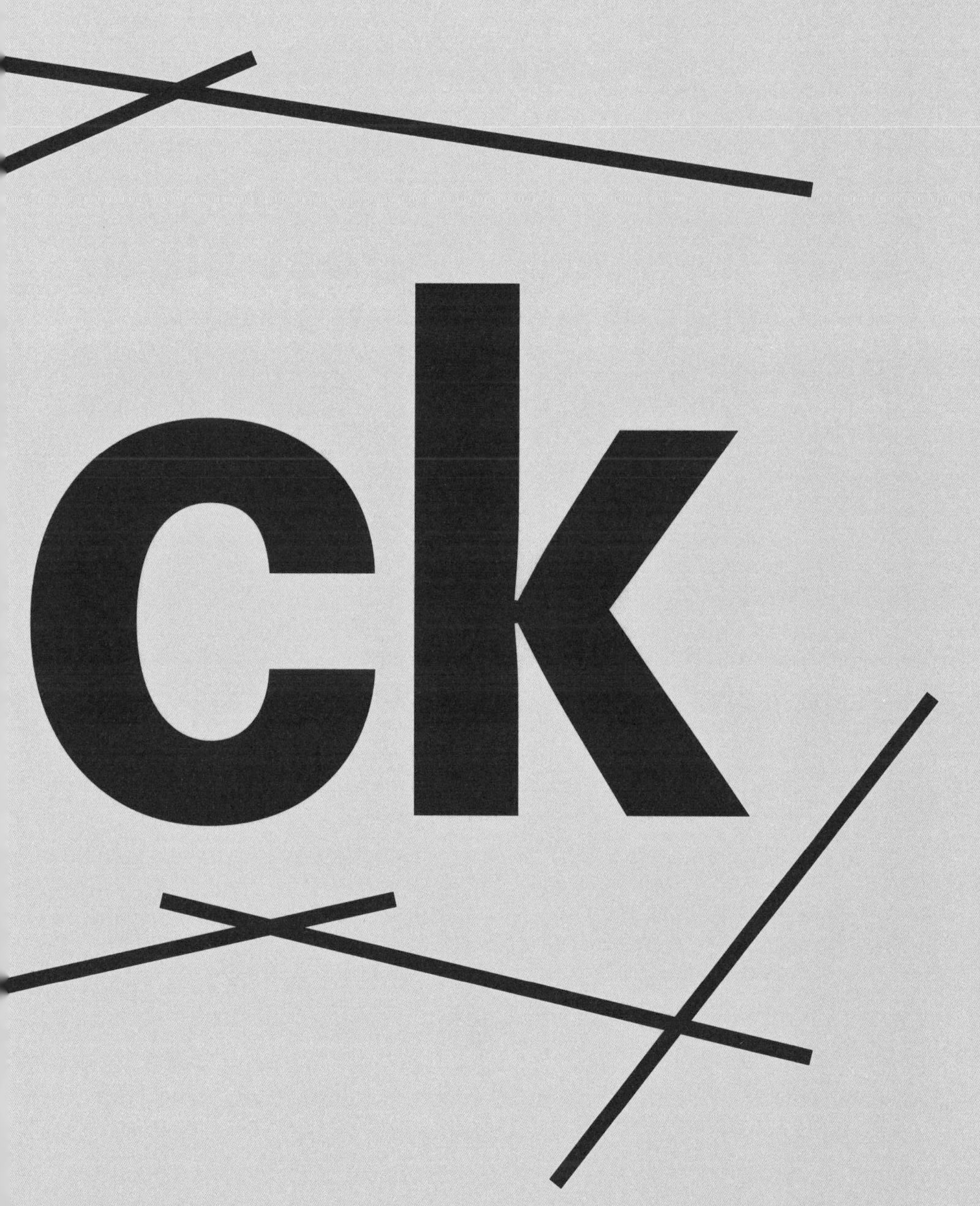
ck

Street View Sculpture

Design a sculpture for a place you have visited only in Google Street View. Make a screenshot and paste your design into the image.

Ronald Nijhof
De Bilt, the Netherlands

When visiting Google Maps, it's easy to get lost if you are in Street View mode. You can go anywhere you want, as long as Google has been there. When moving through the streets one can suddenly feel the urge to add something to a certain spot. For instance, to paint all the buildings green, or to put a sculpture there. Well, you'd better just do it if you feel like it.

Visit a place on earth where you have never been to, search for a good view in Street View mode, make a screenshot, and design a suitable sculpture in any technique you like and make a digital photo collage of how the sculpture would fit into the environment. As an extra step, you can mail your picture to the local authorities and propose this artwork. One day, after trying for years, somebody will say: 'okay, let's go for it'. Trust me. As a warming-up you can play GeoGuesser: https://geoguessr.com.

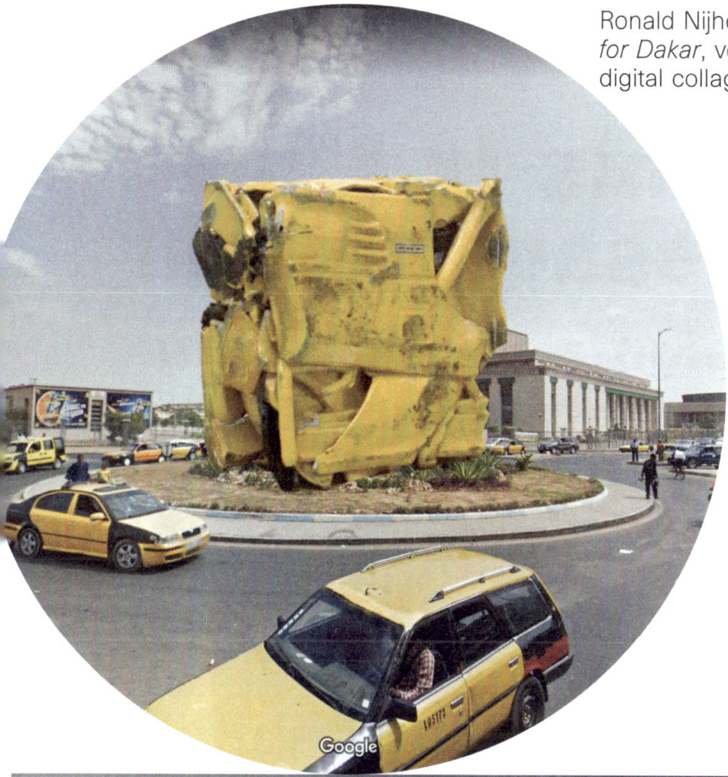

Ronald Nijhof, *Taxi monument for Dakar*, version 1, 2020, digital collage

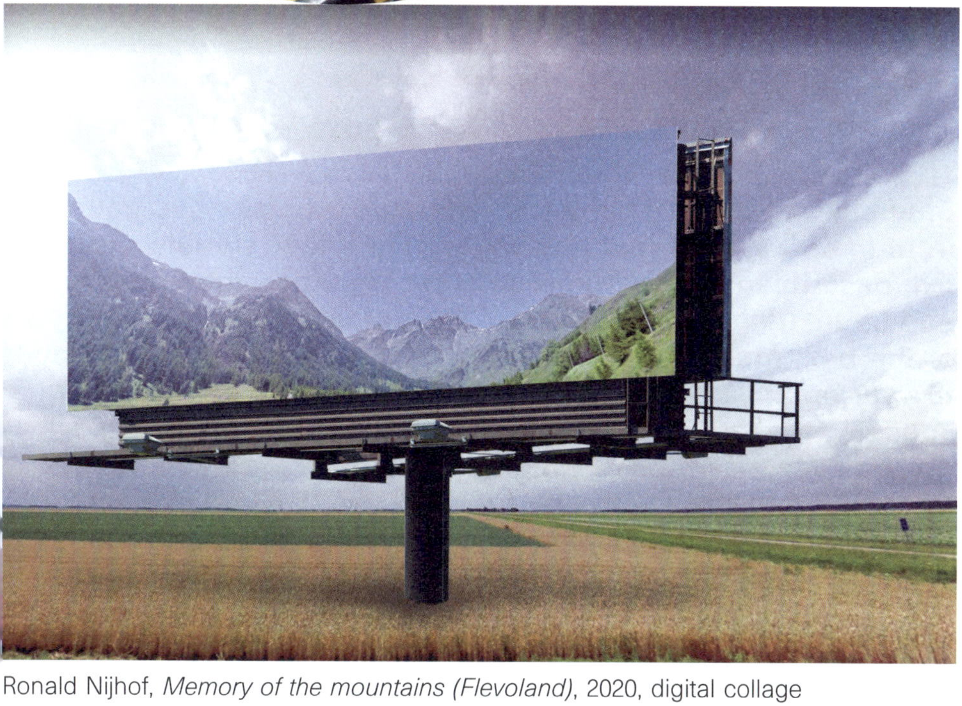

Ronald Nijhof, *Memory of the mountains (Flevoland)*, 2020, digital collage

This Is My Message to You

Design a visual poem by using your last sent text messages.

Saskia van Heugten
Amsterdam, the Netherlands

Students get together in pairs, one student picks five nouns from their last sent text messages. The other student picks five describing words from his/hers. Together, they form new and interesting combinations of the selected words. Think out of the box, make it work visually, let the words speak out loud to your creative brain. For example: wicked grandma, playful Tuesday, darkest gift. Design a visual poem using one or maybe even all of these word combinations. You can choose to design an image with any material you like, with or without using the actual words. Students might come up with the idea to design a poster using mixed media or they might capture the poem in a series of photographs. And remember: don't worry about a thing, every little thing is gonna be alright. This is my message to you!

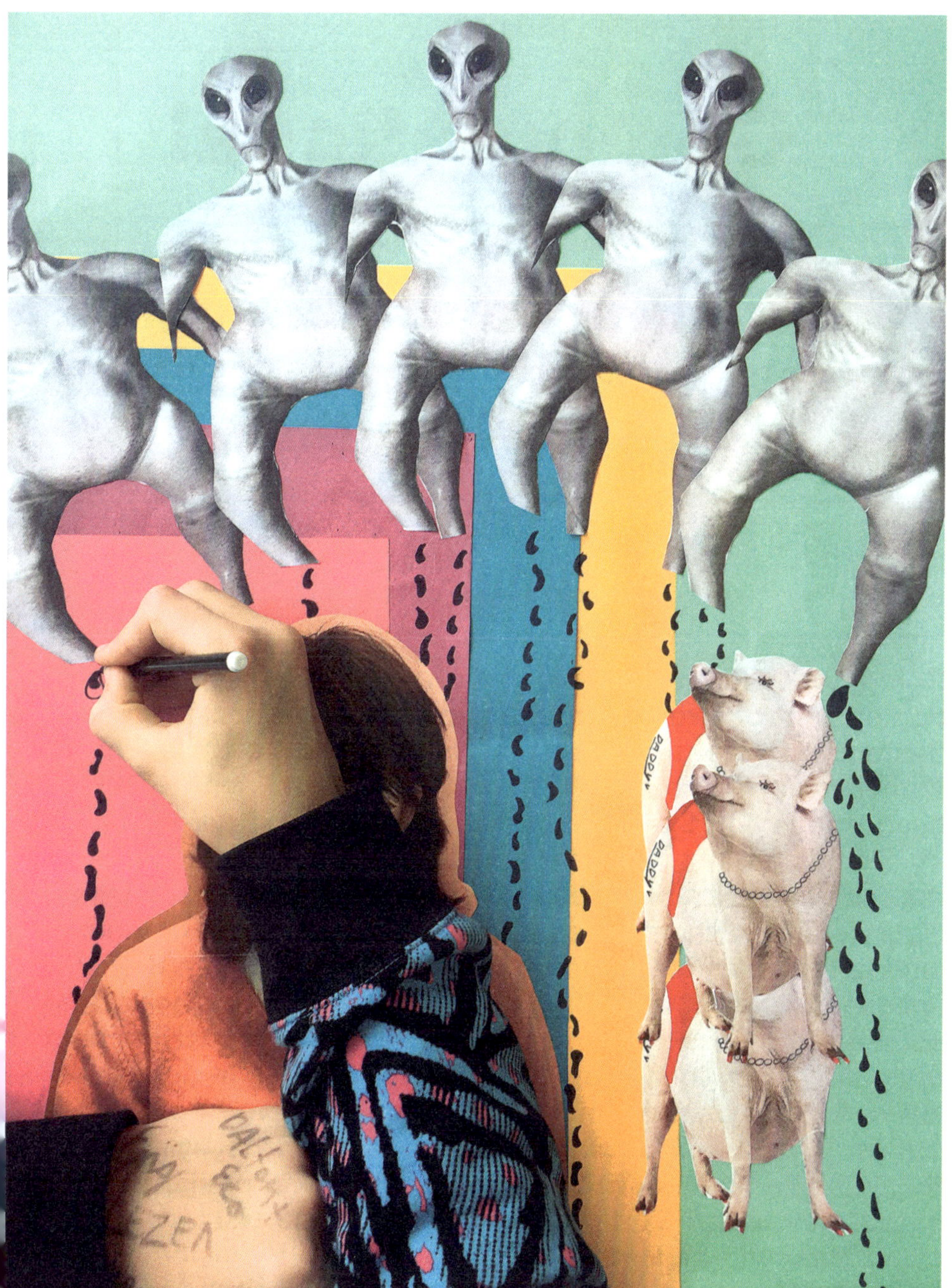

Finn Sceats, *Fat Alien–Happy Emo–Black Rain–Sexy Pig*, 2020, student at work, collage, photo: Saskia van Heugten

Computational Invisibility

Design a way to become invisible to a computer vision algorithm.

Luis Rodil-Fernández
Amsterdam, the Netherlands

Computer vision is now everywhere, from the dystopian deployment of street cameras supporting the Social Credit System in China, to the system used by the Dutch traffic authority to catch speeding cars, to Facebook friend suggestions and Snapchat camera filters. Computer Vision algorithms are notorious for being imperfect. Depending on the task, they can have fail rates of up to 15 percent. These errors manifest themselves in different ways, some of them with potential consequences, like a misinterpretation of a license plate or a raised flag at an airport security check. And sometimes in less consequential contexts like a misalignment in an image, or your Snapchat filter not working in non-white skins. It is in this error margin that we find room to operate as artists. Under what circumstances does the visual system of the machine break down? What does it take to create confusion in these systems? During this assignment you will invent your own strategy to become invisible to a computer vision algorithm by producing unexpected outcomes, false positives, or false negatives. This would be for example, detecting a face where there is none, or not detecting a face where there clearly is one. Work with the error. Find where these algorithms fail to interpret our reality and make a work that exploits this.

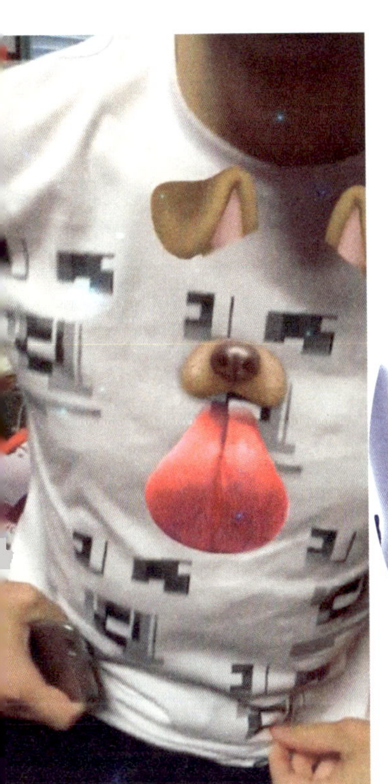

Florian van Zandwijk, *Snapshirt*, 2017

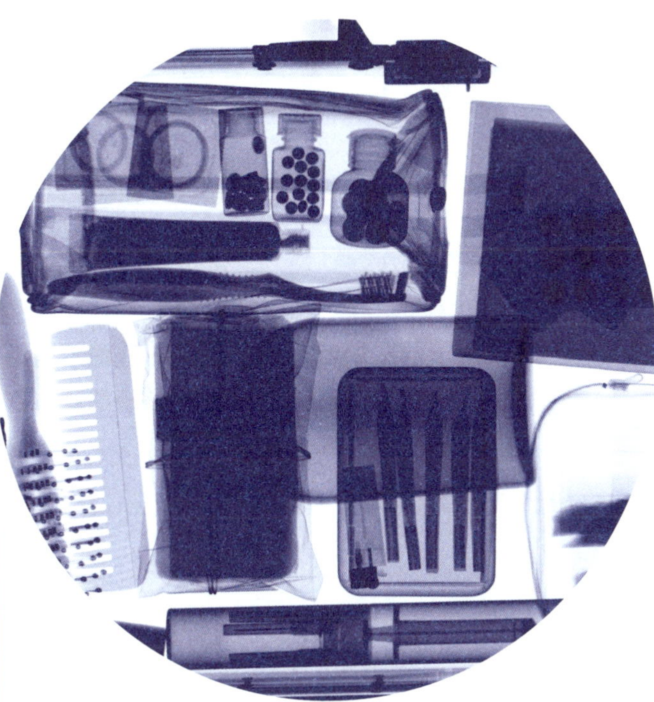

Jippe Liefbroer, *Hello Operator*, 2020

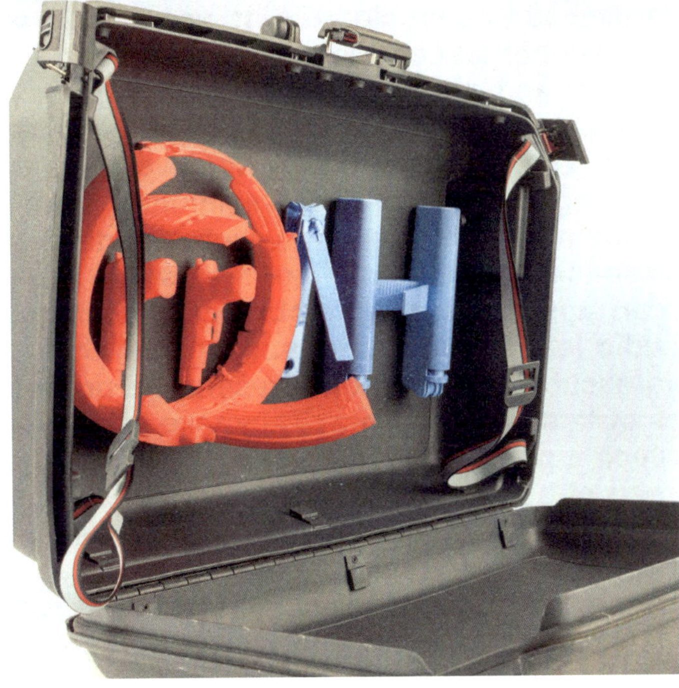

A Clair-Obscure Portrait

Create a clair-obscure portrait with the light of your smartphone in which the technique of chiaroscuro is decontextualized.

Maria Letsiou
Thessaloniki, Greece

With this assignment students familiarize themselves with the decontextualization of artistic strategy and at the same time critique and parody contemporary life, in which smartphones and social media play such a crucial role. It was carried out with junior art high school students of 14 years old and is suitable for both junior and senior high school students (expert level) who have some previous experience in representational drawing from nature. The assignment may be developed as a photography, drawing and/or painting assignment. Students investigate the technique of chiaroscuro, which was developed during the Renaissance. In the beginning, they study and develop skills of art appreciation in Rembrandt's painting portraits. The studio learning includes practice with the technique of chiaroscuro as a way to represent the portraits and other scenes of this particular era. They take photographs of a portrait in which a person, standing in a dark room, stares at the bright screen of a smartphone. During this activity, they can learn aspects of photography with a DSLR camera. Later, they print the photograph and use it as a model in order to create representational drawings and paintings with the chiaroscuro technique. Materials and tools: photography DSLR camera, pencils, acrylic colours, brushes.

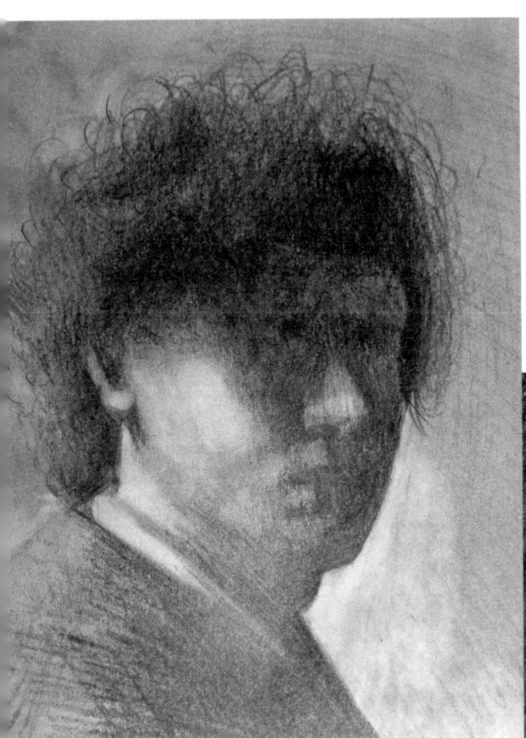

Maria Letsiou, *Reproduction of Rembrandt's Self-Portrait*, 2020, pencil on paper

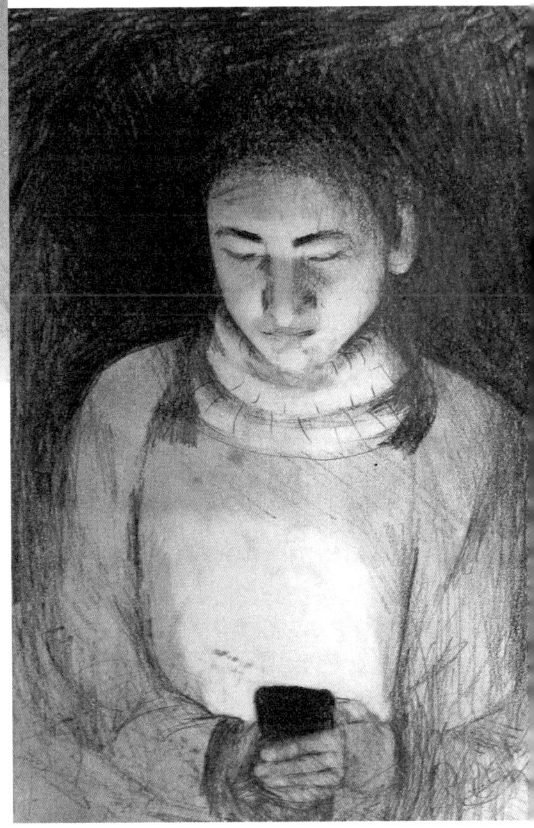

Maria Letsiou, *Portrait with a Smartphone*, 2020, pencil on paper

Phone Sculptures

Make a phone sculpture with your class.

Jen Delos Reyes
Chicago, IL, USA

In 2016 I began to institute a new activity at the start of my classes to address the increasing use of cell phones by students. I found a creative, fun, and participatory solution to this problem: the phone sculpture. At the beginning of each class I would share a Fluxus inspired 'score' that we would create together by using our cell phones. The sculpture would remain until the end of the class. A selection of these instructions:

#5 Exquisite Corpse: Each person is assigned a part of the body so that the total number of people equals the necessary parts to construct a figure. Each person searches an image for their assigned part, and the phones are arranged to make an exquisite corpse.

#6 After Mondrian: Class selects a Mondrian painting to recreate. Each person is assigned either primary red, blue, yellow, or white, and fills their screen with that colour. Phones are placed together to recreate the painting.

#8 After Félix González-Torres: Introduce the class to the work of Félix González-Torres. Search images of his candy spills and enlarge a detail on each phone. Stack phones in corner to create a spill.

#9 Sculpture Garden: Each person searches an image of their favourite example of public sculpture. Class goes outside and arranges the phones as a mini outdoor sculpture garden.

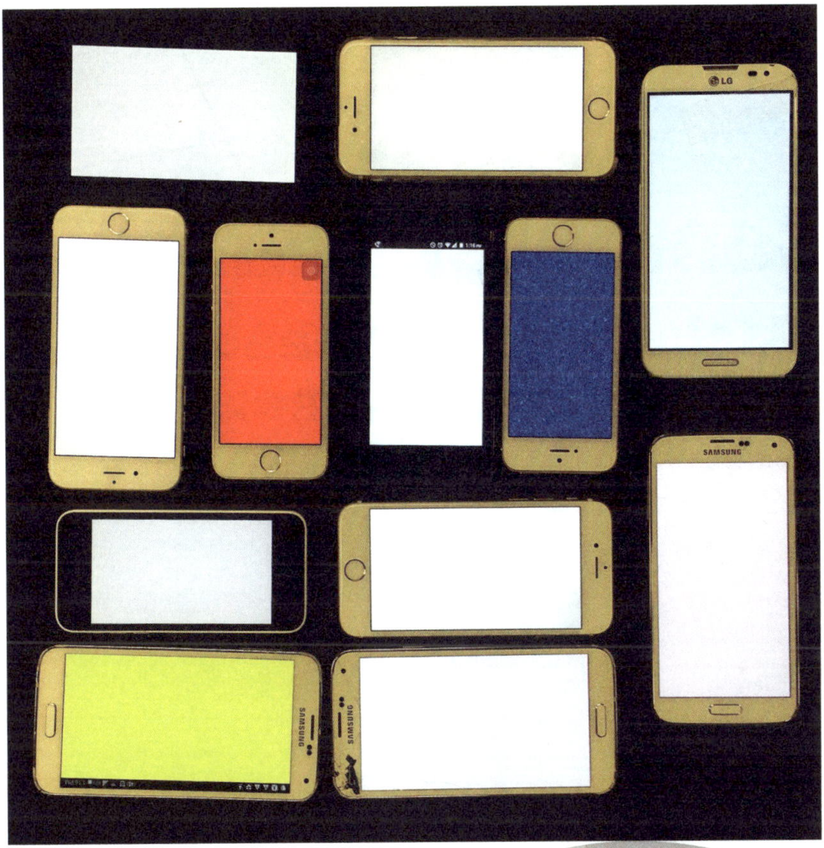

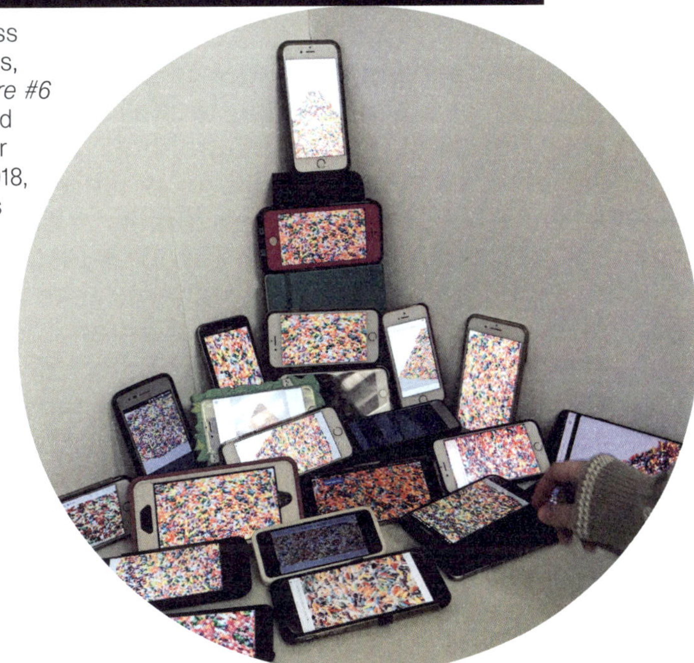

Students of ART 101 class at the University of Illinois, Chicago, *Phone Sculpture #6* After Mondrian, 2018, and *Phone Sculpture #8* After Félix González-Torres, 2018, photos: Jen Delos Reyes

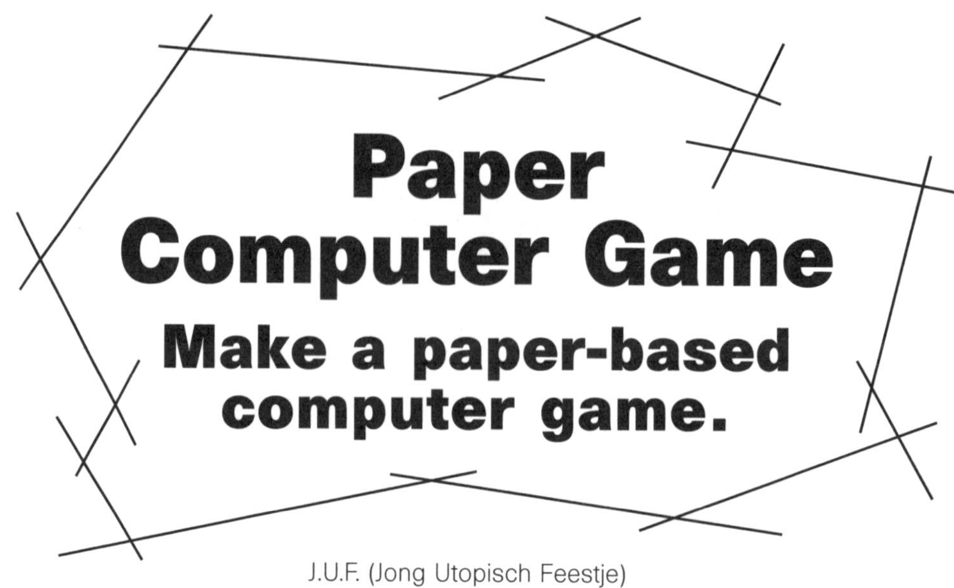

Paper Computer Game

Make a paper-based computer game.

J.U.F. (Jong Utopisch Feestje)
The Hague, the Netherlands

The aim of this assignment is to get students to think about the connection between fiction and reality. Every student draws a hero who undertakes challenges on a scroll of paper, based on the following questions: What abilities in computer games would you like to bring to life? What would you take from your personal life to a digital life? Where does the hero of your game want to go? Who or what beats your hero? What events make her or his journey thrilling? Who are mythical enemies and legendary allies in your quest for life and death?

On a long scroll of paper students take on the role of a hero or become the protagonist of an analogue timeline. They draw their world with the 'pixels' of a school pencil. Students think about: What are the rules of their game? How many lives do they have? Students draw this with eye-catching texts, signs, and symbols on a paper screen. Then they roll up the scroll, put it in a matchbox and present the paper computer game with their own comments and noises to the rest of the class. Optional fun: Make paper emojis and glue them on a stick to make the game interactive.

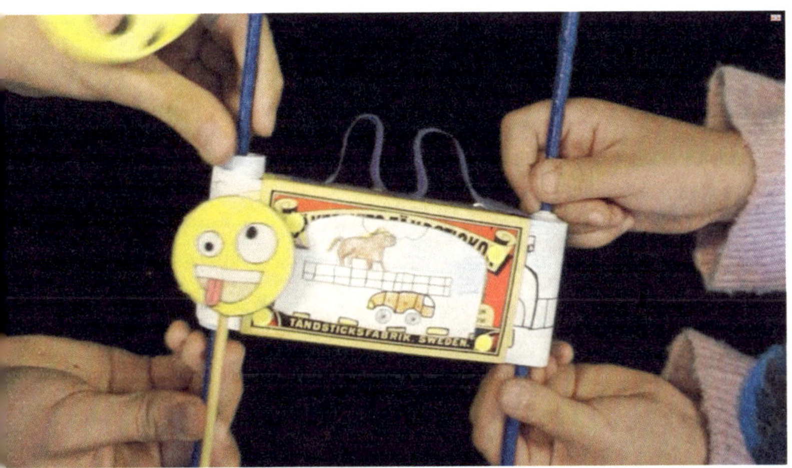

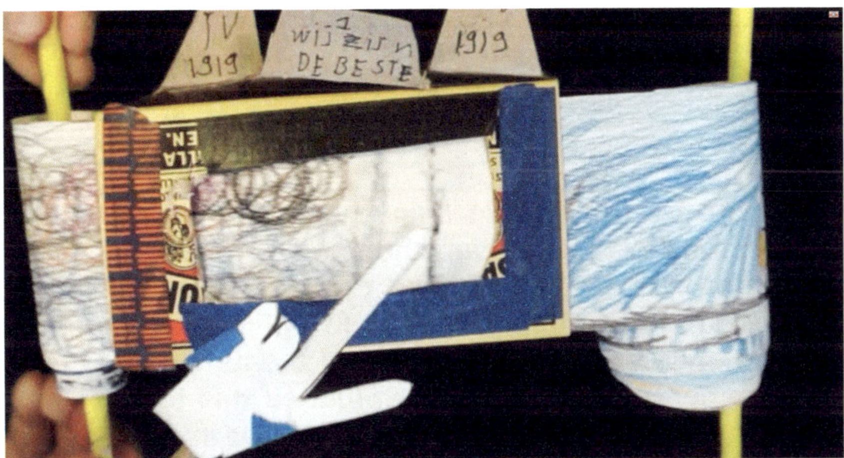

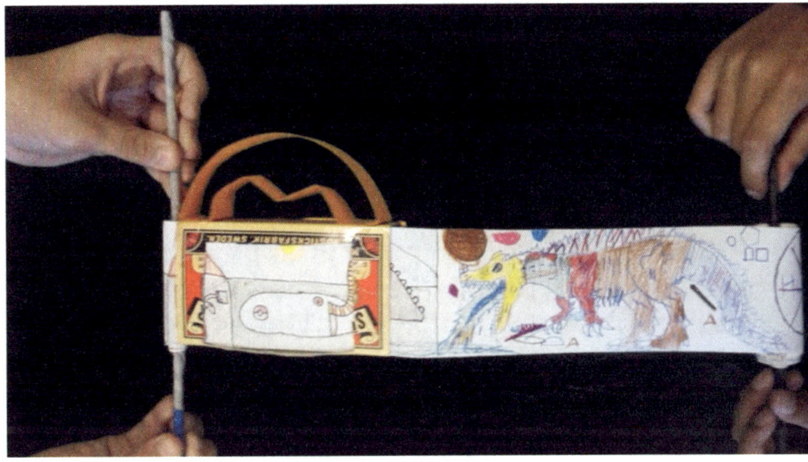

Pupils' work, *Art-S-Cool*, 2019, paper computer game, video still, BS De Buutplaats primary school, The Hague

Let's Talk Computer

Make an artwork in dialogue with Artificial Intelligence.

Arida Bandringa-Hendriks, Hilversum, the Netherlands
Michiel Koelink, Leeuwarden, the Netherlands

Our lives are becoming intertwined with artificial intelligence systems. We talk to our phones, are helped by search engines, get credit ratings based on deep learning and go places handed to us by intelligent online travel agent robots. Artist Merijn Bolink used AI to create *Googles Eyes*. He made a ceramic car tire and uploaded this to googles image recognition system to look for similar images. Google somehow connected an image of a human jawbone to the car tire. He then copied the human jawbone in ceramics and uploaded this image to Google and together they found an image of a human hand, which Merijn copied in ceramics. This process was repeated twenty times and resulted in an artwork made in cocreation with AI.

Students make their own artworks in dialogue with Artificial Intelligence found in apps such as Pinterest, Instagram, or Google Lens. The artworks can be movies, paintings, photographs, etc. The assignment was carried out with students between 13 and 15 years old over the course of three weeks. First, all students draw the same image of a hamburger. They then use the app reverse.photos to find 'similar' images and start their own dialogue by repeating the same steps of drawing and uploading a picture of the result.

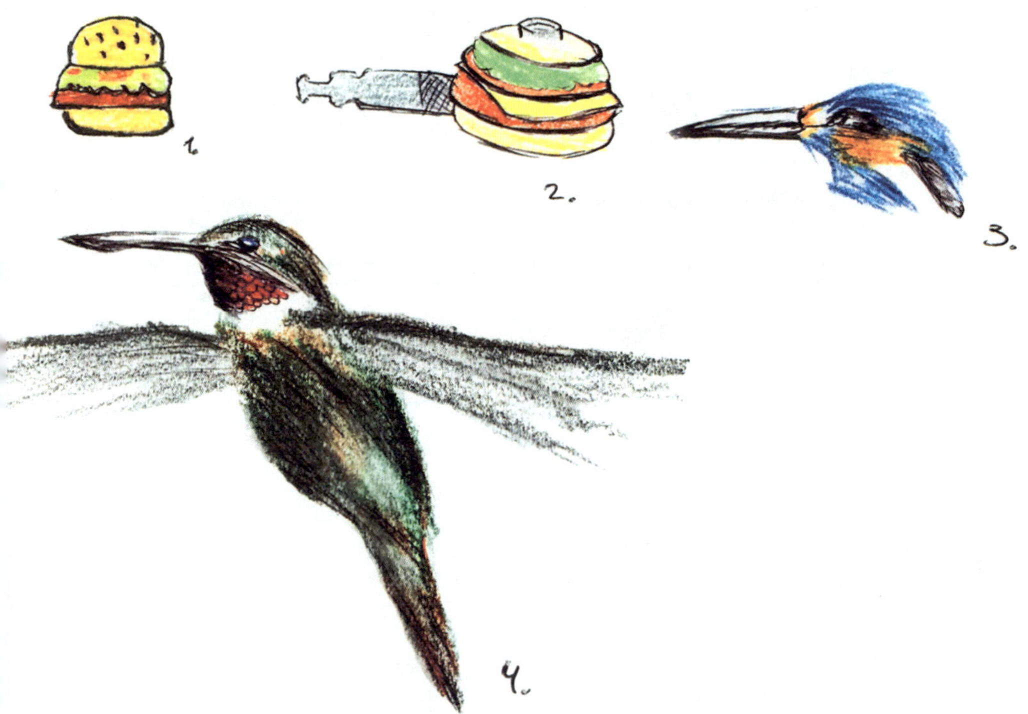

Storm Rombout, 2018, pupil class 2,
Gemeentelijk Gymnasium Hilversum, photo: Arida Bandringa

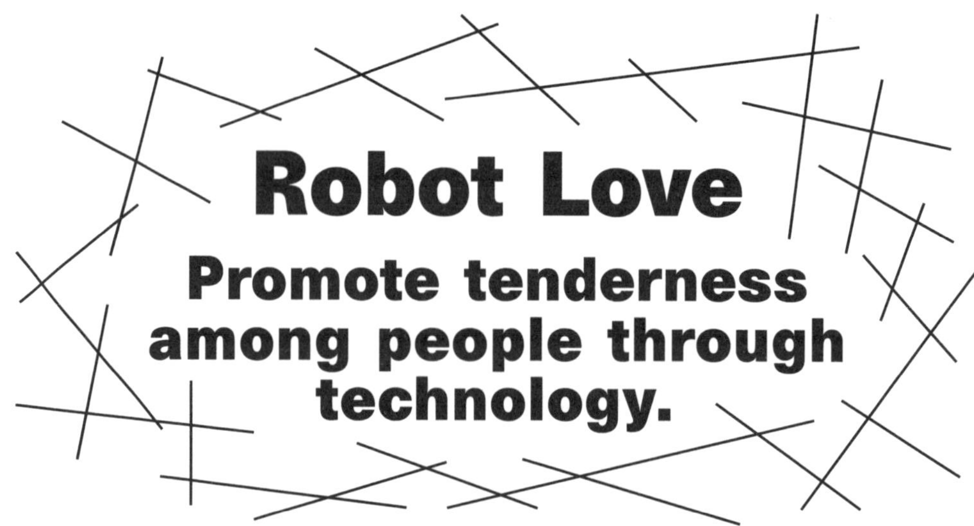

Robot Love

Promote tenderness among people through technology.

Melissa Bremmer, Emiel Heijnen, Anna Hotze,
Emer Beamer, Monique Pijls, Nathalie Roos
Amsterdam, the Netherlands

This assignment took place during the provocative exhibition 'Robot Love' (2018) in Eindhoven, the Netherlands. It was designed as a one-day designathon for pre-service teachers from the domains of the visual arts, STEM, and primary education. During the designathon, these teachers set out to solve the problem of 'How can technology promote tenderness among people' in interdisciplinary groups. This assignment challenges students to approach robotization optimistically, as a process that may stimulate human intimacy. At the same time, the less attractive consequences of robotization may also be investigated. The designathon method—originally developed by Emer Beamer—can be applied to solve trans-disciplinary problems. It consists of different phases, including: introduction (introducing a societal problem that needs to be solved), ideation (exploring possible solutions for the problem), sketching (visualizing a chosen solution) and making (designing a three-dimensional prototype). The students' final prototypes proved to be highly varied: from a bus stop where people slowly move towards each other via a secret conveyor belt to a robot that mediates conversations between grandparents and grandchildren.

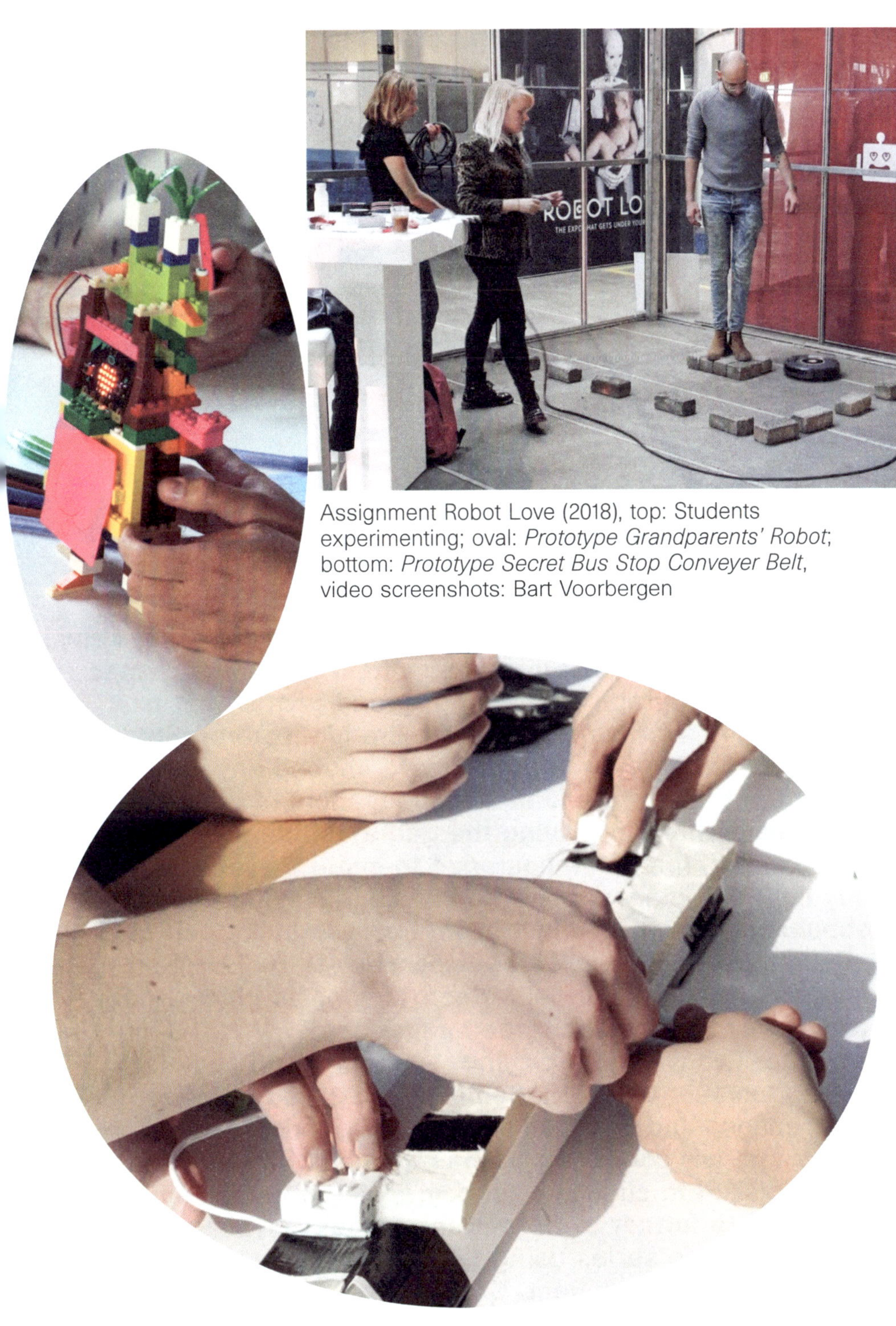

Assignment Robot Love (2018), top: Students experimenting; oval: *Prototype Grandparents' Robot*; bottom: *Prototype Secret Bus Stop Conveyer Belt*, video screenshots: Bart Voorbergen

Digital In-Game Photography

Create a series of photographs using a specific video game as a muse.

Stephanie Veronica Martyniuk
Vancouver, Canada

Students will first be led through a discussion around the question of what is 'Video Game Photography'? (using virtual cameras; screenshots; in-game selfies; looking at games that use photography as gameplay and games that use photography as a fun side-quest/extra fun feature). Students will then be given an opportunity to choose any game they have access to and make screenshots of during their gameplay. Through playing the game and capturing images, students will first be encouraged to capture everything and anything that piques their interest while playing. Students should compile their images and begin to build their own media library. They will also be expected to document their images in a visual journal format (blog or psychical book) with their thoughts about the images.

After two weeks of playing, exploring, and compiling visual documentation, students will be asked to reflect on their images and to try and find corresponding themes and styles that are consistent in their image library. Students will be asked to choose a photographic theme or topic that they wish to further explore in the virtual world, and create a photographic series using the virtual camera as their documentation instrument. Cropping/editing/re-mixing will be encouraged.

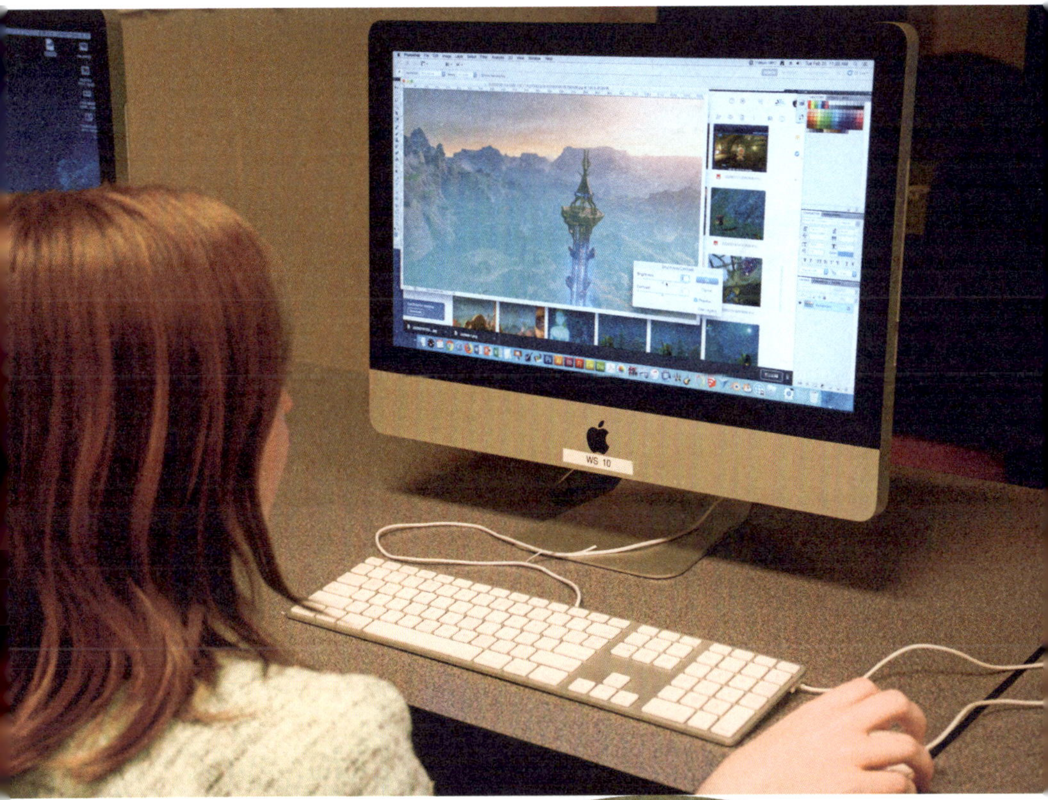

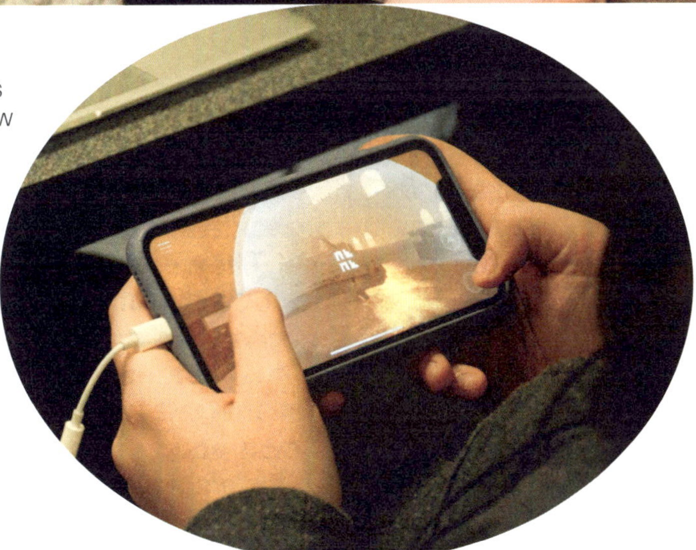

Pupils' work, *Video Game Photography*, 2020, Grade 11 Digital Communications and Technology, Burnsview Secondary School, Delta, British Columbia, photo: Stephanie Martyniuk

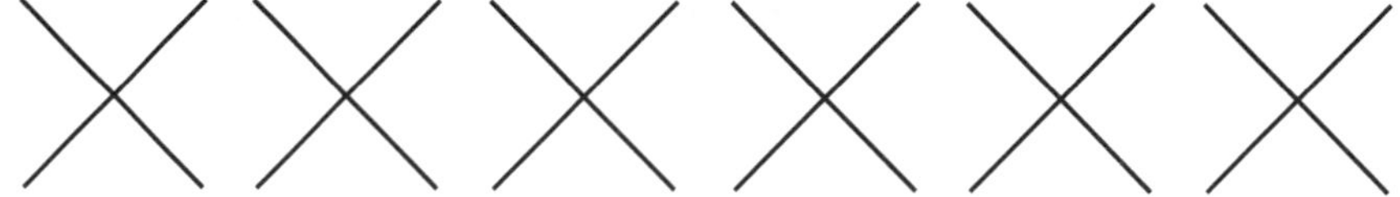

Action Figures

Create your own 3D-printed action figure.

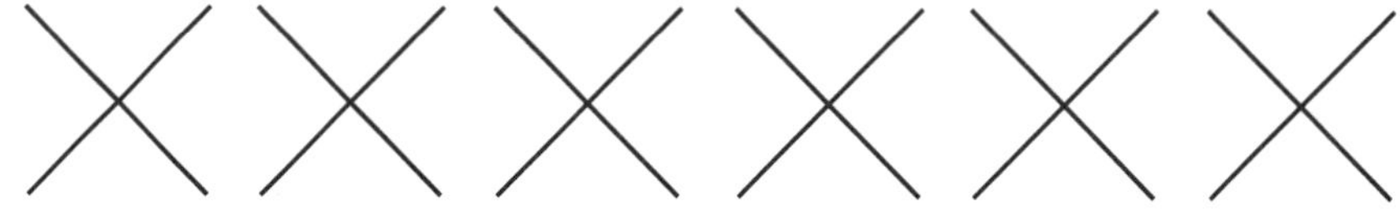

Pallas Linssen-van der Doorn
Breda, the Netherlands

Students first reflect on the action figures they like. What are the powers and skills that make the figures special? What do they look like? What colours are used and which morphology and shapes? They then decide what super powers their action figure will possess. They create their own sketches on paper. The best sketch will be transformed from 2D-paper to a 3D-design. The 3D-designs they create are made with their own school tablets using the free online software Tinkercard. When the 3D-design is finished, it will be printed and students will have designed their own action figures! The designs are printed in white, but it's also possible to paint the white sculpture with acrylic paint. The 3D-models that are made with Tinkercard can be coloured in 3D-paint. This edit makes it possible to convert 3D-printed models to a 3D-hologram. The 3D-printed sculptures made by our students can also be shown through our hologram.

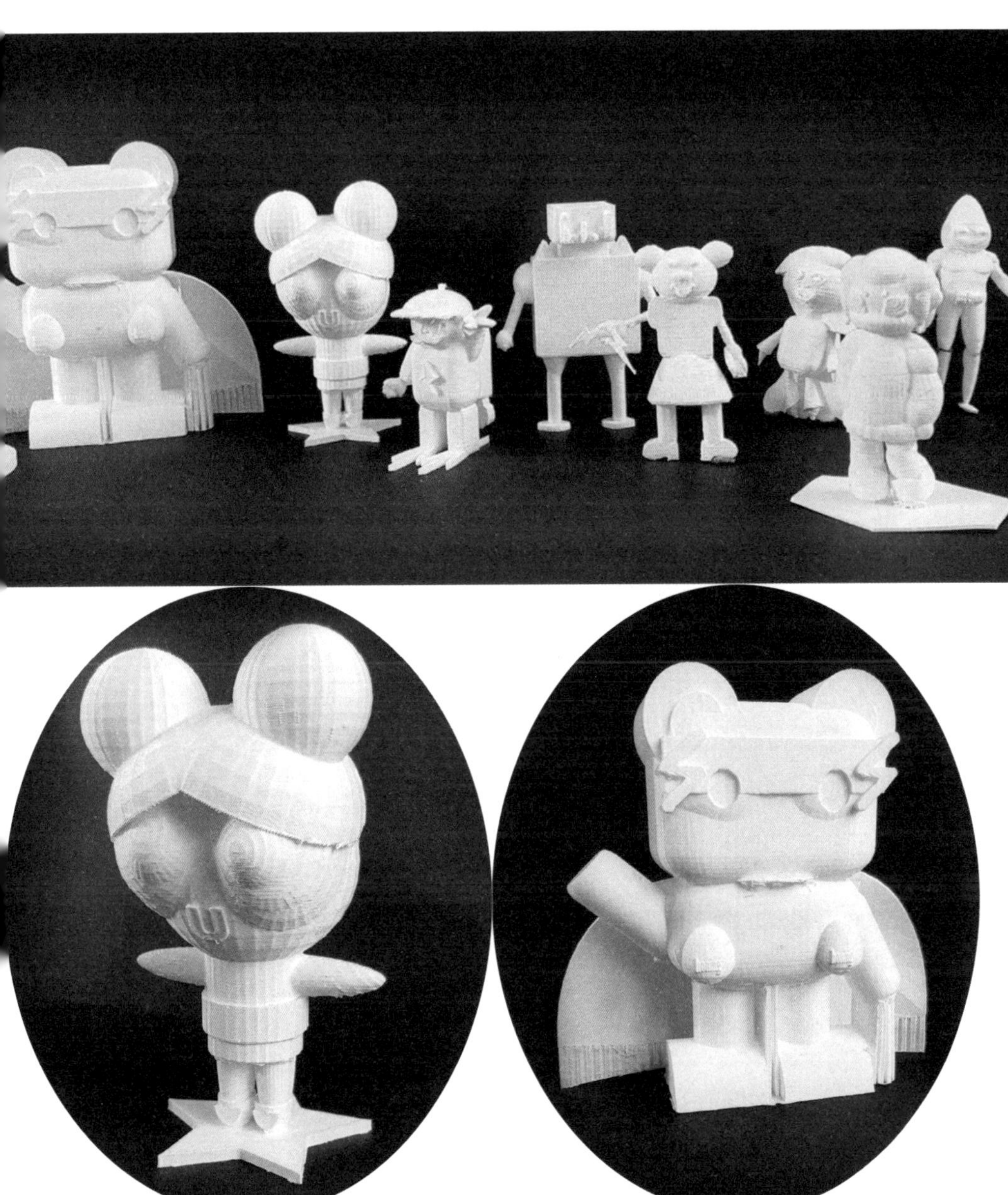

Pupils' work, *Action Figures*, 2019, 3D design,
De Nassau secondary school, Breda

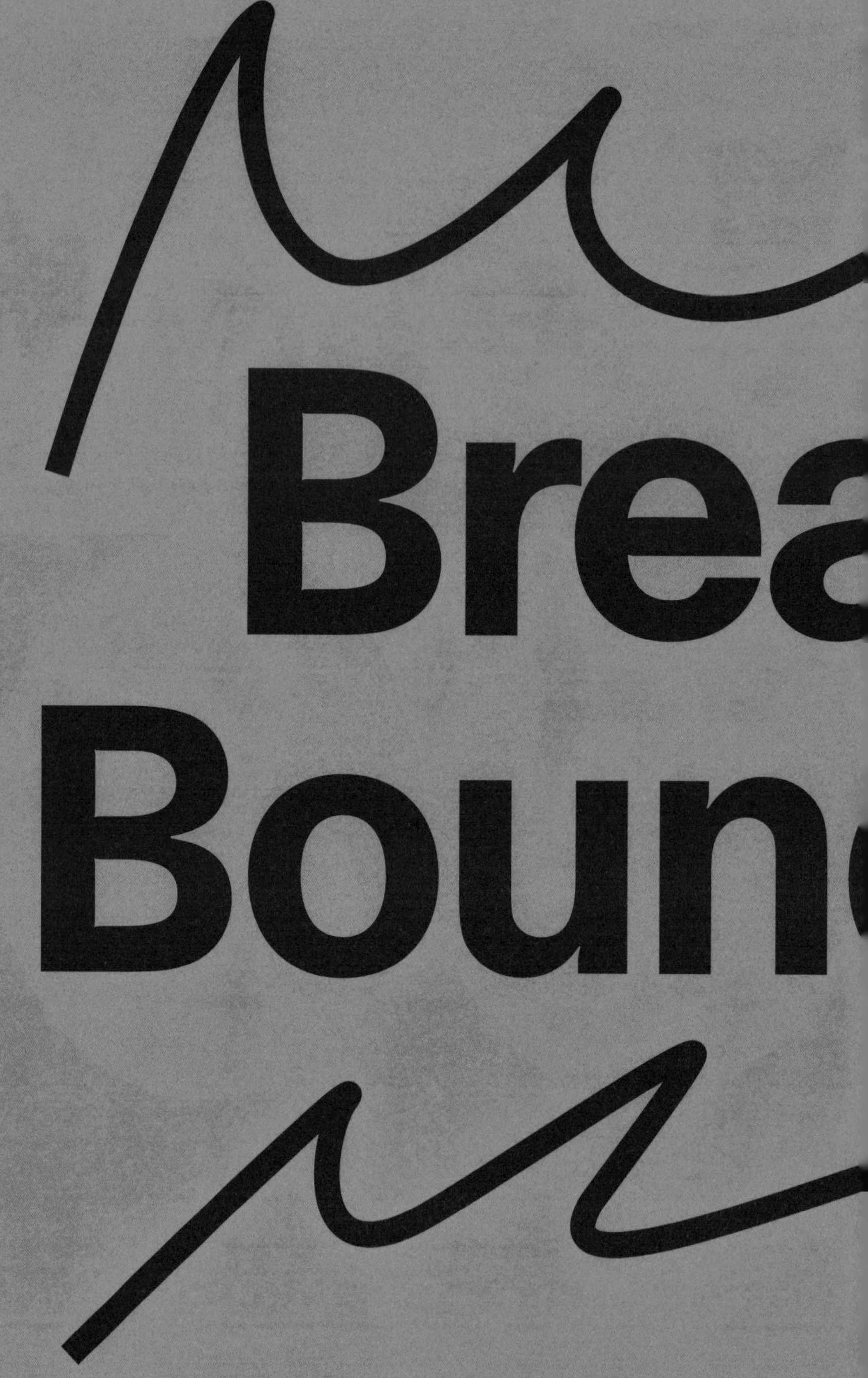
Brea
Boun

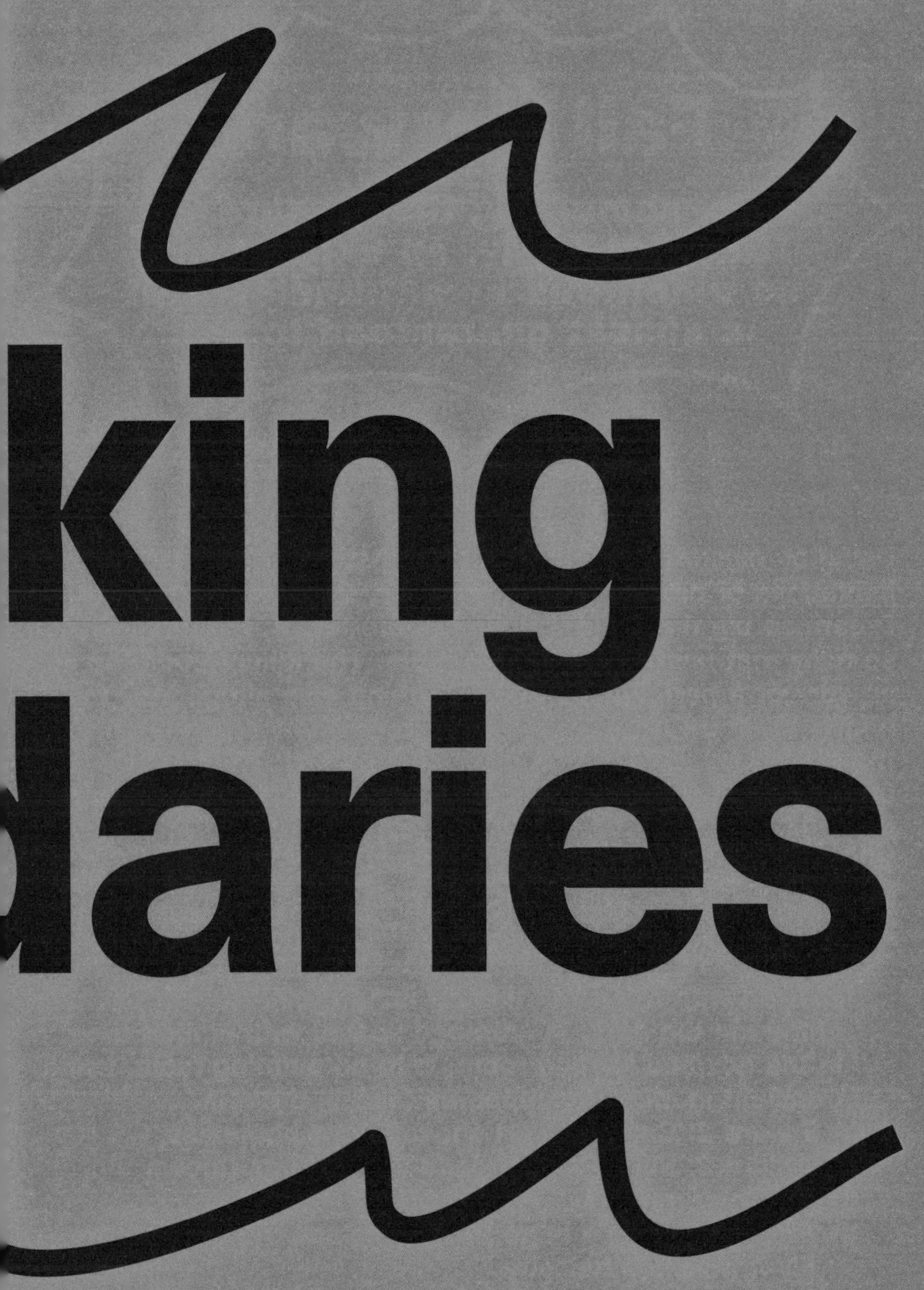
king
daries

Fail Forward

Try something that is sure to turn out badly, an experiment so ambitious or outlandish that is almost guaranteed to fail.

Mark Graham
Salt Lake City, UT, USA

Using an existing or self-imposed constraint or your own limitations or personal boundaries, try something that will fail. Dream so big that you are almost sure to fail, or try something so risky that failure seems inevitable. The failure could be an artwork or a performance or something else altogether. Your efforts must be documented, no matter how embarrassing they might be. Years later one student said: 'I guess the topic has been on my mind because I feel like I'm failing at a lot of things lately. And it has been very discouraging... Your assignment has come to me over and over again because it was the first time that I'd been told that failure was a good thing. Something to seek after.' Examples include:

- **Failure 1: Seeing the invisible: Finding Jesus in paintings painted with mud with the left hand, painted over journal entries in the dark, in cramped space, with limited time, in the hospital waiting room, with no painting tools, using transient medium, dropped and left in the rain.**
- **Failure 2: Create an art show for the homeless.**
- **Failure 2: Blindfolded, evade soft objects thrown at me by my wife.**
- **Failure 3: Build a huge paper airplane from newsprint. Fly it from the balcony.**
- **Failure 4: No possible way a person could gather all the shotgun shells in Saratoga Springs.**

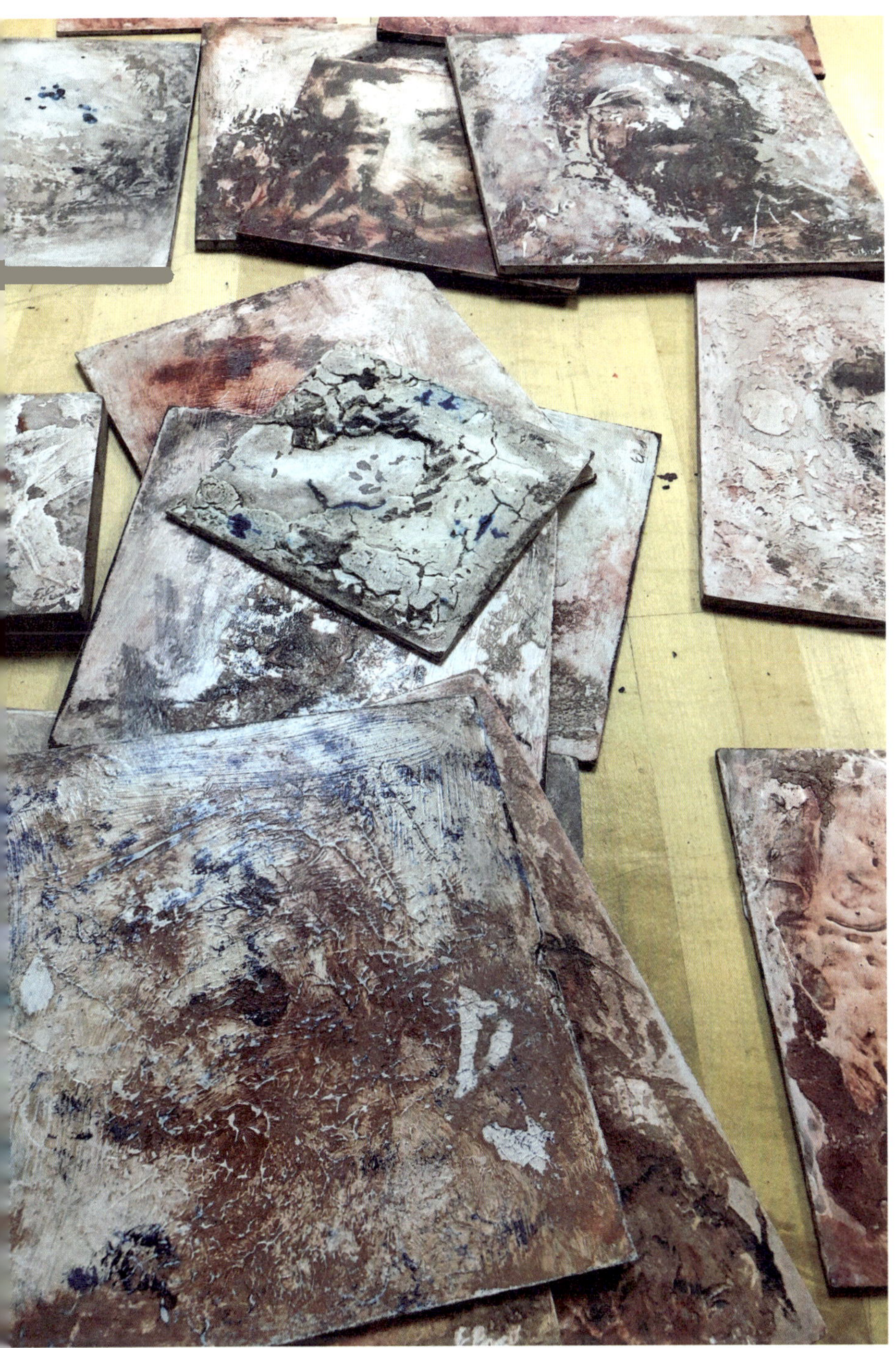

Emmalee Powell, *Seeing the Invisible*, mixed media (ink, paint, mud), 2019

Fictional Product or Service

Think of a unique, fictional, absurd product or service and pitch it professionally and convincingly with images and words.

Ricardo Makosi
Amsterdam, the Netherlands

This assignment is about the narrative behind a made-up product or service. If you tell an incredulous story convincingly and with enthusiasm, people will automatically listen to it, believe you and eventually will want to buy the product! The fictional product is outside reality and has no limitations, technologically or otherwise.

The project has a unique brand name, a slogan, a graphically designed logo, and its use must be clearly described in words and images and visualized in the form of a mood board, product visualization, and photo storyboard. The team (of four students max) that succeeds in seriously pitching and selling the most outrageous product or service, wins!

This exercise is one in a series of concept classes taught in the Media Design study programme of the ROC Amsterdam. Students in vocational training must be able to approach various issues from a conceptual angle, and develop, design, and eventually present them professionally. Students themselves must be part of their photo storyboard, because a story in which you play a part yourself is even more credible! The result is that the most hilarious and inspiring products or services emerge from the imagination of the students.

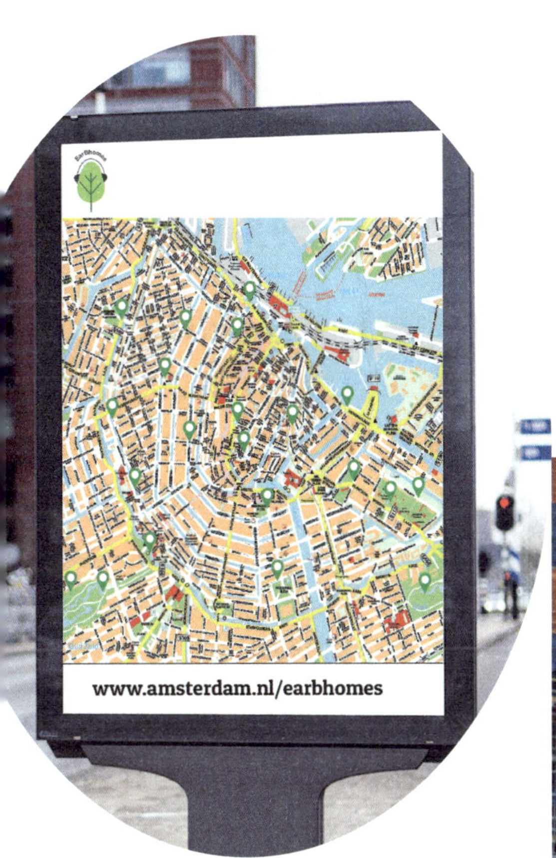

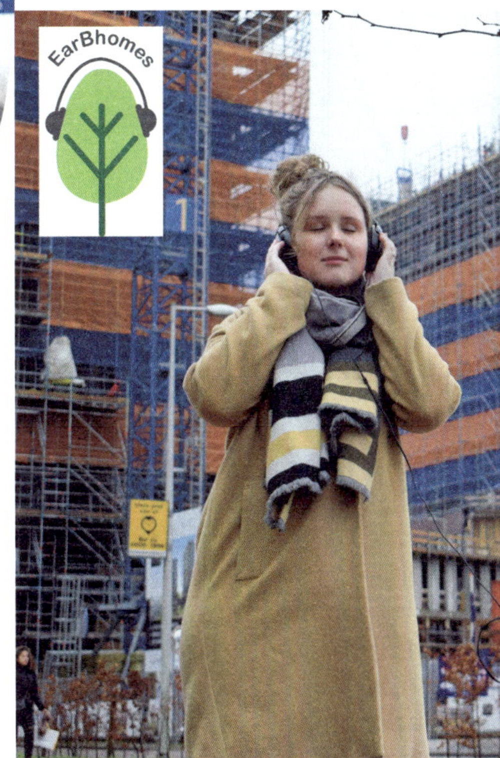

Students' work, *#EarBhomes*, 2018–2019, second year Conceptual Design, Intermediate Vocational Education, Media Design, ROCvA, Amsterdam

#EARBHOMES, a tree with earphones. If you're tired of the flood of stimuli in the city, if you're stressed, or miss nature, you can listen to the quiet and sounds of nature. Think of birds, leaves, a gentle breeze. The tree is equipped with a device that plays these sounds. It's a solution for surviving life in a big, loud city like Amsterdam.

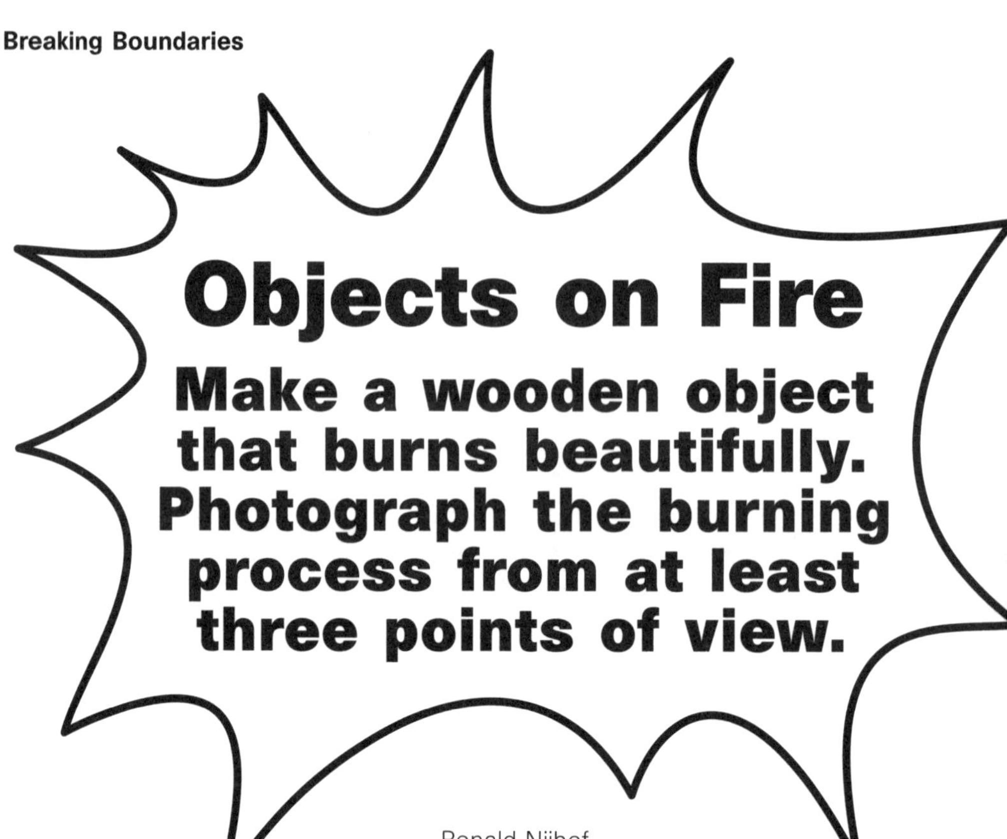

Ronald Nijhof
De Bilt, the Netherlands

Making an object that burns beautifully is an exercise in thinking ahead in the process and working towards an irreversible moment. You are working towards a performative moment, and timing is of the essence. The assignment consists of three actions: making the object, destroying the object, and recording this process. It teaches you that destruction is also principle of expression.

An interesting notion is that not the sculpture, but the series of photographs is the artwork. You leave the source of the image behind and have to make do with the documentation. The photographs are also a memory of the vanished artwork: there is no undo, no ctrl-z. Well, at least we still have the photos. You can also make multiple objects, a series, or a group of sculptures.

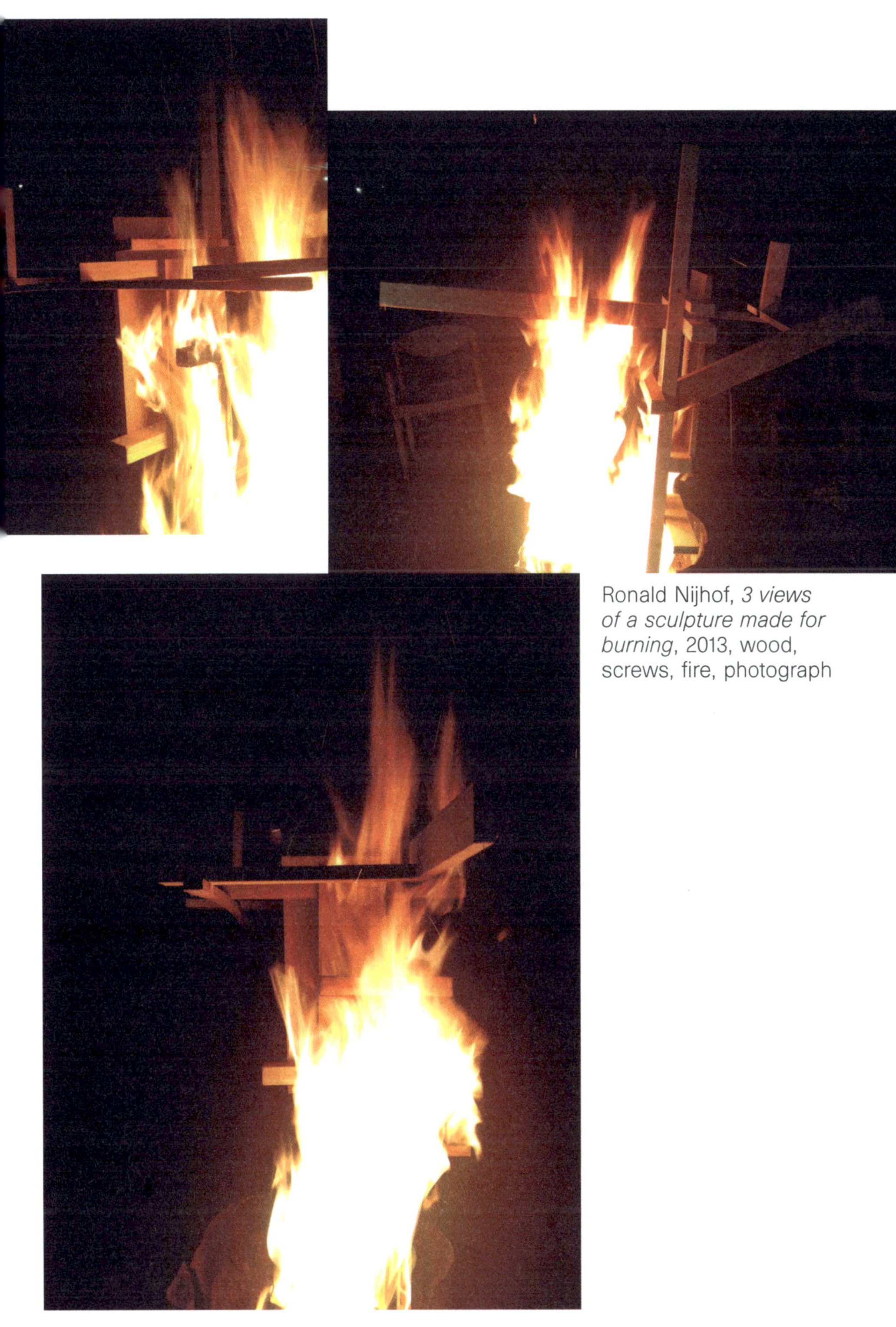

Ronald Nijhof, *3 views of a sculpture made for burning*, 2013, wood, screws, fire, photograph

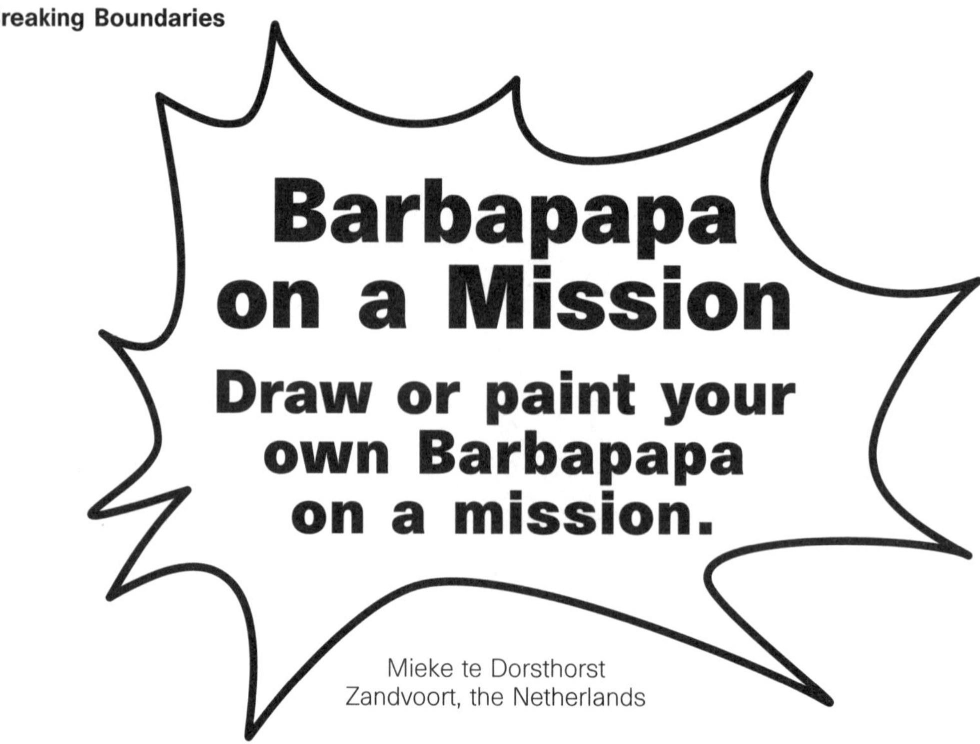

Barbapapa on a Mission

Draw or paint your own Barbapapa on a mission.

Mieke te Dorsthorst
Zandvoort, the Netherlands

You probably know them—Barbapapas can do anything and change their shape at will. They like to do the right thing, help people in need, or make the world a little bit safer. Students will work on imagining their own Barbapapa with special characteristics, starting from the questions 'on what mission will you sent your own Barbapapa?' and 'how will it change its shape to reach its goal?'

Students are called upon to identify with the Barbapapa characters, in combination with solving a personal or societal problem. The assignment was carried out by 12-14-year-old students of a Rudolph Steiner school. One of the principles of this type of education is to be in sync with the developmental stage of students. Children in this age group are still partly living in their own uninhibited fantasy and possess strong powers of imagination. At the same time, the education is in line with their blossoming individuality and interest in today's world. Students are allowed to express what issues concern them. The starting point of this didactics is therefore 'connecting'. Stimulate their motivation to work on content by connecting head, heart, and hands. And also connect to the world and art.

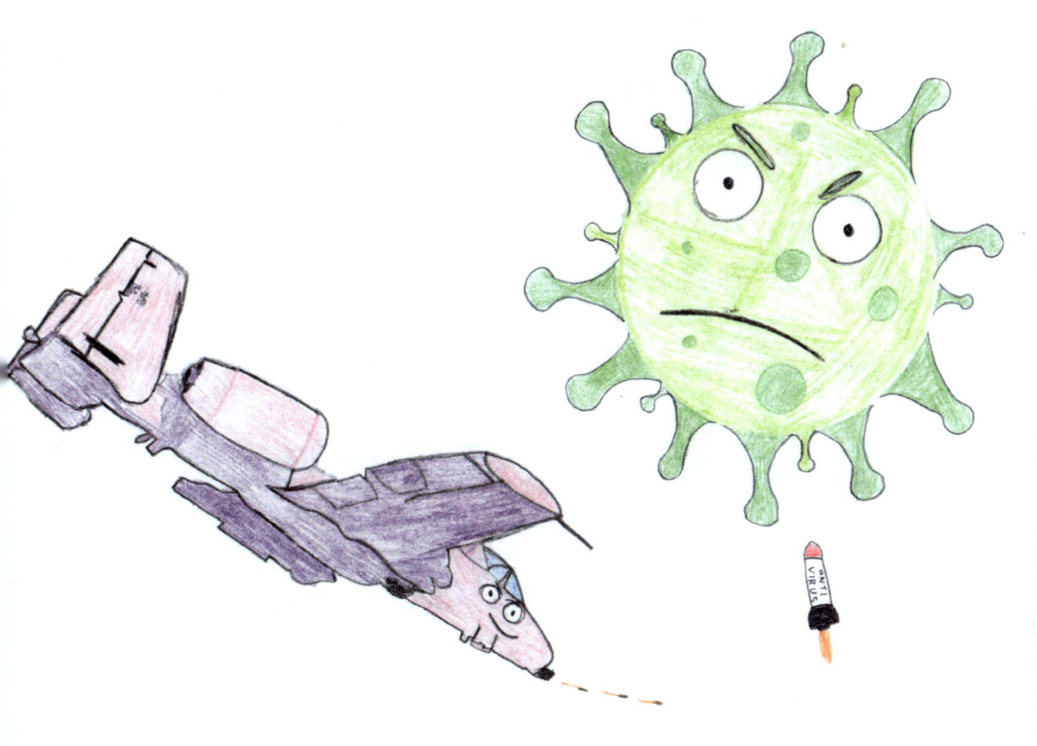

Dylano van Zwol, 2020, 14 years, Kennemer College secondary school, Beverwijk

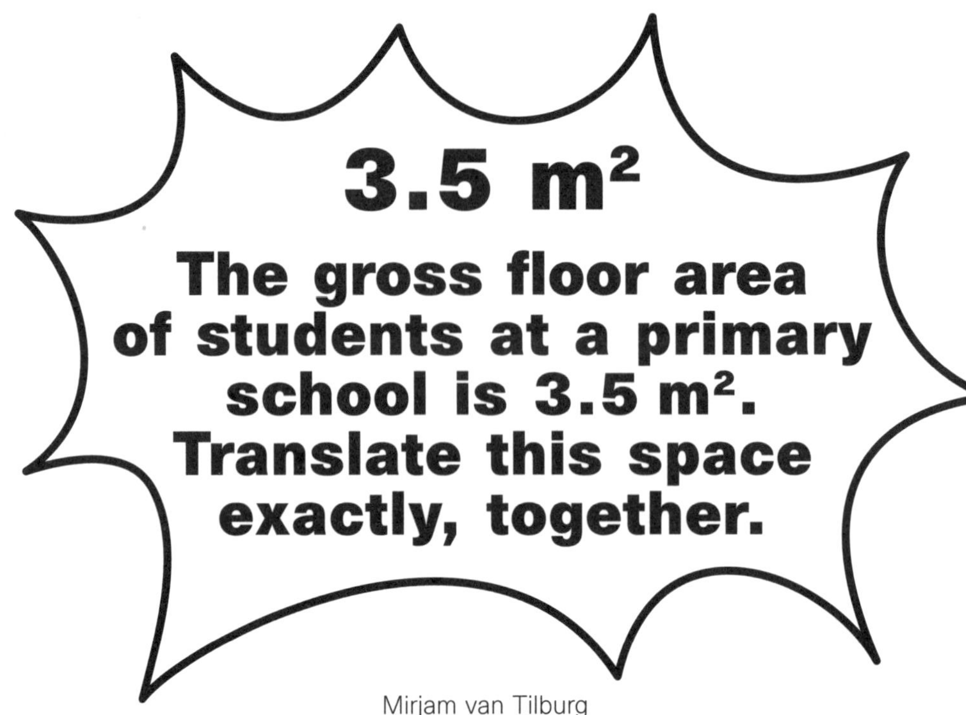

Mirjam van Tilburg
Rotterdam, the Netherlands

This assignment was created together with my colleague Noelle Cuppens and carried out by students of a teacher training course in visual art and design. We wanted to challenge the students to embrace their individuality in art. Take on the role of hacker, of destabilizer of the school order! Play with the concept of 'school'.

This requires to first take a good look. The Dutch norm of 3.5 m^2 per student may seem strict, but all schools are free to determine for themselves how to make use of that space. What is really taking place in the school? What are the rules? How have they been translated into a spatial ordering?

Students then went to work on this 3.5 m^2. By making it sensory, by building, it may become possible to shift things. To destabilize them. Something emerges that plays with this space. We also encouraged them to look closely at the educational context. What can you possibly hack with this 3.5 m^2? What kind of view on education is that?

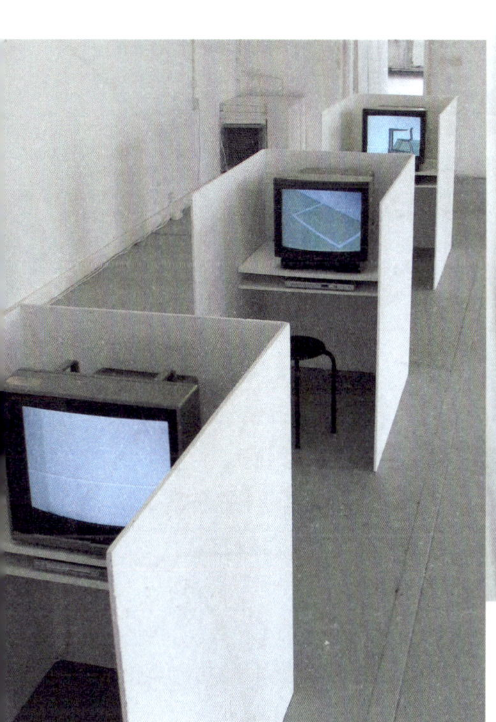

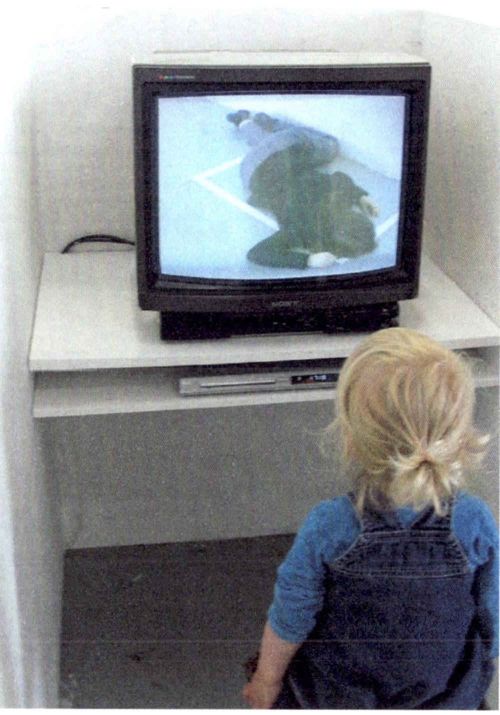

Mirjam van Tilburg, *26 minutes*, 2007

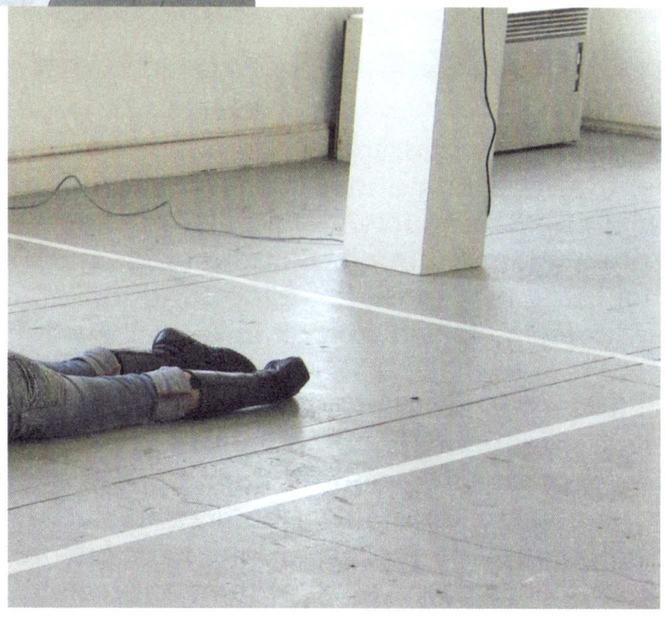

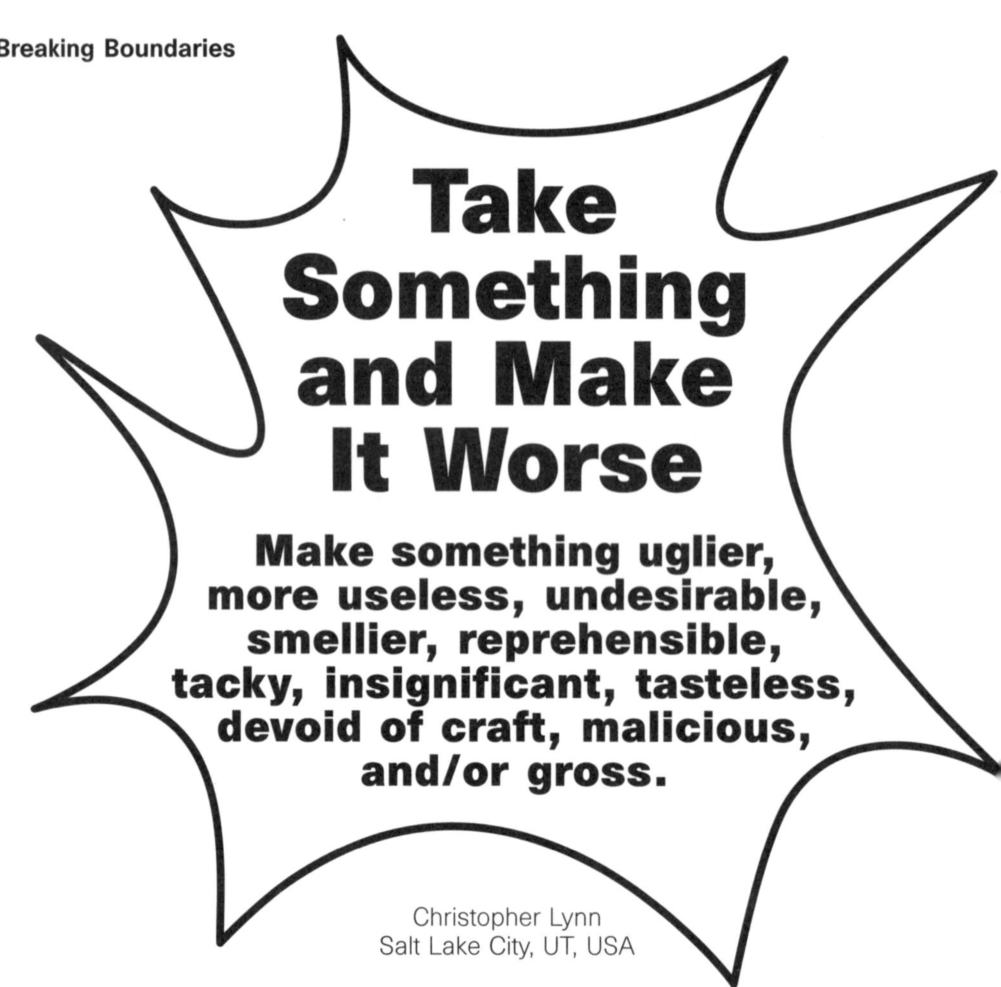

Take Something and Make It Worse

Make something uglier, more useless, undesirable, smellier, reprehensible, tacky, insignificant, tasteless, devoid of craft, malicious, and/or gross.

Christopher Lynn
Salt Lake City, UT, USA

When I ran contemporary art spaces, I would host Bad Art Nights: events where attendees were given basic, low-cost art supplies—watery acrylics, unruly brushes, celebrity gossip magazines, aluminium foil, packing tape, and more—and were told that they were not allowed to make anything good. If their projects started to look to nice, we would stop them and ask them to make it worse. It relieved the stress of needing to feel like a 'good artist' and allowed people to revel in techniques, materials, and content they would normally avoid. Attendees proudly showed off their work to each other rather than sheepishly allowing it to be viewed. Artists discovered new techniques and tools that they later integrated into their regular practices. Everyone came to appreciate aspects of art that they previously found appalling.

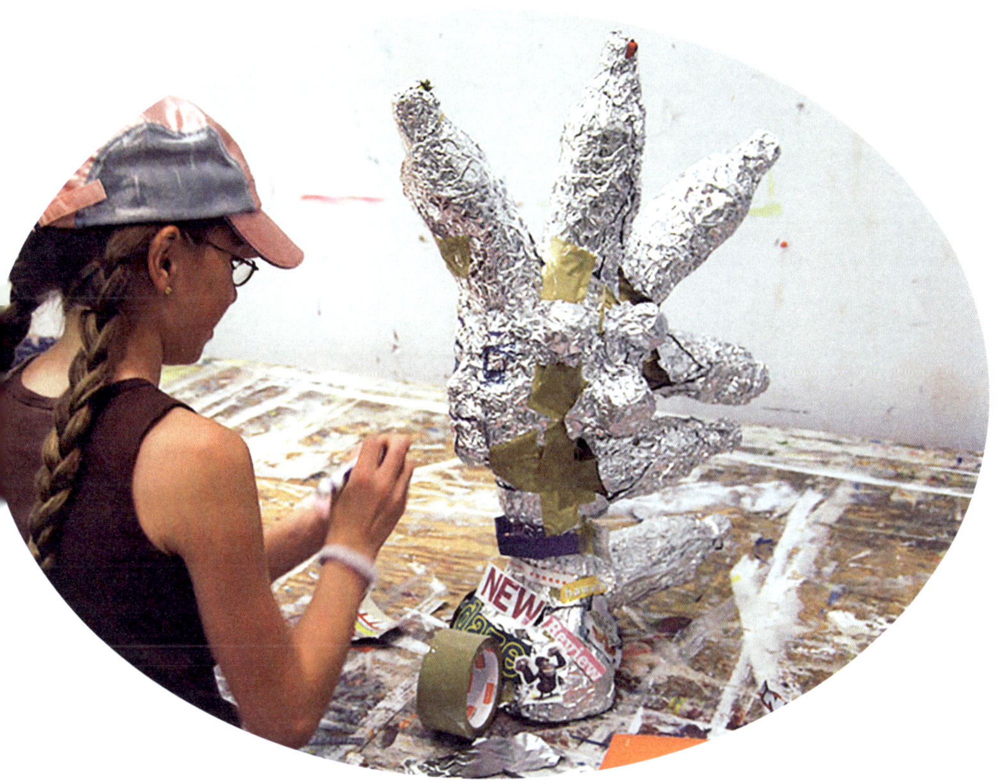

Unknown artist, *Bad Art Night*, 2007, documentation of art making event, photo: Christopher Lynn

Too Wicked to Handle

This section of the book we have named 'Too Wicked to Handle'. This selection of assignments was too unrealistic or 'too outrageous' to be carried out, or the assignments had not been 'tried and tested', but were still worthwhile as a wicked source of inspiration.

YES, YOU CAN!
Design a campaign for your own Presidency.

Coco Ammerlaan, Rotterdam, the Netherlands
Rik Schutte, Rotterdam, the Netherlands

PLANET EARTH RESET BUTTON
Design the button that will reboot our planet in the best way. Of course, it will be the last thing you will see, touch, and interact with in your life.

Claudio Beorchia, Refrontolo, Italy

DYING TRADITION CAMPAIGN
Design a social media campaign for a dying tradition (drawn from the material or immaterial heritage of your own culture or ancestry).

Stéphanie Bertrand, Thessaloniki, Greece

THE PURPOSE OF TOOLS
Draw with your fork, eat pasta with your brush: question the purpose of ‘tools’; within and beyond the studio.

James Gardner, Rome, Italy

THE LONG SHOT

Make an action and document it without editing until the media runs out... of memory, of tape, of batteries. Can you stick with it? What happens, the longer you perform or consider a thing?

Amanda Hamilton, Minneapolis, MN, US

BE A PRIMITIVE FOR THREE HOURS

Set up a situation of being a primitive for three hours.

Nan Hao, Beijing and Shantou, China

GO OUT AND PLAY!

For a whole week, photograph everything that makes you happy / proud / emotional in your city or village. Then present your photos in a way that suits the atmosphere of your images.

Saskia van Heugten, Amsterdam, the Netherlands

WORK WITH STRANGERS!

Place a booth in a public space like a student union's building or library and bring some stuff and lay it out on the table. Talk to the people who pass by the booth and tell them to give anything they have at the moment and / or to take anything from the table.

Sujin Kim, Seoul, Republic of Korea

HIDING, COVERING, CONCEALING
The students are told to hide, cover, conceal, let vanish, etc. something in order to (visually) create social sense.

Anja Kraus, Stockholm, Sweden

THE WORLD IS DROWNING
How would you save Venice (from drowning)?

Anna Kubelík, Berlin, Germany

AIR EDIFICE
Make a building out of air.

Anna Kubelík, Berlin, Germany

TAKE A DETOUR AROUND YOUR ART-MAKING HABITS
Have others assess how you work. They then vote which part of your habitual practice you will not be allowed to utilize. Make a new work, detouring around your assigned obstacle.

Christopher Lynn, Salt Lake City, UT, United States

CROAK!
Explain a joke until it's funny again.

Jesse Malmed, Chicago, IL, USA

ZENO'S WALK
Walk toward something but never arrive.

Chris Moffett, Denton, TX, USA

REVOLUTIONARY SPACE(S)
Find a space where a revolution can unfold or is unfolding. Document this space in whatever way that comes to you.

Laila Saber Rodríguez, Arnhem, the Netherlands

BIG BANG!
Help! The ceiling is lava and gravity works from left to right! Invent your own, new law of nature and show it in a short video.

100% Hedendaags, Rotterdam, the Netherlands

IS IT ART OR IS IT LUNCH?
Is it art or is it lunch? Get your food out of your bag and make your greatest work of art.

100% Hedendaags, Rotterdam, the Netherlands

KINDERGARTEN CURATORS
Children start to think about ownership and power in museum systems, by being a collector and curator.

Anne Thulson, Denver, CO, USA

AN UNCONVENTIONAL GAME ENGINE

Make a video game using only Microsoft Word. In other words, develop a video game using Microsoft Word as your sole game engine.

Hong-An Wu, Dallas, TX, USA

SPIRIT OF THE LAW

Break into your neighbour's home and tidy up the place.

Nathan RPB Young, St Paul, MN, USA

MIRROR, MIRROR

Without notifying friends, colleagues, or loved ones, design, print and distribute missing-person posters of yourself.

Nathan RPB Young, St Paul, MN, USA

Index of Assignment Makers

Gabriela Acosta Camacho (1989) graduated from the Dance Teacher department and the Master of Education in Arts at the Amsterdam University of the Arts. Gabriela works in higher education and for various cultural organizations. It is her mission to improve equality in opportunities for kids and youngsters through arts education.
pp. 134–135

Robin Arnold (1952) is an artist and Professor. She has an MFA from the Michigan State University and teaches painting and drawing at the State University of New York at New Paltz. Her recent paintings focus on environmental and cultural issues; her works have been exhibited nationally.
pp. 80–81

Bart de Baets (1979) is an Amsterdam-based graphic designer. He currently is designing the identity and a bimonthly bulletin for Kunstverein Langenhagen, and *Forum*, an architecture magazine, with Sandra Kassenaar. He regularly conducts workshops and lectures in art schools and institutions throughout Europe, the USA and Asia.
pp. 234–235

Angela Inez Baldus (1989) studies and practices art and art education at the University of British Columbia in Vancouver (BC). As an artist and scholar, she focuses on the experiences of spaces and how art is a way to understand material relationships in different ways.
pp. 126–127

Kira Jo Baldwin (1996) graduated Art Education major at the Brigham Young University in Provo (UT) and completed her Student Teaching at Mountain Ridge in Highland (UT). Her artistic practice includes drawing, acrylic painting, and installation among much else, and she most enjoys making personal artworks for people in her life.
pp. 202–203

Andrea Bandoni (1981) holds a Master in Contextual Design from the Design Academy Eindhoven (NL) and graduated as architect at Faculdade de Arquitetura e Urbanismo da Universidade de São Paulo. She currently works as Designer in Residence at the Aalto University in Finland. Her projects involve objects and spaces, and she is interested in sustainability, technology, and education.
pp. 104–105

Arida Bandringa-Hendriks (1981) studied at the Willem de Kooning Academy in Rotterdam and currently teaches art at the Gemeentelijk Gymnasium in Hilversum (NL). She is the owner of Educatief OntwerpLAB and project member at ArtechLAB Amsterdam, a research lab about how to combine Art, Science and Technology in Art lessons.
pp. 124–125, 256–257

Emer Beamer (1970) studied at the Gerrit Rietveld Academie in Amsterdam and is the founder and method designer at Designathon Works, Amsterdam.
pp. 258–259

Nicolet Bekker (1973) studied at the Breitner Academy, Amsterdam University of the Arts and at the Gerrit Rietveld Academie, Architectural Design. She teaches art and design at several schools in the Netherlands. She works both as interior design architect and social designer. She is interested in collective (democratic) design processes, sustainable design, and digital manufacturing.
pp. 232–233

Hans Belleman (1950) is a multidisciplinary artist and art teacher at the Zaanlands Lyceum, Zaandam (NL). His work is rooted in the tradition of the Dogtroep, a well-known Dutch theatre group that applied various disciplines (visual art, music, dance, and visual media) to create on-site performances. His work consists of paintings, collages, video, photography, on-site projects, and performances.
pp. 108–109

Karlijn Benthem (1983) is a theatre and concept maker. Together with Anouk Rutten, she leads Gebied-B with which they make performances, concepts, education, and interventions. Their focus is to listen, watch, ask questions in an arti-visual environment to make the world a better place.
pp. 156–157

Ewa Berg (1958) holds two MFAs and studied at the Malmö Art Academy, Lund University, and at the HDK-Valand at the University of Gothenburg. She is an artist and lecturer in Visual Art at the Malmö University. Ewa is interested in how contemporary art practice can be woven into educational contexts.
pp. 64–65

Index of Assignment Makers

Jacques Blommestijn (1953) studied at ArtEZ University of the Arts in Arnhem and worked as an art teacher at the Rietveld Lyceum in Doetinchem (NL). Currently he works at two ROC schools with groups taking their finals. He is also active himself in art in various ways: from activist events to conceptual NOT-MADE WORK.
pp. 146–147

Mike Bode (1964) is a Swedish visual artist, researcher, and organizer. His work has been exhibited from the Kunst-Werke in Berlin to the Yokohama Triennale, Japan. His artistic practice frequently takes its starting point in investigations of a place seen in relation to societal, historical, and political shifts.
pp. 236–237

Sterre Boerkamp (1986) is an art teacher in secondary education for children with special needs. She takes an interest in social art, street art, and activism in art. In her classes she uses art to talk with students about the world and to provide them with ways of expressing their own ideas.
pp. 152–153

Anja Brand-Heemskerk (1970) completed the study Art and Design Education at the Willem de Kooning Academy, Rotterdam. She works as an art teacher at the Alfrink College in Zoetermeer (NL). She is also an artist, making paintings, drawings, and land art. She takes an interest in art from the digital age.
pp. 88–89

Melissa Bremmer
[bio see page 302]
pp. 258–259

Wolf Brinkman (1959) studied Psychology for two years at the Utrecht University, and Art and Design at the HKU University of the Arts Utrecht (NL). He is interested in how language shapes the way we think. His main focus is investigating methods to restore art to its rightful place in any educational system.
pp. 214–215

Geke Buis (1977) currently studies Fine Art in Education at the ArtEZ University of the Arts, Arnhem. She is a graduate fine artist, graphic designer, and yoga teacher and is interested in visual poetry, paper art and all things quiet.
pp. 92–93

Liesbet Bussche (1980) studied at the Gerrit Rietveld Academie in Amsterdam and St Lucas School of Arts Antwerp. She teaches at the Jewellery-Linking Bodies department of the Gerrit Rietveld Academie. She explores the meaning jewellery has as a social and cultural phenomenon, often resulting in interventions in public space.
pp. 112–113

Kirsten Busse (1999) is studying Theatre & Media Arts at the Brigham Young University in Provo (UT). When she is not hiding away in the tech booth, she loves to spend time observing the natural world. She is currently inspired by art's power to drive social change.
pp. 110–111

Cabello/Carceller, Helena Cabello (1963) and Ana Carceller (1964) are artists and teachers at the Faculty of Fine Arts, UCLM University in Cuenca (ES). They have been working together since 1992, producing interdisciplinary projects that use appropriation, performance, and fiction to provoke unsettling situations, texts, or narratives that displace normative discourses. They have used tools from queer, feminist, and decolonial studies, based on reciprocal collaboration mainly with amateurs.
pp. 138–139

Anastasia Chaguidouline (1993) is a curator based in Basel. She currently works for various art institutions, including Museum Tinguely. She graduated from the Royal Academy of Art, The Hague and the Art Institute at the FHNW Academy, Basel. Her curatorial focus lies on multilingual and marginalized or overlooked (female) artistic practices, and subversive art in post-Soviet Russia.
pp. 162–163

Tamar Clasquin (1988) graduated from the HKU University of the Arts Utrecht (NL) and the Master of Education in Arts in Amsterdam. She teaches pedagogy at the Universities of the Arts of Utrecht and Amsterdam. She is a visual artist and has been working as a visual art teacher in secondary schools for ten years.
pp. 134–135

Index of Assignment Makers

Ross Coulter (1972) is a visual artist with a BFA and MFA from the Victoria College of the Arts in Melbourne. His practice is about an exploration of photographic portraiture, performance, participation and the office worker. Coulter lectures in Fine Art and Photography at the Monash University and Deakin University (AU).
pp. 194–195

Jen Delos Reyes (1981) is a creative labourer, educator, writer, and radical community arts organizer. She is the director of Open Engagement. Delos Reyes currently lives in Chicago, where she is the Associate Director of the School of Art and Art History at the University of Illinois at Chicago.
pp. 252–253

Disseminart Collective, founded in 2012, was initiated by Nadine M. Kalin (1968) and Daniel T. Barney (1968). Nadine and Daniel studied at the University of British Columbia, Vancouver. Nadine teaches Art Education at the University of North Texas, Denton (TX), while Daniel teaches Art Education at the Brigham Young University in Provo (UT).
pp. 82–83, 140–141

Lili Liane van Doorninck (1996) studied at the Breitner Academy, Amsterdam University of the Arts. She is an art teacher at the Gerrit van der Veen College in Amsterdam, a secondary school for students with an art and culture profile. She also does artistic and educational projects for various organizations.
pp. 100–101

Mieke te Dorsthorst (1971) studied Fine Arts at the Royal Academy of Arts in The Hague, and Art in Education at the Breitner Academy, Amsterdam University of the Arts. She works as a teacher at the Geert Groote College in Amsterdam, a Rudolph Steiner school. She also gives painting classes through her own art initiative KunstProces.
pp. 272–273

Petra Drost (1979) graduated from the Minerva Art Academy, Groningen, in 2005 as a teacher in visual art and design and has been working as an art teacher in CKV and as cultural coordinator in secondary education since 2006. In her classes she values individual input by her savvy students. In 2019 she obtained her Master's degree in Art Education.
pp. 90–91

Sabina Enéa Téari's work unfolds between emergent transversalities of cultural, educational and artistic practices. She is a founding member of Foresta Collective (founded in 2015), a fluid collective dedicated to the research and co-creation of experimental formats of learning, working, and meeting, rooted in multi-layered sustainability, poly-creativity, and embodied culture.
pp. 144–145, 164–165

Margreeth Eringa (1982) completed the study Scenography at the Minerva Art Academy, Groningen, and Art and Design Education at the Willem de Kooning Academy, Rotterdam. She works as an art teacher at the Dalton Voorburg, Voorburg (NL). She is interested in theatre, media art, and art in the public space.
pp. 88–89

Natalia Espinel (1988) is a Colombian artist who works at the intersection of visual arts, performance, somatic practices, and movement improvisation. Natalia teaches drawing and body-space practices at the School of Art at Pontificia Universidad Javeriana, Bogotá. She completed an MFA in Integrated Practices at Pratt Institute, New York.
pp. 198–199

Maura Flood (1983) is a Midwest designer and educator at the Art Institute of Chicago. She engages art as a relational medium to disrupt systems of power, connect individuals, uncover beauty, and illuminate wonder in the everyday.
pp. 62–63

Clark Goldsberry (1987) is a public high school educator and Adjunct Professor. He studied at the Brigham Young University in Provo (UT). He teaches advanced placement art, design, and photography in secondary school, and a technology & new media course at the university.
pp. 228–229

Mark Graham (1952) is an Art Professor at the Brigham Young University in Provo (UT). Graham is an internationally known illustrator of children's books. His research interests include teacher education, place-based education, graphic novels, ecological/holistic education, secondary art education, design thinking, STEAM education, and Himalayan art.
pp. 266–267

Index of Assignment Makers

Anne Graswinckel (1965) and **Jeffrey Deelman** (1976) started out as drama teachers. As highly motivated and inspiring education makers they developed a method for dealing with language, narrative, and imagination in the classroom. In 2016 they compiled their expertise in the book *De kunst van het verdwalen*, supported by the VSBfonds.
pp. 196–197

Nadieh Graumans-Tigchelaar (1989) studied at the ArtEZ University of the Arts in Arnhem and completed the Master of Education in Arts at the Amsterdam University of the Arts. She works as a theatre maker with young people, as a theatre teacher and singer. She is interested in the aesthetic experience and the intersection between arts and entertainment.
pp. 158–159

Sam de Groot (1985) works as a freelance graphic designer and teaches typography at the Gerrit Rietveld Academie, Amsterdam. Under the name TRUE TRUE TRUE he publishes books and music in collaboration with artist Paul Haworth.
pp. 84–85

Olivia Gude (1950) is an Endowed Professor at the School of the Art Institute of Chicago and founding director of Spiral Workshop. Her practice combines her work as a collaborative public artist and as an art educator, creating spaces in which teachers investigate and re-invent the social practices of art education.
pp. 66–67

Graphic designer **Hansje van Halem** (1978) gathered recognition with her distinctive typography and geometric, almost psychedelic illustrations built on complex patterns. Her work is in the collection of the Stedelijk Museum Amsterdam and Museum für Gestaltung Zürich. Since 2017, Hansje is the head of design for music festival Lowlands.
pp. 240–241

Patrick Earl Hammie (1981) received an MFA from the University of Connecticut. Through painted portraits and allegories, he explores the complexities of identity, emotion, and family by layering existing histories with new narratives. Hammie is currently an Associate Professor at the University of Illinois at Urbana-Champaign.
pp. 200–201

Riley Harmon (1987) is an artist and social engineer and was a resident of the Rijksakademie van beeldende kunsten. He has exhibited at institutions such as the Nederlands Instituut voor Mediakunst, FACT in Liverpool, De Appel in Amsterdam, EYE Filmmuseum in Amsterdam, the 32nd Biennial of Graphic Arts in Ljubljana, and the Festival of Dangerous Ideas.
pp. 94–95

Emiel Heijnen
[bio see page 302]
pp. 106–107, 258–259

Bianca Hester (1975) is an artist who completed a PhD at the Royal Melbourne Institute (2007). She is a Sidney Myer Creative Fellow (2017-2018) and a Senior Lecturer in Art & Design at UNSW, Sydney. Her projects engage place as a complex constellation of human timescales, nonhuman durations, objects, histories and geologic materialities.
pp. 216–217

Saskia van Heugten (1984) studied at the Amsterdam Master of Education in Arts and since 2016 teaches Art and Design with lots of love and enthusiasm to students aged 12–18 at the Spinoza Lyceum, Amsterdam. She has a practice as photographer and is a singer.
pp. 246–247

Lisette de Hooge (1991) studied Photography at the Willem de Kooning Academy in Rotterdam and worked as a graphic designer before she decided to pursue her ambitions in art education. Her humane approach towards students teaches them that everyone can join in the practice of making art.
pp. 160–161

Anna Hotze (1976) studied at the Leiden University and is Professor of Science and Technology at the University of Applied Sciences IPABO, Amsterdam/Alkmaar (NL).
pp. 258–259

Index of Assignment Makers

Pavèl van Houten (1984) studied at the Gerrit Rietveld Academie (BA) and the Sandberg Instituut (MA), Amsterdam. He is a visual artist and also teaches at the Fine Art & Design Teacher Training Department at the Willem de Kooning Academy, Rotterdam. He does research into the possibility of seeing education as an artistic medium.
pp. 168-169

J.U.F. are artists Manouk Hasebos (1987) and Sara Pape García (1980). They join forces as art & nature teachers for children between 4 and 12 years old. Manouk is a Fashion Design graduate of the ArtEZ University of the Arts, Arnhem. Sara graduated with her Master's degree Artistic Research from the Royal Academy of Arts, The Hague.
pp. 254-255

Ramesh Kalkur (1969) is an artist and educator. He holds a Master in Fine Arts from the Royal College of Art, London, and has been teaching at Srishti Institute of Art, Design and Technology in Bangaluru since 2001 and holding a position of Dean of School of Foundation and Preparatory Studies at Srishti since 2010.
pp. 206-207

Oliver Klimpel (1973) is working at the intersection of design, art, and extra-academic research. He gained his degrees at the Academy of Visual Arts Leipzig and the Royal College of Art in London and was Professor of System Design in Leipzig from 2008-2015.
pp. 204-205

Paul Koek (1954) is a Dutch percussionist and music theatre director. Together with Johan Simons he formed the artistic leadership of Hollandia (later ZT Hollandia) and founded Veenfabriek, a socially engaged music theatre ensemble in Leiden. He has also taught at the Royal Conservatoire, The Hague, where he initiated the Master Music Theatre T.I.M.E.
pp. 180-181

Michiel Koelink (1972) studied Media Art at the AKI ArtEZ Academy of Art & Design in Enschede and Interactive Media and Environments at the Frank Mohr Institute, Groningen (NL). He is the founder of ArtechLAB Amsterdam and is also a lecturer at the Breitner Academy, Amsterdam University of the Arts and at the Master MADtech in Groningen.
pp. 122-123, 186-187, 238-239, 256-257

Gila Kolb (1979) is a researching art educator. She lectures at the Bern University of the Arts and the Bern University of Teacher Education. She is co-founder of the Kassel-based agency art education and edits the trilingual interview blog thearteducatorstalk. Her teaching focuses on a critical art education, and strategies of unlearning.
pp. 142-143

Caspar Lam (1985) and **YuJune Park** (1982) are Assistant Professors of Communication Design at Parsons School of Art and Design, New York City. Their studio, Synoptic Office, has exhibited internationally and works with cultural institutions and companies in the space between design, technology, and education with particular emphases on brand strategy, digital archives, and typography.
pp. 118-119

Eunji Lee (1979) is an artist-educator, curator, and researcher based in New York City. She explores the participant experience at the intersection of contemporary art practices, public engagement, and education. She received her doctorate in Art & Art Education at the Teachers College, Columbia University, New York City.
pp. 74-75

Matt Lee (1980) is an artist and illustrator. He holds a Master in Visual Arts: Digital Arts from Camberwell College of Arts in London and has taught at the Srishti Institute of Art, Design & Technology in Bengaluru, Arts University Bournemouth, Open College of the Arts (Online), and Camberwell College of Arts, London.
pp. 206-207

Maria Letsiou (1972) is a visual artist, educator, and researcher. She earned a PhD in Art Education at the Athens School of Fine Arts and teaches Art Education at the School of Early Childhood Education, Aristotle University, Thessaloniki (GR). Her research focuses on topics related to contemporary culture and identity.
pp. 250-251

Index of Assignment Makers

Pallas Linssen-van der Doorn (1986) completed her Bachelor Illustration Design at AKV|St.Joost, Breda. She received her Bachelor's Degree of Fine Art in Education at Fontys School of Fine & Performing Arts in Tilburg and teaches art 2D and 3D at De Nassau, an innovative secondary school, located in Breda.
pp. 262-263

Jorge Lucero (1976) is an artist, teacher and Associate Professor of Art Education at the University of Illinois. He was born, raised, and educated in Chicago. One proposal Lucero makes in his work is that the teacher can be a conceptual artist through the permissions of conceptual art. Through the same thinking, the conceptualist is also a teacher.
pp. 114-115, 230-231

Christopher Lynn (1974) is an Associate Professor of Art and Design at the Brigham Young University in Provo (UT). His research and artistic practice are about borders, differentiation, and collective action.
pp. 166-167, 276-277

Oskar Maarleveld (1968) is a visual artist and art teacher. He teaches art at the Montessori Lyceum and fine art and education at the Breitner Academy, Amsterdam University of the Arts. In his work he looks for a playful and unexpected connections between making art, experiencing art, and teaching art.
pp. 72-73, 136-137

Ricardo Makosi's (1978) background is in game design, animation and illustration. He is a teacher at the study programme Media Design of the ROC Amsterdam. He also produces various interactive (game) productions and calls himself 'education designer'. His passion is for educational innovations such as the 'analoggram', design thinking, and of course his students!
pp. 268-269

Stephanie Veronica Martyniuk (1987) is high school visual/media arts and English teacher, in Vancouver. Stephanie also is an academic scholar and enjoys researching and writing about video game pedagogy, digital design and technology, and designing her own video games.
pp. 260-261

Chris de Man (1984) is a teacher in social work at the Deltion College. Prior to that, he was a teacher at the academic primary school De Sprankel, where, as culture coordinator, he dedicated himself to a broader approach to creative subjects.
pp. 70-71

Linda Mekkes (1974) studied Textile Art at the Royal Academy of Fine Arts in The Hague before she obtained her Bachelor in Education at the Amsterdam University of the Arts. She teaches Art and Design at the Willem Blaeu secondary school in Alkmaar and works as a visual artist.
pp. 210-211

Wilke van der Molen (1979) is a teacher of Drama at the Teacher Training College Viaa in Zwolle. In 2017 she graduated from the Master study programme Art in Education. She has worked in primary education with the remix model in the project 'Art in Education'.
pp. 70-71

Ronald Nijhof (1976) studied at the HKU University of the Arts Utrecht and teaches Art at the School of Media, HKU University of the Arts Utrecht (NL). As an artist Nijhof focuses on the systems of everyday life. Using spatial constructions and photography, he operates at the intersection of two-dimensional and three-dimensional imagery.
pp. 128-129, 170-171, 244-245, 270-271

Andrea Palašti (1984) is a visual artist and lecturer at the Department for New Media Art at the Academy of Art in Novi Sad (RS). She works across artistic, pedagogical, and curatorial boundaries, concentrating on issues of cultural geography, history, and the everyday life.
pp. 192-193, 218-219

Monique Pijls (1970) studied at the University of Amsterdam and is Senior Lecturer Inquiry and Design-based Learning and coordinates the minor Maker Education at the University of Applied Sciences, Amsterdam.
pp. 258-259

Index of Assignment Makers

Sam Ramos (1982) is a writer and educator at the Art Institute of Chicago. His practice emphasizes risk, experiment, and experience, with an emphasis on interdisciplinarity, social justice, and the profound.
pp. 62-63

Marja Reniers (1965) studied Fashion Design at St. Joost Academy for Visual Arts in Breda and holds a Master's degree in Education in Arts. She is the founder of Beeldlokaal and develops art education and community art projects. Connecting, sustainability, and taking care of your environment are important themes.
pp. 134-135

Ber van de Rijdt (1954) teaches Drawing, Art and Art History/Cultural History at the Minkema College in Woerden. Over the past forty years he has seen Drawing become an examination subject, witnessed major overhauls in the educational system as a teacher of Drawing, Arts, 3D printing, and Sinology, and the advent of computers and the Internet.
pp. 154-155

Joachim Robbrecht (1979) is a theatre maker and playwright. He studied Literature at the Ghent University and Theatre Directing in Amsterdam. His work is driven by the desire to experiment with the performativity of words and structures of story-telling. In addition, he is tutoring at the DAS Graduate School, Amsterdam.
pp. 96-97

Luis Rodil-Fernández (1977) is an artist, teacher, and programmer with a mixed background in computer science, art, and design. He teaches at the ArtEZ University of the Arts in Arnhem and is a teacher and researcher at the Amsterdam University of Applied Sciences in the Master Digital Design.
pp. 248-249

Rolinda Rook-Heetebrij (1970) works as an assistant teacher at primary schools Eben Haëzer in Sint-Jansklooster (NL) and De Vuurbaak in Urk (NL).
pp. 220-221

Marijke Rook-Lassche (1980) works as an assistant teacher at primary school Eben Haëzer and is pedagogic coach/policy assistant at day-care centre J/M in Sint-Jansklooster. Both have graduated from the University of Applied Sciences KPZ in Zwolle.
pp. 220-221

Nathalie Roos (1979) studied at the Fine Art Teacher Training course of the Amsterdam University of the Arts and Anthropology at the University of Amsterdam. She is a teacher and researcher at the Amsterdam University of the Arts.
pp. 258-259

Hanna Salonen (1968), **Marloes Nieuweboer** (1986) and **Annelies den Boon** (1989) graduated from the Master of Education in Arts at the Amsterdam University of the Arts. All three of them are interested in what technology has to offer to the arts and vice versa.
pp. 184-185

Erik Schrooten (1966) studied guitar at the Royal Conservatoire Antwerp and Pedagogy at the Free University Brussels. He teaches guitar, coaches art academies in Flanders, and writes a blog about artistic competencies for future competent teachers.
pp. 176-177, 188-189

Johanna Schweizer (1949) is a Dutch visual artist. She teaches ceramics, but recently she has been working with crochet. She often makes life-size figures, in which her fascination for the strange and abnormal becomes visible. Her work combines a meaningful reflection with humour and play.
pp. 130-131

David Serra Navarro (1976) (alias Kenneth Russo) studied at Fine Arts at the University of Barcelona and teaches Art and Design at ESDAP Catalunya. He has a practice as a visual artist and he is interested in social innovation, interactive communication, and the debate over the ethical criticism of art.
pp. 116-167

Marijke Smedema (1977) studied Arts at the Applied Universities of Maastricht and Amsterdam. She teaches music at Olivijn, a school for children with special educational needs in Almere (NL) and is a trainer for Musicians without Borders. Her focus areas are inclusion and using arts for social change.
pp. 178-179

Index of Assignment Makers

Erin Tapley (1969) is an artist, teacher, school director, and dreamer at the Western Carolina University in North Carolina. Her own work focuses on fibre, printmaking, and installation.
pp. 68-69, 148-149

Rein Jelle Terpstra (1960) studied at the Rijksakademie van beeldende kunsten in Amsterdam and teaches Fine Arts and Photography at the Minerva Art Academy, Groningen. He investigates the relationships between perception, memory, and photography. His work is held in collections of the SFMOMA, San Francisco, EYE Filmmuseum, Amsterdam and Nederlands Fotomuseum, Rotterdam.
pp. 86-87

Anne Thulson (1961) studied painting at the Cranbrook Academy of Art (MI) and teaches Art Education at the Metropolitan State University of Denver. She has taught art to children in Denver Public Schools and in her camp, School of the Poetic City. She alternates between post-studio and studio practices.
pp. 60-61

Mirjam van Tilburg (1980) studied at the Maastricht Academy of Fine Arts and did a Master's at the Piet Zwart Institute in Amsterdam. She works for KCR in Rotterdam, regularly publishes in specialist journals, and teaches at the Master of Education in Arts at Fontys School of Fine & Performing Arts, Tilburg. She is pursuing her PhD at ARIA, Antwerp. Mirjam approaches art education from the arts.
pp. 222-223, 274-275

Hanna Timmers (1987) graduated from the study programme Theatre Teacher in Amsterdam in 2010. She has since been working for Theater Na de Dam, Frascati Theater and Het Nationale Theater as a teacher, artist or coordinator, and maker. Hanna makes all of her work in the social-artistic context and often in public space.
pp. 76-77

Seher Uysal (1983) is a visual artist and researcher based in Istanbul. She is interested in participating in discourses on Turkish art education and alternative teaching practices. She is presently part of the teaching team at the Nesin Art Village Visual Arts Summer School where she gives interdisciplinary classes on Visual Culture and Storytelling.
pp. 236-237

Susanne Venbrux (1989) studied at the ArtEZ University of the Arts in Arnhem. She finished her Bachelor in Fashion and started the fashion and accessories label 'Suvenirs'. At the moment she studies Art & Education at ArtEZ, to become a creative teacher in high school.
pp. 208-209

Catherine Willemse (1991), studied Communication and Media Design at the HU University of Applied Sciences Utrecht. She makes illustrations, videos, and animations. At the moment, she studies Fine Art and Design in Education at the ArtEZ University of the Arts, Arnhem.
pp. 98-99

Job Wouters (1980) is a practitioner of the lost art of psychedelic and delirious penmanship, a letterer whose precisely honed technique hides behind a world of unbridled alphabetic experimentation. His international practice bridges the applied field of (typo)graphic design, with the autonomous disciplines of drawing and painting.
pp. 182-183

Eser Yagci (1979) studied Architecture at the Yeditepe University in Istanbul and is teaching theory- and practice-based classes related to environmental discrimination at the Mimar Sinan Fine Arts University in Istanbul. She has been involved with an autonomous art collective and urban-based grassroots groups in Istanbul.
pp. 172-173

Davy Yong (1988) is an art therapist and educator, currently working for the British Association of Art Therapists (BAAT) while also maintaining an artistic practice. He studied at the Willem de Kooning Academy in Rotterdam and obtained an MA in Art Psychotherapy from Goldsmiths, University of London.
pp. 224-225

Index of Other Names

Index of Other Names

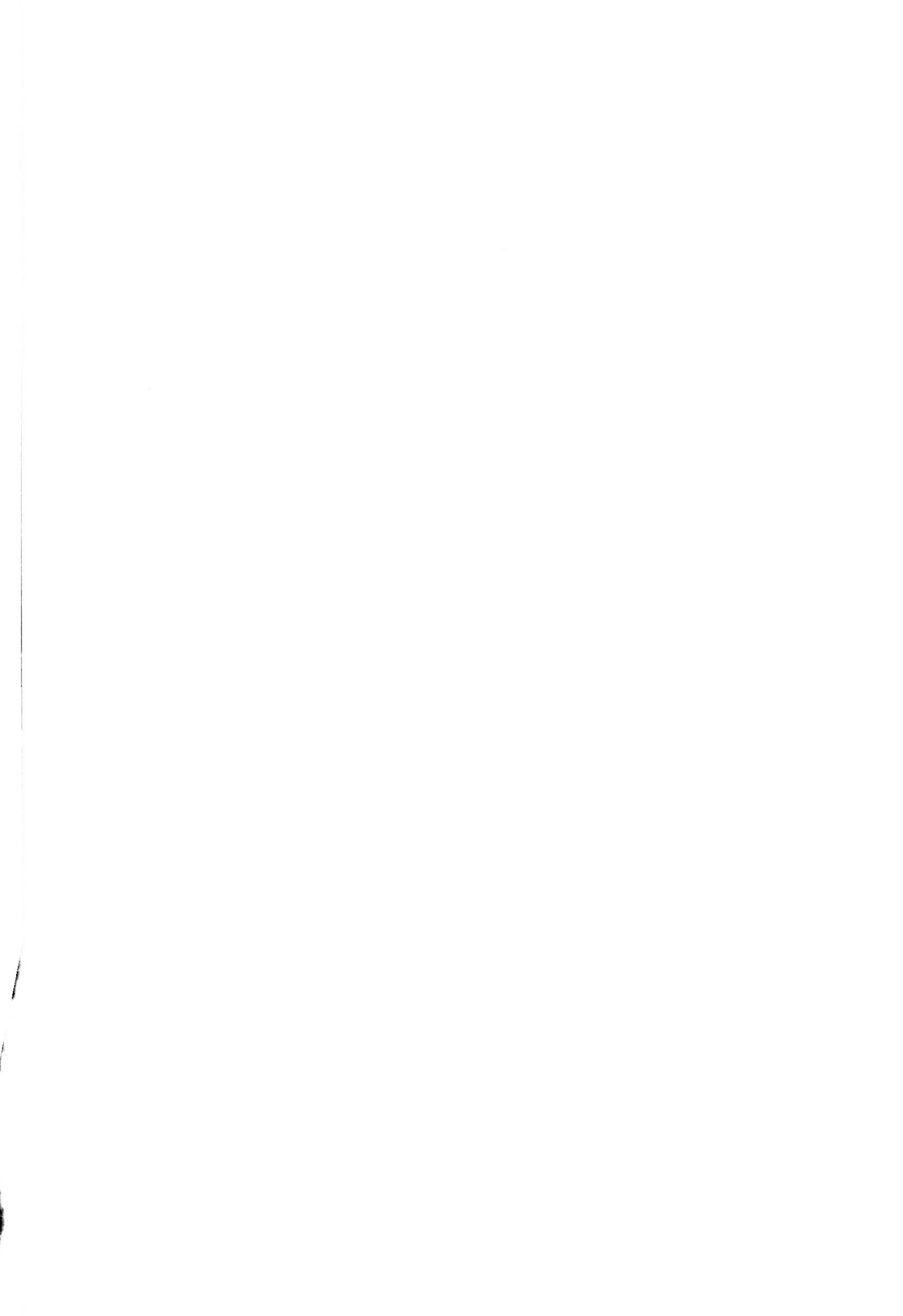

Acknowledgements

The editors would truly like to thank the members of the selection committee for their critical and creative perspective on the assignments: Folkert Haanstra, Gable Roelofsen, Oskar Maarleveld and Laura Pappa. Also, a big 'thank you' to the people who generously activated their networks to showcase the project and who gave us stimulating feedback during the making of the book, in particular Jorge Lucero, Arthur Herrman, Jappe Groenendijk, Folkert Haanstra, Madelinde Hageman, Sterre Boerkamp, Channa de Vries, Aldo Kroese, Roderick Laperdrix.

Research Group Arts Education, Amsterdam University of the Arts, the Netherlands
This publication stems from the commitment of the Research Group Arts Education of the Amsterdam University of the Arts. This Research Group is focused on developing knowledge, designing research-based curricula, and innovating professional practices in the field of arts education. It publishes and organizes symposia and events around two main research strands: Interdisciplinarity and Social Engagement.
www.ahk.nl/en/research-groups/research-group-arts-education/

Biographies

Editors and Co-editor

Emiel Heijnen has worked in various contexts as an arts and design teacher and is now Professor of Arts Education at the Amsterdam University of the Arts. Trained as a teacher in Visual Arts and Design at Fontys (Sittard), and at the Utrecht University of the Arts, Emiel obtained his PhD at the Radboud University Nijmegen. His research focuses on authentic arts education, popular culture and media education, curriculum design, and ArtsSciences education.

Melissa Bremmer has worked at various institutes and schools as a music teacher and is now Professor of Arts Education at the Amsterdam University of the Arts. Melissa obtained her Bachelor in Music Education degree at the Conservatory of Amsterdam, her Master in Educational Science at the University of Amsterdam, and she obtained her PhD at the University of Exeter. Her research focuses on embodied music teaching, inclusion in music education, and ArtsSciences education.

Sanne Kersten is the coordinator and research assistant of the Research Group Arts Education of the Amsterdam University of the Arts, where she previously worked on research regarding the theme of 'Teacher as Conceptual Artist'. She is also coordinator of the third cycle programme THIRD, part of the same university. THIRD focuses on artistic research in the performing arts at the DAS Graduate School (Academy of Theatre and Dance). She has extensive experience in publishing books.

Designer and Publisher

Laura Pappa is a freelance graphic designer based in Amsterdam. Her clients include Valiz, Biennale Matter of Art in Prague, Het Nieuwe Instituut, Rotterdam, Kunstverein Toronto, the Museum of Estonian Architecture, and several artists. She teaches at the Royal Academy of Art in The Hague and the Estonian Academy of Arts, Tallinn.
www.laurapappa.biz

Valiz is an independent international publisher and addresses contemporary developments in art, design, urban affairs, and visual culture. Their books offer critical reflection and interdisciplinary inspiration in a broad-based and imaginative way, often establishing a connection between cultural disciplines and socio-economic questions. Valiz is based in Amsterdam and connects to authors, artists, designers, institutes, bookshops, distributors, and readers worldwide.
www.valiz.nl

Colophon

Editors: Emiel Heijnen, Melissa Bremmer
Co-editor: Sanne Kersten
Translation (Du-Eng) and copy-editing (Eng):
Leo Reijnen
Proofreading: Els Brinkman
Index: Elke Stevens
Design: Laura Pappa
Typefaces: Neue Haas Unica,
Century Expanded
Paper inside: Munken Print White 90 gr. 1.5
Paper cover: Invercote 200 gr.
Lithography:
Mariska Bijl, Wilco Art Books, Amsterdam
Printing and binding:
Wilco Art Books, Amersfoort
Publisher: Valiz, Amsterdam,
Astrid Vorstermans & Pia Pol,
www.valiz.nl, 2020/2021

This project was generously supported by

Amsterdam University of the Arts

Distribution:
NL/BE/LU: Centraal Boekhuis,
www.cb.nl
Europe/Asia: Idea Books,
www.ideabooks.nl
GB/IE: Anagram Books,
www.anagrambooks.com
USA, Canada, Latin America: D.A.P.,
www.artbook.com
Australia: Perimeter,
www.perimeterdistribution.com
Individual orders: www.valiz.nl

This book has been produced on
FSC-certified paper.

ISBN 978-94-92095-75-6
Printed and bound in the EU, 2020
Reprint, 2025